On Being a Disciple of the Crucifie

Ernst Käsemann
1906–1998

On Being a Disciple of the Crucified Nazarene

UNPUBLISHED LECTURES AND SERMONS

Ernst Käsemann

Edited by
Rudolf Landau, in Cooperation with Wolfgang Kraus

Translated by
Roy A. Harrisville

WILLIAM B. EERDMANS PUBLISHING COMPANY
GRAND RAPIDS, MICHIGAN / CAMBRIDGE, U.K.

© 2010 William B. Eerdmans Publishing Company

All rights reserved

Originally published in 2005 in German as *In der Nachfolge des gekreuzigten Nazareners:
Aufsätze und Vorträge aus dem Nachlass* by Mohr Siebeck, Tübingen, Germany
This English translation © 2010 Wm. B. Eerdmans Publishing Company
All rights reserved

Published 2010 by

Wm. B. Eerdmans Publishing Co.

2140 Oak Industrial Drive N.E., Grand Rapids, Michigan 49505 /

P.O. Box 163, Cambridge CB3 9PU U.K.

Printed in the United States of America

16 15 14 13 12 11 10   7 6 5 4 3 2 1

Library of Congress Cataloging-in-Publication Data

Käsemann, Ernst.

    [In der Nachfolge des gekreuzigten Nazareners. English]

    On being a disciple of the crucified Nazarene: unpublished lectures and sermons /

Ernst Käsemann; edited by Rudolf Landau in cooperation with Wolfgang Kraus;

translated by Roy A. Harrisville.

        p.   cm.

    Includes indexes.

      ISBN 978-0-8028-6026-2 (pbk.: alk. paper)

      1. Bible. N.T. — Criticism, interpretation, etc. 2. Bible. N.T. — Theology.

      I. Landau, Rudolf. II. Kraus, Wolfgang, 1955- III. Title.

BS2290.K3713 2010

225.6 — dc22

                           2009040900

www.eerdmans.com

Contents

PART TWO: CHURCH CONFLICTS

Editor's Foreword

In a handwritten fragment of text entitled "On Discipleship and Faith," Ernst Käsemann replied as follows to a review of his book *Kirchliche Konflikte*, volume 1: "My theological work steered toward a problem I would now like to examine in a thematic way as the relation between discipleship and faith. No doubt, my exegesis served the summons to discipleship, but could define it only by way of examples from historically transmitted texts and historically settled answers. As a result, I was legitimately questioned about my hermeneutic, since I actually had to explain why these texts and answers should be or had been exemplary for me and my time. What united the Bible's past with the present or my personal situation, with the biblical summons to discipleship, a summons also (ms. possibly: first) addressed to me? And to what extent had the summons thus addressed been subjectively interpreted and accepted or rejected by me, but was to be inflexibly set forth as the teaching of the church, more yet as the gospel for persons today? . . . Hermeneutics allows for inquiry into the meaning of historical texts and their relation to our present time, and by doing so necessarily explains the conditions under which such significance can be essential for us."

The existential unity of historical research into biblical texts and the will to hear the voice of the one God speaking now in the Bible, the summons to discipleship of the crucified Nazarene to be heard in it — unavoidably for the one who hears it — makes Käsemann's theology a theology from, in and for the Christian community.

The community following the Crucified, the leading of Christians toward a radical life on the basis of the first commandment, possibly incurring martyrdom, the unrelenting listening to the judging and alluring, warning and admonishing voice of the God who calls his children to the freedom that is the gospel, the incessant struggle and conflict over God's right to his whole world unremittingly linked to it, stamp the research and teaching, the speaking and acting of this exegete.

The inseparable unity of doctrine and life can be recognized in all his work. Such makes clear "that I have tried to hear how a disciple should listen according to Isaiah 50:4. Furthermore, I have become more and more conscious that the Bible is a subversive book. . . . It judges the churches so severely that their criticism of those who do not simply submit to them wholesale seldom still has any weight. Authority is legitimized only by service. . . . No hierarchy and no bureaucracy may limit the freedom of those who still want to follow the Nazarene in a radical way."[1]

The fact that the theologian Ernst Käsemann, concerned in his exegetical work for the truth from which alone the community lives, received the Sexauer Community Prize for theology in 1985 was entirely consistent. (The lecture and sermon are printed in this volume as the last two contributions.)

From the meeting with Käsemann, occasioned by that event, there emerged a late, intensive friendship that he extended to me and that was strengthened in conversations and correspondence. The editing of this volume of literary remains is a fruit of those years.

In the controversy over and with Ernst Käsemann, his core exegetical, theological, and practical utterances were often disregarded. They were not given credit, and since no one paid them any mind, the truth and irresistible pressure caused by his central observations were avoided, and the call to change contained in his writings faded away.

Käsemann's exegetical insights and his theology of the cross can wait. They still have their time before them and will gather community and theology into a common new obedience to the first commandment in the discipleship of Jesus.

I owe a huge debt of thanks to Dr. Eva Teufel, daughter of Ernst Käsemann, who was generous and obliging enough to give me access to the literary estate in her father's house, whose trust in me allowed me a free hand in the composition of this volume, and who helped and advised me in its creation.

The present volume would not have appeared without the untiring, meticulous, and involved labor of co-editor Professor Wolfgang Kraus, Saarbrücken. Ernst Käsemann's exegesis and theology became ever clearer in conversations held with him on the texts published here.

---

1. E. Käsemann, *Kirchliche Konflikte*, vol. 1 (Göttingen: Vandenhoeck & Ruprecht, 1982), p. 5.

I have Professor Kraus to thank as well as his staff: Nadine Richter M.A., Coblenz, put the manuscripts in digital form; Sarah Donsbach and Heike Panter, students in the Philosophy of Religion Department; Dr. Georg Gäbel, coworker; Assistant Dr. Martin Vahrenhorst (all from Saarbrücken), assisted in organizing with proofreading and setting up the index.[2] These young theologians thus fulfilled the desire and awareness of Ernst Käsemann that coming generations would recognize his concerns anew and pass them on.

I am thankful to Frau Andrea Siebert for preparing the typescript.

Dr. Henning Ziebritski accompanied the publication of this volume with a zeal that contributed great clarity and help. In the true sense of the word he cared for it! Thanks are due him and the staff of the Mohr-Siebeck publishing firm occupied with producing the book.

The essays printed in part 2 (not arranged in any particular order) were intended by Ernst Käsemann for the publication of a second volume of *Kirchliche Konflikte.*

May this entire volume be heard in the guild of theologians, as well as in Christian congregations! Ernst Käsemann once said to me that, like no other, the hymn of Gottfried Arnold "O Durchbrecher aller Bande" (O Breaker of all bonds) expresses his concern, his struggle, and his battle. Let it be the hermeneutical key to his life and work. In his lecture on receiving the prize at Sexau on November 30, 1985, appearing next to last in this volume, he comes to speak of it: "This would be the place to cite in its entirety Gottfried Arnold's magnificent chorale 'O Durchbrecher aller Bande'. . . . One verse may suffice: 'Oh, raise the feeble powers to tear loose all at once, free and pure to break through all the world's affairs! Away with fear of men and hesitation! Retreat, reason's consideration! Dread of shame and worrying, be off! Frailty of flesh, away!' God's kingdom here is freedom bursting out of heaven to earth."[3]

May this freedom seize those who read and study these literary remains collected here.

RUDOLF LANDAU
Schillingstadt, June 26, 2005

---

2. The peculiarities of E. Käsemann's diction were retained; obvious errors have been silently corrected.

3. See page 313 below.

Translator's Preface

Some will disagree, as some have always disagreed, but for many the old lines from Hebrews 11:4 apply to the author of these essays: "He being dead yet speaketh." In these essays the Ernst Käsemann that speaketh is less the critic than the herald, the proclaimer, the *professor,* though he would have insisted it was precisely his critical reading of the Bible that gave him what it was he needed to speak. And the passion, the fire in the belly that accompanies what he said, leaves no doubt that he believed with all his heart what he had to say. As to the relevance of these essays, even those "parochial" references, say, to the situation in his own country, are easy of application elsewhere. One would have to be blind, deaf, and dumb to ignore the divide between people of the Northern and Southern Hemispheres, to ignore a Europe and an America totally devoid of the imagination needed to sue for peace, to overlook mainline, top-down hierarchical Christianity perilously close to extinction; one would have to be too fogged over not to see the pietist's everlasting introspection or the overconfidence of the orthodox in a permanent theology, too thick to miss the average Christian's identification of Christian faith with bourgeois, middle-class affluence and aspiration. These things Käsemann deplores, but he does not for that reason throw the baby out with the bathwater. The reader had better note that, whether toward state or church, middle class or underclass, pietist or orthodox, Käsemann's stance is dialectic, a view compounded of attraction and repulsion. He could scorn the pietist's navel-gazing and incessant reaching for the pulse but at the same time assign his own origins to Pietism, insisting that it rescued the heritage of the Reformation.

As to Käsemann's style, staccato comes to mind, and the hope is that, despite the damage done in translation, it will have left to his friends something of what they saw in the heart and mind of one of the twentieth century's most unembarrassed confessors of Jesus Christ, the Crucified, through whom life is manifest, not only in heaven, but already here on earth, and not just for me, but for the other, perhaps for the other most of all.

With the exception of those attached to the titles, the footnotes have been supplied by the translator. Here in the front matter, Eerdmans Publishing Company has included "A Theological Review," a theological retrospective by Ernst Käsemann on the occasion of his ninetieth-birthday celebration at Tübingen in July 1996.

Many thanks to William B. Eerdmans, Jr., for his interest in making this volume available, and to Craig Noll for needed assistance in preparing the manuscript for publication.

Finally, if such a thing as a translation could ever have a dedication, it would be to all Ernst Käsemann's former students and friends in the United States. You know who you are. . . .

Roy A. Harrisville

May 2008

A Theological Review

For seventy years theology has determined my life. In the stormy twentieth century one adventure has followed another. Such cannot be avoided in church and theology. At times we even get embroiled in the political struggle. In any event, I have had to alter my course from time to time, but have always kept faith with my beginnings.

My father fell in Russia early in 1915. From then on my mother, really isolated in the city of Essen, had to tough it out with her two children. On my arrival at the castle gymnasium, on the border between the Krupp[1] colony and the more rural suburb, I had no friends. I could have found them only in the inner city, where the school was also located. Even after the war we had to queue up in front of the stores to buy anything. Then when there was homework, there was little time for play or the outside world. I was left to reading my father's books, thus at thirteen discovered Shakespeare, and in curious succession two years later Karl May,[2] and at a similar interval discovered the German classics and romantics. Put briefly, my youth was lonely and rather joyless.

My life first took on clarity when in my last years at school (in a way I no longer remember) I came to know the Essen youth pastor Weigle[3] and his Jugendhaus [youth center] situated in the city center, which I visited twice a week after lunch. This was a preparation for, and narrow entry into,

1. Family name of the famous arms manufacturer.
2. Celebrated German author of American Wild West novels.
3. Wilhelm Weigle (1862-1932), leader in the German evangelical youth movement.

Professor Käsemann penned this retrospective at Tübingen on August 12, 1996, which his wife, Margrit, mailed to me following his death in February 1999.

the study of theology. Weigle was a charismatic such as I have not known since. Till his last breath, before and after World War I, he took care of and, magnetlike, drew thousands of youth from the working class. When isolated from them, he drew others from the secondary schools. His theme was to bring Jesus to the youth. I venture to say he succeeded with thousands. He made clear to me what I had unconsciously sought, a Lord to whom I could give myself, and he showed me life's way and goal. Prior to all the existence theology that later captivated me, and ignorant of the St. Christopher legend,[4] I came to know that each one's uniqueness, or in modern parlance, each one's identity, is experienced only through the Lord or through the demons to which one surrenders. No one belongs to himself or herself. In various ways a person exists only in a participation to be discovered. It is not enough to demythologize texts with Bultmann.[5] Before doing such, the world and human beings need to be demythologized, in, say, their self-mastery, their ideology, and the religious superstition to which they have surrendered. This takes place in the power of the gospel. This power streamed forth from Weigle. I will never forget his funeral. The procession began from the youth center, which the last mourner left only when the first arrived at the grave twenty minutes later. Two rows of youths and the elderly crowded both sides of the street, once more to thank the one who had helped them to a radical change in life. In a way I will never forget, Weigle showed me that German pietism preserved the Reformation heritage — provided, of course, it was not fanatical or egocentric. I have always defended that point of view, though my theology has often been condemned by pietists in many lands.

In May 1929 I became a student. Bonn lay nearest, and there too I found the friend I most respected in my student years. Coming from Bultmann and Marburg, he planned to take his first exams at Coblenz but still had time to ease my entry into academic life. His concern was not unjustified. In the university I attended all the lectures that piqued my curiosity, even those outside theology. On the third day, Peterson's[6] Romans

4. According to legend, an ancient warrior carries an unbearably heavy child across a river who is later revealed as the Christ. From this story the warrior becomes the patron saint of travelers, and from it derives his name, Christopher (lit. "Christ-bearer").

5. See Bultmann's 1941 essay "New Testament and Mythology," in *Kerygma and Myth: A Theological Debate,* vol. 1, ed. Hans Werner Bartsch, trans. Reginald H. Fuller (New York: Harper, 1961).

6. Erik Peterson (1890-1960), professor of church history and New Testament at Bonn, a convert to Catholicism in 1930.

lecture-course fascinated me, so I also took his seminar on Augustine's *Confessions*. In addition, I took the one hour a week history of religions course on Hellenism, without realizing how quickly Gnosticism was to become a chief problem of liberal New Testament exegesis. I sensed that Peterson was resolved to convert when during his lecture six Catholics kept stomping their feet in applause and the six irritated Protestants scraped theirs. From the first moment on, his ecclesiology had me in its spell. I was used to a church that treated youth as if it were a religious club. Now I was confronted with the worldwide Body of Christ, on the theme of which I later took a degree in 1931. Never again, as the leadership of my church pietistically and in its programming actually still does, would I describe the care of souls as the center of theology. Now too, Bultmann's anthropology became problematic for me, an anthropology viewed by both Pietism and the Enlightenment as the obvious exegetical perspective. With Bultmann, however, anthropology was not a way to psychological mastery. Existence theology occupied him, and not as a worldview. Today I incline toward the venturesome thesis that the entire Bible must be read and interpreted Christologically, thus not even from a theology-of-creation point of view. When Bultmann wanted to spoil my use of the term "humanity" as abstract, I retorted almost insolently that speaking of the "individual" was just as abstract.

In any event, the central theme of the New Testament is the worldwide lordship of the Crucified. Even the cure of souls, which I have never relativized, must make that lordship concrete in pastoral practice. According to Paul, the task of a particular theologian is to discern the spirits. The pious person is not to become more and more pious, nor obliged to pursue or demonstrate one "religion" among others. What is required is the discipleship of the Nazarene. The individual may function as a model in the fellowship, but the priesthood of all believers is not to be replaced by devotional individualism. Every Christian exists vis-à-vis an entire world and, even when isolated within one part of it, must resist both idealism and materialism. The Christian must always confess the Lord where idols rule on earth, whether under the sign of lust for power, of superstition, or of Mammon. From the Christian point of view, the first commandment is personified in Christ. It is this *solus Christus* that separates the gospel from all religions and worldviews, often even from a bourgeois or proletarian Christianity. On his way to Rome, Peterson laid bare the weaknesses of an idealistic Protestantism. I have always been grateful to him for that.

My friend was suspicious. In Marburg he witnessed Peterson's power to attract in Heinrich Schlier,[7] who followed Peterson's route to the end. I was in danger of going that way myself. So, after the first semester, I swallowed Bultmann's historical criticism as antidote. I naively agreed to go to Marburg, since I was lured to find in Schlier there the best interpreter of my Bonn master, and thus to be able to make a reasoned decision for my future career. I asked Bultmann to take me into his seminar on Pauline anthropology. He replied that the usual limit had already been reached. On the recommendation of my friend, however, I was to be viewed as an exception if I could justify my acceptance with a sketch on the anthropology in Paul's letter as gleaned from Peterson's lecture course. I learned then that when success beckons, risks are not to be avoided. The risk was worth the trouble where Bultmann was concerned, though I am still astonished by it even today. Of course, in the seminar I had to pass a second test. My Christmas vacation was ruined by the requirement that in the new year I submit a report of Kierkegaard's influence on Barth's exposition of Romans 7. When I managed this, I became a recognized member in the circle of the Marburg school. As such, I had daily to master Heidegger's philosophy[8] as well as Bultmann's theological criticism.

My labor was rewarded in the early sixties when the Geneva leadership of the ecumenical movement discussed the problem as to whether and, if so, what latitude was to be given New Testament criticism. As a representative of the Bultmann school, I was asked to give a main address at the next session of Faith and Order in Montreal on the theme: "Is the Unity of the Church Based on the Unity of the Bible?" The general secretary, Visser 't Hooft, never forgave me for deriving the variety of confessions from the variety of the biblical message. Thankfully, my thesis was ultimately adopted. The result was obvious: Discerning the spirits is a theological necessity, for which historical criticism is indispensable and, with the course of church history, more and more urgent. Now, of course, I had to face up to the question as to how I could unite my pietism with radical historical criticism.

In the fifth semester I changed schools again and, unlike most Marburgers, did not go to Barth at Münster, though I had devoured his writings ravenously. I expected greater clarity at Tübingen, above all with Schlatter,[9] but was disappointed. This tale cannot be told here and now in

7. Heinrich Schlier (1900-1978), professor of New Testament and ancient church history at Bonn, a convert to Catholicism in 1953.

8. Martin Heidegger (1889-1976), cofounder of the German philosophy of existence.

9. Adolf Schlatter (1852-1938), from 1898 to 1922 professor of New Testament at Tübingen.

any detail. Schlatter loved to provoke but was not eager to engage in public dispute. He had functioned in the same way at Berlin, when, in contrast to Harnack, he was to maintain the balance between conservative and liberal. He never let himself be diverted from his own point of view. I profited much from him and regard him as my third teacher in the New Testament. Still, he detoured around my problem. I made use of the free time left to me. The Tübingen faculty chose the present status of Johannine research as the subject for a prize competition. Again, I naively plunged into one of the most difficult exegetical themes and, often till midnight and much too young, came to deal with a gigantic flood of literature embroiled in dispute. A semester earlier I had, however, heard Bultmann's first lectures on the Gospel of John. I received the prize, though with the spiteful comment that I had criticized everything but Bultmann. The comment was justified. When thirty years later I held my own lectures on John, I was well prepared and could give my own view more depth.

Since my study had reached its peak, after a year in an area of theology I had neglected till then, I could apply for my first exams at Coblenz. This also turned out happily, aside from an accident: I failed totally when asked about the difference between Reformation and Orthodox ethics. I had never concerned myself with the theme but shamefacedly made up for it in the years to come. I'll not be silent about my conclusions, although — or perhaps just because — they might be provocative. As far as I know, the concept of ethics stems from Hellenistic tradition and is the basis of the modern idea of performance. A theory of duties makes clear what we must do or avoid, led by reason, conscience, situation, and convention. When we do not adhere to that theory, we are guilty. So we are constantly responsible in thought and deed, provided we do not challenge the distinction between good and evil.

I cannot derive such a discipline, and thus its watchword, from the Bible. The Bible knows of no one responsible for salvation or independent within it. The Pauline theology announces the justification of the godless and in place of "ethics" sets its doctrine of the charisms, which in turn reflects the first commandment. God is the Lord who commands, but he is the One who delivers from Egypt and forbids giving his place to other lords and gods. In this prohibition, promise is dominant. One need no longer serve other lords and gods and, like Israel once in Egypt, is freed from all idolatry. Precisely this is at issue when Paul speaks of the charism. It is the concretion of the *charis* that pardons us. At the outset of our worship, then, stands the God who serves, who sets us free. When he commands that we serve him, he wants us to remain in the freedom from ideologies and illusions he has given us. Now the recipient of *charis* becomes at the same time its bearer and its being let loose in the world. In the individual instance and always this service becomes a witness to and realization of the divine power of human liberation — a charismatic activity. The first commandment is truly a gospel. It calls to us to hand on what was given us, that is, the freedom of grace. But the first commandment is made concrete in the Nazarene, and in the discipleship of the Crucified it preserves the divine power of liberation in a world beset by demons. Reason, conscience, and understanding of the situation must play a role. In this respect, we approximate the ethics of paganism but are distanced from it by the fact that our freedom is expressed first of all and in a flatly revolutionary way in our resistance to the world's insanities. This was the fundamental experience of my generation. In the radical German Confessing Church we were stigmatized because, as disciples of Jesus, we had to become partisans of the gospel, risking death from tyrants for the sake of Protestant freedom.

I will omit the period of my education in the church, in order as briefly as possible to report the church struggle in my congregation at Gelsenkirchen-Rotthausen, spun off through a territorial exchange among the mines from the Rhineland toward Westphalia. I have admitted earlier that from 1930 to 1933 I too voted for Hitler. My work in the congregation and for my dissertation left me little time for involvement in politics. Every night, and for an entire year-and-a-half, while synodical vicar in Barmen, I was forced to experience the civil war at my very door. I eagerly longed for order. In family and school we continually heard that the Treaty of Versailles shamefully humiliated us Germans. Finally, the war left behind six million unemployed in our country. So my friends and I agreed that only a strong government could help us. I did come to mistrust Hitler after his intervention on behalf of a criminal storm trooper in Silesia. But I was naive enough to suppose that we could get rid of him at the next election in four years. In the meantime, the party of the German Christians was formed.[10] In the summer of 1933 it grew from four to forty-five members among the representatives of my congregation. Then, when the so-called Reichsbishop incorporated the evangelical youth groups into the Hitler youth,

10. A movement in German Protestantism, originating in the nineteenth century, closely connected with the rise of National Socialism and leading to the German church struggle and the creation of the "Confessing Church" (Die Bekennende Kirche).

and when the Roehm putsch eliminated disputes within the Nazi leadership through mass murder, we could no longer ignore our having been handed over to thugs who unflinchingly used force and would yield only to force.

The founding of the Confessing Church at Wuppertal led to political opposition. As early as the fall of 1933 I declared that the Reichsbishop was a traitor to the evangelical church. From then on I was hated by the Nazis, later was denounced in the marketplace as a national traitor by the Gauleiter (district leader) in Gelsenkirchen, and was recommended to the higher authorities for assignment to a concentration camp. The chairman of our congregation lent support in an appeal to headquarters at Berlin. For either side there was no turning back. This became clear in sessions of the congregational representatives. As president of the congregation, I denied that those sessions had any authority in the church and assigned them a merely secular importance. In the fall of 1934 I secretly learned that the Confessing Church was thinking of separating itself officially from the German Christians. With two colleagues and twelve members of the Confessing Church, we now resolved immediately to go on the offensive, and on the Day of Repentance and Prayer of November 15, 1934, we resolved to dismiss the forty-five German Christians from church service. In accord with church protocol, the announcement was made public at worship on the three Sundays prior and was carried out in a solemn service on the Day of Repentance and Prayer. Before the altar forty-five members of the Confessing Church were presented as substitutes for the discharged German Christians. We were in fact the first congregation in Germany to venture such action.

What we dared to do would of course never have succeeded if what seemed miraculous to us had never happened. On the Day of Repentance and Prayer a riot was about to occur on the plaza in front of the church. Nazis from Gelsenkirchen had decided not to allow our action. The pastors were to be flogged out of the church and the worship service discontinued. Many women from our ladies' aid, the backbone of our congregation, formed the opposition. They obviously did not threaten the men with brooms but promised to participate aggressively. Curiosity seekers of all ages and levels bordered the battle arena. Then Graf Stosch, advocate for church affairs in the district of Westphalia-North, suddenly appeared with about fifty policemen and ordered the area cleared in the name of the state. He himself took part in the worship, which now proceeded as planned. I preached on Jeremiah 7:1-15, an unusually compressed attack on the house of Israel, and then introduced forty-five members of the Confessing Church as substitutes for the discharged German Christians. We could see the older people weeping there. Graf Stosch had informed us the previous day that he would be commissioned by Berlin to arrest the pastors and prevent the service. When we answered "yes" to his query whether we would still keep to our resolve, he assured us of his protection. He had informed Berlin that he would guarantee order. I do not know what motivated him. Family tradition in the Silesian nobility may have prevented him from using force against the church. Perhaps he had learned from the Roehm putsch and the Silesian storm troopers' crimes to distance himself from tyranny. He was later removed from district leadership and became president of the Minden administrative district. I must always remember him. For me the climax of our struggle is bound up with him.

The struggle continued. Not even our synod in Westphalia regarded us as its vanguard. They wanted first to wait and see how our experiment would turn out, or so they wrote to me. Our action really isolated us. There should be no talk today of an ethics of resistance in the church of that period. We were partisans.[11] Even after the war our inheritance was buried at Treysa[12] for the sake of the national church of the nineteenth century. Reconciliation, in the religious sphere as well, became the watchword worldwide. That kind of ideology was driven out of me when in 1937 Niemöller[13] had to enter a concentration camp and seven hundred evangelical pastors also had to go to prison. At that time I had to preach at a service of intercession on Isaiah 26:13: "O Lord our God, other lords besides you have ruled over us, but we acknowledge your name alone." Angry and in pain, I determined then that God's reconciliation with us could not be accomplished by compromising with our enemies. In the church the obverse side

11. By "partisans," Käsemann here refers to their struggle against the German Christians, and in the face of the timidity of the national churches.

12. Treysa was the site of the provisional founding in August 1945 of the Evangelische Kirche in Deutschland (EKD, the Evangelical Church in Germany), which was inhibited by denominational differences. Note the reference below to Treysa (p. 272).

13. Martin Niemöller (1892-1984), one of the most noted and most disputed church leaders of the twentieth century. For his resistance to Nazism, Niemöller was imprisoned as the Führer's "personal prisoner" at Sachsenhausen and Dachau from 1938 to 1945. Following liberation he occupied various leading positions in German Protestantism, opposed the founding of the German Democratic Republic, and polemicized against rearmament and the church's adaptation to the ideology of the Cold War.

of freedom is and remains resistance to idolaters. On the following day, the Gestapo came and got me. They were very cautious and went thirty steps ahead of me. Miners can still be violent; they can deny authorities the respect the average citizen will never refuse.

I clearly recall 1937 because on Good Friday I had to hold out for seven hours in four worship services, as well as give communion on Easter week to the children and grandchildren of members of the East Prussian Prayer League. But in 1937 no less than one-third of my congregation voted for the Social Democratic Party, a communist front. At that time I did not detect any "reconciliation," but rather a fellowship of Christians and proletarians, which had not existed before in Germany. Some came to worship because the pastor had visited them; others came out of curiosity, to see if my neck would finally be on the line. Night after night, for three long years before the war, we knew nothing of the security that existed only for citizens who played along. But with the exception of one co-rector who would not let me into his house, I was secure among my communist Masurians[14] and will not forget what they did. The almost twenty-five days I spent in jail before being released without a hearing were actually restful. I did not have to rush daily from one house to the other, or at night give communion to the dying. No one said an evil word to me. The prison inspector got me a box of Brazilian cigars and allowed books, excerpts, and paper to be sent to me so that I could finish my study on Hebrews, *The Wandering People of God.* Now and then a guard visited me in the evening to ask how a pastor could get himself behind bars, and how I happened to be the first in the history of Gelsenkirchen. On Sunday morning the brass band from the hospital opposite the jail played "Wach auf, wach auf, du deutsches Land, Du bist genug geschlaffen" [Wake, wake, O German land; you've been long enough abed] and other rousing stuff. Only the fish bones in the herring soup on Wednesdays and the anxiety at being arrested by the Gestapo on the prison steps after my release disturbed my peace.

Up to the war, and finally with the visit of six nice women and six hardy miners to the High Consistory at Berlin, the congregation refused to be put on the defensive. When the visitors were not admitted, they sat on the steps and refused to leave till the president, vice-president, and consistory council had to leave their rooms and be informed about Rotthausen, gently by the women, roughly by the men. We succeeded in having our rec-

14. Inhabitants of former East Prussia, now northeast Poland.

ords mislaid till the end of the war. How that would turn out I never doubted, not for one moment.[15]

I should like to break off here. It would lead to a full-scale autobiography if I were to tell how I had to be a soldier for three years, perhaps to get out of reach of the area command and seizure by the Nazis; how I finally survived the camp at Kreuznach, in which 70,000 prisoners starved, then returned to a heavily bombed congregation; and how I at once learned that I had been chosen as a New Testament scholar for Münster but, because of a denunciation, landed at Mainz instead. My students and my writings can tell about the theological problems that arose at Mainz, Göttingen, and for thirty-seven years at Tübingen. I thank them all for having patiently heard me and even more for honoring me today. I would gladly give each of them my hand and my thanks, though I cannot. Age hinders signs of friendship maintained. As a last word and as my bequest, let me call to you in Huguenot style: "Résistez!" Discipleship of the Crucified leads necessarily to resistance to idolatry on every front. This resistance is and must be the most important mark of Christian freedom.

Many thanks!

ERNST KÄSEMANN
July 1996

---

15. Käsemann appears to be voicing his confidence that, when finally made available, the records would justify the congregation's resistance.

PART ONE

BIBLICAL ESSAYS

Beginning of the Gospel:
The Message of the Kingdom of God

1. Let me begin with a *preliminary critical remark.* I am happy to open your new lecture series on apocalyptic. At the same time, the theologian, particularly the New Testament scholar, must take it as a challenge to do so in light of the overall theme of this series, "The Danger and Meaning of Anxiety." First of all, and perhaps in fact, only psychologists and psychotherapists should speak of it as they actually will do in the weeks following. They are more competent than others where the problem of anxiety is involved among individuals, groups, or in nations and continents. Theologians will not avoid conversing with them in this area. They would be of no use to their craft if they failed always to remember their duty of soul care. They would ignore real persons whose reality involves continually falling prey to anxiety. Less than earlier should we close our eyes to the fact that today psychoses actually help to determine world politics. Only a poor theology devotes itself to church dogmatics, as if the responsibility for having to enter the anxieties of the world around it should be left to the experts of other disciplines. In any event, the Bible deals basically and relevantly in concrete situations with the danger and meaning of anxiety. We would be liquidators of the Christian inheritance if this did not call us to our place and task.

What I as theologian object to as regards the theme of our series and what thus forces me to begin my report with a critical preamble concerns the fact that our program seems more or less clearly to assume that the person of today can speak appropriately of apocalyptic only when discuss-

---

A lecture given on September 30, 1985, in Hospitalhof, Stuttgart.

ing the problem of anxiety. For the New Testament scholar, apocalyptic is a basic phenomenon of the discipline. Without it the history of early Christianity cannot be understood. For a theology bound to the Bible the question must be put as to whether Christian proclamation may ever forget that its roots reach deeply and stoutly into such native soil. Today, almost 2,000 years after the beginning of the Christian era, we may be forced to treat our heritage in a more intelligent way and perhaps, as is now given formulation in many places, to demythologize it. We will not place under taboo or hand on as sacrosanct indigestible scraps of bygone ways of perceiving, since without intelligibility our message of faith would no longer be convincing. Even less can we allow it to be mutilated for the sake of modern taste by declaring its original concerns to be outdated and meaningless in our day. In my opinion, exactly this occurs when early Christian apocalyptic is reduced to the aspect of a world anxiety familiar to us all. Then it is a sickness, and about it psychologists as well as therapists would necessarily have the first, perhaps even the last, word.

The New Testament scholar, however, must passionately oppose this, if he or she intends to remain a theologian, thus to defend the gospel. Only the scholar of religion who attempts to conduct impartial analyses can, on my view, judge apocalyptic as a depressing worldview, such as politicians and the mass media for the most part suggest, and as Christian church authorities and congregational members on occasion unthinkingly concede. Such an apocalyptic — that is, the idea that cosmic catastrophes should threaten us or at least should end the global preeminence of the white race, perhaps actually annihilate all humanity — does not square with the concept of faith in progress as handed on to us. For this reason an apocalyptic that actually conjures up such visions is branded by the protectors of public order as a frivolous and dangerous alarmist tactic. The argument reads that where anxieties are aroused, economic growth, political serenity, and the citizen's mental balance are disturbed. Doom, of course, can also be glibly ignored. Hence those in government suppose it is precisely their duty by way of propaganda to oppose the prophets of doom, to stigmatize them as fools or as subversive pests. Whoever has read something of the Old Testament recalls that such conflicts existed 3,000 years ago between those in power and the messengers of God. Something similar can easily be detected in the history of nations. But in our days we see that even atomic weapons and a possible star wars can be touted and believed in as instruments of planned security and worldwide stability. The human being is the only living creature who can shut out eyes, ears, and reason when reality is unpleasing. Afterwards the excuse is that one meant well, that we must still trust the competence of those in power if we would not turn every community into a chaos of conflicting forces.

Thus a twofold task lies before the theologian who would render early Christian apocalyptic intelligible. First, the illusion must be repressed that imagines that our personal life and the condition of the world today are no longer prey to volcanic outbreaks, which for millions of years shattered and plowed up the earth. In a certain respect it would be good for us if we began to fear again, rather than to allow our eyes, ears, and understanding to be fogged over. No one remains human who chases after the heroic ideal of fearlessness or lets oneself be seduced by demagogues and then gives trust to idols instead of to the Father of Jesus Christ. No one remains human who has given no room to death or failure in one's account book, who is not ready and willing with Abraham and Israel to join the exodus from the familiar world of Chaldea or Egypt. Biblical apocalyptic reminds us of this. Second, the theologian with early Christian history in mind must make clear that there, in any case, apocalyptic was primarily a promise of salvation. The theologian cannot allow counterfeiting and falsifying into a depressing worldview that which proclaimed resurrection of the dead and the life of the future world to the damned of the earth as the God-willed liberation from their anxieties and distresses. Apocalyptic, Christianly understood, is a theology of liberation and salvation, not of anxiety.

2. *The beginning of the gospel: the message of the kingdom of God.* A glimpse into the history of earliest Christianity should confirm what was just asserted. This history begins apocalyptically, that is, with a summons that, according to the report of the first gospels, signalized the appearance of John the Baptist in the very same words as those of Jesus: "Repent! The kingdom of heaven has come near!" What "the kingdom of heaven" means here — that is, according to the Jewish view, and as clearly appears in the New Testament as well — is not primarily something beyond earthly reality, into which souls are gathered after death. What is meant first of all is that event in the end time in which God openly makes known his lordship over the earth, a lordship rightly due him as Creator and Lord of the world, because he overcomes all other powers. The eternal reign is then the consequence of such a revelation of his glory, which historically was mostly hidden and thus forgotten, denied, and claimed by idols. According to the message of the Baptist, the breaking in of this lordship is directly at hand, putting an end to all demonic deception, mischief, and even the tyranny of earthly persons in

authority. This is clearly announced in threat. The Baptist, as most Old Testament prophets, is a witness to the divine wrath about to be discharged in judgment. Thus the Baptist begins with the call to repentance, which means, as in the Bible throughout, a turning from godlessness and unrighteousness. Where, like a consuming fire, the majesty of the Lord of the earth brings to light his sole power over his creation and reckons with his adversaries, only one escape is open: return to the condition to which everything earthly finally belongs, that is, to the condition before his face, in obedience to his word, in hope of the promise of his blessing. This is symbolized in the act of baptism. The rebel who considered himself his god and lived out from the illusion of his own will and power must drown. The one who allowed himself to be sealed by baptism as God's possession, as it were, and to be called to a new service in the divine lordship must rise from the water, judged and purified. So there is deliverance only in judgment, but only for a minority, as once during the flood.

Jesus appears with the same summons as the Baptist. According to the unanimous witness of our Gospels, he himself was a disciple of the Baptist when he allowed himself to be baptized by him and thus joined with those who sought deliverance in the face of impending judgment. But when we survey the entire story of Jesus as told us by the Gospels, we must state that, with the Nazarene, the same words have another meaning than with John. There is not the least doubt that Jesus was not a preacher of judgment. He brings the good news of salvation, for which reason the reports concerning him are called Gospels. Of course, he too can speak of the divine Judge and summon his hearers to repentance. But this is only the reverse side of his proclamation, according to which whoever does not hear the call to salvation and accept it incurs disaster. Thus the God of Jesus is the Lord, whom one may call Father and storm with petitions. He waits for the lost son and allows the poor, the outcasts, the sinners to hear his beatitudes. He allows the sick and the possessed to be healed and extends the covenant of reconciliation beyond the boundaries of Israel to everything on earth that has need. We can say that Jesus sets the message of the Baptist on its head. Where John spoke of the wrath of the world Judge and leaves open only a crack for rescue of the converted, in the words of Old Testament prophecy Jesus' so-called inaugural sermon at Nazareth in Luke 4:18-19 reads, "to proclaim the year of the Lord's favor." It is intended as "good news to the poor . . . to proclaim release to the captives and recovery of sight to the blind, to let the oppressed go free." It is precisely of this message that our Gospels tell.

With Jesus the prophetic promises are fulfilled. But this means that the inbreaking of the rule of God is no longer merely announced as imminent. The breaking in already ensues, though the consummation is still outstanding. The coming kingdom of God is already manifest on earth where the Nazarene appears and is accepted. He is thus no longer a pupil of the Baptist. He began as such. But in the meantime has occurred what John still awaited. The baptismal narrative in Matthew 3:16-17 portrays it in sharpest colors: heaven is opened over the One sent by God. The Spirit descended on him, and a voice from heaven announced, "This is my Son, the Beloved, with whom I am well pleased." This is how New Testament apocalyptic looks at its core. It does not deal in a mood of world ruin, as is asserted today, because the Bible has more and more become an unknown book. Naturally, the Baptist prophesies world ruin, and Jesus likewise appears to have reckoned on it in the near future. But the end of the world is the horizon against which the gospel stands out. In the twentieth century no one would any longer seriously deny, as perhaps our grandparents still could, that the world is hastening toward its end. Where atomic bombs have already been exploded and both sides of Germany create a huge arsenal for them, no one would tell bedtime stories, hand out opium pills, and say that the end might come in a thousand years. Still, we would wish for a bit more taste for reality on the part of politicians and propagandists, since in this century they have already twice deceived us.

So we state first of all that Christian apocalyptic has stood the message of the Baptist on its head. According to the New Testament, the end of the world does not begin with the imminent, cosmic wrath of God, as surely each of us can experience the true God in our life as a wrathful Judge, provided we do not harden our heart and mind. But the Baptist was only a forerunner of Jesus, who began as his pupil and thereafter became his master. According to the New Testament and its apocalyptic, the end of the world begins with the appearance of the one on whom the heavens opened, on whom the Spirit descended, and of whom it was announced, "My Son, the Beloved." He drives out the demons, opens eyes and ears, wakens the sleeping and the dead, and brings freedom to all of us who lie in chains of unreason, passion, weakness, and guilt, of an earth gone mad and its tyranny.

It is the tragedy of Christianity that, after almost 2,000 years of its history, people of all educational levels see it as the bearer of a depressing worldview, or as the consoler and prescriber of religious opium. Where there are Christians and heralds of their Lord, life and death, salvation and ruin, judgment and grace — in brief, all the truly ultimate and most important, all the literally apocalyptic experiences — should begin and end as at the Isenheim Altarpiece in Colmar.[1] There stands the Baptist, who points with his gigantic index finger to the man of the cross, with whom everything just told is connected. He is the end of the old world insofar as he is the end of the old Adam. As the new Adam, he is also the breaking in of the rule of God in midst of his enemies, the godless, and the devout. Since his earthly appearance apocalyptic theology always and everywhere denotes a theology of liberation in an earth that is dying and plagued by evil powers. Whoever maintains otherwise may appeal to an apocalyptic outside the New Testament, about which I need not speak here, and about which not many in this hall may have accurate knowledge. Evangelical theology is solidly and uncompromisingly opposed to it. An apocalyptic reduced to a mood of world ruin and promoting desperate anxiety has nothing to do with the gospel. There, according to the Revelation of John, the most apocalyptic book of the entire Bible, Christ is the Alpha and the Omega, the beginning and the end, and the rule of God come near is the kingdom where the beast from the abyss is conquered, where God himself will wipe away his servants' tears, and where those set free will sing the praise of the Lamb, who was slain for them.

3. *The crucified Lord and his liberated servants.* Meanwhile, we have pushed too far ahead. From the perspective of the gospel we would have had to begin quite differently, that is, with Easter. We too easily forget that the Gospels were written only after Easter and that they tell everything that happened earlier from the optic angle of the Easter experience. No doubt, much that was noteworthy occurred earlier, to which we may later assign apocalyptic weight. A pupil of the Baptist took up the message of his teacher regarding the imminent kingdom of God. Against everything allowed a pupil, he stood the message of his teacher on its head: the kingdom of God is not just coming; it has already broken in, and in fact with him, the Nazarene, who is making a forerunner of his master. In fact, he treats Moses in the same way as the Baptist when he contrasts his sovereign "But I say unto you" with the commandments from Sinai and with Jewish rab-

---

1. The reference is to the center portion of a retable painted by Matthias Grünewald (Mathias Neithart, ca. 1480-1528), an acquaintance of Philip Melanchthon but ambivalent toward the Reformation. Prepared for the hospice at Issenheim, it is now in the Colmar museum.

binic interpretation. Here a Jew relativizes the authority of Moses and the scribes, an authority that had to be sacrosanct for every Jew. Can he then still be a Jew? Accordingly, he attaches his preaching in such a way with his person that the company of his disciples must see in him the promised Messiah. No doubt, he has assigned himself a unique position when he allows the history of salvation to begin with his appearing, when he performs healings of the sick and possessed, events the historian can scarcely contest, and precisely from his casting out of demons concludes that the final rule of God has broken in. Obviously much that was noteworthy occurred that is not to be dealt with now. From what is there we can see that a company of disciples formed about the Nazarene, that, remarkably, it included the devout as well as crude sinners, and, most unusual for a Jewish rabbi, a group of women of a not-too-tidy origin. But when we have said this, we must keep in mind that his way ended on a Roman cross. Devout Judaism rejected him as a blasphemer, and the Romans condemned him as a political rebel. He died among zealots as a criminal, and in view of this end his disciples fled to Galilee. Apocalyptic expectations may have been connected with his earthly journeys and perhaps were even shared by himself. On Golgotha they were thrown to the winds. "But we thought," say the disciples on the way to Emmaus. Only over the ruins of all their hopes does Easter occur. Thus at bottom this event must be described as the beginning of the gospel. In place of the disciples who follow a most unusual Jewish prophet there now appears the church of Christ.

The oldest document of this church is contained in 1 Corinthians 15:3ff. To prove his apostleship Paul reminds the community there of a fixed tradition, listing the witnesses to the resurrection of the Crucified. Perhaps the convert was inculcated with such a tradition at baptism. It contains what is most important of Christian faith and may be summarized in a single Greek word that, translated, reads, "He was seen." This term has technical significance, that is, it means as much as, "He appeared." Better yet would be, "He was revealed." This brings us again to the theme of apocalyptic. Quite literally, apocalyptic denotes nothing but "tidings of revelation." The resurrection of Christ has become the basic apocalyptic event for Christianity, as it is for each of its members. Our faith rests on it. He was seen, he appeared, he revealed himself, and — take note — as the Crucified. His story did not end at Golgotha. In fact, it only begins there and at Easter, which may not be separated from the cross. Now the Nazarene is no longer a prophet and teacher. From now on his name is "Lord." Paul thus reduces his message in 1 Corinthians 15:25 to a single denominator, "He must reign." Now, more than ever, it is necessary to hear and repeat that this is and must remain the basic message of Easter. For in the course of time what has become more and more important to Christians is what happens to them and not to their Lord. Too often the church has assumed his place and behaved as if it were evangelical to believe in what it declares and thinks it can prescribe. Even in Protestantism whoever does not do homage to current theology is often excommunicated or at least hereticized. Here, of course, the office does not enjoy as much power as in Catholicism. Still, orthodox or pietistic minorities the more easily arrogate to themselves the right to judge others who do not act in conformity with their doctrine and morals. Bishops and popes rule in every community and seek to impress their surroundings with their own image.

The more the church became middle class, the more middle class became the ideal of the Christian way of life, and the more the gospel became a middle-class worldview. But since it is characteristic of middle-class citizens that they, their values, and their possessions should survive all crises, Christian hope at the grave has predominantly become the expectation that we shall also survive death. Beyond this there may still be speculation as to how this can happen. Certainly many will be irritated when their personal interests, yearnings, and eventual anxieties no longer dominate. It is so hard to learn what the Baptist says according to John 3:30: "He must increase, but I must decrease." Still, the life of the disciple of Jesus stands and falls by the fact that Christ increases in, over, and through us, and that we learn to decrease in discipleship to him. In just this way it is verified on earth that he reigns since Easter, and that even applies to the grave. We need no longer be concerned with our personal fate because he does not abandon his own but retains his rule even when we decrease and return to dust. "His kingdom's ours forever" where our kingdoms end.[2] Of course, it is important that such speaking is not merely heard and understood in a devotional way. According to the New Testament and especially 1 Corinthians 15, Easter has apocalyptic dimensions. To the horror of the pious and the heathen there now occur miracles of which the Gospels tell. The ears and mouths of the deaf and dumb are opened, the lame walk and prove they are no longer bound, the possessed are freed of the spirits of Mammon and egoism, the downtrodden raise their heads and spite the tyrants, the poor are aware they are chosen and praise the Lord, who resists the mighty, the sated, and the self-secure. There is much talk today of the fact

2. A citation here of the last line of Luther's "A Mighty Fortress."

that our churches are becoming more and more empty, and that is true. But we should not overlook the fact that meanwhile the driving downpour of the gospel of which Luther spoke has fallen on the Third World, while the desert around the white race is spreading inside and out. The resurrection of the dead has its prelude in time.

I have argued that, in the New Testament, apocalyptic is an event that begins with the Nazarene and finds its midpoint with the reigning Christ. Whoever reduces it to world-anxiety does so as if the rule and glory of Jesus Christ no longer existed in our time. From a message of salvation Christian apocalyptic becomes a depressing ideology. If the theme of apocalyptic since Easter is "He must reign," then since Easter it necessarily has a worldwide horizon. For the most part this is no longer taken seriously, though it is constitutive of our faith. When Christianity was almost totally lost in middle-class values and less and less able to begin with apocalyptic, the slogan heard everywhere was that religion is a private affair. This slogan, at least with reference to Christianity, is absolutely false. The gospel is intended for every individual. And this is so because it will have the whole earth and reclaim the creation of our God within the first commandment's sphere of power. The resurrection of the dead does not merely apply to pious souls. It is a revolutionary event alongside which all other revolutions appear harmless. Idols fall where God's kingdom seizes space on earth. Demons and demoniacs are driven out where one begins to live and believe as a disciple of Jesus. Easter sends one out of the closet into the world. A private affair is and remains a tiny corner affair, which still does not explain whether such a thing as a private life is not just imagination. We are all part of the world, in body and mind continually entangled in the occasions of earth. In any event, Christians are neither able nor permitted to hide or barricade themselves, because their Lord enlists them as messengers in his great mission and does not relieve them from it till death. His kingdom is not so invisible that one would fail to get any trace of it. Luther maintained that there would be tumult where the gospel is preached. He thus seized on Jesus' prediction to his disciples. Jesus called them to discipleship by way of the cross. They cannot possibly be his disciples when his opponents are naturally provoked by the Master but not by his disciples. No more than he do they model the honest citizen, and they are not deposited by him on an island of the blessed but are sent to an earth that, for the majority of its inhabitants, is a hell.

For the allegedly modern persons, of course, hell no longer exists, and where they ought to look for heaven is also unclear to them. Even the world itself is seen only from the nook or cranny of their worldview, their ideologies, their entanglement in goals, tasks, and troubles. Neither the Bible nor the newspaper and television can in general deliver them from apathy respecting the victims of our civilization. They repress the experiences, even more the crimes of a generation now dying off. Hell simply lies distant from those who no longer allow themselves to be reminded, who in any case will not open their eyes and ears to the misery of Lazarus before their own door, or of those dying in distant lands. The officially elected soothsayers or those who parade as such declare that anxiety is imagined and never tire of whispering or trumpeting that everything will be fine again and in the long run actually better. There were such soothsayers in the Old Testament, as well as in our past. I can still hear the song of the dance halls disturbing our sleep in the hot summer nights of 1939: "Es geht alles vorüber, es geht alles vorbei. Auf jeden September folgt wieder ein Mai" (All goes away, all passes by, every September is followed by May). May of 1945 came, and as early as September of 1939 reasonable folk knew how it would look. The ruin of the world we knew was clear before the first atomic bomb fell. We absolutely cannot miss the flaming script on our walls announcing the arrogance and stupidity of today's soothsayers, "weighed on the scales and found wanting." These are actually apocalyptic utterances. On this account may we take them to be horror visions of a sick fantasy? Once more, politicians and the media assert, just as did the youth who marched into ruin singing, "Wir werden weitermarschieren, wenn alles in Scherben fällt" (We'll keep on marching, though everything goes to pieces). The heap of shrouds has only partially been removed. But it is not so in the underdeveloped world, and among us there appear in its place a pile of rockets, a hidden cache of chemical weapons, only allegedly outlawed, and in addition forests, ground, water, and air whose poisoning no longer can be denied. Are they really insane who will not be diverted from such conditions by phrases about security, balance, superiority, deterrence? Today, hysteria and possession have more power over the propagandists of the affluent society than the minority that sees this earth of ours increasingly handed over to the powers and forces of darkness. Christians should courageously defend the truth and the right of a biblically apocalyptic worldview. At least in our time they should be and act apocalyptically.

This is the reality of the earth in which Jesus Christ wills to establish his rule and the witness to it. When we engage with this earth, we must relearn every day that our Lord is and will remain the Crucified even after

Easter, that his people are not set within a tranquility the average citizen loves on Sunday and expects of Christians. The peace promised us that passes all understanding means that we can confidently walk with the Nazarene through distress and hate, supported by his word and learning to know him as the Liberator in midst of an earth plagued by demons. Once, as the Pentecost narrative states, Easter was understood as the sending of witnesses to the resurrection power into a world ruled by darkness and the fear of death, but at the same time as the opening of heaven, as the gift of the Spirit of its Lord to his community left behind on earth, making it certain of his abiding presence and fit for its service. At Easter is repeated that apocalyptic event which the Gospel reports Jesus himself underwent in the Jordan baptism. At Easter the Son, proclaimed as such by the divine voice and equipped with the Holy Spirit for his mission, creates sons and daughters of the heavenly Father who follow him in his mission throughout the world and to whom he gives the Spirit as the power for their earthly service. What he defined as his task in his inaugural sermon at Nazareth they must pursue in discipleship, that is, set on the way with him under the sign of the cross, in the transport of the Spirit bringing the promise of freedom to those captive to demons. In this way, according to Romans 8:21ff., the true church of the gospel enjoys solidarity with all creation, which groans from its transitoriness for the freedom of the glory of the children of God. Thus, apocalyptically, it is something to the praise of the divine glory and the inbreaking of God's kingdom on earth. The ruling political and religious powers may want to make of Christians protectors and preservers of middle-class order and in so doing tolerate them. Evangelical freedom cannot be bureaucratized. It lives and acts where the Spirit of their Lord reveals himself on earth in his disciples, in the expectation of a "new heavens and a new earth, where righteousness is at home." What apocalyptic means from the Christian point of view cannot be more clearly stated than in this quotation from 2 Peter 3:13. It cannot be clearer that true Christianity must always be seen as apocalyptic, not as a carrier of anxiety, but of the freedom of the gospel and everywhere as bearer of a theology of liberation.

4. *Conclusion.* I have not even begun to touch on everything that needs to be analyzed of New Testament apocalyptic. We have not gone beyond early Christian beginnings. But they would have made clear that to construe early Christian apocalyptic merely as a preachment of imminent world ruin is an intolerable mutilation of the evangelical message. Church groups may have contributed to such a misunderstanding, and it may be

that particularly in Swabia they contribute mightily to it. It would follow, then, that we cannot dispense with a critical theology if the gospel is not to be falsified into a pious worldview, particularly in West German middle-class society. Against such a worldview psychologists and psychotherapists may have to defend themselves under the theme "The Meaning and Danger of Anxiety." No doubt, in our world and era the need and problematic of widespread anxiety should be taken up thematically. But where Protestant theology conceives apocalyptic as the message of God's kingdom revealed in Christ and as the worldwide liberation of the children of God, world anxiety may not be derived from it. A beginning should rather be made with the demons in politics, economics, and the worldview of the white race in the modern age, with the aim of promoting their expulsion and restraining.

The Righteousness of God in Paul

The New Testament scholar cannot treat the theme of "righteousness" in one brief hour — in fact, cannot do so at all if the political dimension of this theme within the biblical message is to be discussed. So we must limit ourselves from the outset. The Reformation recognized the justifying righteousness of God as the heart of Scripture and found it formulated most acutely by the apostle Paul. My lecture will remain within the confines of this topic. I intend here not to present a professional-theological monologue but to introduce a discussion. We begin deliberately with what we generally have in mind concerning the term "righteousness," so as to be aware of its difference from the Pauline proclamation. No doubt we have all seen the image of the woman who, blindfolded, holds the scales in her hands as a symbol of earthly righteousness. She is blindfolded in order not to be influenced by rank, appearance, or behavior of the parties appearing before her. She particularly cannot have an eye to her own advantage or, in the case of ticklish decisions, to her personal peril. She must judge impartially whatever the result, and the scales in her hands may fall or rise only according to the weight of the determined guilt or innocence. Leave undecided whether this beautiful idea corresponds to or at least approaches the daily reality of our justice. What is only of concern now is that we actually have such an ideal. In this case we follow in the footsteps of classical Greece, for which the goddess of justice sat high enthroned above all other gods and particularly over humans. All were subject to her judgment, neutrally handed down solely in accordance with norms of guilt and inno-

---

A lecture given on February 1, 1985, to the congregation at Leonberg.

cence. Only when she behaved in such fashion was there actually justice in heaven and on earth. Otherwise, the whole world would sink into chaos, into total disorder. Individual mitigating or more difficult circumstances might be considered in connection with a crime, so that the punishment of an evildoer could turn out lighter or harsher. To righteousness was thus attached the regulative of fairness, that reason not be excluded. At issue wherever there was to be judgment was the upholding of the order of common life. By its rule separation was to be made between good and evil, and acquittal or sentencing would make sense.

For at least two thousand years we in the Western world have had this ideal in view, and by it measured our judges and the governance of our political rulers. It should be underscored that this image of righteousness was political in character, since it was concerned with maintaining universal order in the various spheres of communal life. Whoever separates politics from valid rights unavoidably abandons reality to the arbitrariness of the stronger. Now, in view of this ideal, how is it with what Paul calls the righteousness of God? Inquiring in this way, we are immediately struck by a difference that cannot be overlooked. For the apostle, righteousness is not punitive. It does not hold the scale of earthly justice in its hands and wears no blindfold to protect it from partisanship. For Paul, righteousness effects salvation. This was the basic insight of Luther that paved the way for the Reformation. The righteous God is not the wrathful and punishing Judge but the gracious Lord, who offers his creatures salvation. Of course, this does not at all mean that he will not claim his rights or enforce them. His righteousness is not a moral attribute that unites him with the good and separates him from the evil. Persons who live and think based on the morality usual among us have understood nothing of the gospel. They must always have the scale in mind and take it in hand to indicate the difference between the better and the worse. And as in business, they would have to share without end in the competitive war of all against all, a war in which all passions are unleashed, deception and self-deception, arrogance and despair spell one another, and the great rush for the best seat takes place in body and soul. Finally, they would never know the grace of God and their own salvation. None of us will ever be free of guilt, regarding which we need to note that, along with our daily failings, there are the unnumbered dangerous snares that, for the most part unnoticed and unwilled, drag us into the demonic darkness of our earth. It sounds incredible and yet is true that genuine piety makes one self-critical, ends the moral competition in which one everlastingly feels one's pulse and that of others, ends the religious struggle in which all the strong seek to outstrip one another and reach the heights on the way to the kingdom of heaven. If this should not be clearly recognizable in Christian history and present existence, it would only prove that Christians can ruin Christian existence, can distort piety into a playground scene of egotistical pushing and shoving, hypocrisy and inhumanity.

We summarize: Whoever is wise leaves the scale out of the game where God's righteousness and our relation to it are concerned, especially when we look at our neighbor and suggest comparisons. When we do this, we always look foolish and must end in delusion instead of in grace and humanity. To put it pointedly, the Father of Jesus Christ, in whose revelation alone we learn the truth about him, our neighbors, and ourselves, is in opposition to what we require of earthly justice. It is thoroughly partisan. The Beatitudes tell us this. God resists the proud and descends to the poor, the shattered, the despised of the earth. None could be saved if he were impartially just. The whole world would otherwise be lost, a world that we even today can see is an inferno for the majority of its inhabitants. It is such even where it is not evident and the demons disguise themselves. There can be salvation for us all only when Paul summarizes the gospel in provocative and polemical fashion to read that God justifies the godless, always and everywhere. The truly devout are aware of our own and their godlessness and thus pray the Our Father: "Hallowed be thy name, thy kingdom come, thy will be done on earth as it is in heaven! Forgive us our trespasses! Deliver us from evil!" Our God must intercede with partiality on behalf of his lost and godless creatures if we shall be helped. And we must emulate him if the earth is not to remain an inferno everywhere. Love must displace the judge's scale where salvation is to seize hold of our world. Impartial justice never achieves this. At best it will create and preserve order, thus hem in evil. But the reflection of the new heaven signals a new earth only where another righteousness than that of Pharisees, scribes and jurists makes its home with us.

I cannot omit anticipating a portion of what should be dealt with only at the conclusion of my lecture. Clearly, the political dimension of the biblical message must come to light if God's righteousness does not measure according to the norms of guilt or innocence but rather, for the sake of the godless becomes man in Christ and intends to be their God and Savior. Consider our situation first of all. It is a political fact that there is global conflict over true Christianity, that individuals, groups, parties, confessions, and worldwide communions are involved in erecting walls against each other that do not even allow common celebration of the Lord's Supper. Economic, cultural, and military interests foster dissension on earth, but no less so do religious and intra-Christian conflicts. Non-Christians can thus play us off against each other, can heighten the conflict of worldviews with Christian support, can give title and space to a worldwide polarization reaching into families, even with the support of Bible interpretation, such as in the synod and congregations in the region of Baden-Württemberg, or as in South Africa, where racist fanaticism of a particular white Christianity treads human rights underfoot.

Second, we may not ignore the fact that the message of the God who with great partiality descends to the lowly and the exploited and, according to Mary's song of praise in Luke 1:53, sends the rich away empty, represents a huge annoyance for the whole world. This message must appear revolutionary, and it is so in fact, as the story of the massacre of the innocents in Bethlehem and even more the cross of Golgotha make clear. When heaven actually overturns our morals, when the gospel attacks our basic values, it is no longer directed toward our performance, merit, or ideals. When God makes a pact with his enemies, then indeed moral world order comes to grief, and as a result not even the status quo in the material realm remains inviolable. There are reasons why church decrees oppose the theology of liberation, as once did the scribes and the lay movement of the Pharisees following them. There is also a reason why Protestant theologians would like to separate salvation and earthly well-being from each other, though Jesus not only received souls to comfort and edify, but healed the sick and possessed, thus made earthly well-being a sign of the coming resurrection and kingdom of God on a new earth. A theology that does not proclaim liberation, even of bodies from demonic slavery, is heretical ideology. It abandons the world to tyrants and, in illusion, offers salvation in the beyond behind the clouds, no longer to disturb politicians or jurists. Of course, a Christianity that speaks softly of freedom but loudly of order is opium for the masses and, for this very reason, is everywhere beloved where rulers lay claim to what is on earth and where heavenly intervention in worldly affairs is regarded as suspect. All temporal power clings to a scale tipped to moral or arbitrarily decreed laws. Religion is then to legitimize such practice but may not jumble the weights normally used in trade. We concede that God often allows undeserved mildness to prevail. This is very beautifully illustrated in the rabbinic teaching which disputes that believers can create their own salvation but at the same time obliges them to do their utmost in producing good works. When guilt and merit more or less correspond, the divine mercy will lower the scale to the believer's advantage. In this case, there is mercy for the one who in continual striving has sought salvation and to that extent complied with what even earthly justice admits is a mitigating virtue. But according to 1 Corinthians 1:18ff., Jesus' cross, with its proclamation of salvation for the godless, becomes a political scandal.

Returning to our theme, what was said needs to be more clearly supported. According to Paul, God's righteousness does not punish. Rather, it grants grace to all who accept it. It likewise counts for justice. How can the apostle call it such? We must keep in mind that as a Jew, he follows the trail of the Old Testament. Divine righteousness is seen in the fact that the One who concluded his covenant with Israel remains true to it. And he does so even when Israel behaves otherwise, turns to idols, and must be punished by him. His judgments serve pedagogically the salvation of the elect. He for his part holds fast to the promise once given at Sinai, remains its God who does not reject his people for ever. In the New Testament what was limited to Israel in the Old is extended worldwide. God claims the whole earth for his lordship. He concluded an original covenant with it when he made it and breathed his breath into the human being. In the end time, broken in with Christ, there returns what God's act determined at the beginning and through Israel was preserved vicariously for all nations. The Creator does not abandon his creation. In all places and at all times the whole creation hears what once was heard at Sinai: "I am the Lord your God . . . you shall have no other gods before me!" As the final clause indicates, this is primarily promise, and I venture to add that it is concretized and personified in Christ. For this reason, John 1:18 can call *him* the exegete of the otherwise invisible God, and to this in 2 Corinthians 1:20 Paul adds, "For in him every one of God's promises is a 'Yes.' For this reason it is through him that we say the 'Amen,' to the glory of God." None who bear Christ's name or are his disciples need any longer place trust in other powers or themselves, or need fear other lords. Though there are many gods and lords in heaven and on earth, according to 1 Corinthians 8:5-6 we have only the one Lord Jesus Christ, and to everything with a human face he says, "I am the Lord your God," and no one else.

Precisely this and only this is the righteousness of God, which reaches out to the whole creation and creates salvation already on earth. This is the justice of the Creator, that he fetches us back to his kingdom from which Adam fell. This is our salvation, that for time and eternity we may give ourselves to the One who called us into life and then in Christ repeats that call, brings about a new creation with a new covenant, and in the inferno of our earth makes the cross of Golgotha the sign of his undying claim to us. The justice of God and our salvation become identical when Jesus Christ becomes our Lord, who, according to 1 Corinthians 1:30, "became for us wisdom from God, and righteousness and sanctification and redemption." Thus and only thus are we justified, we who can never justify ourselves with our performance. Over us is a Lord who holds us dear, important, and does not merely misuse us. Since he sets us in the sphere of his justice, he fetches us from nothingness into being, just as he did on the sixth day of creation, beginning the story of the resurrection from the dead already in time and on earth, a history that, according to 1 Corinthians 15:25, stands beneath the Easter message, "But he must reign."

The watchword of the coming Kirchentag[1] reads, "The earth is the Lord's." *This*, in promise and demand, is God's justice and the center of the Pauline doctrine of justification, properly understood — the center of the biblical message as a whole. With this gospel that God does not abandon us to other powers or to the arbitrariness and rebellious obstinacy of our egotistical hearts, the apostle founded his mission to the Gentiles and built the ecumenical church. In doing so, did he understand Jesus correctly? We must answer "Yes!" He understood that his Master was not, nor intended to be, head of a religious clique, that he cannot be expropriated by a pious party. Not by accident did Paul become the apostle of Christianity hardest to understand, as, incidentally, was already affirmed around the middle of the second century in 2 Peter 3:16. Even that early, one had occasion to urge congregations to a careful reading of the Pauline letters. The doctrine of a righteousness of God imputed to us without our merit and worthiness has forever been misused. For this reason it was never quite at home in the churches, while far and wide justice with her scales was free of suspicion, sympathetic to pious groups and whole confessions. Not even Christians and synods were always certain that one need not assist God's mercy to a degree, at least assign it somewhat more intelligible grounds. Congregational teachers have seldom allowed their pedagogy to be radically repressed and for the most part have mixed *something* of our good will with God's grace. A totally alien righteousness given to sinners, tax collectors, whores, and the godless is all but uncanny in its proportions, in which gifts

---

1. The biennial forum (lit.: "Church Day") of German Protestants, established for the purpose of strengthening and equipping the laity. In the year of this writing, the Kirchentag was held at Düsseldorf.

without conditions attached seldom have worth and at bottom can only harm the morality of performance. Jesus, of course, already connected the word of the other, better righteousness with the Beatitudes, and thus broke through the wall of our prejudices for the sake of the basic values just named; for his part, Paul merely projected in ecumenical fashion what his Master had anticipated subliminally. Neither of them fared well. At Golgotha, scribes, Pharisees, and politicians avenged themselves on the One who placed them entirely on God's mercy and did not take their piety seriously.

As my first teacher, Erik Peterson, formulated it by way of the extraordinary word in 1 Corinthians 15:8, in Christianity Paul for the most part remained an "apostle of the exception," ever since the heretic Marcion[2] collected his letters in the middle of the second century, and thus laid the basis for our New Testament canon. The message of God's righteousness is a very dangerous affair. It injures our human pride and contradicts all reason when it bases earthly salvation on grace alone, once more making of us the clay the Creator must mold and help to take on life. The slogans "by Christ alone, by faith alone" have an edifying sound. But it is very annoying to hear and learn in every moment that of ourselves we are incapable of doing good and, even in the most favorable instance, must admit, as did the servants in the parable, "We have done only what we ought to have done!" Until Golgotha, humankind and the world have never been so harshly judged. When Christ must be crucified that we might be rescued from the power of darkness, then there is no longer room for an idealistic worldview. Then, rather, the old Adam in us and everywhere about us dies together with his illusions.

Then too, sanctification ceases to be the second step in the Christian life after the beginning of justification. Of course, churches have always taken pains to be educators of the human race, to make the pious ever more pious, and to allow only respectable people at Jesus' table and in the congregation. In any event, in the white man's world they have often been merely religious societies for the improvement of public morality, thus generally treasured by officials and state protectors of order, since they begat brave subordinates and avoided rebels and subversive elements. But in doing so they fell prey to a crude misunderstanding and supported others in misinterpreting Christianity as a religious society of useful citizens.

2. Marcion of Sinope (110-160), celebrated Gnostic whose canon included ten of the Pauline epistles, a truncated version of Luke's Gospel, but none of the Old Testament.

According to Paul, sanctification is nothing but a holding fast to the justi-fying grace of God, trusting ever anew in the One who must fetch us again and again from nothingness and the earthly inferno. Christians cannot pull themselves out of the bog by their own hair, with Baron Münch-hausen,[3] though it is our profoundest temptation to want to do precisely that, thus to be incessantly occupied with it. To phrase it as clearly as possi-ble, evangelically speaking, sanctification is nothing else than to have one Lord, who must carry and preserve us, body, soul, and spirit, in time and eternity. Sanctification is nothing but the keeping of the first command-ment in a world in which many lords and gods offer themselves to us, promise us salvation, and want to enroll us in the ranks of the mighty, wise, rich, and pious, where they pretend to set us on our own feet and lead us to liberty by our own understanding or by subordinating us to the norms of the given ruling powers. According to Luther's explanation of the second article of the Creed, "that Jesus Christ is my Lord" is Christian sanctification, nothing else. The Heidelberg Catechism made this clear in the words "that in life and death I belong to my faithful Savior Jesus Christ, and am his own." In this way the message of the divine righteousness is held fast, according to which Christ alone is our salvation.

Here, no doubt, we have reached the political dimension. The theater of the contest between God and the idols, which is imposed on all mem-bers of the people of God by the first commandment, is naturally also our heart and our so-called private life. But we may not forget that God's in-struction from Sinai applies primarily to a people wandering through the desert, a people that will collide with the Gentile world and thus must prove to whom it belongs and to whom it may in no wise entrust itself. The first commandment applies basically to the political realm and only deri-vatively to the manifold temptations and decisions of the individual be-liever. Now, if it is correct that this first commandment is concretized in the New Testament by the promise and call to the discipleship of Jesus, it is no different here. The Christian community also always exists in a political environment and within it must continue that struggle with idols to which Israel once was summoned. Therefore, Ephesians 6:12 reads, "For our struggle is not against enemies of blood and flesh, but against the rulers,

---

3. Freiherr von Münchhausen, an eighteenth-century German baron who told a num-ber of tall tales about his adventures during campaigns against the Turks, which included riding cannonballs, traveling to the moon, and escaping from a swamp by pulling himself up by his hair.

against the authorities, against the cosmic powers of this present darkness." For this reason Paul compares himself to gladiators in the arena and calls his life a spectacle that the world and angels and humans look on, shocked or fascinated.

Insofar as all Christians must be messengers of the gospel, they share in the apostolic work in their conflict and responsibility for whatever portion of earth they occupy. They cannot live isolated or remain anonymous. On the path of the Crucified they unavoidably stand out from others and reflect the image of their Lord to those who see and surround them. From the outset, whether they know and want it or not, Christians are political creatures, a fact confirmed by the doctrine of God's righteousness and our justification. Those who in their place and surroundings must represent the righteousness of their God and themselves live from that righteousness toward his creation, necessarily collide with all the forces that also claim a right to them. Till death they will have to resist the temptation to entrust themselves to other gods and lords or to hearken to them. This resistance is the reverse side of faith. Those who believe live unavoidably in strife with the powers ruling this earth. Otherwise they do not belong to the community that always and publicly confesses, "There is salvation in no one else, for there is no other name under heaven given among mortals by which we must be saved" (Acts 4:12). Note that it says here, "under heaven" — that is, not in our private chamber or wherever we are protected from foreign seizure. "Under heaven" means everywhere on earth and continually, wherever we find ourselves, whether alone, among friends, or in view of our enemies. For heaven always hangs over us.

I can no longer enter into the profusion of details and view all the consequences to be drawn. Nevertheless, what was just stated in rudimentary way needs some developing. We accept too much on principle; only what is made concrete incurs risk. First of all, it should be emphasized that the point of view just expressed strongly contradicts our inherited opinions. Because the Enlightenment and Pietism oriented Reformation tradition more and more to individual life they followed a tendency that of course was already inherent in this tradition. Yet both over-emphasized the relation to the individual to such extent that the splitting of Christianity into churchly institution and so-called private piety led to religious schizophrenia. There never was a "private" life. All persons live in and from relations to the world around them that will determine their inner life. Other than in death, we are never quit of involvement in the fellowship of the creation. Otherwise we live in illusion. This is more radically true of the disciples of

Jesus because true discipleship sets them more forcibly than others in a continual contest with earthly claims. When we learn to speak again today of the political dimension of the biblical message, we return from pious ideology to reality. Only fanatics imagine they can leave earth behind and invade the heavenly. Only fanatics lose sight of the place of the cross of Golgotha, which marks the earthly wandering of the people of God and may not be replaced by the personal inconveniences of everyday human life. For this reason fanatics were also incapable of perceiving the inferno entrapping millions of brothers and sisters in hunger, invalidism, torture, murder, and every kind of exploitation. It is salutary that we are becoming realistic again, that we understand the Beatitudes of the exploited literally, discover the political dimension of the divine righteousness — that is, God's right to our bodies and the misused earth.

To this first thesis a second is directly to be added, that is, that the world today, thanks to technology, economic dependencies, and the media, has become small. The polarizing of the whole earth is not only tearing West and East apart but, more and more threateningly, North and South as well. Directly or indirectly it influences every individual life, but particularly the future of our children and grandchildren. The ravaging of nature and the military engineering of space are visibly on the increase. All this is slipping from the grasp of governments and experts, and all the more the longer it goes on. We can no longer afford to stand passively by and look on. A Christianity becomes contrived that proclaims in solemn declaration that "the earth is the Lord's," confesses as its Easter faith "But Christ must reign," but does not throw itself against the fearful stupidity and criminal frivolity that exist in the sphere of the white race. We can no longer afford to promote our own well-being and that of our friends to the extent that the work of our days and the sleep of our nights are not disturbed by the death agonies in the underdeveloped world. We may not allow the circle of our responsibility to start out small at first and then extend to the most remote. We must learn to think and act globally and on that basis shape our behavior in the personal sphere. Who we are and what we do is at present reflected most clearly in the countries of Africa, Asia, and Latin America, which accuse our politics and our Christianity. Do we really imagine that we may preach the righteousness of God for our salvation and at the same time abandon our brothers and sisters beyond the sea to demonic darkness? There is no provincial and regional salvation. We are not its recipients if we will not also be its bearers.

In conclusion, I would like to hark back to the beginning. There I drew a contrast between (1) righteousness in our Western tradition in the image of that woman with the blindfold and the scales in her hands, and (2) what Paul calls the justification of the godless. This indicated the opposition between the goals of the two points of view. While the apostle is concerned that through the lordship of Jesus Christ salvation comes to all creatures in every corner of the earth, worldly justice — at least in middle-class sectors of the democratic type — seeks to establish order. It is understandable, but it imperils Christianity as well as politics when the two goals are confused or so approximated that they appear almost identical. This may actually be the peril of our time, toward which we must be most on our guard. We must respect earthly order wherever credibly represented, and as regards our civil obligation, we neglect God's will when we do not support it with all our might. But it must be just as clear to us that earthly order may not be confused with divine salvation. The political behavior of Christians is precisely to be measured by the fact that they do not equate the two, nor, of course, that they radically separate them. Earthly order, when uprightly sought, is concerned to bring society's powers and the interests of individuals, groups, parties, nations, and cultures into balance, so that no one within the realm of what is humanly possible is violated. In doing so, it understands itself to be a service to humankind, and insofar corresponds to the divine will, which calls each of us to common and mutual service.

Christians must nonetheless be mindful of the fact that since the fall, thus historically, concern for order in terms of the balance between manifold powers and interests was always utopian, in the best instance realized only in impeding the war of all against all. No life comes without recognizing certain rules of the game in family, profession, communication, economics, nation, and the international community. Conversely, not only criminals upset existing order. Rather, competition between various forces and interests indicates that ideas of desirable order differ at all conceivable levels. We live in a world whose history is an incessant conflict between diverging and opposed schemes and systems of order. Every practicable rule of the game has its time and place, and is thus not repeatable. At times its representatives must seek to implement it with force and, in so doing, encounter rebellious counter schemes. This is the danger — that the desire for a particular order becomes defense of a particular status quo, about the validity of which only power and force can decide, and in disputing which, revolutionaries can argue that nothing on earth lasts, that everything is relative, and thus to be corrected anew in every generation. Christians cannot avoid this conflict of worldviews. Wherever rights and laws are of use,

Christians must be on the side of the conservatives, knowing they are in the service of God, who will have all to be helped.

Conversely, Christians allow themselves to be misused when they give themselves to defend the property of ruling classes where their brothers and sisters in the wider world are exploited by the mighty and made slaves of their egoism, their ideology, and their idols. Christians know of the God who will create the new heaven with a new earth, who forever puts down the mighty from their thrones, calls blessed those who labor and are heavy laden, and has become Advocate of all the damned on earth. If it should be revolutionary to state that the Father of the Crucified is not a God of the possessors and enforcers, for good or ill Christians must take the side of the revolutionaries because they are called to serve humankind and not the partisans of those who cry for order, by which they mean the preservation and continuance of their own power, their traditional prejudices, and their economic, cultural, and political privileges.

To summarize: Neither individual Christians nor churches are exempt from the task of critically testing what is the good and gracious will of God on earth today, and thus their service to God in everyday life and the world. They should not be taken in by demagogic models, and certainly not by orders that find expression in a fanatical polarizing of camps and worldviews. Just as their Lord between the fronts in no-man's-land, they will proclaim the right of their God to his creatures. They will enter the lists on behalf of this right with all their powers, even when existing earthly orders must be unmasked and shunted aside as a mockery of divine justice and the divinely intended service to humankind. The righteousness of God intends and creates salvation for the poor, the oppressed, the misused, the dying. The utopia of balance between societal powers and interests, even under the aegis of earthly order, may not bring us to the point of existing and working against those for whom the Crucified died and to whom we must bring the gospel of salvation not merely with words but with our life and solidarity. As disagreeable as it is to say, the true church was never a fellowship in which decent people formed the majority. The church of Jesus is a new earth by the fact that, and insofar as, the masses scorned by upstanding citizens find room and asylum in it. Where we do not respect legitimate and necessary order, the earth becomes chaos. But where, for the sake of earthly rules of order, salvation and the divine righteousness are not allowed to be the final measure of our service, we betray the lordship of the Crucified already begun on earth. Our political behavior does not recognize order as the last word, but rather love, which sets free.

Evangelical Truth amid Radical Change in Christian Theology

A spectacle marks the radical breakthrough of methodology in the study of religion and hermeneutics in the German Protestant philosophy of religion. In 1896 Die Freunde der christlichen Welt (The Friends of the Christian World), who were representatives of church liberalism, were assembled at Eisenach for their yearly conference. A noted historian had lectured on the Logos doctrine in primitive Christianity. The discussion was opened by the then thirty-one-year-old Ernst Troeltsch, who for two years had been full professor of systematic theology at Heidelberg, later the leading member of that younger generation, resolutely devoted to the science of religion. He well nigh swept the lecture from the order of the day and shocked the audience with his opening remarks. What was heard was like a proclamation of radical change at the turn of the century, "Gentlemen, everything is tottering!" The lecturer whom Troeltsch attacked dismissed the impetuous offensive with the remark, "A shabby theology!" Thereupon Troeltsch left the hall. He needn't have quit the field on which German Protestantism was seriously tottering. Today, though restoration, apologetic, and unreality are widespread everywhere, not merely in the church, it is still true that everything is tottering.

From the systematic perspective, with the entry of the science of religion into theology, historical relativism emerges as the basic problem of Protestant liberalism. Troeltsch can maintain that all truth and ethic are historically conditioned. For him this means that truth first of all and at any

---

A lecture given on February 10, 1983, on the occasion of the University of Tübingen's Science of Religion series.

given moment exists only "for us," though this naturally always has consequences for the world around us. Truth is basically polymorphous. It is not enough to speak of the various stages of its development. Rather, it is encountered in various forms and types. Historically, everything lives from a development long in preparing, but no less by way of unavoidable decline. Where there is talk of revelation, what is in view is really a problem, not the final solution of a vexing riddle. We are summoned to recognize and acknowledge what is permanent in the transitory, to fix values and norms, though the mighty stream of history continually washes them away. The absolute exists only in the garb of the relative. The ethical task consists in the problematic as to how historical relativism ought not end in nihilism but can, as it were, be checked. If that were not possible, we would not be able to speak of truth at all, which at least symbolizes an absolute, and summons us to responsible decision in the process of a life incessantly facing hindrance.

Where this question is raised and assumed to be the order of the hour just struck, it must be announced that "everything is tottering!" There, the authority of a church organization and its dogmatic-historical teaching tradition can no longer be accepted as invulnerable but must be examined respecting its historical meaning and insofar set within the context of waning and waxing.

More intensely than its forebears in 1896, current Christianity has occasion to deal with the provocation I signaled by naming Troeltsch. Actually, the Bible does not protect us from it. The saying in Ecclesiastes 12:8 was directed precisely to the devout and to theologians: "Vanity of vanities, says the Teacher; all is vanity." What liberal criticism once reflected on and discussed in an academic way has in the meantime become the problem of our world. Nothing more brutal could have happened than occurred in the twentieth century, shaken by wars, revolutions, and catastrophes without measure. The breathtaking scientific discoveries and the technical development that made use of them rather intensified than limited it. Western churches that do not continually keep in mind the horror at their doors and in the Third World, a horror reflecting the delusion and tyranny of the white race, do not so much represent the Body of Christ as a middle-class society whose conscience and self-critical understanding have been ideologically benumbed, so that specialists of every provenience have a free hand for experiments with human being and nature. These churches would at least have to recognize how much everything about them is tottering that for centuries had stability and awakened fascination as irrevocable, in any case, as subject to organic change.

This holds true statistically, since persons of color now make up the Christian majority. This fact alone would have to shift the angle of vision 180 degrees where all church matters are concerned. Of course, just as in the colonial past, the political, technical, and economic superiority of the white race still hinders emancipation of the underdeveloped peoples. Their leadership class has to great extent been given Western shape. In their congregations they cannot for the most part do without financial support and foreign advisers, and only slowly and with difficulty do they get free of adopted worship traditions. Still, this cannot last. The European-American umbrella of a worldwide Christianity is a fiction entertained only by the ignorant. It is liable to open contradiction and even to aversion in the ecumenical movement, which at times does not accept contributions for areas of need and more and more gives leading positions to people of color. What weighs most heavily is that Western theology unmistakably finds itself in retreat along the whole line. The themes of the great conferences do not allow this to be seen as clearly as the discussions held locally. We should be soberly prepared for the fact that in the immediate future there will be discussion of what under all circumstances is to be retained of our tradition, a kind of emergency rations, as it were, and what will prove to be more complex, and how all this can be made clear to all participants. It is to be expected that more will go overboard than will be saved. Africa, Asia, and Latin America will not appropriate a history of dogma that took its systematic force from the logic of Greek antiquity, still less the historical-critical method of Western science, and not even the forms of organization that have proved purposeful or at least sound with us. It would be useful if every Christian among us were supplied with the map handed out at the Commission on World Mission and Evangelism in 1980 at Melbourne, indicating the North-South divide made by the equator. However strong or weak it may be, Western Christianity is accordingly no longer the midpoint, but the periphery. Only distance from reality and permanent self-deception can fail to draw from this decisive consequences in every possible area.

This, of course, is not so flatly stated as to overlook the decisive change that, as an ecumenical movement made its way early on in the epoch of white preeminence, and that, with the exception of the Roman Church and a few extremely confessionalist fellowships, has almost entirely encompassed Christianity. It might be the most important event in the church history of the twentieth century. It likewise proves that the global is the nonrepealable mark of a church worthy of its name. On the other hand, it proves that Western development is coming to an end in which national, regional, and provincial thinking helped materially to determine theology. A Christianity that, in all its dimensions, does not aim at *oecumene* and understand itself from that point will become a sect, and in a time when politically and culturally the earth is taking new shape and everywhere the great religions and the most variegated cults begin to attack what has been dominant till now. Unfortunately, from the inception of their specific traditions church bodies do not sufficiently grasp what is to be gained and surrendered thereby. In this respect the so-called lay and clergy at the lowest level are often far ahead of bishops and the theological guild.

Of course, the price to be paid for amalgamating is higher than enthusiasts can see. *Oecumene,* which should be more than a space for intrachurchly dialogue or for Christianity's assuming greater influence within the various areas of tension of our time, necessarily conflicts with the structures determining its environment. In evidence I refer to the intense debates over decisions involving antiracism or disarmament. The discordant echo on this subject in West Germany must be taken as an indication of the fact that a really ecumenical Christianity, no longer oriented just to its own continuance, provokes the middle-class, which supported it for many centuries as its societal basis. To the extent he or she judges realistically, the severest critic of this symbiosis, still characteristic of the entire Western world, will admit that in our relationships and for the foreseeable future no alternatives need be taken seriously. Naturally, Christians can withdraw into what today is called "base communities." This form of community will actually have to be continually nourished, the more clearly the character of churches as associations of religious minorities within a secular context becomes visible. Nevertheless, these basic communities will actually be marked by the fact that, in the long run, they are more and more radically alienated from middle-class behavior. Not even in the Enlightenment period did the middle-class understand those biblical narratives that depict our life as a journey, or how, illustrated by Abraham, they describe it as an ever-new departure from the houses of one's fathers and friends, how they let Israel be led from the legendary fleshpots of Egypt into the wilderness, then later into exile, and how they call the disciples of the Nazarene beneath the cross. Almost always the churches have worried more about their members' peace of soul and tended edification from the cradle to the grave than given courage for resolute discipleship in everyday life. God's revolutionary activity, which resists the proud and takes up the cause of the lowly, may have been cozily considered in the closet, but anxiously concealed in society and politics.

According to prevailing opinion, Christianity was not meant to awaken unrest. Where possible, it had to preserve the status quo. Occasionally, corrections and reforms had to take place. Extreme behavior was tabooed. To behave properly, in all situations of life to give moderation the last word, and to deliver bitter truths in homeopathic dosage were the most treasured Christian virtues, and correspondingly honored by the various authorities. Christians agreed with the average citizen that radicality is dangerous, and radical changes seldom useful. Intellectuals as well as the proletariat commonly went astray over such mentality. On the other hand, the petty bourgeois and the middle class more stoutly shaped the image of the worshipping congregation, and of course in the direction of a conventicle, or private gathering for worship. Just as the middle class had forgotten those times when, as in 1848, people took to the streets and actually erected barricades against the power of the state, in the Third Reich the resolute wing of church resistance could least get foothold with the bourgeoisie. Then, at that time, introversion resisted the risk. Contact and openness to currents signaling future revolutions were minimal and, to great extent, were inhibited by pressure from the top.

In such churches there was scarcely any place for ecumenical thinking. Generally, in those churches Christianity was regarded as a private affair. There was personal and mutual feeling of one's pulse. Behavior in worship, as in everyday life, was directed toward the norms of inherited tradition and the morality of a given milieu. The dominant desires related much more strongly to a nation gaining strength than to heaven, perhaps the clearest indication of the degree to which the churches in our country were clenched and interfused by the middle class. This also explains the development after the two world wars. The underdeveloped world was now made visible by the mass media and a tourism penetrating every corner of the earth. But in essence, despite Brot für die Welt (Bread for the World) and Misereor (lit. "I take pity"),[1] it has remained the recipient of charity, even among Christians. Confrontation with those who, compared to us, vegetate like lepers and die like animals without owners, occurred only within special groups, especially of youth, and in congregations irritated by the concentration on wealth in their environment. The decisive break

1. *Brot für die Welt* is the name for an action undertaken by German evangelical and free churches on behalf of the poor, and in response to world Christianity's aid to Germany following the Second World War. The first call to action in 1959 resulted in the greatest ingathering of funds ever assembled by German Protestants. Similarly, on the Catholic side, *Misereor* was founded by German bishops in 1958 to combat world hunger and disease.

did not occur, in which each of us everywhere would see Lazarus before our own door and feel solidarity with him. Usually, we fail to hear the gospel that enlivens the weak and calls to freedom. We have adapted the biblical message to our desires and relationships, or, as for example in South Africa and among the ruling strata of both Americas, we have even made it the religious ideology of the white race, without calling ourselves to account for it. We are convinced that, just as our privileges hold good on earth, so also in heaven, which gives legitimacy to our plans and at least does not unmask our interests as egoism. The schizophrenia of our piety and morality is disguised by the general ideological polarization.

This polarization that penetrates society and the church ultimately roots in a mind-set oriented to possessions. As our parties which call themselves democratic raise rhetorical objections to open or covert weapons deals with dictators, invoke peace over the whole earth, but themselves join in inciting civil wars within their sphere of power, so the churches of the West pillory force from below but suffer murderous despots as divinely willed authority. The political dimension of the gospel, as, for example, in the Sermon on the Mount, is denied. The political dimension of the capitalistic ideology of a free economic market that fosters exploitation in the Third World is shamefully rendered harmless under the slogan of "development assistance" or "support for indigenous workplaces." Anticommunist sentiment is not without legitimate motive or background, insofar as armament in the East is no less threatening than in the West. But only hypocrisy ignores the fact that everywhere our society is dancing around the golden calf and hopes to gain an illusionary security with its illusionary superiority. The god Mammon reigns. The citizen of today is forever occupied with possessions, whether in the workplace, in affluence, or in the claim to good fortune or the defense of power. One wants to survive with what he or she possesses and, as a Christian, even beyond the grave. Thus, by way of a striving for possessions, one is possessed, and as everywhere in the countries of the white race, so also with us, and without the resolute resistance of our provincial churches.

The question is whether, in view of these circumstances, the education of the next theological generation must be decisively altered. Obviously one cannot and must not deny that the church of Christ lives from the gospel, that this gospel is linked to the Bible and has its deposit in confessional writings. Exegetical, historical, dogmatic theology is not to be replaced by ideology and need make no concessions to it. But precisely because ideologies are luxuriating everywhere around us, theology and theologians should be radically open to reality. There is no lack of pious feelings or edifying speeches, but nothing of preparation for service and sacrifice. There is lack of courage throughout and of the capability for diagnosing quite soberly and without navel-gazing the kind of world in which we live and how we must actualize the gospel today. A sermon delivered at random is not gospel, though larded with Bible quotations. In 1 Corinthians 14 the apostle Paul demands that the bugle give a distinct sound. The worship of the Christian community should not be dominated by fanatical ecstasy or profound oracle, but by prophecy as a contemporizing of the message of the past. The gospel concretizes and actualizes. It does not feed people with warmed-over broth. No theological study is meaningfully begun, no churchly office conducted in truly evangelical fashion when temples of the past are adorned and the slums of today forgotten. Though Protestant bishops may advocate a new spirituality and suppose they must play the God-theme off against the social impulse, as has recently occurred in Hamburg, their dogmatics may be called into question. Such antitheses are the white elephants of an idealism that separated God and humankind, soul and corporeality, the Nazarene and his brothers and sisters, the pious and the exploited. Christianly viewed, a heavenly salvation that does not also and, as its distinguishing mark, set out as earthly help is a pious deception. This is the basic perception of the ecumenical movement, namely, that our God lays claim to our earth in all its nooks and crannies, as well as to our everyday existence, that he intends to lead from all sorts of demonic possession into his lordship and, in so doing, provokes the bourgeois religion of the white race. Again, everything is tottering. We can see it when we dare to leave the ghettos of traditional Christianity for our world become chaotic.

We do not need to state this with such pathos. True, our time is more violently shaken than other epochs, and to the inhabitants of earthquake-free zones volcanoes appear to be an exception to the status quo on which they base their way of life. Yet everyone can appreciate that the entire inner earth is aglow and anywhere can burst open its crust. We could also realize, provided we have been conscious throughout the twentieth century, that people are incalculable and with incredible speed tumble out of the civilization of the Enlightenment into the inferno. If others are blind to this, theologians may never be so if they want to avoid making their God an idol of delusion. There has never been that harmony we dream about, and there never will be. The Christian church has always experienced one revolution after the other, has never possessed a *theologia perennis,* a unified confession, which, to quote Vincent of Lérins,[2] "has been believed everywhere, always, and by all." Troeltsch was absolutely right. The truth is polymorphous wherever it meets us.

As early as in Jerusalem there were two rival Christian communities, different in their forms of organization, as well as in their dogmatics. The twelve gathered around Peter seem to have understood themselves as the sacred remnant of Israel, the people of God of the end time, while the seven around Stephen very early engaged in a mission among the Diaspora Jews and Gentile God-fearers, a mission unrecognized by the Jewish religious association. The alleged prince of the apostles is displaced by James, brother of the Lord, and dies as an exile in Rome. Apostolic succession of the hierarchy lacks evidence. It exists only in a discipleship that represents the universal priesthood of all believers. The charismatic order of the congregation, theologically established by Paul and in John's Gospel defended against a clerical dominance institutionally enforced by the Pastoral Epistles, cannot ultimately protect from heretics. In the never-ending conflict over pure doctrine and unity of organization, a great church is constituted that takes itself to be mother and teacher of the nations, yet is continually split into schools and confessions, into regional, national, and continental societies, can never maintain itself in its own space without force or political support, and finally today, alongside four confessionally separated basic types and their numerous independent denominations, aims to merge hundreds of young churches. There can be no talk of organic development. In this respect also history is manifest as scandalous. Its reality hides what we call meaning and truth, if we do not actually have to assert resignedly or nihilistically that it proves the absurdity of world history, and precisely in the area of religion. In view of the many radical changes we have merely touched on in theology, morality, and organization of Christianity, dare we still speak of evangelical truth by which what is historically divisive is to be measured and to which it points in its pluriformity?

Respecting the development in ecclesiastical history or dogmatics up to our own time, the New Testament scholar perhaps has the right and duty to refer to a word that stands at the beginning of this development and was more buried than illumined by it. According to the Gospel of John, Christ declares in 14:6 and in a clearly exclusive way, "I am the way,

---

2. Vincent of Lérins (d. middle of the fifth century), author of the norms of Roman Catholic orthodoxy influential in the sixteenth and nineteenth centuries (including Vatican I).

and the truth, and the life; no one comes to the Father except through me." This word, which, of course, can be shunted aside as mere pious chatter, deserves to be set at the center of theological reflection on evangelical truth. If we take seriously its exclusivity, it raises a claim that is not only marked off from rivals in the area of religiosity or moral worldviews. It also maintains something unconditionally valid and unalterable in opposition to all historical relativism. The admittedly scandalous history of Christianity and the theological upheavals in constant rotation since its beginnings are no decisive argument against the claim raised here. They merely describe the arena where truth is manifest, as well as the manifold and, in certain instances, doubtful or even negative reactions of those stigmatized by encounter with it. Over this surface lies an uncertainty that always needs rechecking and control. If it is said in response that one should "come to the Father," this indicates the goal of all earthly searching and straying, the end of doubt and despair, a salvation encompassing clarity, freedom, and help, thus making possible a life in blessing. What is decisive is that all this is presented not as a transcendent hope or a distant utopian goal but as a present possibility and reality. It is incarnate in the Nazarene in face of his Jewish contemporaries, and to all who come later it is promised that this Nazarene will also encounter them in the word of his witnesses. The absolute in the relative is proclaimed here, as Troeltsch postulated in his theological program. Troeltsch was concerned that this paradox not be weakened. He was not concerned with a meaning behind what on earth always appears relative. For him truth was concrete, thus not a hidden meaning.

This is precisely the concern of the gospel, whose word just cited must now be made doubly precise so as to separate it from a religious worldview.

Where it reads "I am the truth," faith is not tied to a doctrinal system, but to a person. Salvation does not consist in one's believing something but in having a Lord whom one follows, from and toward whom one lives. Salvation does not even consist in believing something correctly and proclaiming it as salutary. It was always the greatest peril of the Christian churches and devout communities that they abstracted the truth entrusted to them from the person of Jesus Christ and made it a religious doctrine. This could happen in two ways. One could make of the Lord one had to follow, from and toward whom one had to live, the object of a dogmatic that in turn became the criterion of a right, imperfect, or false faith. But that tradition could also be extended to an ethical principle, with some probability traceable to Jesus, making him a religious teacher and his disciples observers of an order hallowed by his name and authority. Orthodoxy and liberalism differ fundamentally in their preference for the one or the other, though in practice both could be connected in the most varied way. In either instance the Lord who appointed his disciples became his community's possession of faith. It took control of him in its dogma and morals and became his earthly representative on which access to and conformity with him depended. So it is no accident that as early as in the New Testament the central dispute is not with heathenism. Rather, genuine discipleship is critically described as always imperiled. It is not by chance that the Old Testament is used as instruction in the New. With the first commandment it defined the human being (and all persons) as a creature continually directed to one Lord, but also continually tempted to rebellion, thus to an idolatrous substitution of its Lord for other powers. As curious as it may sound, the real danger to evangelical truth is not invoked by pagans and alleged atheists but by the pious and their groups who hand themselves over to idols by no longer serving the One who created them and who set them in his lordship under their rule, but modeling him after the pattern of their longings or apprehensions, their worldview, or morality. Precisely for this reason the Johannine Christ proclaims himself the truth by calling himself the way. Evangelical truth exists only in discipleship. It never becomes our possession to be exchanged at will or combined with another. It abides with us only when we begin with it again each day, hear its voice for our time and hour, remain its pupils, learning it ever anew. We possess it always only and as long as it possesses us, draws us into its realm.

So, it is not enough merely to be underway, to remain a searcher and learner, ready to depart from self, the house of the fathers and the warmth of old friends and in some foreign land of the future to await our Lord. What unites Christians with all those wandering about, waiting, and breaking out of the status quo is that their salvation is present only on the way. The established society is never and nowhere a protector of evangelical truth. It is not even in a church community that supposes it must take control of the truth dogmatically or pedagogically, as confessionalism usually does. Only its Lord determines where Christians must make a stand or retreat. He does not remain their Lord if he is not also the judge of their teaching and organization, if he may not command reform and change of direction. Churches cannot bring freedom when they confine their Lord to their ghetto and, as often enough occurs, to a pious prison. Precisely for this reason their dignitaries, the guild of theologians included, are always to be reminded by nonconformists that every official office has and retains authority only when it serves the freedom of the Christian community and openness toward all. Evangelical truth is not the privilege of an elite. And it never appears in uniform, though even in the religious sphere there is no lack of uniforms of every sort. Actually, the mode of its appearance, to cite Troeltsch, is polymorphous. By virtue of time and place, inheritance, cognitive faculty, and opponents, evangelical truth is as varied in the direction of its thrust, radicality, and intelligibility as the four very different Gospels alongside, say, the Pauline letters and the various confessions, which often appear to the so-called laity as incomprehensible or disturbing and unnecessary in daily life.

This raises the question concerning the most common and simplest denominator of evangelical truth. Here, of course, we can only consider it in quite nonacademic fashion. It is not a deposit in a heavenly bank. It is the discovery of an earthly encounter, the result of which stimulates to radical changes in one's own life, to the most partisan participation in the radical changes of our time. The Reformation spoke of humanity's unrelentingly and radically becoming human in order to show what the Nazarene intends and what he creates, among us personally, as well as in his sphere of rule on our earth, represented by the ecumenical church. He became the brother of the poorest, like the Samaritan on the way from Jerusalem to Jericho. He became man into the inferno so that, ever since, Golgotha became the place where God is present and gathers his people to himself. He is, as John 1:18 states, the exegete of this God. For he reveals who his Father is and at the same time reveals our own true nature. He does so with the Beatitudes, which speak of a mercy that (interpreted literally!) turns its heart to the poor, exploited, and lost, that promises the eternal kingdom, Beatitudes that speak to us in the creatures' need. So the Our Father sets our salvation solely on petition. For this reason, the gospel characterizes genuine life not by the categories of being and having but, rather, as a fellowship of sharing, as a service taken up and handed on ever anew. The creation is repeated where heaven is opened and people become open to one another in a freedom that no longer allows circling about oneself or fearing the powers and forces of this world, but allows room to love the neighbor and the enemy. Freedom and love, humankind's becoming human, are not measured by dogmatic and pedagogical yardsticks. They are signs of God's encounter with men and women, of the discipleship of the crucified Nazarene. Our world needs it as never before because we are entering a radical change as never before. At least, the world of the white race is tottering as never before.

Corporeality in Paul

In advanced age we sometimes see ourselves faced with problems with which we first began. So it is with me and the theme I chose fifty years ago in my dissertation *Leib und Leib Christi*,[1] and with which I began my exegetical work. Into the arena of liberal Protestantism Erik Peterson had hurled the question "What is the church?" His then youngest pupil has not gotten free of this question all his life, though, in the intoxication of his first encounter with scientific theology, it did not remain the central question of his career. In the semester following, Rudolf Bultmann put the question characteristic of him alongside that of Peterson, "What is it to be human?" and was not able to answer it without having to define existence radically by the revealed word of God, just as Karl Barth and the Reformation. I myself discovered only decades later that, for me and my time, the ultimate and most important theological question would have to read, "Who is the Nazarene?" Adolf Schlatter, the theological freebooter, had already formulated it. But in the altered landscape of the ecumenical movement, it was to be actualized in terms of a theology of liberation. In 1931 I was already deeply disturbed by the various battle cries of the various theological schools. Still, Peterson's question stuck like a thorn in my flesh. What is the meaning of the Pauline statement about the church as "Body of Christ"? The pupil who neither would nor could become a Roman

---

1. Ernst Käsemann, *Leib und Leib Christi: Eine Untersuchung zur paulinischen Begrifflichkeit* (Body and the Body of Christ: An Investigation of the Pauline Conceptuality) (Tübingen: J. C. B. Mohr, 1933).

A lecture given on February 3, 1985, at the Catholic Academy of Freiburg and on May 6, 1985, at the University of Bern.

Catholic like his teacher had to find a "Protestant" answer to be able to remain a Protestant.

While amused at my youthful foolishness, clumsily equipped, crudely ignoring the dangers and labors of the undertaking as well as my own insufficiency, and wanting to storm a height at its steepest ascent, in retrospect I am moved by the courage and resolve to connect independent thought with faith. The gospel was to be verified in my own everyday life so that it should remain credible. Pious tradition had to be inquired into regarding its sense and the degree of its reality. How did it emerge? What had allowed it to hold and hand on? What could it still do today? Was it indispensable? To what extent did it deserve to be called evangelical? Was it not just a piece of past ideology? It was easy to tell beforehand that the beginner had taken too much on himself, had run into walls and ditches, returned to the valley broken and sobered. But afterward he knew that the attempt was worth repeating if he gathered strength and the prospects for success became more favorable. Even more than in life, in science and especially in theology one must be trained in stubborn patience and, if need be, prepare fifty years for the longed-for goal. In any event, I think I am finally so far that I can clearly outline my problem of former days, render it intelligible to others, and solve it in a fruitful way.

1. *The problem.* How did Paul come to call the Christian church the Body of Christ? What is his theological intention? To what extent is the gospel reflected in this formulation? To be worthy of the name, the exegete of Romans 12:4-5; 1 Corinthians 10:16-17; 12:12ff. must answer this question. But in my opinion, an exegete is not worth the name who chooses the simplest answers from the outset. In our case, the simplest answer is to see in the Pauline motif of the Body of Christ a mere edifying image, as many expositors do. They can actually appeal to the apostle himself. In Romans 12:4-5 he draws a comparison between our human body and the Body of Christ of the church. In 1 Corinthians 12:12ff. he does so with broad brushstrokes to describe the church as a worldwide organism. So we may not deny that he made room for a metaphorical interpretation of his reference to the Body of Christ, and it will still have to be carefully explained why this is so. Of course, the question is whether by interpreting it in this way the entire problematic of the view presented here is grasped and explained.

Please pardon a small digression. In dealing with the Bible, theologians must consider that in our time everywhere, even in scientific discussion, language is mishandled without limit. It is used as though it were a tool for mutual understanding in which only function matters. At bottom, it is regarded as replaceable, say, through a maximally reduced system of signs and numbers. We forget that it is the transmitted inheritance of a society that supports us, which we may not arbitrarily pick up like a dirty bill in a business transaction. In a society determined by interests and purposes, words may have only the daily exchange rate resulting from their use in the service of universal profit. Where party and circumstances are concerned, words may actually express contrary opinions, thus becoming ciphers of a technical regulation of speech. Theologians, at least, should consider that our God reveals himself speaking and encountering the world, that the certainty of faith as well as of love grows only from the word, be it in the religious or secular sphere. Whoever no longer takes words seriously and is not attentive to the precision of hearing and thinking sacrifices his or her own humanity to the technical bustle of the modern world. Such a person has nothing more with which to hope for an encounter with the truth and must be content with probabilities and what might be gained from speculating. It may be that we do not get beyond what is plausible. But from the outset to content ourselves only with what is plausible would allow our research, as well as our life, to become a game of chance. In any event, theologians must decide between images and realities, aware of their responsibility in Bible interpretation, of their service to the discipline transmitted to them.

Applied to the church, the phrase "Body of Christ" is too unusual to be understood as simply metaphorical. If the apostle was merely concerned with describing the Christian community as an organism, it would have been enough to say in 1 Corinthians 12:12, "As with the human body, so also with the church." But instead it reads, "so it is with Christ." We may not ignore the fact that an admonition ("behave accordingly!") does not follow. One would think an imperative would fit after the comparison. But what continues is in the indicative: "You are members." One given reality is thus identified with another, not merely compared with it to establish a postulate. Then the following verse is unequivocal, "For in the one Spirit we were all baptized into one body — Jews or Greeks, slaves or free — and we were all made to drink of one Spirit." Baptism thus sets one within the Body of Christ, just as, according to 1 Corinthians 10:17, the Lord's Supper, renewing the sacramental beginning, does exactly the same through its reception. The comparison that refers to the type of organism is possible since earlier, through the events of Baptism and Eucharist, a sacramental unity was created between Christ and his disciples. This unity is so real and

world-embracing that it actually abrogates the usual ineradicable differences of religious, political, and social affiliation. A new world of the members of Christ replaces the old, in which, disastrously polarized, Jews and
Greeks, slaves and free, and, according to other texts, men and women
were emancipated from, and were at war with, each other.

What the apostle is after with his comparison is not the admonition,
"If you want to be a body, then behave as is necessary in an organism."
Rather, he opens the community's eyes to a reality that can only be an-
nulled when one cancels out a baptism already occurred and a Eucharist
daily received. One is in an organism when placed in the Body of Christ,
whether one knows and wants it or not. This is how the first pupils of Paul
understood it in the Epistles to the Colossians and Ephesians. For them the
ascended Christ is the heavenly Head of a body continually growing on
earth and forming a new world, that is, the body of ecumenical Christianity. The apostle did not so sharply detail Christ's lordship as Head as did
his pupils. For him Christ, present on earth in his Spirit, is as it were the
soul of the body, thus the Lord who rules it. Variations on this motif in
Colossians and Ephesians give the apostle's idea precision. In each instance
the Body of Christ is what later dogmatics called the *corpus mysticum
Christi* and proclaimed as the earthly reality of a new world, that is, as existing in the end time of history. Our theological problem consists in what
this doctrine may mean for us.

2. *What does the word "body" generally mean in the Pauline writings?* For a
radical Enlightenment theology that regards ancient mythology as irrelevant for us, the description of ecumenical Christianity as the Body of
Christ might also have become meaningless. We may make allowances for
it, perhaps as a metaphorical way of speaking, designed to depict the
church as an organism of its members, that summons us as individual
Christians to our moral duty of mutual service. Yet it seems to me that the
program of demythologizing can be exaggerated. There is no theology
without dogmatics. The gospel is not served when a dialectic of existence
has the last word. Babies are not to be thrown out with the bathwater. How,
then, do we get further? It appears to me even today that what was most
important in my otherwise quite dubious dissertation is that I did not investigate the motif of the Body of Christ in isolated fashion. The motif
must be set in the context of the Pauline utterances concerning the body
and corporality to get at its meaning. But what is meant by "body" is not at
all obvious. So, for example, in German the word "Leib" (body), which

originally denotes a living thing, can alternate with "Körper" (body), a term that generally denotes what is objectively there — in anatomy, the corpse; in geometry, what is measurable; in ancient economics, a head count, for example, of slaves.

We reflect too seldom on the fact that, depending on time, place, and tradition, human history is reflected variously in our words. A particular perspective facilitates a particular aspect. The Greek enlightenment examined the human body in analytical fashion. One may divide it into parts. The whole then forms an organism within an individuality that can be abstracted from its environment. On the other hand, the Hebrew Bible has no linguistic equivalent. In it the human being is never seen as a creature made up of its members, as an isolatable being. The human being is never an *individuum*, but — as we would say today, when viewed totally, say, psychosomatically — a projection of the world that determines him or her. What we currently enumerate as parts of the body is represented in the Old Testament as the total person in a given particular orientation, thus in relation to its environs, and of course according to its concrete possibilities and capacities. As this environment affects persons in continually changing situations, they act and react to it in different ways according to their insight and volition, their personal gifts and weaknesses. By this they evidence that membership in a comprehensive community is the underlying character of their existence. What they are is always in relationship to a particular world.

Only when we have become clear about this do we understand that for Paul corporeality is not reduced to a single denominator. It exists only in the continual alteration of its underlying structure. That underlying structure consists in a relation to and a dependence upon a particular world, upon its projection, so to speak. Factually, this is realized in totally different ways of behaving. Without question, the body is earthly existence as a work of the Creator and thus called to serve God's creation. In an earth that since the fall is in rebellion against this Creator, according to Romans 3:12 every one forfeited the glory of the original state, denoted by the biblical key word "image of God." The creature's body, thus its earthly existence, is from now on subject to sin and death. Even among Christians the body is subject to temptation and transitoriness. All creation must now cry for freedom from "this body of death" (Rom. 7:24) and wait for "the redemption of our bodies" (Rom. 8:23). Finally, that event occurs in which the risen Christ draws us into his Godlikeness and grants to his own a share in his resurrection corporeality (1 Cor. 15:42-49). Such final redemption is guaranteed in the earthly present, where God's Holy Spirit is given as the earnest of the consummation (2 Cor. 1:22; 5:5), consequently, by incorporation into the Body of Christ of the church. Even in this state, Christians in their corporeality continue to be earthly existence under attack. They must therefore tame their bodies, according to 1 Corinthians 9:27, actually punish them; according to Romans 6:16ff., allow them to be made slaves of the divine righteousness. The Christian lives in obedience to the first commandment and is thus continually tempted to want to live from idols, to live from the power and reasoning of this world. Christians are no longer prey to sin, insofar as Christ's Spirit rules them and sets them in service. But they are not yet withdrawn from the pull of earth to emancipate themselves, are set in the world-wide struggle between God and Satan, called to sanctification.

The survey just presented was abbreviated and summarylike. The point was to show that Paul observes corporality under various aspects, that he defines it variously, even in apparently contradictory ways. The concept cannot be explained when we try to base it on a modern understanding shaped by natural science. Paul argues in such fashion that the historical nature of the creature determines his utterances at any given time. We must still put it more precisely. Corporeality is interpreted from a concept of salvation history, concretely, from the perspective of the basis of creation, fall, redemption, and consummation. In this way the perspectives of anthropology and cosmology — of doctrines concerning creation, fall, salvation, Christology, ecclesiology, eschatology, sacramental language, and parenesis — continually intersect. The unity of the basic structure threatens to be lost in the variety of ways of viewing the subject. It will thus be useful at the conclusion of this section to draw a sharp contrast between the perduring basic structure and the variety of statements respecting concrete situations.

Corporeality is the nature of the creature. First Corinthians 15:35ff. reflects on the fact that plants, animals, stars, thus what is earthly and cosmic, differ in the manner of their corporeality, that thus the resurrection body in its singularity must be regarded as the likeness to Christ, no longer perishable or under attack. What is important about this statement first of all is that corporeality, other than in classical Greece, at least, or according to our usual view, is not seen as a part of the creature, that is, as its external part. It does not so much "have" a body. It "is" corporeal, by which we may leave open the question whether the apostle, as child of the syncretistic Hellenistic period, paid tribute to dualism, say, in 2 Corinthians 5. Un-

shakeable principles exist only in theory. In practice we must content ourselves with the main accent and tendencies. In any event, Paul does not legitimize spiritualism. If forced to a decision respecting appreciation for
spirituality so widespread again today, we should rather term the apostle's
worldview materialistic. In all its possibilities and capacities what is earthly
is corporeal and actually fleshly. The resurrection world determined by
Christ, however, is no longer fleshly but "corporeal" in a new pneumatic
way. If death should leave us "naked," according to 2 Corinthians 5:3-4, we
will not remain so. For Paul, "inwardness" is not a dimension or quality
towering over or transcending the natural. Corporeality, however, does not
mean we are determined solely by the material. We have eyes, ears, reason,
and conscience; more precisely, we are certainly all of that and therein altogether capable of development.

With these last sentences I have leaned heavily on my teacher Rudolf
Bultmann and his *Theology of the New Testament*,[2] so that I am at least
obliged to indicate where I can no longer follow his interpretation. It
seems to me that he sacrifices a holistic view of human corporeality to idealistic tradition, because he does not find his way out of existential analysis
into the breadth of the Pauline motif. He does not inquire to what extent
utterances about the believers' bodily existence are connected with those
about the church as Body of Christ and the resurrection corporeality of
the consummation. From out of this context he would surely have had to
interpret more clearly those difficult sayings about the body of sin and
death. Instead, based on his presuppositions, he defines human corporeality as the "relationship to oneself," in which one may be at odds with oneself or be under one's own control.[3] The problem is compounded when,
alongside the possibility of getting oneself under one's control, Bultmann
sets the other of losing control and being at the mercy of a power not one's
own. Finally, it is expressly stated that in the latter instance that power can
be experienced as hostile, as estranging one from oneself, or can be its opposite, a friendly power that brings the self-estranged self back to itself
again. It is clear that demonic and divine power are contrasted here. But
then, human, corporeal existence is understood as the battleground of
powers. How can the interpretation of the body as a "relation to oneself"
be connected with that? Is not that relation lost when an alien power is be-

2. R. Bultmann, *Theology of the New Testament*, 2 vols. in 1, trans. Kendrick Grobel
(New York: Charles Scribner's Sons, 1951).

3. Bultmann, *Theology of the New Testament*, 1:195ff.

yond my control? May we speak of "having oneself under one's control" when we see our existence handed over to alien powers? I no longer understand this interpretation, not even its wording.

I suggest that the dilemma arises from the fact that the Pauline motif of corporeality cannot be limited to the area of the interpretation of existence. Without being able to enter into this special problem here, I would at least like to remark that the technical meaning of the word "body" as "person" does not appear to me to be Pauline and, without thoroughgoing investigation, should not be assumed to be present in other Hellenistic texts. Only if there were this technical meaning and it could be proved to be in Paul could Bultmann's definition of the Pauline motif of the "body" be given consideration. However, Bultmann's definition proceeds further when it calls us to note that, in Paul, "body" constitutively has the structure of a relation. This is a basic insight for me as well. Put pointedly, just one single word separates me from my teacher. For the apostle, "body" or "corporeality" does not denote a relation to oneself. It cannot, because Paul assumes an extrahuman corporeality. But it can indeed be asserted, as I have already done, that the apostle understands all corporeality as the relation to a world and as a specific projection of it in the given instance.

No text strikes us more forcibly on this uncommonly important matter than 1 Corinthians 6:13: "'Food is meant for the stomach and the stomach for food,' and God will destroy both one and the other. The body is meant not for fornication but for the Lord, and the Lord for the body." What is tersely stated here is that for all corporeality the structure of relationship with others is decisive. This relationship has its culmination in bondage. The radicality of the utterance allows whoredom to be more than one sin among others. Rather, it represents the demonic, anti-Christian world. It can do so because it lays claim to our body and brings it into subjection. For Paul the body is other than the belly, which merely has to do with eating and drinking and, like its nourishing, belongs to the transitory; it properly belongs to Christ alone. For this reason there is that exclusive either-or of Christ and the whore, in which the first commandment is concretized. In the area of sexuality the struggle for world rule is fought out in the life of every individual believer. Christ intends to have the corporeal for himself, since he intends to have the world that is manifest in corporeality. In a final clause Paul sharpens the expression: Not merely the body belongs to Christ. In an unheard-of provocative way the apostle formulates what is perhaps the most offensive sentence in all his letters: Christ belongs to the body. This is still to be considered. For the present let us resume. In its broadest sense corporeality is existence in communication; more concretely, it is the relationship to a particular world and the powers ruling in it. Insofar as Christ is the designated world ruler (1 Cor. 15:25ff.), he lays claim to human corporeality as the concretion of our belonging to the world. The struggle for world rule, which the first commandment has in view, is daily carried out as the struggle between Christ and the demonic powers for our corporeality. In it as in nothing else Christ is at work redemptively. Thus it can be said that he belongs to corporeality. The obverse side reads no less radically: corporeality means to have a lord, to be ruled, whether by Christ or by the demons as representatives of our world's autocracies. No one is excepted here. Each has only this alternative as his or her destiny. In the reality of life each can belong to only one lord. So, conversely, no one is lord in one's own house. In the sphere of corporeality and in it alone is decided who at any given time is our lord. Thus, in truth, self-determination is a utopia. None exists in and for the self, none in the struggle for the world can be neutral, none can emancipate the self. Because and insofar as we live bodily, and even in God's kingdom will live in this way, we are always members of a specific world, whatever its rulers may be.

3. *Members of the Body of Christ.* It has now become quite clear that Paul does not merely speak or speak in a chiefly metaphorical way of the Body of the exalted Christ in his church on earth. As in the analogous phrases "body of death" or "the power of sin," a reality is in view in which the relationship to a particular world and dependence upon its given rulers appear. For Paul, corporeality always has the nature of an "ontological structure," as Bultmann formulated it. This expresses the "worldliness" of existence that is different on earth, yet is manifest in the corporeality of the resurrection. Thus the individual as well as human societies belong and witness to a history full of change, a battlefield with its victims and signs of victory in the struggle between God and idols. They are reflections of the power to which they belong or are subject, enmeshed in earthly and supra-earthly conflicts. Their nature — or, put idealistically, their "authenticity" — is not something they paradoxically have from or in themselves, but rather outside themselves in their lord and the cosmic sphere claimed by him. Constitutively the human is never of age, is always and everywhere determined by what is alien.

The Body of Christ of the Church, however, is the earthly sphere of the lordship of Christ as the destined and ultimate world ruler, following his exaltation mightily at work in the world through his Spirit. To this extent, the dogmatic phrase *corpus Christi mysticum* corresponds to the Pauline intent. But to this extent the phrase is also "demythologized." The apostle did not at all mean that Christ is absorbed in his church as the idea of the *Christus prolongatus* (the extended Christ) suggests. Christianity is not the authority that, in the name of the Exalted One, continues the earthly existence of its Lord with its hierarchy. It may not without limit arrogate to itself his authority. It does not have to spare him direct intervention into earthly relationships, as it were; it may not sacrally domesticate his Spirit. The church is and remains nothing but the earthly world sovereignly ruled by Christ, chosen and directed by his voice. Its chief characteristic is acceptance of his word in daily obedience and willingness to suffer. In the extreme instance this obedience is to be actualized in rebellion against the ecclesiastical institution and its official leaders so as to proclaim Christ's sole lordship. Such rebellion has in fact accompanied church history since its beginnings. Today, in the interest of the universal priesthood of all believers, and against bureaucratic organization, we should emphasize the right and obligation to rebel, since the lordship of Christ is frequently more strongly imperiled by its alleged representatives than by its enemies.

This last remark implies that glory is not at all the dominant characteristic of the earthly Body of Christ of the church. It cannot be more emphatically called to mind that the exalted Lord is and remains the Crucified, who calls his disciples to follow his earthly journey toward the cross. To this both Baptism and the Eucharist point, which incorporate and hold us fast to the earthly Body of Christ. We do not constitute that Body by entering into it as into an association. We are set sacramentally into that new world in which Christ is sole Lord even on earth, and the sacraments mediate a share in the crucified body of the exalted Lord, as Paul emphasizes with a singular acuity. The new world of the Body of Christ, while on earth still in competition with many other worlds and spheres of rule, is distinguished from them all by the *signum crucis* erected over it. To do justice to the importance of this statement, let me pose it provocatively. Ultimately, from any other kind of world with its alluring heights, depths, breadths, wonders, and glories, this world is distinguished by the *signum crucis* alone.

But in order that this may not lead to the most current and, often enough, to the seductively propagated mythology about the church, such a description must apply to the entire body as well as to each of its members. It has long been observed that Paul varies and concretizes the motif of the

Body of Christ of the church when he states that Christ lives "in us" and that we are drawn into him. This has nothing to do with mysticism, though such is incessantly maintained. The exalted Lord concretely seizes hold of the world, which belongs to him. Just as once as the Nazarene, so now with his Spirit, he is present through his members on earth. But he is present on earth at all times as the One who takes up his cross and allows his disciples to share in it. The apostle boasts that he is a member of the lordship of Christ when he confesses in Galatians 2:20, "I have been crucified with Christ; and it is no longer I who live, but it is Christ who lives in me." Then he interprets this statement in Philippians 3:10-11, "I want to know Christ and the power of his resurrection and the sharing of his sufferings by becoming like him in his death, if somehow I may attain the resurrection from the dead." In an earth over which demonic powers and forces tyrannically reign in manifold shape, Christians witness to the coming resurrection of the dead when they daily and throughout life bear the cross after their true Lord, an act inseparably bound with resistance to idols. With their resistance and from their discipleship of the Crucified Christians for their part announce that the earthly Body of Christ is not merely an edifying picture of a bloated church triumphalism. Rather, in midst of the inferno of a creation terrorized by ideologies and despots, demonically disfigured by hunger, exploitation, torture, and murder, there exists the reality of a lordship of Christ that looks toward the resurrection of the dead and that thus resists demonic violence, concretely and bodily.

This lordship is no longer determined by the categories that usually apply, that is, "being" or "having." It is not oriented to the utopia of human self-realization and the urge to subject God and world to the creature's self-will. Rather, in it there occurs something like a cosmic revolution. God's Spirit sets people in motion to win the earth for their Lord, to recognize in the neighbor as well as the stranger the claim and promise of the One who created us in his image and in Christ will reshape the fallen creation in that image. "To take part in" and "to share" gain ground as categories of the end time and the resurrection where Christ's kingdom is realized worldwide and makes one-time rebels his servants. At Pentecost heaven opened over the earth. The fact that even now the barriers between humans are falling, that, according to Galatians 6:15, a world everywhere sealed off has been opened as a new creation for mutual service, allows Paul to compare the sphere of Christ's lordship with an organism. Of course, we must note that he does so in critical fashion, for this lordship is imperiled, not only by the enemies around it, but no less by fanatics and the scrupulous within. On earth the new creature still remains the tempted creature, as such always inclined to set Adam's image, hence worldly reason, power and metaphysics, in place of the likeness of Christ.

Religious ideology among church leaders, pious groups, and theological concepts is not content with a unity that denotes solidarity of the various members in service for one another. Rather, conformity in thinking, willing, and acting is assumed, though uniformity allows all service to become meaningless and favors the privileges of the highly endowed in the community. The most foolish polemic is directed against pluralism in the community and the *oecumene,* though there is no other life than one that is differentiated and "pluralistic." New Testament texts can actually speak of differences in heaven. All creation grows only where a variety of possibilities and capacities are visible, where the alternation of becoming, ripening, and decline takes place, where talents and defects are united in individual life as well as in community, where the morals and traditions of past generations are slowly changed or, in times of crisis, changed overnight. We are not speaking here of political, social, and moral polarization, nor are we sanctioning partisan intolerance. Still, ideological fanaticism turns the earth into a desert when it aims to render everything alike. In the church at least, each one must be permitted to retain one's own hue. Where there is religious leveling, love dies, boredom spreads, and only navel-gazing remains. Jesus trafficked with the most varied types. For the most part, the men and women of the Bible are not singled out for their lofty morality. Not even the apostles were ever at one theologically. We tinker with God's affairs when we measure his creatures by self-fabricated or traditionally valid norms and conventions.

It is no less perilous for the Christian community when the weak wish to be less than God would have them be, when they bury the talents given them and are still theirs in resignation, sloth, and cowardice, when they fold their hands dispiritedly in their laps, leave thinking to others, and, as it were, feign death. Neither God nor the neighbor in need allows us to make our way to the isolation ward before we die. The solitary person already goes through hell on earth and drags it along when refusing to participate actively in life and in community. A passive Christianity leaves the path and space open to demons and thus blasphemes the Lord, who endured the cross and conquered the demons. There are no superfluous members and no fellow travelers in the Body of Christ, though the churches continually seem to prove the opposite. Where no one is served one lives as a monad under a closed heaven, in a world more and more steadily closing itself off; one denies the Holy Spirit, who frees for resurrection from the dead and eternal life even those who before death dig their own graves and are cut off from fellowship and membership. According to Paul the Body of Christ is like an organism because the disciples are called to service and, in serving, experience anticipated blessedness. Where the earthly communication of love has not reigned, in which members are made of "individuals," the basis for the communication of the perfect in the kingdom of God is removed. There is no heavenly continuation of what has not been begun on earth. The corporeality of the resurrection is grounded in the fellowship of service within the Body of Christ on earth. Whoever was not for the neighbor and the stranger in our world was not for Christ, whatever was believed, offered, or prayed, and in eternity Christ will not be for that one. When the Body is despised, the Lord is despised.

This leads us to a final insight: As Paul understands the Body of Christ primarily as the earthly rule of the exalted Christ, thus as the presence and communication of Jesus in the world after his departure from earth, so the statement regarding the organism of the church in its turn points back to this primary meaning of the motif of the Body of Christ. Each one is served in fellowship of the church and, as far as it is possible in our world, each one is assisted to the freedom of the creature by the others. Where the individual Christian and Christian fellowship do not serve to liberate the creature and preserve it to the deepest and most secret needs of corporeality, there is no true church. It does not exist without the new earth's coming into view as preview of the new heaven. In an unmistakable and unforgettable manner, 1 Corinthians 6:13 proclaims that "the body is meant . . . for the Lord, and the Lord for the body." This means, for the earth. For this reason he became man. For this reason we proclaim the gospel of the resurrection. And with this statement the apostle establishes the other, that is, that the body belongs to the Lord and must be and become alive to his honor. This occurs when and where the worldwide dimension of Christian service is recognized and realized. Just as there is no Christian who is not used in the service of his Lord, so there is no creature that could do without this service. Each one needs the helpful, cooperative, sympathetic fellowship, and each needs the earthly presence of Christ as Liberator in service to his community. Its members carry on his lordship and his glory ever wider and deeper into the earth. Because their talents are inexhaustibly manifold, they adapt to all relationships. Because they must receive particularly those who are weak, despised, and heavy laden, they penetrate to the most distant corners. By its very nature, the Christian church is ecumenical. Its service is not limited by the confines of confessions and denominations. According to 1 Corinthians 15:25ff. its Lord will rule worldwide, and his church is to manifest his earthly omnipresence in a service applicable to all and needed everywhere. It is the Body of Christ as the sphere of his ubiquity and omnipotence in midst of a world that is hostile to him but still belongs to him and is loved by him.

So, here too Paul construes corporeality once again as the medium of communication and participation with a view to the world. But the unity and totality of the cosmos is envisaged beyond the reality and possibilities of other organizations. The Body of Christ denotes a radical and global revolution of an earth enslaved since the fall by demonic forces. In it the Exalted One is revealed as its true Lord. The bodily service of his servants in fellowship with every creature is the demonstration and realization of the claim and promise of the One whose resurrection in 1 Corinthians 15:25 is interpreted as a worldwide revolutionary and explosive event: "For [Christ] must reign." This far exceeds humanitarian and caritative activity. If anywhere, then here one may and must speak of world politics. The power of the resurrection creates a new earth under a new heaven, an anticipated kingdom of God as liberation from the tyranny of the cosmic powers that have reigned until now. In the power of Christ's lordship service is offered to all in the Body of Christ. But this service is misunderstood if it is not construed as a manifestation of the lordship of Christ the Liberator, bodily penetrating all the breadths, depths, and corners of the world. The corporeality of the church spells the dimension of the lordship of the exalted Christ. It is the space in which at last the first commandment in its promise and claim is proclaimed over all the earth.

Justification and Freedom

Whoever wishes to speak today of the Pauline concepts of justification and freedom unavoidably encounters three great difficulties among his hearers. First of all, what the apostle means by the righteousness of God and our justification is no longer understood by most members of a Reformation church so that they could give a precise answer. Even the Lutheran World Federation at its 1963 Helsinki Assembly felt this so strongly that it no longer dared speak of it. Its profound lack of comprehension was revealed when the assembly announced that this theme was of course once the heart of the Reformation message but today is no longer relevant and is better replaced by the question of the certainty of God. The World Federation should then have been dissolved as out of date.

Second, there is difficulty with the Pauline concept of freedom. Each of us understands it to be a watchword, and in all the world there are a crying after and a struggling for freedom. But we must see and clearly point to the fact that, for the most part, Paul means something else by it. The revolutionary slogan of the Enlightenment overshadows what the apostle meant, and not merely with the white race. The self-determination and coming of age of persons and nations to be won by emancipation and insurrection against the fetters of tradition is now the ideal, the presupposition, and the goal of a meaningful life. But Paul never and nowhere advocated emancipation. He did not recognize or intend the person come of age. He would have regarded such a device as a satanic caricature of the gospel.

A Bible study given on December 12, 1996, at the Evangelisches Stift (Evangelical Institute) in Tübingen.

The third great difficulty of my theme results from the fact that in theology not only practical life but thought as well can no longer be contextually oriented. Details overrun our capacity to see and isolate us from other people and the world. We batten ourselves down on the narrowest plank against the breadth and confusing variety of life so as not to lose ourselves in it. In this way the past becomes more incomprehensible than the present. We neither can nor want to live with it, though we come from it. We content ourselves with a few islands we have discovered in its sea. The adventure of descending to its depths and finding our own reality modeled there as in a mirror no longer fascinates. But in our time whoever avoids the toil of the way back to ancestral fathers and mothers will view the neighbor and the stranger in a merely schematic and ideological fashion. A propos of our theme, we must understand Paul from the center of his message, not from the distance of the onlooker who in archaeological fashion is content with the shards of history.

On the basis of these insights my task is now marked out for me. First of all, I will briefly set forth the provocation residing in Paul's concepts of justification and freedom. I will then attempt to indicate the contexts from which such provocation emerged and which could allow them to be worth our consideration, perhaps even tempting, for us today.

1. The idea that we understand others is so far from obvious that the greatest concentration, devoted preparedness, and most extreme patience are needed to arrive at it. We would have had to know of it from our experience with parents and friends. Again and again we enter the adventure of an expedition when dealing with a foreign language. Only in the dictionary does it appear that there is a single definition for every word, that it has precise correspondences among other people everywhere. Whoever listens to the Bible leaves familiar territory and should be prepared for something like a Pentecost event. What righteousness and justification mean to us does not at all capture the meaning Paul connects with it. We follow the Greek tradition according to which the goddess of righteousness is enthroned above all the other gods as impartial judge who creates the order of each community by distinguishing justice from injustice, the good from the bad, levies punishment as well as reward, and sets us under fixed norms. Whoever recognizes and furthers such order is made righteous, thus is not liable to punishment.

For Paul, however, righteousness is not primarily an earthly affair. It has to do with salvation, and of course exclusively with salvation, never with punishment. It is hard for us to grasp this. We cannot help but observe God and our relationship to him, as well as his relationship to us under moral categories. But for the gospel and Christianity, morality is more dangerous than all blasphemies. The parables of Jesus make this clear. Annoying to anyone concerned for respectability, order, or settled basic values, they allow the prodigal son, the publican, and the prostitute, none of whom can exhibit anything but a lawless life, to be redeemed. The unrighteous steward is praised, whereas the rich young ruler remains outside the door. Throughout the whole Bible it is precisely the pious who are forever harshly attacked. In Romans 4:5 Paul reduces this to the offensive unit of value that our God differs from earthly judges by making the godless righteous. He is God precisely when he reverses what is felt by us to be just and valid, devout, and necessary. The watchword of the gospel reads "grace for sinners." Long habit may allow us to agree with the watchword, but with a small improvement: "Grace *also* for sinners." The improvement ruins everything. For the God of Jesus does not let grace pass for justice *in addition* to those who really do not deserve it. Rather, his justice always and only reads, "Grace for those who do not deserve it." No longer does morality have significance here, nor even religiosity. There is no objection to finding devout people and people concerned with morality and custom at worship. On the contrary, it is much desired if the church is not to come more and more into disrepute. But it nevertheless applies that the devout and so-called respectable people possess no privileges with our God, can make no claims to justice. They also, and they precisely, are dependent on grace. Before the Creator and Judge, no one can lay claim; all his creatures are poor and as such dependent on mercy, thus on the fact that our God opens his heart to the poor. He justifies the godless, always only the godless, because none of us can pocket God or deposit him in our private bank. There is none so good and pious as to create access to the Lord God by one's own power, merit, or understanding. Godlessness is the mark of the one who needs God for living and dying, since none can ever make God one's own possession.

My statements may sound unexpectedly pietistic to many here. They are designed to do just that. Put flatly, in our country the gospel has been preserved only to the extent that Pietism carried on the Reformation. We have occasion to be thankful to it and wish it well. We should, of course, not overlook the fact that this Pietism, especially in our country, has been infected with the illness of the evangelical church within the area of the white race. In this area Christianity has become so middle class that other levels of society scarcely cooperate actively with the church or are to be observed at worship. From of old the characteristic of the middle class was the will to possess, to protect and to preserve. The middle-class church is oriented to the affluent society, since it too proclaims the right to property and resolutely defends its possessions from foreign seizure. In a certain sense Christians have now become the protagonists of the capitalistic economy dominant in white society. They not only defend their little house and account at the bank but also their religious, ideological, and moral property. They so energetically affirm the resurrection because above all else the bourgeois want to live on and thus they must outlive even the grave. In this way those in possession come into conflict not only with communists but with God and his gospel, which never becomes our inalienable possession, which always lies ahead and must be seized ever anew.

The bourgeoisie desire security, though all creation lives on volcanoes and death teaches us how little we may trust in possessions or understand ourselves as possessors. According to 1 Corinthians 15:25, "Christ must reign" is the meaning of the resurrection message proclaimed over earthly graves. "Er reißt durch den Tod, durch Welt, durch Sünd und Not. Er reisset durch die Höll. Ich bin stets sein Gesell" (He bursts through death, through the world, through sin and need. He bursts through hell. I am forever his ally) we sing at Easter as the host of those who have nothing solid in hand, who are and remain poor and needy in terms of the Beatitudes and the Our Father, who must always leave the camps of our fathers for an unknown future and, according to Hebrews 13:9, take along as the costliest thing that our hearts should be strengthened by grace. We must pray for *daily* bread, since even today manna hoarded spoils in the desert. We do not remain creatures if we no longer need to stretch out our hands as always in need, waiting to rely on help from outside. The church that boasts of its religious possession and adapts itself to affluent society hinders the course of the gospel more than the hatred and persecution of those who oppose it. God's righteousness may not be requital according to merit or debt. It must always create salvation, bring grace, forgiveness, and new beginnings. Not even the church is a world that owns God, but a world crying after God, confident of his help.

From the history-of-religions perspective this definition of righteousness is best understood from the Old Testament idea of covenant, according to which God joined in partnership with his people. Since he remains true to the covenant, he proves he is righteous. Since he returns his fallen partners to the covenant, he sets them again where they must stand, in the right. His righteousness can only be a justifying power, setting one in the right, in salvation. What related Israel to its covenant with God Paul extended to the covenant of creation. Each stands beneath the promise that God will be and remain a partner, a mark of the righteousness of the One who remains true to himself and thus does not allow his promise to go aground on our unfaithfulness. His righteousness is continually underway toward setting us again in the right, in justifying us.

2. It is easier for us to grasp what Paul means by "freedom." To avoid the notion of human arbitrariness, we had best proceed from a parallel concept, from the Greek term *parrēsia*. *Parrēsia* is the lot of the full citizen of the *polis,* who may share in the public gathering at the marketplace, vote with others there, defend his rights, and participate in deciding the weal of the commonwealth. *Parrēsia* is thus a juridical as well as a political concept. It denotes the status of one who does not need to hide, as well as the claim to free speech and responsible decision touching all the questions of common life. Thus also it denotes the trust of the one who has no fear or does not slink away into anonymity. In the Bible this is what marks Christian freedom. We can put it very briefly. It is the condition under the open heaven, in an earth in which barriers, fixed camps, jails, and even graves must be opened, in which the resurrection has already begun, so that the disciples of the Risen One fearlessly follow their Lord in the earthly realm opened by him and are sent out by him to all the corners of the earth as his messengers. The free church is the open church, opening itself to all sides.

Interpreters of the Bible have often anguished over the question whether Christian freedom is first of all freedom *from* exploitative powers or freedom *for* service in love and for being shaped after the likeness of Christ. I think we must answer the question in the first sense. Christian freedom is first of all and always liberation from the yoke of slavery under the powers and forces. Israel's exodus from Egypt is the model of discipleship that the Master rescues from the chains of fallenness, to set it in his service. Otherwise, as church history proves, we fall too easily into an idealistic rut. Then we forget from whence we came, that it was God who dealt with us as the Creator when his righteousness justified us and set us under an open heaven. He must daily have the first and last word, and he must daily free us from that in which we have ensnared ourselves or been ensnared. We no longer know this, no longer experience and practice it, if we begin to fantasize about emancipation, self-determination, and coming of age; if we fall prey to illusions and ideologies, no longer perceive the reality of our earth and of our own existence. It is only too clear today that the loss of reality marks the Christianity of the white race, which for approximately 1,800 years has confused the gospel with an idealistic worldview and ended up in a ghetto.

3. Now it is necessary to pose the third difficulty we spoke of in the beginning. We must set the definition of justifying righteousness and Christian freedom within the contexts that characterize the reality of our life. Since I have no dogmatics in view, I will choose a section especially important for Paul. As nowhere else in the Bible, for Paul the theme of corporeality is the point of intersection of almost all theological problems. I will attempt first of all to sketch what the apostle means by corporeality, then conclude with viewing the consequences of the evangelical message of justification and freedom for our time.

Presumably only a few will see a serious problem when corporeality in Paul is up for debate. We are in error, however, if we assume it can only mean what we describe as a bodily condition or allow to be the conveyor of individuality or the phenomenon of human personality. Paul does not follow Greek tradition, on the basis of which *we* are defined. He is not thinking of what is marked off from everything else, something offered to our senses as the object of our observation or management, to be divided up by anatomists into its parts or researched respecting its peculiarities and functions. For the apostle, corporeality is the basic structure of every created creature, thus from the outset constitutively related to a God-given condition within a specific environment. It is thus viewed theologically, and it is more strongly oriented to history than to what we call nature. Since this is so, human corporeality, at which we are looking now, is referred to in very different areas and conditions. For the apostle "body" can denote a yet uninjured world of creation, but also a fallen and sinful sphere, or the fellowship of the redeemed, that is, the Body of Christ of the church, and finally the resurrection glory. For this reason what corporeality means in the concrete is not fixed once and for all. The meaning depends on the circumstances that at times characterize our existence, and definitely on the powers to which we are handed over or which protect us.

This also means that Paul in no way recognizes the person as an isolatable creature. Insofar as the person is a creature, it never exists in and for itself, as an individuum, but always only in a society as its member. In saying this we should note again that the apostle regards societies as spheres of power. Societies are ruled by powers and forces that may be radically hostile toward each other, such as the Creator and idols; such as life under the aegis of the Risen One or under the law, sin, and death; or such as the rule of the earthly Adam and the glory of the eternal kingdom. Human existence is always dependent, even when in rebellion — perhaps then most of all. We can come to a definition: Whoever we are is manifest in who is really and actually our lord. Only ideologues speak of human autonomy. So it is evident that, without exception, we always live under the claim and promise of the first commandment, that precisely in this way and without exception we always live in inner conflict and in the threatening or actual subjection to idols. One cannot define oneself by oneself. One is defined from outside the self, whether by grace or by the demonic. The first commandment is in fact not primarily prohibition but promise. Whoever is subject to the Creator not only should not, but need no longer be captive in body or soul to other lords. Such a one is saved, for salvation means to have the one Lord, who gives himself to us by becoming man, who establishes his right to us and calls us to freedom, no longer to be compelled to fear, love, and trust idols above all else.

Earthly and eternal ruin is correspondingly always only one thing, as the Christopher legend illustrates, that is, subjection to false lords. The human, a rebel since the fall, will not accept this but fashions other gods from ideals and ideologies. Even the Christian must daily learn and be trained in the fact that the entire gospel consists solely in holding to the true Lord and turning from the false. In this way the promise becomes a ceaseless claim. To have a Lord, then, always means to be obliged to serve. The difference between salvation and damnation consists only in whether or not the "must" becomes a "may," whether love or fear moves us to obedience. How it is with us is lived out in our corporeality. The prattle about spirituality is in any case nonevangelical when it exempts us from or intends to supersede bodily service. We are not pure and free spirits; we do not hang suspended in the air. According to Paul, corporeality belongs to existence and reality, all the way to heaven itself. To avoid idealistic fanaticism, it would do us no harm if we tried to think and live in purely materialistic fashion. God, like the demons, wants our body, because he will have us totally. This is the conflict that agitates all of world history. To whom do our bodies belong, both now and in eternity?

From what has been said it follows that corporeality denotes not only a particular sphere of rule but also its enlargement at any given time. For the Jew, the body is not, as for the Greek of the classical epoch, the prison of the soul, the mortal ballast of our authentic and immortal nature. Rather, the body is the medium of communication. Life is no longer out from or under the categories of "being" and "having," but under those of sharing and giving a share, of mutual and common membership. This is made clear in the apostle's theology of the sacrament. If in the Lord's Supper the body of the crucified Lord is offered as gift for our salvation, the exalted Christ communicates with us, seizes possession of us, and draws us into the realm of his Body, that is, the church, so that we become its members, sisters and brothers of one another. This should not be heard in a devotional way. According to 1 Corinthians 12:12ff., Christian fellowship means that, since we are gifted by a Lord and obliged to him bodily, that is, totally, we must and may grant each other our corporeality, so that in the everyday life of discipleship we, as it were, go out of ourselves and surrender ourselves in order to assist the other to life, joy, courage, salvation, and growth in grace. But as a whole, the Body of Christ as the church of believers is nothing but the means for the exalted Lord's entering into communication with a rebellious world, to proclaim his promise and claim to every corner of it. According to Matthew 28, 1 Corinthians 15, and above all the Apocalypse of John, the Lord of the church will be Lord of the earth. For this reason he needs the church as his Body, as his means of communication with the world. He needs our corporeality, the corporeality of those who as members of his church are members of his Body and his rule.

I will stop here. We are not at all at the end of the Bible and dogmatics. We have only made a beginning. Yet this much suffices to summarize. We began with the key words "justification" and "freedom," which may not become isolated catchphrases. They are indicators, not of a worldview but of a theology and our faith. A worldview allows bystanders to inform themselves about the course of history and of the history of salvation and then to set up a program. Justification and liberation refer to what has happened to us, that we are used, daily, bodily, earthily, totally, and radically. These are the contexts for our two key words. Our God will win back his earth. For this reason he became man. For this reason he seizes hold of our corporeality, sets it justifying and liberating within the realm of his justice, that is, of grace that does not leave its creatures to themselves and certainly not to demonic enslavement. He frees us not only for coming of age and self-determination but for the glory of becoming his instruments and of serving one another. Viewed evangelically, freedom means, not merely that we are set once in the kingdom of grace, but that we live in it. God has set us in his kingdom and, by so doing, has set us in the right place, in a place where we belong. Love understands that we are not to remain there as in a ghetto. It drives us toward the earth, which belongs to our Lord, toward the oppressed who wait for his kingdom. We are to go out of ourselves as messengers and servants of the liberating God, in the discipleship of the Crucified, to give our earthly life to those who experience earth as a hell. Put contrary to all merely theoretical demythologizing, the war with the demons for the earth has begun. We participate in it on one side or the other.

The Theological Relevance of the Word "Possession" in the New Testament

Jesus, so the Gospels tell us, healed the possessed. If anything in New Testament tradition is as historically well attested, as, say, the baptism by John and the cross on Golgotha, it is that Jesus, as early Christian language would have it, fought with and drove out demons, freed the possessed from the realm of darkness, and set them under his lordship. For good reason Mark, first among biblical authors to write a Gospel, which in its first section gives special emphasis to the deeds of Jesus, gives considerable space and emphasis to the healing of the possessed. We should not see in this a mere device of composition for contrasting Jesus' mighty deeds with his passion, however important that aspect. The One who with heavenly power brought God's mercy to human misery is, paradoxically, handed over to men and earthly powers. We must also emphasize that here we have come upon a prehistoric Christian rock, upon the history of the Nazarene. Mark 3:22 allows scribes to arrive on official deputation from Jerusalem and declare outright that Jesus is possessed: "He has Beelzebul, and by the ruler of the demons he casts out demons." Clearly, Jesus' activity in the Jewish community creates unrest and in this way gains adherents. His opponents cannot contest this reality, but they construe it as demonic conjuring. Satan, they claim, uses his envoy to blind the people; magic feigns divine healing that can cure body and soul, thus leads even the pious astray.

According to Matthew 12:46, even Jesus' mother and his brothers be-

---

A lecture given on May 6, 1988, at the Evangelisches-Lutherisches Missionswerk in Lower Saxony, Hermannsburg.

lieve he is possessed and therefore want to divert him and fetch him home. Thus occurred Jesus' rift with his family. He solemnly states that only those are related to him who hear and do God's will. According to Matthew 12:31ff., whoever obscures what hour it is commits unforgivable blasphemy against the Holy Spirit. Jesus' activity marks the breaking in of the end time of the old aeon promised by the Baptist. The Nazarene is not just one of a host of Jewish exorcists. In conflict with his Jewish opponents, he recognizes the gift given him and the task appointed him. According to Luke 11:20, he states in triumph, "If it is by the finger of God that I cast out the demons, then the kingdom of God has come to you." The text continues that Satan's armor is taken from him and can be divided as plunder. He has nothing more on which to depend. The two last strophes of Luther's hymn "A Mighty Fortress" are anticipated here. The enigmatic word in Luke 13:32, to be delivered as a message to Herod, resumes the thought, "Listen, I am casting out demons and performing cures today and tomorrow, and on the third day I finish my work." Jesus' earthly work flows into his resurrection and exaltation. It prepares for Pentecost, the festival of a heaven no longer closed but opened to all the world, and at the same time of an earth in which the message of salvation can no longer be hindered by powers, forces, or human tyrants. God has appeared at our level and claims it as the area of his eternal lordship. Wherever he advances, the idols are in retreat.

In the theology of the white race since the Enlightenment this aspect of the gospel has only seldom been given the significance due it. For the most part, in modern parlance, it was "demythologized." It was conceded that Jesus intended to heal the body and could do so, that he returned sight to the blind, hearing to the deaf, upright movement to the lame, and in addition to the senses opened hearts and understanding. It is likewise admitted that he returned the isolated, outwardly and inwardly confused, to the fellowship of daily life, restored humanity to those who previously, put figuratively, housed among the graves, who already on earth were trapped by the solitariness of death with clouded hearts and heads and with crippled wills. Still, no one wanted to hear of demons any longer. Specters in the ancient and medieval worldview had to yield to the rationality of moderns. Even today the horoscope is still consulted, secret magical practices are still performed. Considerable portions of Christianity cannot and will not surrender their conviction of the existence of a personal devil without endangering faith in a personal God. Nonetheless, modern Enlightenment supposes we must regard this as the nightmare of frightened children. The "possession" of which the Bible speaks exists only in terms of mental illness. Today, such belongs to the practice of the psychiatrist, with whose handiwork the church should not tinker.

First of all, the right to such "demythologizing" is not to be contested. In the Bible an ancient worldview is actually connected to the gospel. Christian faith should not be based on this ancient worldview. A theology that must discern the spirits must also for its part participate in evangelical freedom and liberate people from the delusion and superstition of past worldviews. The disciples of Jesus belong in the present; they may not live off the canned food earlier generations have left behind. God's Spirit daily renews the earth and humankind, daily calls us to a new morning. His concern is that his servants are open to this renewal, that in body, soul, and spirit they are not turned to the specters and constraints of those already buried, or that they fall further prey to them. Such demythologizing is the irrevocable component of Christian theology and the evangelical freedom of faith. None should jostle it.

The faith and theology of the disciple require no less than that we once more leave the fleshpots of Egypt and, just as Abraham, leave the houses of our forebears and take to wandering into the future determined by God. To this it also pertains that we test our forebears' interpretation of the Bible, do not concede their formulas and insights, as it were blinded by them. We may throw the baby out with the bathwater and confuse radicalism with illumination. Where evangelical freedom rules, enlightenment also follows. But there is also an ideological, nonevangelical enlightenment. With the right to demythologize comes also its limit. Evangelical freedom is not without limit; it is located first of all not in our heads but in an obedient heart. Not only an ancient worldview must be demythologized but also that optimistic, rationalistic delusion about human progress in the economic, spiritual, and moral sphere, the myth of goodness at humanity's deepest core, of the right, possibility, and duty of self-liberation from the fetters of immaturity. To put it concretely and provocatively, that condition must be diagnosed which in the history of dogma is usually treated under the rubric "original sin."

Today, this state of "original sin," at least in Protestantism, is just as controversial as the concept of possession, and not at all by chance. Naturally, by "original sin" we are not to think with old church tradition of sensuality, especially human sexuality, which by inheritance thrusts us into the lusts of the world and separates us from the heavenly. Sensuousness is a divine gift and an indispensable possibility for earthly communication that only an eccentric idealism may disregard. Conversely, we may not reduce the state of "original sin" to a variety of individual legal and moral transgressions. Such is neither biblical nor justified by our modern view of human nature. The heaping up of guilt in life is not to be overlooked, nor is the personal responsibility of every person for evil done being contested. But sin denotes more than an act against God and harmful to persons. This idea would favor a purely moral way of looking at things and would impair the aspect of rebellious attack against the holy will of God. Sin is always and primarily the creature's rebellious urge to assert itself against its Creator, whether in thought, word, or deed. This urge toward self-assertion is incessantly concretized in what we intend to do and actually do, but it cannot be reduced to this. It is not only a deed; it is also power and destiny, which involves the individual, willingly or not. There is also guilt as fate thrust upon us by our environment or our forebears, a fate that cannot be avoided and continues to work as curse and that we repeat. We are never merely "we ourselves" but always a part of our world and history.

In Romans 7:7ff. Paul described this condition with the greatest theological precision. Even today Adam has his worldwide effect on all his children. We sin not only when we behave immorally. At bottom, that is only a projection of the power that most profoundly deserves to be called sin. It allows us to do what we do not want, even when we long for life. It lets us arrogantly desire to create our own salvation or in despair give up hope of it, and seek a substitute for it in earthly lust. The more pious we are, aspiring to know and realize God's law and moral norms, the more imperiled we are. For then we almost necessarily build on the tower of our own righteousness or resign in view of our weakness and no longer trust in God's mercy. In either case we fall prey to the demonic. We are prisoners of sin, which acts through us and reigns sovereign in our members. If we understand the apostle's utterances correctly, then what we customarily call "original sin" from the perspective of the history of dogma is in reality "possession." Sin is then no longer exclusively anthropological, but all through the world it takes possession of us as power and destiny. We must no longer see the devil as having cloven feet or superstitiously scent evil spirits everywhere but recognize that the world and human beings of every age are constantly exposed to demonic seduction. Possession also lurks behind the alleged rationality in science and technology and determines our personal behavior, as well as social and political events. We dare not reserve its treatment for physicians and psychologists, nor does it concern only theologians. By this we can see that the place of Christ and his church is not the soul of the pious but the realty of the world — in short, that the gospel has political and cosmic dimensions. It cannot be otherwise if we have understood the first commandment.

"I am the Lord your God . . . you shall have no other gods before me!" This sentence has meaning only when I am never "in and for myself," when I can never really "emancipate" myself. I am always and everywhere subject to a lordship that brings God and the idols always and everywhere into conflict. It is this alternative that determines individuals and groups, as well as the entire world. Here, and here only, is it decided what sin is. In saying this, we should not forget that the first commandment is primarily promise, decreed by the One who leads his people to freedom from servitude. Thus "you shall not" basically means, "you need not serve other gods. You already have a Lord whom you are called to fear and trust, because he alone saves and sets free, loves you and is your Creator." What is commanded is to hear the promise, to let oneself be led by it. Accordingly, sin is always grace rejected, a despising of the Redeemer, who, according to Colossians 1:13, rescues us from the power of darkness and transfers us into the kingdom of his beloved Son. Sin is then put an end to by a change of lordship. Redemption is nothing but a change of lordship, meaning that it brings us home from the tyranny of supra-earthly and earthly powers to the arms of the Father, who waits for his children. As Father, he can only be a God *for*, not a God *against*. Now, of course, those brought home are not left to themselves. To be freed from idols does not mean to be free for oneself. In the new world of the Son and divine love, we are no longer violated. But everything still remains under a lord and king, thus in service. Paradoxically, the yoke of love characterizes evangelical freedom. What we have received must be further handed on. The disciple is modeled after the Master, who voluntarily humbled himself and, according to Luke 12:37, even as Judge of the world will put on the towel of the slave to serve his own. Love gives everything, but in precisely so doing, it takes from us our own will. Its claim is radical. It will perfect us according to the Sermon on the Mount, and that means "totally." For this reason, in Galatians 2:20 Paul must say, "It is no longer I who live, but it is Christ who lives in me." So little do Christians belong to themselves that their heart has been possessed by their Lord.

This takes us to the result of our survey of the first commandment. Just as there is demonic possession, so, analogously, the disciple of Jesus is taken into possession by his Lord, namely, as an instrument of his grace in a demonically perverted creation. There is no such thing as human autonomy. One is never simply oneself but always the projection of an all-encompassing power, the copy and image of whichever lord has commandeered one for service. In this sense Christians and non-Christians are no different from each other. In fact, it is the lords and masters that differentiate themselves and their servants. Believers remain what they were as unbelievers by the fact that they never belong to themselves, never can be understood otherwise than as dependent. Who we are is merely a reflection of our lord, the one to whom we are most deeply obliged. These lords need not necessarily be other humans, though they can be. Ideals, utopias, and systems, each with their compulsions, can also rule us, can thus be gods for us. But no one can escape the condition common to all persons always and everywhere of finding ourselves in one position or the other. The fact that we always embody and concretize the lordship that possesses us also means that we always live in a confrontation fixed by the first commandment, that is, between the true God, Creator and Father of Jesus Christ, and the alleged gods, which in reality are idols, images, and representations of the demonic. One may laugh at this, but it applies. Each of us lives in an earth determined by demons and demoniacs.

For this reason it is never unequivocally clear who God is. The one for whom we live and die, whom we love or hate, who possesses us in our inmost being, yields the evidence. If this is so, then Christianity is not merely akin to a conviction, even less a mere religious doctrine, or conversely a particular morality within a limited social sphere. Rather, it is worldwide service in the discipleship of Jesus and in resistance to superstition. What is determinative is the tie to the Lord, who was crucified on Golgotha. From this a believer's self-understanding may be derived, and concrete ways of behaving from the outset affirmed or denied. On this basis a worldview may be accepted, another rejected, or a third tolerated. What must be clear is that neither theory nor practice, neither principles nor so-called basic values may be regarded as the criteria for what is Christian. As people in general, so the disciple in particular is characterized by the Lord. The Christian is thus always engaged. What is permitted and what is forbidden may change according to place and time. But what must always be clear is that one takes sides *for* something and *against* something else. The key phrase in Philippians 1:27 reads, "worthy of the gospel," which concerns our Yes as well as our No. This can in one case recommend tolerance and elsewhere make tolerance impossible. Contrary to many admonitions from church authorities, the amicable settlement of differences is not the Christian's most important business. In view of the Crucified, neutrality, leveling, and edification, if at all, are seldom possible and, especially in view of our mortality, all but totally inappropriate.

There is no moment in our life in which we may forget what Ephesians 6:12 impresses on us: "Our struggle is not against enemies of blood and flesh, but against the rulers, against the authorities, against the cosmic powers of this present darkness, against the spiritual forces of evil in the heavenly places." I would prefer to know nothing of those exorcisms sometimes reported in the newspapers. Yet it must be emphatically stated that the preaching of the gospel and true discipleship always deal in exorcism. According to the first commandment, it cannot be otherwise. Golgotha makes that evident. In this fashion, members of the earliest Christian community entered upon the mission field and, according to the instructions of Matthew 10:8 and the appendix in Mark 16:17-18, gave evidence in word and deed of the breaking of the kingdom of God into an earth inhabited and perverted by demons. Not without reason the Bible closes with the Johannine Apocalypse, much too seldom read, meditated on, and interpreted, a powerful hymn to the day when hellish power meets its cosmic end.

From this we must conclude that the program of demythologizing did not spread widely enough. We would have to describe the uproar this program created in Germany as almost comical, and label those pietists who stumbled on it as much too harmless. Demythologizing may not be construed as merely fostering a theology oriented to the Enlightenment. It cannot be separated from the gospel itself. Admittedly, it must be radicalized. It may not merely propose to orient ancient texts and their worldview to a modern understanding of human existence and the world, as doubtless must occur theologically and as has always been done. Exegesis of biblical texts done in scientific fashion is only part of a more comprehensive understanding of the gospel, to be achieved on the basis of the missionary service of Christianity. Enlightenment, or expressed in New Testament fashion "enlightening," should not first of all be assigned to the past, for example, to the traditional material of the community, but particularly in the area of mission to people living now and in their particular circumstances. They need illumination because the present is generally darker than the earlier period; the demons can feel more at home in the present and be busier than when they were confined to inside book covers.

Demythologizing is to be conceived as part of the task assigned to the Christian of expelling the demons, thus giving definition to our service. The spirits are to be tested and distinguished theologically, even in the past, because they outlive the generations and, fascinating or horrifying, still haunt us today. Perils derive from them that still threaten us, even when hidden in print. Written tradition renders untold numbers possessed. But we can see this only when we are awake to the threat to our existence by the now-regnant principalities, powers, and tyrants, when we know we are called to resist wherever in our time human rights, human dignity, and human community are violated. All this is demonic activity in opposition to the Creator's work and intent. Wherever God's creation is threatened, misused, or ruined, whether through persons, systems, theories, or techniques, the devil and his company are at work. According to 1 John 5:19, the whole world lies under the power of the evil one. Idealists may call this exaggerated and unforgivably pessimistic. At any rate, German idealism has too often deflected us from sober realism to allow us, after two world wars, to succumb to such political propaganda slogans. After our experiences, ridding our world and time of demons should lead to considerable mistrust toward all idealism. In fact, we have reason for finally turning to the reverse side of the idealistic worldview, for unabashedly tackling what has too long been discredited as materialism. Historically, idealism too often grew on a soil tilled and made fruitful by slaves. It is high time that Christians at least become cognizant of this and draw consequences from it for themselves and their relationships.

As to ridding our world and personal life of demons, Christian theology in particular, whether or not it suits our setting or is decried as an illegitimate invasion of the social and political sphere by the religious, must distinctly assert that the gospel recognizes something of the sort, just as does the first beatitude. The kingdom of God is promised to the poor. Here "poor" means everything that must live oppressed, without hope on earth, without justice, everything dying that neither spiritually nor bodily shares in the status quo of an affluent society, everything called the Third or Fourth World by the presumptuous sovereignty of the white race. It was a misfortune for the whole earth that Christianity became more and more inward, private, and alienated from the world, that it held morality high against supposed subversion and came to defend its own privileges. Contrariwise, we must learn theologically today that, from the very beginning, the gospel had a political dimension and, as early as the first century, was persecuted as revolutionary. In most of the confessions our church leadership is intent on spiritualizing. Its delight is to discover and praise new spirituality. It would be better and, at least within the white race, more appropriate to Christianity to call the first beatitude to mind and draw its criteria no longer from the tradition of white citizenry but from the reality of the Third and Fourth Worlds.

The description of the last judgment in Matthew 25:31ff. should make us uneasy. There the Son of Man names as his kin and our neighbors those who are socially and politically most removed from us. There we can learn why demythologizing is necessary, what "the gospel" and "possession" are. There the pious and the moral of every nation stand before the One who has the last word and brings final enlightenment regarding good and evil, regarding what is necessary and what is unimportant. They have not noticed what is involved and think they can defend themselves without having noticed it in time. Finally, everything depends on our becoming human. We may possess and may practice a dogmatics, an ethics, and a proper worldview such as the given tradition requires but still leave Lazarus lying before the door to be licked by dogs. This brings the curse of the Judge of the world. Ridding hearts, conscience, and head of demons in order to conquer human apathy, resignation, and presumption, in order to hand on God's mercy shown to us, and in it all to preserve the discipleship of the Crucified is the criterion of the last judgment. At bottom, there is nothing special about this. Those who are blessed regard it as the possibility and duty of their everyday life. But everyday life is precisely the place where the Creator and his creation are recognized, witnessed to in service, and torn from the violence of the possessed.

In conclusion, we return to the beginning. The healing of the possessed is only one part of the gospel, relatively seldom spoken of in churches and theologies of the white race — that is, provided one is not actually ashamed of it and deems it appropriate and necessary to demythologize. Jesus, however, founded his own position on this part of his mission. From this it must and can be seen that he is and will be the eschatological bringer of salvation for all who have fallen prey to possession. Earliest Christianity took up Jesus' activity into its service and carried it on. The power of evil rules everywhere on this earth in the most varied forms, and Christians are sent to resist it and, insofar as they are able, to wrest its victims from it. They are thus sent into all the world to proclaim the risen Lord as the liberating conqueror. We must still do so today. A Christianity that has not set out to do so and does not see in this its task is no longer the salt of the earth but just one among many religious affiliations. It may be marked by a particular devotional character, but it is no longer an instrument in the structure of the kingdom of God, only one of private piety.

In our congregations theology is no longer carried on seriously enough. We nurse religious feelings and take care that the youth do not throw overboard the dogmas and moral traditions of our forebears. But we no longer take the Scripture seriously to the effect that we feel called and obligated to the priesthood of all believers, for which reason we must theologize. There is abundant pious absorption, at least on Sunday and at the turning points of life. But what is becoming less and less frequent, even in Protestantism, is dialogue with Scripture and each other concerning its meaning. At times we are tempted to bemoan the confessional squabbling that reaches a critical point in our provincial churches with the dispute between pietists and liberals. Actually, there is not enough dispute at the right place, where we are ready to hear and learn and, conversely, are passionately engaged on behalf of recognized truth. At the "right" place — that does not mean to be busy about what seems obvious and only needs repeating, but about the questions of today and the divinely intended answers to them.

We suppose that, given the legacy of our forebears, we no longer need the Holy Spirit for our time, and we look to what still suits us, as though we were at a second-hand store. This too belongs to demonic tactic, that in congregations and churches outdated controversies are continually being fought out, the fronts of yesterday are being spied out, today's debates are carried on with the formulas and arguments of yesterday. The Johannine Paraclete need no longer be concerned. Possession is also expressed, particularly so in a stupidity that avoids labor and holds to conventions where the spirits would rather have to be tested. Naturally, this begets boredom. A Christianity marking time is the habit of the one who, according to 2 Corinthians 11:14, depending on time, situation, and audience, disguises himself as an angel of light and feigns charismatic fellowship where, apart from openness to the world, a Christian ghetto is renovated and repaired and where thought is at an end. There is a narrowing of the field of vision. Interest in what occurs worldwide disappears in our middle-class communities, just as, remarkably in the same measure as, trade in exports increases and military entanglements involve us in the most distant corners of the earth. Deaf, blind, and lame to the dangers threatening the entire creation, too many calling themselves disciples of Jesus contemplate their own navel and alone or in groups feel their own pulse.

Mark 5:1ff. tells of the demoniac who lived among the tombs. Metaphorically, we may apply this to the behavior of many Christian groups. They are encamped in isolation near and among the graves of inherited traditions and conventions, have only their own resurrection in view, and are no longer aware that in 1 Corinthians 15:25 Paul interpreted the Easter message with a view to the whole world: "For Christ must reign." Lack of communication is a characteristic of possession, and whoever does not desire a new creation should not speak of rebirth. Such persons confuse their own wishes with the will of the Lord and dream of their own private gospel. Of course, we know and are conscious of crises in our affluent society. But we do not see that, for the great majority of humanity, the earth has become a hell in which hunger, torture, murder, oppression, and exploitation rule. We do not see that our affluence rests on forcing our wares on the underdeveloped world, selling it our weapons and chemicals, taking from it its raw material. This is a broad field that cannot be illumined now, but one example may illustrate the reality. Just as we who after 1945 wanted to have nothing more to do with armaments or with selling our weapons where nations are at war, even so we do not avoid supplying, say, Iran and Iraq, with the result that the war there goes on, and we profit from it. White Christianity also profits from it, as does each one of us. But this means that, whether or not we want it or know it, we are most deeply entangled in delusion and possession, that we are giving space to hell, though we preach the kingdom of God. We have reason to reflect on "possession" in the Christian community as well, and on how we as disciples of Jesus resist it.

Galatians 1:1–2:10: The Freedom of the Apostle

At the beginning of our Bible study I cannot avoid making a few prelimi-nary remarks. In three evenings, a New Testament epistle cannot be dealt with in its most important parts and in any detail, surely not the Galatians epistle, which in particular poses many problems. So I will attempt as quickly as possible to advance to its center and leave to right or left what does not directly lead to it.

The epistle is difficult not only for the theologian but even more for the contemporary congregation. It affirms much that has become foreign to us or what we at least no longer regard as so important and would not formulate so bluntly. This is especially true of the covert theme of our epis-tle, that is, Christian freedom. I am rather certain that in a poll of our con-gregations only a very few would call Christian freedom "the truth of the gospel," as Paul does in Galatians 2:5; only a few would regard freedom as its chief point, its true characteristic or ultimate norm.

As no other writing of the New Testament, Galatians is a call to Chris-tian freedom. Perhaps this explains why it is no longer as well known in our congregations; even in godly homes it is less read and reflected on than anything else in the Bible. It announces that wherever the gospel appears, there is freedom. Where freedom disappears, the gospel is no longer at work, for the gospel is nothing but the message that the Father of Jesus sets free and that none is a disciple, servant, or kin to Jesus Christ who does not extend freedom on earth.

This not only sounds political but is actually such. Here Paul takes up a

---

A lecture given on March 7, 1979, at the Kirchentag in Zweibrücken.

word that in its Hellenistic environment denotes the right of the full citizen. In contrast to the slave or the immigrant, the full citizen may appear and vote unafraid in the public gathering. Freedom is a democratic right and, where oppression takes hold, actually becomes the right of the rebel and resistance fighter. Whoever calls freedom evangelical truth brings the community into the fresh air and open field, does not leave it in the closet or behind the windbreak, behind thick church walls in the pious company of the like-minded. Such a one does not merely tie it to heaven but connects it firmly to its place on earth, since heaven intends to appear precisely there, on earth. We must actually say that it calls us out of occupation with ourselves and our friends, out of our longing for rest of heart, soul, spirit, and body in the strife. Freedom exists only where powers and forces struggle for earthly rule. The freedom of the gospel is incorporated in a discipleship that has set out to resist the powers and forces of oppression in solidarity with all the enslaved. It not only proclaims, it lives God's kingdom and rule wherever the enemies of God and of his creatures erect their own kingdoms and rule and lay claim to the earth. I am assuming that it is clear now why I call this message unusual and even offensive. Lest it be supposed I am merely reciting my own personal views, let the text of Galatians 1:1-10 next be read.

Three things strike anyone who compares the introduction of this epistle with others. Unlike elsewhere, there is nothing in it of thanksgiving for the Galatian community's standing firm in faith. Quite the opposite. The apostle angrily accuses his readers of falling away from his proclamation. If thanks there be, it does not apply to the fidelity of the congregation but to the Lord, who gave himself for sinners and delivers his people from the bondage of the present evil age. Finally, nothing short of a colossal curse is uttered in these very first verses, and in fact not only against earthly seducers but in a passionate arousal against angelic powers that falsify the true gospel. All this takes on meaning when Paul sees his congregation exposed to devilish temptation. In it Christ's work threatens to be undone. Once more is being driven into the evil world what was driven out of it. Evangelical freedom is used to reestablish demonic rule. Where it takes hold the apostle curses. Thus these first verses of the epistle attest, first, that freedom is regarded as the central gift and power of the gospel; second, that this gift and power is a possession of the Christian that can be lost or endangered — it is always imperiled, must be defended throughout life, and is won daily anew; and third, by the very fact that it was given grace, Jesus' community becomes a battlefield on earth in which each of its members needs protecting.

A Christian community is worth only so much as it announces, preserves, and increases evangelical freedom. Is it too much to say that I think this statement should move all our lives and churches to repentance, to a downright revolutionary reformation? By no means should we ignore what occurs among us of devoted thought and action; of prayer, preaching, and love for one another; and of the diaconate near and far. But what is at issue now is that, in a crisis, it can all be shoved aside, as it were, so that one single thing emerges as the indispensable characteristic of the Christian community and all its members — that is, standing in evangelical freedom, needing to remain in it, and extending it all around us according to our ability and energy. Are we not in such a crisis so that we must lose sight of everything else for the sake of this one thing, just as the apostle does here? Are we such disciples of Jesus Christ as wish to stand and remain in the state of freedom, defend it, and make it accessible to others? Are we able and willing to seize the gospel as the message of divine freedom for ourselves and the world, to allow our Christianity to be measured and evaluated by what we did or omitted to do for evangelical freedom?

Now, we could begin a conversation that cannot be concluded in a few hours but must be carried on throughout our entire life and that applies to each of us. To repeat, wherever evangelical freedom is not debated or reflected on; where its tasks, dangers, promises, and hindrances are not tested with care; where all of us are not enlisted in its service unabated and in our own way, there, according to our epistle, Paul recognizes no Christian community but a falling away from his message and his Lord, a relapse into the present evil age, and a subjection to demonic powers and forces.

Till now, however, we have spoken rather offhandedly of this freedom. Now we should describe it more concretely, thus hear and reflect on our text up to 1:24. Here the apostle illustrates the matter of evangelical freedom by his own life. Later, we will see that he has good reason to do so. His opponents, who confused the Galatian community and who publicly criticized and twisted his preaching, upbraid him as having no right to appeal to his personal freedom as apostle. We do not know exactly whether, by doing so, they meant only to cast doubt on his authority and credibility, or whether they actually intended to describe his message as suspect and insufficient. They probably intended both. They try to achieve this by portraying him as one we would call a freebooter, someone who has given up all previous, perhaps even legal and legitimate, obligations, and has in mind and achieves his own profit at all costs. We do well to make clear for a moment that, in that earliest Christianity we have for the most part glorified, true and false Christianity were no less passionately fought over than among us today, that even a person such as the apostle Paul could be suspected of being a false preacher, that such calumnies actually found a hearing and credibility in his own congregations. This is a mightily sobering instance. Obviously, the Christian community was never a peaceful playground. It has always included conflicting parties, so that the world around it discovered that it too is no better than its environs. Not even apostles were free of criticism and denunciation. This proves that Christian freedom is not practiced without risks, anxieties, and pains. Whoever is involved in it must pay for it, with friend and foe, possibly with everything one has and is. Let us put it pointedly: Christian freedom leads beneath the cross.

The reproaches of his opponents have something to do with the notion of Paul as dependent on the Christian mother community in Jerusalem. Only from this can it be understood that, in the text just read, the apostle sets forth in minute detail how seldom and briefly he came into contact with the Jerusalemites. If he were in fact dependent on them, he would have had to get instructions more often from them, would have had to let himself be more basically informed by them than was the case. Here is the place to insert the unusually solemn asseveration of the epistle's first verse: "Paul an apostle — sent neither by human commission nor from human authorities, but through Jesus Christ and God the Father." What is striking is the otherwise never-occurring demurral, "neither by human commission nor from human authorities." An apostle, obviously, is called by his Lord; human beings have not brought that about. Still, Paul's opponents must have been of another opinion and, as Luke did, must have regarded an apostle as an eyewitness of the life of Jesus, which Paul was not. We may put it more tentatively. They must have linked apostolic status to recognition and commissioning by authorities of the arch-community. The introductory verse resists this idea. Paul is an apostle not because men have installed him, say, in a kind of ordination, or have confirmed his task. His Lord and his Father alone granted him his authority, decreed his service. His Lord and his Father alone thus revealed to him the gospel that he conveys to the world. It is ultimately to them alone that he must render account for his activity.

The debate we are viewing has a theological background. The question at issue is who may legitimately be called an apostle. Paul's opponents will allow him to be regarded as such only when he recognizes the supremacy of Jerusalem, that is, of the arch-community there, and carries on his service in concert with the Jewish-Christian capital. This is altogether understandable. The gospel went out from Palestine, and the first Christians made Jerusalem the home of their leaders. Is it not right and proper that all Christian missionaries yield to the control of the arch-community, at least adjust and justify their work to and before it? When Paul later journeys to the so-called apostolic council in Jerusalem to give a report of his mission among the Gentiles, he himself, at least to a certain degree, recognizes something like the arch-community's preeminence. For this he had particular reason, if what Acts tells us is accurate. According to Acts, Paul allowed Barnabas, a member of the arch-congregation in Jerusalem, to bring him to Antioch, and there with Barnabas he began missionary work, for which reason he accompanied Barnabas to the apostolic council. Human mediation thus appears to have been in play when Paul took up his actual service. At least a representative of the arch-community appears to have introduced him to this service. The Galatian opponents might be referring to this.

Now we have laid out the historical background of the conflict, which helps us understand what is at issue for Paul's Galatian opponents and how they influenced his congregations. They assert that the only one who can be an apostle and missionary is one whose work the Christians in Jerusalem recognize, whose message they authorize, who remains in agreement with them and subjects his activity to their control. Whoever will not or does not do all this is nothing but a freebooter, whose motives and teaching must at least be subject to testing, perhaps actually to correction. No one should from the outset or flatly consider him trustworthy.

Paul reacts to these assertions by emphasizing his freedom — more exactly, by demonstrating his independence toward persons in general, and toward the community in Jerusalem and its authorities in particular. The apostolic council furnishes evidence that Paul wholeheartedly engages in compromises, provided his rights are not contested. But here he defends himself against the radical attack on his authority and service, and we may not forget he is also defending the congregations he founded. If he is suspect as an apostle, then they are also suspect as Christian congregations. Then also their legitimacy is to be put to the test. And in fact Paul's opponents at least add corrections to the doctrine and practice prevailing in Galatia, if we are not actually to speak, as Paul does, of a fundamental alteration of Christian existence. Not by accident, the Galatians letter, if we exempt the Revelation of John, documents the bitterest conflict in primitive Christianity of which we have any knowledge. Ultimate truth is at issue. What concerns the apostle first of all is the struggle for the legitimacy of his message. At issue is the status of his Gentile Christian congregations, the very understanding of Christianity. So we arrive once more at the statement that, from the evangelical point of view, everything is at stake where the theme of freedom is discussed.

Let us give it loftier form. What princes earlier maintained of themselves applies to the Christian community and all its members. They are what they are by God's grace. If this no longer applies, they are nothing but one tiny part of the religious world. Whoever intends or allows the curtailment of this grace sins against God's will and our salvation. Everything else can and perhaps must be renounced when persons and circumstances require it. Christians can never be expected to surrender, nor may they themselves dare to surrender the truth that they are creatures by God's grace. God has dealt with them in such a way that what an old hymn movingly expresses becomes true: "Der Glaub steht immer im Schein" (Faith ever exists in light), that is, in God's light, so as to be his reflection in the world. If we read the verse of our text superficially, it appears as though the apostle was concerned only with his independence, with his own integrity over against Jerusalem and those who were Christians and authorities in the community before him. This may be the consequence, but it is not the issue itself. Paul most stoutly defends the grace he has received, a grace traceable to God alone, which may not be overshadowed by human cooperation, classified under the rank and file of our usual values and regulation, normalized, and where possible even bureaucratized. Grace cannot be managed; one cannot use it to arrive at a hierarchy of offices or principles or an unalterable continuity of tradition. Once and for all grace bursts our self-fabricated arrangements and value-structure. It relativizes the traditional because God daily acts in a new way and cannot be overrun by our doctrines. Whomever grace would make its instrument can no longer be harnessed to the cart of convention but is truly free, since through this one God himself will speak to our time and world. Ever since John the Baptist evangelical freedom means that space is given God's voice in all the world and thus in every Christian community. It is the freedom of the witness that is invulnerable and to be measured solely by the truth of the gospel. It is ultimately the freedom of God in his witnesses.

This theme is so important that Paul devotes to it the most detailed description of his life that we possess. On the other hand, verses 11-12 once more make clear that biography is at issue only to the extent it is determined by the gospel. The apostle understands his existence as a kind of incarnation of the gospel and its history within the limits of a single human life. This is an enormous assertion for us to consider. Here is already stated what is made explicit in 2:20: "It is no longer I who live, but it is Christ who lives in me." There have always been persons who were possessed, were totally subject to a single idea, who lived for only one goal. We can almost count Paul among them. In a certain sense he too is possessed — not, of course, by an idea, but by his Lord, who takes new shape in him and gives a human body to the gospel. Later, Ignatius of Antioch called himself Christophoros, a Christ-bearer. This would hold true of us all if we were actually serious about the gospel. For this reason there is opposition again, just as in the introduction to the epistle: "Not by human commission but through revelation." Here we have an allusion to the story we all know about Paul's conversion before Damascus, where he perceives the exalted Lord, hears his voice, and is called to be an apostle.

"Not by human commission" may serve as the heading for this story, and the revelation of Jesus Christ as the content of this experience. It is probable, however, that the sentence hides a polemic. The Galatian opponents appear to have appealed to the fact that they stood within a set doctrinal tradition and would be legitimized by it. Paul also knew and valued such traditions, for example, those of the Lord's Supper, Baptism, and the Easter witnesses. He does not at all intend to reject them. None of us as Christians lives without doctrine and tradition, and we do well to continually meditate on them, as occurs in theology. One thing, of course, Paul will not do. For him, doctrine is not the deepest and ultimate ground of his apostolate, and he will not base his work on tradition alone. This is a provocative and dangerous thing to say, for without tradition we are rootless and homeless. Was it not the Reformation that led us to preserve pure doctrine and to recognize a church as Christian only where such occurs? Yet, it may be precisely this that hides our current defect. We can conceal Christ and his Spirit with tradition, make pure doctrine a kind of canned food with which to maintain ourselves religiously without the need for God's daily intervention in our life. Without the presently acting God, with a plethora of inherited doctrine and tradition, but without the living gospel, the church is a place in which Christian freedom no longer flourishes. For this reason Paul appeals to a revelation he received.

It is worth giving close attention to what Paul is emphasizing here. Not by accident he begins with the past, in which he was a persecutor of Christians, one who laid waste to the church of God and in this way sought to excel those of his own age and, as he then thought, make progress. His opponents do not know with whom they are dealing. They reproach him for disregarding the tradition and doctrine of his people. But once all he aspired to, and what made him stand out above all the others, was that he was zealous for the traditions of the fathers and advanced in them, leaving behind all those of the same age. His religious and theological zeal made him an enemy of the disciples of Jesus, a persecutor and destroyer of their congregations. Yet, on such a path God visited him, the God who, according to Jeremiah 1:5, separated his prophets from their mothers' wombs for his call and their task. Against all the expectation of the scribes, it pleased this God to convert Paul, the pious and zealous model pupil. God did not do so to lead him deeper into the doctrinal tradition of Judaism, to furnish him new illumination regarding it. God revealed to him his Son, the crucified Jesus, whose disciples Paul was persecuting. He showed him and all the world that even the pious must be converted and that religious zealots can be godless. Even today and within all Christian churches, it is too often supposed that piety satisfies God and that conversion applies to the acceptance of particular dogmas, traditions, and propositions respecting a given worldview. In this way thousands and millions of Christians prove that at bottom they are pagan. According to our text, for Paul everything is pagan that does not know and recognize Christ alone as Lord. Evangelical freedom thus consists in seeing only this as truly necessary and salutary. At Damascus God himself proves that the piety of the religious zealot is godlessness, and all his knowing and preserving of the traditions of the fathers is weighed against this one thing: that Jesus is Lord and as such must daily be learned, confessed, and praised.

Paul's breach with his past is expressed in his receiving a new task. As early as in Isaiah 52:7 it is said of the Servant of God that he must proclaim the gospel. The apostle, however, is commanded to do this from now on among the Gentiles. His calling is at the same time his installation as missionary to the nations. The gospel entrusted to him leads him away from the devout in Israel, and therein has its peculiarity. With Paul there begins a history of God with the world that reaches to our own time and sets *oecumene* in place of the ancient people of God. Thus, along with the beaten tracks of previous tradition, this new task bursts the boundaries of the Palestinian community that had not gone beyond the Jewish Diaspora. The grace revealed at Damascus sets free for the world.

The conclusion of our text puts this pointedly. From what Paul has experienced, he cannot be returned to Jerusalem and the apostles residing there in order to converse with them, get their counsel, or receive their blessing. Flesh and blood need no longer have any say where the Lord has shown him the way and the goal. He is turned toward the area we today call Jordan, then makes Damascus his headquarters, as it were, makes it the central point of an independent Gentile mission — the very place where he had previously persecuted the Christians.

Unfortunately, we learn nothing more of this period. It did not appear to have been particularly successful, since after three years at the latest, Paul changed his field of work. He may have done so even earlier, since in the ancient world the year from which one began to count was reckoned as the first. At any rate, for at least two years the apostle delayed his first visit to Jerusalem, a visit we would have expected to occur long before. He limited the visit to two weeks and, as he solemnly asserts, did not seek out the whole arch-community but only Peter and James the brother of the Lord. Furthermore, he sought them out in private, thus in most unusual fashion held himself aloof. Acts was no longer able to grasp this. I will not deal with its report, however, which gives an entirely different reading. It would lead too far afield, and Paul surely deserves greater trust than the later generation from which Luke writes. The fact that so few sayings of Jesus and no narratives at all of him are found in Paul's epistles likewise indicates that the visit to Jerusalem was less for the purpose of information than it was to meet the chief members of the earliest community, however incredible that may seem to us today.

Paul obviously kept zealous watch over his independence and thus in his description takes pains not to give such weight to the encounter. This is the answer to his opponents who reproach him for his dependence on Jerusalem and the arch-apostles. In what may be an exaggeration, Paul allows for only one brief contact with two pillars of the Jerusalem community, and that only years after his conversion. He insists that only his Lord remained his standard. This is underscored in verses 7 and 9 by the use of the passive voice (a frequent allusion to divine activity). But here we must note what the apostle does not say. From Acts we know that Barnabas brought him to Antioch and that for a longer time Paul was a leading member of the community there and together with Barnabas, a missionary from Cyprus. We hear nothing at all of this apart from the fact that instead of its chief city, Antioch, mention is made of Syria. This must seem strange, since we will encounter this silence later on. It may be enough to state that in this context Paul intended merely to refer to his connection with Jerusalem and so even at the conclusion speaks of it again with emphasis. The earliest community was so little an authority for him that neither it nor its Palestinian setting learned to know him personally but only came to hear of the conversion of the onetime persecutor and could praise God for it. We must, however, go at least one step further. Just as Paul made clear his independence over against Jerusalem and Palestine, so it is no less his concern to assert the same independence toward Antioch, and especially toward Barnabas, though he no doubt was more closely connected there than with the arch-community.

The section in 2:1-10, which we are now to enter, tells of this connection in thematic fashion. An official meeting between Paul and the Jerusalemites actually did occur, which, if we observe the ancient habit of reckoning, was eleven or twelve years after the first private visit. Evidently the apostle did not consent to it voluntarily; he speaks of the revelation that moved him to it. This suggests something like a vision in a dream such as later led him to Europe. Yet Acts narrates that the community at Antioch felt the trip was necessary, so it may be that the revelation occurred in the congregational assembly and was experienced in the instruction by one of the prophets functioning there. It was necessary to firm up the connection with Jerusalem as the site of origin and center of earliest Christianity. This was necessitated, as was clear from the action at the so-called apostolic council, by the question of the Gentile mission carried on from Antioch. There was unrest in Jerusalem and even dispute over this question. Rigorists, whom Paul angrily calls false brethren, held the view that no one should be accepted into the Christian community who had not previously undergone circumcision and thus personally accepted the Jewish law and had been incorporated into Jewish Christianity.

The significance of this requirement is obvious. It is possible that, in the entire history of the church, a decision more pregnant with consequences was never to be made. If the requirement of Paul's opponents held, only Jews could be Christians, in which case the community would have been and remained a Jewish sect distinguishable from others merely by its recognition of Jesus as Messiah. As suburb of the developing Gentile Christian church, Antioch had to urge for clarity here. For this reason it not only dispatches Paul to Jerusalem but gives him Barnabas as actual leader of the delegation. Paul takes along his pupil and friend Titus, who is uncircumcised and thus a representative of the Gentile Christians, as, so to speak, a living object of dispute. On and with Titus the decision must be made whether in the future there shall be a church of Jews and Gentile Christians or merely a Jewish-Christian sect with proselytes from paganism, of which there were many in the Diaspora synagogues. Paul makes clear his need of a council, as well as his anxiety, in the words, "in order to make sure that I was not running, or had not run, in vain." Though he may be ignoring the details and shifting his own role to the foreground, he had occasion to see all his work, his preaching, and his apostleship endangered. So he not only angrily calls his opponents "false believers secretly brought in," thus Christians really unworthy of the name who ought not at all give counsel or decide. He also reproaches them with having intended to spy out on and denounce his and his congregations' freedom. Again, in the word "freedom" he summarizes the entire matter of the Christianity he represents. And again, for him the gospel, as well as discipleship, stands or falls with it. All this is of course oriented in a church-political way. At issue is the right of the law-free community, of a mission among the Gentiles uninhibited by Jewish Christians and Jerusalem. In other words, it is about ecumenical Christianity.

The apostle trumphantly identifies the action and its result. He did not submit to them even for a moment. He had in view the truth of the gospel, which he owed his congregations, and this allowed him to remain firm. This stance was also respected by those in Jerusalem who had the authority and the last word, and about whom he now speaks almost contemptuously. Just as God is no respecter of persons, so no one impresses the apostle when forced to defend the grace entrusted to him. The result was a fortunate compromise set down straightway in a formal treaty. His treaty partners were the three apostles called the "pillars" in Jerusalem, since they were, so to speak, the columns of the earliest community — Peter, James, and John. These three disregarded the opinion of the radical, legalistic Christians and conceded to Paul the independence of his work in the Gentile world, just as they saw their task in the Palestinian area. The gospel tolerates different types of labor and a division of labor, the *oecumene* of Jewish and Gentile Christians and, what was decisive then, the fellowship of the circumcised with the uncircumcised, thus a discipleship that preserved the Jewish law of the fathers and another not measured or bound by this law. To become a Christian, no one had to join the Jewish religious community beforehand. Both could freely live out their faith and were not limited by the other's type behavior. They only owed each other love, given expression in Paul's promise in the name of the Gentile Christians to leave the mother community in Jerusalem with the collection we often hear of in his letters.

This said, we can conclude for today the story of Christian beginnings. But we should not do so without taking from it specific insights and questions that deserve careful reflection. 1. Will we wholeheartedly agree that the truth of the gospel consists in the freedom we desire for our own conduct of life and not merely concede but actually bring to others? 2. Will we acknowledge that in Christianity uniforms are not appropriate but that various types of behavior have a place, and that in this very fact evangelical freedom becomes visible on earth? 3. Do we thus remain in the ecumenical church, which is not a closed society such as a political party but, as a community of Jewish and Gentile Christians, remains open to all persons and their traditions? 4. Do we know that Christian freedom must be maintained and defended in conflict, and are we personally prepared to shoulder and suffer its risks? 5. Do we keep sufficiently in mind that discipleship may not be limited by authorities and privileges, and that inherited, or, say, confessional doctrine cannot avoid continual testing? The universal priesthood of believers knows only one ultimate and unbreakable rule: Jesus is the living Lord, and he rules his community through his Spirit and promises it ever anew his revelation and its understanding for the changing situations of our life. Are we ready to hear him ever anew, or are we living from and by our dogmatic canned goods?

Galatians 2:11-21: Law and Gospel

Life is always more complicated than theories assume. Even agreements among Christians often have their snags. The apostles themselves had to learn this, as the first four verses of our text make clear. At the council in Jerusalem a final peace seemed to have been arrived at between the community of Jews and that of Gentiles, between Peter and Paul as the mutual representatives of the mission. The agitators in the earliest community had achieved nothing. Suddenly, and in fact very rapidly, it became clear that not all possible differences had been considered. The new conflict broke out in Antioch, the Jewish-Christian filial of Jerusalem in Syria, the new suburb of the Gentile mission. In this Diaspora colony Christians among Jews and Gentiles lived peacefully together, nor were they disturbed when Peter, chief apostle of the mother community, arrived there on his travels, which later led him to Greece and Rome. On the contrary, he strengthened the Antiochenes in their harmony by participating in their common meals. The situation changed when intimates appeared from the circle around James, the Lord's brother, the one who had most to say in Jerusalem after Peter's departure. We learn further that James was a particularly strict Jewish Christian. Evidently, the rigorists who had already attacked Paul at the council regarded James as their real master.

We see again that in primitive Christianity things were not much different from the rest of church history or even from events of today. Jesus, of course, had commanded that his disciples should not allow themselves to be called master, as was the practice among the rabbis. Still, in Chris-

---

A lecture given on March 8, 1979, at the Kirchentag in Zweibrücken.

tianity there were always parties, schools, and sects. These had their leaders who did not bother with Jesus' command but allowed themselves to be so venerated by their adherents as if Jesus were not sole Lord and Master. Cliques never arise, in any event do not long persist, if they cannot gather about them protagonists who in good faith or from desire for power and ambition take the field against others and for that purpose furnish the necessary slogans. Thus the Body of Christ is continually divided and made ridiculous and incredible before the world. There were always schoolmasters who forced all to be holy after their fashion, who barred rebels from the kingdom of heaven without troubling themselves over the fact that Jesus was much more generous and admitted sectarians, traitors, prostitutes, and Pharisees of all stripes to his discipleship. In the community one has always wanted to make the pious more pious still, leaving in the wilderness all the others who were not religious idealists and could not be saints. The history of Christianity is a history of the exploitation of those who were not allowed to remain creatures after God's image but were conformed, uniformed, and trained after the image of the party chairmen and drafted into the religious war of competition.

Were not James's people at all concerned for the truth of the gospel, though they hailed from the circle of the Jerusalem rigorists, belonged to the "false believers" and denounced their brothers' freedom? It is altogether probable that they came to Antioch only for the purpose of closely examining the practice of the Gentile Christians in the community — in particular, that of Paul and his adherents. There will always be those pious folks who believe they are Zion's watchmen and thus pay more attention to others than to themselves. Still, they found what they were looking for. Peter, Barnabas, and the other Jewish Christians took no offense at the common meals with Gentiles and thus were exposed to the almost unavoidable peril of rendering themselves cultically unclean, whether by eating food not permitted by Jews or by coming in contact with persons who had not observed the prescriptions of the law and thus had become unclean. We can scarcely imagine how serious this problem seemed to the devout in Israel, a problem with which Paul also had to contend in 1 Corinthians 8–10 and Romans 14. Jesus had already been reproached by his opponents because he did not hold strictly to the laws of purification. After Easter this might have encouraged a more liberal group such as those around Stephen to become careless. Conversely, other members of the community learned that, as Jesus' disciples, they had all the more to prove to their compatriots their fidelity to the law and their zeal in preserving the traditions of the fathers. A conflict among the Jewish Christians was thus already in process, and the ever-increasing number of Gentile Christians on the mission field fanned the flames. Strict observers of the law necessarily became fewer and fewer. The time could be foreseen when they would be an insignificant minority in the church, when all Jesus' disciples would appear as despisers of the laws of purification, thus of the entire Mosaic law, and as a result could no longer be regarded as a Jewish sect but represented a new religion. Was Christianity a new religion that had most profoundly detached itself from Judaism? This was the issue at Antioch, and the answer to this question could no longer be postponed, when even Peter participated in the common meals and no longer bothered with the Mosaic law of purification. What the first apostle and leader of the earliest community did had significance for all Christians. His behavior also decided the theological problem. How could James's people not have reproached Peter for that?

It is understandable that Peter began to hesitate. He might not have given sufficient thought beforehand to the consequences of his act; perhaps he had merely wanted to show brotherliness and hospitality. Yet even in Jerusalem he had at times been exposed to attacks from the party of James and might actually have left the earliest community to avoid these disputes. Whatever may have been the case, he is on the defensive and draws back, no longer participating in the common meals. Barnabas and other Jewish Christians join him. Understandably, this arouses Paul's towering rage. He might have put up with the situation if Peter and his entourage had initially taken their meals by themselves so as to document their fidelity to the law. Paul would surely have conceded this to James's people. But Paul must regard as defection and hypocrisy Peter's attaching himself to the party of James upon its arrival. Now, thanks to that party, the occasion has developed into a matter of principle. It has become the object of dispute over Christian freedom, over the nature of the community and the relation between its Jewish-Christian and Gentile-Christian members. Now the situation alone can no longer decide regarding the change in behavior. It must be unequivocally made clear whether Gentile Christians have the full truth of the gospel behind them or whether they are disciples in an exceptional situation. Paul is particularly embittered because his old companion Barnabas, with whom he carried on the Gentile mission and who was his companion at the Jerusalem council, attaches himself to Peter and yields to the party of James, thus denies his own work, leaves Paul in the lurch, and sets legal regulation above Christian freedom. Verses 15-21 make this clear. There, and of course with reference to the Galatians, Paul explains why he hurled at Peter the reproach of hypocrisy and defection from the gospel at Antioch.

The reproach is colossal. It is all the more so as applied to the prince of the apostles. If anywhere, here it is clear that, even in primitive Christianity, men could come to blows, that even apostles recognized the yawning abysses separating them, that, as was the case with Barnabas, they could be alienated from their most intimate friends, benefactors, and one-time patrons. A decade later they were still musing angrily over their mutual disputes, and in no wise regretted or reversed them. This makes sense only if being a Christian is not, as is too often assumed, a quality gained with baptism or conversion, at times disturbed, but at bottom persisting. To the extent something persists, it spells God's faithfulness. On the other hand, Christian existence is an existence forever prone to falling and sinking, to denying, and, as the truth most clearly reveals, to idol worship. There is no neutral zone between gospel and idol worship. Whoever is not for the one lives for the other. A Christian remains such only in resistance to idol worship, and whoever neglects this resistance or shoulders it casually pays homage to idols, however pious, even if he himself is an apostle or the prince of apostles. One is a Christian always only by becoming one. If this were known and accepted today, the world around us would be dumbstruck. A fellowship only of resistance fighters, of believers continually on the way, resolved to cause no shame to the name of their Lord, a gospel seized and preserved ever anew — this would scarcely be heaven on earth, though God would perhaps regard it as such, but it would change the world and shock it more than terrorists could. That our earth accepts Christianity so casually, partly in a friendly and agreeable manner, is possible only so long as the truth of the gospel, that is, Christian freedom and Christian resistance to idol worship, is not sufficiently practiced.

Now we leap to the heart of Paul's argument. Many sermons and lectures could be held on these few verses. We will extract only a few key words from them. We must always keep in mind that the apostle stands on the threshold between Judaism and Gentile Christianity, and therefore both inwardly and outwardly he must continually endure and overcome this tension. He describes it as the tension between law and gospel and formulates the revelation he received at Damascus as the content of his missionary preaching: "Justified not by the works of the law but through faith in Jesus Christ." We have understood nothing about him if we do not understand this. Since we are no longer, like the apostle, on the threshold between Judaism and Gentile Christianity, we must continually be clear about the meaning of these words if we want to understand the Pauline message today. This may confront us with the most difficult problem Western theology as such must pose to its congregations. In fact, we must add that our congregations scarcely think of and understand anything less about Christianity than they do this word, and that it indicates what Paul is insisting upon when he speaks of revelation not "from a human source" but through God. It is possible, though not without difficulty, to understand what is at stake for the apostle. But according to Pauline and Reformation insight, none can affirm it by one's own reason or understanding, but solely through revelation of the Holy Spirit.

This was the attitude of the Israelites who were not yet persuaded by Jesus: "We ourselves are Jews by birth [better: originally!] and not Gentile sinners." And this is the attitude of the Christian persuaded by Jesus: "We know that a person is justified not by the works of the law." How to leap this chasm that separates more than classes and races, one that grew out of religious belief in election — "not Gentile sinners"? God himself separated person from person, and here too the gulf between heaven and earth is yawning. According to the Pharisee, whoever does not know and keep the works of the law is damned, no matter whatever else may be said of him. At this point we need not decide whether in the apostle's time all Israelites passed sentence in this fashion. In any case, as a Pharisee of the straitest sect, Paul once thought in this way and thus persecuted the Christians because they regarded Jesus as more important than Moses and wanted to replace the works of the law, at least in part, by their faith. For him this was blasphemy against divine revelation.

From that point we can now take up the first assertion, which helps us better understand what the apostle means by the law in contrast to the gospel. The law is the guide to a piety characterized by good works. Several elements are to be noted. At considerable remove from our situation and vicissitudes, Paul does not have to engage in fundamental dispute with those who have no regard for religion or have come to despise it. As a matter of fact, on Gentile soil his adversaries are the pious who insist that Christians are above other people morally, cultically, and ritually. This is at the center of the piety with which Paul must contend, that it imagines it must stand aloof, be separate from others, must not be sullied in conscience or in the view of strangers by fellowship with them. In the most varied way it is the old question as to who is clean, what renders clean or unclean — or, in other words, when it is that one behaves vulgarly or is seen behaving as such by God and others. On this view the law of Moses is regarded as a fence separating the world of the clean from the unclean, the lawful from the permissible, order from disorder, a fence warning against transgressions, facilitating control of lapses, and everlastingly impressing on the devout that they look to themselves, do not allow themselves to be contaminated with blasphemies, and remain within the sphere of virtue, duty, and propriety.

It appears to me that here we can be most profoundly aware of our solidarity with Jewish believers. Our Western Christianity has long been defined by idealistic tradition and the reality of the bourgeois world. The watchword of our education has almost universally been to give spiritual precedence over the material and our impulses. On the other hand, at least since the nineteenth century, the middle class saw itself faced with the double peril of despotism and anarchy and thus fell prey to the anxiety of those who must defend in every direction inherited wealth or wealth earned through labor. Strive for self-perfection and retain what is worthwhile in family, society, and nation! For many generations this was and remained the decisive task and goal of competition. The will to perform was implacably urged. In the case of the individual, it resulted in accenting one's own development; in the case of society, in accenting the increase of goods; and in the case of the nation, in emphasizing glorification of the ideals of duty and readiness for sacrifice. Ultimately, persons became what they could make of themselves and their circumstances. Their good deeds were decisive for life, to which they were continually summoned by the bourgeois-idealistic world around them. We can scarcely deny that this is a reflection of what Paul describes as being under the law, and that piety could and actually did adapt itself easily to this middle-class idealism. Here too could be located the practice that from the long tradition of the West was demanded and realized, and on which the Jewish law was based. Here too a conservative posture was unavoidable when one's own views appeared endangered by collision with another ideology. One's surroundings were measured by whether or not they suited one's own manner of life and worldview. As the legalistic Jews cut themselves off from the Gentiles, supporting their action with ritual and cultic criteria, so in the middle-class meritocracy outsiders and rebels were shunted aside into the sphere of chaos and for this reason could actually be called chaotics. Here too the criterion had to do with how much through performance one met the ideals of middle-class surroundings, furthered its traditions, or collided with them.

I hope it has become clear why I attempted to describe the world from which we have more or less emerged, together with its presuppositions and goals. In a certain sense this brings us face to face with what the apostle describes as being under the law, though only in a secular reflection. Still, what came to light here can be elevated in the most apt religious fashion by setting it under the sign of the divine will. This too has everlastingly occurred in the past from which we have all more or less emerged. We all have continually come to hear that God wills that we become respectable, do our duty, do not break out of the given order, have regard to the tradition. To be pious means above all to respect middle-class morality and convention, to belong to the relatively closed, so-called better society, with its idealistic basic values, because the God who is preached to us — Providence, the Highest World Order, or whatever else it is called — has required this of us. In this understanding, piety was the crowning of a traditional middle-class view of life and of a meritocracy that measured persons by their deeds and made God require good deeds of them.

If I have succeeded in describing the reality of our own past and of what may still be our own time, then we would have experienced the gospel Paul preached as a shock, and we could therefore sympathize with his Jewish opponents. The chief tenet of this gospel reads that God does not first of all and finally want your good deeds, but you yourself, just as you are. He is not an employer with an eye to the performance of his employees, and certainly not a despot who compels his subjects to do their duty. He is the Creator who fetches his creature home to himself, the Father who mourns over the lost son, the Redeemer who makes his way to earth, in which idols have more to say than he and are thus more revered. First and last, the gospel proclaims to us an unknown God, though we have learned to obscure this. We speak of the "dear God" and imagine he must at least be loving toward us. But when we look at the earth around us, the message of the love of God is replaced with the so-called basic values of obedience, respectability, order, and performance. How we treat our neighbor shows who our God is. For no one knows the Father of Jesus who measures the neighbor with the ruler of his or her own worldview and middle-class idealism, who judges persons based on their deeds. Conversely, the unknown God is not the God who, as we learn or assume from the Bible, peeks through his fingers and strikes a pact with our evil will. He is the God of truth, of whom Paul declares that before him no flesh becomes righteous by works of the law.

He sees us as sinners, without exception, while representatives of the law always call only a segment sinners, that is, the immoral, the rebels, the atheists. God sees us all as sinners because he knows that, on our own, none fulfills the first commandment, none with the whole heart fears, loves, and trusts him above all things. This is the real sin from which all others emerge and lay waste the earth. Not to acknowledge him as our true Lord, and not to recognize him as the Father of Jesus who seeks us and, for our sake, descends into the inferno down to Golgotha allows us to live in falsehood and stupidity, arrogance and cowardice. Where possible, we want to be our own lord and master, achieve our own goals, and seek out our own paths. Naturally, there are powers and forces we fear, to which we subject ourselves willingly or in anxiety, an entire scale of values we make obligatory for ourselves and others, so that we are constantly occupied with forcing our laws, customs, usages, and economic regulations on our children, pupils, subordinates, neighbors, and strangers, even on other nations and races. Whoever is acquainted only with the idols that enslave us will likewise enslave others, and such idols can lurk behind worldviews, ideologies, norms, and social conditions. Those who pay homage to them will appear in the name of those idols as lords who take command in a narrower or wider sphere, who establish regulations according to their will and understanding, who mold others after the image of the idols whose image they bear.

The gospel tells us that we are in fact destined to be the image of our God on earth. But that is an image of the One who formed us for his creatures and children. He called to discipleship of the Crucified, of the One who was the most despised and unworthy, who wished to help the lost, and who served scribes and Pharisees, harlots and tax collectors alike. Whoever does not bear the image of the loving, gracious God who binds himself to the hopeless, poor, and outcasts — that person does not live in the gospel. But to this the Old Testament and the law of Moses must also be subject. We should not read first and foremost in them that God is highest Judge and Protector of order, who sets all our life under his command. Rather, we must let these writings tell us that he redeems his people from Egypt and the wilderness, from the power of the enemy, and from error and guilt. We must interpret the Old Testament and the law of Moses from Golgotha, not Jesus and his disciples from Moses and the scribes. The first commandment reads, "I am the Lord your God" before it continues, "You shall have no other gods before me." This second clause is properly understood only when we hear the first tell us, "You need no longer have other gods before me!" It is our lot on earth, as Isaiah 26:13 has it, that other lords rule over us, that we must fear them, that they kill us with their commands and their tyranny. But this is the promise that, as early as in Isaiah 26:13, anticipates the voice of Jesus and the New Testament, "but we acknowledge your name alone." They fall on us like robbers, yet our heart trusts only the One who went to the cross for us; it gives him love and calls only him true Lord and Master. There are other gods. But now we no longer fear them more than we fear anything else. We defy them. We are most profoundly free.

The conclusion of our chapter contains such an abundance of equally important and difficult statements that we can single out only a few key phrases from the context. The first reads, "crucified with." If we look to the churches of the white race and to the life we Christians normally lead in our land, scarcely anything is less understandable or credible. It is generally expected of disciples of Jesus that they be brave, peaceful, and friendly citizens, good fathers or faithful mothers, reliable comrades and resolute defenders of discipline, duty, and order. All this was and is commanded by the law of Moses, as well as by our secular laws, and is meticulously observed by most believers. We have no objection to this and must even give it powerful support, insofar as all this occurs with upright hearts and for the actual well-being of our neighbors. On the other hand, we must keep in mind how scandalous this word of the apostle is. He does not direct us first of all to our place in society or admonish us to behave appropriately there. He calls us instead to Golgotha, for every pious Jew an unclean place, where revolutionaries were hanged and Gentiles carried out their executions of evildoers. The shrieks of pain, hate, and blasphemy were loud there, nor was there anything resembling order, mercy, or humanity. If Paul speaks of our being "crucified with," he must be assuming that at least from time to time Jesus' disciples may be removed from their middle-class circumstances and at last be forced to see the world from Golgotha.

This statement may be shocking to us. Yet it does not even do justice to the apostle's statement, for he insists that every Christian has been crucified with the Lord and lives under this sign all life long. Otherwise the gospel has not been rightly heard and accepted. For Paul, Golgotha is not merely the place where the Savior dies for our sins and gives evidence of his love for us in the very inferno. It is not merely a place of devotion and self-awareness. In a certain sense the gospel is harsher than the Mosaic law. It kills our old Adam, as the Bible says, and as Luther formulated it in the Small Catechism, it draws every one baptized into a daily new dying. We are not to regard this as a memorable or exaggerated figure of speech. Christianity becomes unworthy of belief when it construes such words as images, gives others the impression that its proclamation is something like pious poetry and not to be taken seriously.

Now we must determine precisely to what extent Paul can speak of being "crucified with" and what this really means. The second key phrase of our text helps us better understand: "that I might live to God." This sounds harmless enough, but it contains a comprehensive doctrine of human existence. The human is never, as the philosophers sometimes say, in and for one's self, never an isolated and isolatable creature without a surrounding world. To be human means always to have a friend and a foe, an earth and a heaven, to have anxiety and yearning. Alive and in the body, a person is always related to others and other things, as is most clearly shown in the relation between husband and wife. Every science or personal relation that ignores this renders the human a thing, is inhumane and most profoundly alienated from reality. Religion discovers that, in addition to all other relations, there is an orientation to God or to something regarded as God, something on which the person places ultimate trust, for which the person is prepared to live and die. I believe that everyone has something in which to place ultimate concern and for which he or she is ready to sacrifice everything else, for which reason there are no real atheists, except in imagination. In despair or pride many maintain they are without a god. But as long as they experience love and fear and yearning, according to my conviction they still have a god, albeit unknown to them. So, Christian theology dares to assert in the face of all contradiction that everyone lives for a god, for one's own god. It is only a matter of who that god is. If one can answer that question, one also knows whatever a person's concern may be. Everyone is the image of a god, it may be only in caricature, and in every thought and deed must point to that god. In saying this, we stand once more before the first commandment. In a certain respect everyone has heard it, "I am the Lord your God, you shall have no other gods before me." Each one is a creature, however much that may be denied, and on the strength of it each one is open to communication.

Thus for everyone, not just for the Jew, the decisive question is whether to place oneself under the law or the gospel. As one must distinguish God from idols, there is also the possibility of seeing the biblical God in two ways and relating to him in a twofold way, that is, from the point of view of the law or the gospel. When Paul speaks of those devoted to the law, he has in mind the believer who makes of the Creator something like a referee who notes one's good and evil deeds, judges accordingly, summons one daily and hourly to show fitness, and sets religious alongside secular competition. We may not overlook the fact that the apostle does not merely intend to describe the pious Jew. In our text he speaks about and to

Christians, and we all know how easily, even in the religious sphere, we take our own pulse or fall to navel-gazing, or compare ourselves with others as if they were contestants needing to be outstripped one way or another. Whoever acts in this way is cross-eyed, not concentrating on the task but expecting praise or fearing reproach. Such a person robs the other of creaturely dignity and makes the other a means by which to exhibit or increase one's own proficiency. This finally results in deception regarding oneself and the true God. For whoever makes God the referee of performance also makes him an onlooker of what people do, no longer allows him to remain our Creator, who daily must give us life, power, counsel, and help, without whose grace we are unable to live. For Paul "to live for God" means something else, since at Damascus his eyes were opened for the truth of the gospel. He summarizes it in the beautiful and yet hazardous word, "it is no longer I who live, but it is Christ who lives in me." This word is hazardous because it can lead to a level of edification that imagines it is situated in heaven and no longer takes earth seriously. In such a way God, neighbors, and the world are betrayed, and one is deceived respecting one's own reality. To avoid this danger the apostle altered his first sentence by a second: "and the life I now live in the flesh I live by faith in the Son of God, who loved me and gave himself for me."

Christians live in their flesh, that is, in their entirely earthly being, as though their own heart no longer belonged to them, as though they in no way whatever had to make determination regarding themselves or their relation to others. In and from them Christ will live on earth and in this manner prove he is Lord of those who follow him. For as we can see most clearly here, this most profoundly spells faith — that is, no longer to exist for oneself but to reflect Christ's image on earth and in the world around us. The only measure of his disciples in time and eternity is how deeply and to what extent Jesus' image has been made known on earth through them. This is their promise and salvation. It is also their task and the final question about them. This is what they could, ought, and should do. For many, this may sound like a new law, and all too often the pious have made of it a new law. But Paul says that he has died to the law and that no righteousness comes through it. Where does the decisive difference lie? Faith has a lord for which it lives. But it does not have a lord who judges on the basis of performance or harnesses one to the yoke of pious duties. The believer lives for the Lord because the Lord first lived for the believer, loved and offered himself up for the believer. It is true that Jesus calls now as he once did, "Follow me!" He takes his disciples along on the way toward

Golgotha and does not spare them from crucifixion together with him. But he does both that they might be worthy of keeping his image alive in the world around them, of being something to the praise of his glory. With their life and death they make clear who their God really is, that is, the One who does not remain enthroned in the heights of heaven and appear only as Judge of our deeds, but the One who, out of love for us, descended into the human inferno and allowed himself to be crucified by his creatures. He is the One who keeps faith with us, remains Father to us, and takes us to himself when we have alienated ourselves from him and lost our neighbor. The faith of the Christian hears the first commandment as the sum of the gospel. The Lord speaks to the Christian, thus points to the Man of Nazareth and Golgotha, "I am the Lord your God. You need no longer have other gods besides me, need no longer make for yourself idols out of anxiety and yearning, need no longer place yourself at the center of the world and, through your image and the image of your performance, make others dependent on you. Christ will live in and out from you. Accept it!" This is the whole gospel.

Galatians 3:1-9, 26-29: Children of the Spirit

In this hour we will treat only one question: What does it mean to be children of the Spirit? This is the new slogan Paul now takes up like a watchword in his debate with the law, and which for him unites the two other expressions: "Abraham's offspring" and "children of God." Israel of course believed, and it sought to corroborate its faith by works of the law. The Old Testament prophets show us that Israel continually came under the power of the divine Spirit and awaited his outpouring over all people at the end of days. Since Pentecost, primitive Christianity maintains that in it the last time has broken in and the promise of the abiding gift of the Spirit has been fulfilled. On this point it is completely at one with Judaism. In Romans 8:9 Paul can therefore maintain that no one is a Christian who does not have the Spirit. In 1 Corinthians 12:12ff. he goes on to explain not only that all members of the Body of Christ have the Spirit in common, but that each has received a specific gift of the Spirit wherever placed, and enabling for special service.

Since this is so, our text regards Christian faith and existence in the Spirit as actually interchangeable, and just as it contrasts faith and law, so also Spirit and law, or miracles occurring in the community and works of Jewish piety. Whoever founds life on performance no longer hearkens to the truth revealed in Christ, denies the beginning God made at baptism, and takes matters into one's own hands. It is as though the crowning conclusion of the disciple's journey could be reached by one's own power and insight, and as though at the end of life the disciple would no longer need

A lecture given on March 9, 1979, at the Kirchentag in Zweibrücken.

the help and grace of the Lord but could rather be witness to one's own glory and perfection. Paul calls this falling prey to the flesh, giving it the last word, and setting one's trust in it.

This makes clear what the apostle understands by Spirit. Everything depends on knowing what this is precisely, otherwise everything becomes unclear, and mere edifying feelings take up space in us. The Spirit creates clarity, and in fact in seeing, thinking, and acting — thus in all of life. Today, too many Christians allow clarity to be ignored, move about like sleepwalkers, and are moved inwardly by dreams and imaginings alone. A reformation of our church would have to begin with setting Christians and evangelical communities in a state of watchfulness again. According to our text, this means being torn from a neutral stance. The Spirit is not given where one strives to remain neutral, which explains why many congregations and Christians must be called spiritless, bereft of the Spirit, no longer to be spurred on to rational thought. They think that being a Christian means being peaceful, avoiding strife, being accommodating and not partisan, mollifying, sticking one's nose into one's own little closet, not into the wind. The unavoidable results are crystal clear: the Christians are marching in the ranks of the greater crowd. But within its ranks no one arouses an unpleasant stir. And if it should later appear that one marched under the wrong flag, one can make the excuse that, in the final analysis, the majority would not have known better. It is always risky to belong to the minority or actually to take to the field for what appears unpopular, unconventional, or radical. But this is what must occur when the gospel has brought us so near to the crucified Christ, as though Golgotha were situated in our own time and society. Paul maintains that the Galatians had come to learn of it in this way from him, which of course means that every Christian should learn of it in this way. At Golgotha there is no neutrality, no treating with the raging, blaspheming, murderous rabble. If anywhere, then here the disciple of Jesus is set within the little flock, an object of finger-pointing, whose devotion and loyalty to the state are suspect, and in the first centuries was accused of enmity toward God and man. We must ask why all this has become different today. Is the Crucified now accepted on earth, or do we no longer stand where he died? Do we live, say, in the flesh, as Paul calls it?

What he means by the phrase cannot be misunderstood. Clearly, "in the flesh" does not merely mean to have a body. For the apostle and for much of the remainder of the Bible, humans, insofar as they are defined by the world, measure everything by their personal needs, orient their thinking and acting to their own interests, wishes, or anxieties. The world as a whole is flesh, insofar as it denotes existing by and for oneself, therein denying its creatureliness, no longer giving heed to the first commandment. Briefly put, it is the creature who, turned from its Lord, orbits about itself and intends to make its own way. This can be the case intellectually and in fact religiously, and is such when we force our worldview on others, just as the white race has done to other races through the centuries, or when we make our concepts of order and morality universally obligatory, or treat our piety as a uniform that alone allows true faith to be recognized. The flesh has as many reflections as the Spirit. In every generation it is necessary to reflect anew on the mask behind which self-seeking flesh, crucifying Christ and falsifying Christianity, is hiding. This must be done not only in individual life but by Christian communities; it is an unarguable component of the daily sorrow and repentance required of us. Where there is no neutrality, danger threatens from all sides. We must be conscious of this and together investigate what is necessary and salutary today.

We can live only in the Spirit or in the flesh, not in both together, when what is at stake is whether the Crucified or I myself and the autocratic creature have the last word. Above all, we need to consider that such dispute between Spirit and flesh does not occur in a vacuum, thus not merely in our ideas or our little chamber or in the circle of the like-minded. We may not only believe inwardly, with the head or the feelings, as though there were no neighbors or strangers about. The contest between Spirit and flesh occurs on our earth or not at all; it occurs in our body, so that we are totally affected by it. Whether it suits us or not, we cannot free our members of it in the communities in which we were set in our place and time. We must finally be free of the superstition that Christianity is a private matter and chiefly related to our inward life. The cross on Golgotha is not enclosed in church walls and social halls if it is not to become a pious resting place. The Nazarene never had to do merely with those souls of which we speak in our religious jargon. God has already lost his kingdom if we surrender the earth and leave him only heaven. Precisely the opposite is the case. If he will give us heaven, he commands that we be faithful on earth, not bury our talent there, but multiply it. Jesus calls his community the city on the hill, the light that is not put under a bushel, the salt of the earth. The Spirit will never blow where we do not hoist our flag or let ourselves be chased into a corner by the powers and forces, fenced in behind the temple walls. The Spirit of God will have the world because it is the work of the Creator.

Previously we staked out the area where we can intelligently speak of children of the Spirit. In doing so, we emphasized that there must be readiness for serious reflection and the will to state things clearly. Second, we insisted that there are no neutrals as onlookers there, and third, that God's lordship over our earth must be contended for in full sight of all. But it is now time to put the question that continually agitates many congregational members, particularly in remembrance of Pentecost: "What does the term 'Holy Spirit' really mean?" One has the feeling that at Christmas, Good Friday, and Easter one would be more easily informed than at Pentecost, though that certainly is not true. But it can scarcely be denied that in general it was left to pietists to speak of the Spirit of God, and that we too often think of it as a matter for theologians and the initiated. This has a painful result. First, this Spirit of which the Bible speaks is set within the sphere of so-called spiritual things, with the corporeal and the world being left to their own powers and forces. Second, we are no longer able appropriately to define what its opposite ("flesh") means in Paul and elsewhere. This leads to a narrowing nigh on to blasphemy and allows the gospel to deal with fostering morality and universal order. In either instance piety as such appears spiritual and corroborated by the Spirit. In either instance we stand in a long tradition of the Western middle class, unwittingly confined within the prison of its ideology, which lures or forces others across the earth and every confession into the same prison, obscures the gospel, and substitutes this tradition for the Spirit of God and thus proves to be "flesh." We cannot say it often enough. There is also pious flesh, and just as in Galatia, Christians are always tempted to exchange the Spirit for it. Christianity, which in our zones has become especially middle class, has most extensively succumbed to this temptation.

Our text sets forth clearly that the Spirit of God is defined by pointing to Christ, keeping him in mind and heart, and laying down a witness with one's life. There is Spirit only where the Man from Nazareth and Golgotha rules. Where this is not the case, no piety suffices, however attractive. We are most simply and impressively told this in the farewell discourses of John's Gospel. The discourses call the Spirit the Comforter in whom the exalted Lord returns to his disciples left on earth. Accordingly, our Pentecost hymns continually pray: "Lass mich den Vater kennen schon, dazu auch seinen lieben Sohn" (Let me know the Father truly, and as well his own dear Son). Luther writes in the same vein when in his explanation to the Third Article he states, "I believe that by my own understanding or strength I cannot believe in Jesus Christ my Lord or come to him," but for this I need the Spirit. Where the Spirit is at work, Jesus becomes visible and present as my Lord and as Redeemer of all creation. This is the only legitimate, clear and complete definition that we may also reverse: Where Jesus is visible and present as my Lord and Redeemer of all creation, God's Spirit has done his work and reveals himself on earth as at Pentecost. We may object that Luther exaggerated, that we absolutely *can* come to Jesus Christ by our own understanding or strength and in him recognize a Redeemer and a gift of God, just as devout Gentiles actually did at all times and still do today. After all, we have the Gospels, the reading of which has always seized the heart, and there are reflections of Jesus in painting, poetry, and music, which like an echo of the biblical message glorify the Nazarene, even where faith in him has not occurred. The Pentecost hymns anticipate this misunderstanding when they speak of knowledge of the Son, thus of the one true image of God, of the Revealer. Luther does so when he says "my Lord" in the sense of his "only" Lord; there is no other. Finally, Paul expresses the same thought in his way by pointing to the Crucified.

To the old Adam, in whatever shape he appears, it is simply incomprehensible that one shamefully hanged on a tree as guilty of high treason, obviously not protected from such a fate through the intervention of divine omnipotence, should be our Lord, the salvation of the whole world. Is it conceivable to us? Just as the disciples on the way to Emmaus, must we not sadly state, "But we had hoped," and join with those who call to Jesus to save himself and come down from the cross if he is the Son? Do we ever come to terms with the One who as Lord calls his own beneath the stake of Golgotha, calls them in their own present existence, each in a particular way, but each in such fashion that the old Adam must die and in precisely this way we experience Christ as Lord? Theologically, we can highlight this as absolutely meaningful and necessary, but only the Spirit allows us to affirm and acknowledge it as the Father's will. As so often in life, the most beautiful and lucid theories are useless against what our heart fears and desires. What we allow to apply to others we bitterly repulse when we are involved. That the Crucified may become and be our Lord is the Christian's central problem, and it remains so every day till death. Here God's will and our will, God's power and our power collide, and we must decide who has the last word.

Here we will make a brief excursion into the theological debates of our generation, to the eminent and genuine program of demythologizing. Bultmann was entirely correct to throw out this catchword that so horrified and enraged his opponents. There must be demythologizing. It was only that Bultmann was much too soft when he applied it principally to our worldview and called us from ancient Christian ideas to modern thought. Without question God does not intend that we run about as living mummies of the ancient world, everywhere assuming and making use of the technology of our time, but spiritually and religiously setting ourselves back 1,900 years. Faith must be lived today, and this means it must give thought today and give an account of itself. The dead bones of the past remain ghosts if there are no living witnesses oriented to the present to take up their message. Nevertheless, demythologizing may not only denote speaking in new tongues and with modern speech. For such we did not need to look to Golgotha and allow ourselves to be summoned from there.

Let us look further into our text. What Paul does there deserves to be called demythologizing. Abraham is the progenitor of Israel and, about which we must think soberly today, of the Muslim as well. For he is the ideal believer who has been blessed by God and declared bearer of promise for all the world. The apostle agrees. God reckoned the patriarch's faith for righteousness, found him worthy of being his child and ancestor of all the future blessed. But now, as so frequently occurs in the apostle's letters once the Old Testament Jewish tradition has been taken up, there comes a great reversal. For Paul, just one single word stands at the center of the biblical tradition, the word "believe." Still, for him, to believe no longer signifies the simplest but most comprehensive work of believers who side with their God and become protagonists of all the eternal virtues on earth, heap up merit not merely for themselves but for all their people, and cast a long shadow for all the elect. We have documents that depict Abraham according to this Jewish view, and James 2:21-23 has retained and accented it in the New Testament and against Paul's disciples: Abraham was "justified by works." Once more we encounter with especial clarity basic theological contradictions as early as in primitive Christianity, as well as in our Bible. The Bible did not fall from heaven a perfect whole but is rather the collection of witnesses to faith across 1,200 years and thus gives expression to very different voices, convictions, and even confessions. We will return to this subject later. For the present, however, we will get clear in mind what, in contrast to Jewish tradition concerning Abraham, the apostle understands by and extols as "believing."

Again, by way of the patriarch's example, Paul has brought it to its sharpest point in Romans 4:1ff. Abraham sees realistically that, in their age, posterity is denied him and Sarah, that the promise cannot be fulfilled in them. Nevertheless, he relies on God's word and in so doing is blessed and becomes the ancestor of all believers. Faith is recognition of one's own weakness, a hearing of the promise that views the world and the creatures in a totally realistic way, just as they are, but allows God to remain Creator, then in Christ learns to reckon with the resurrection of the dead here on earth and in the present. One devotional hymn expresses it in this way: "Nichts hab ich zu bringen, alles, Herr, bist du" (I have nothing to bring; you, Lord, are everything). Now we have arrived at the contrast already called to our attention. On earth, humans are worth as much as they are able to perform and are tossed aside like dirty rags when they can no longer make themselves useful. God, on the other hand, sees his creature in the lost son, in the harlots and tax collector, and never stops loving us, searching for us, waiting for us with open arms. Faith lets itself fall into these open arms and will not exhibit its efficiency but stakes everything on love, as it must always be between lovers. It does not play the hero, the sage, or the pious one who deserves reward. Such a one is a child toward the Father and before this Father lays aside all merits as if they were filthy rags. So, the matter is quite the reverse as obtains on earth. Here, persons are tossed aside when their power is dissipated and their deeds no longer matter. But God turns away from those who make him their eternal arbitrator and seek to impress him. He will have the creature who remains directed toward him, will have the children who live from his goodness, the poor whom he can satisfy; he will have the dying, becoming their comfort and hope. For Paul, this means "justification by faith," and this is what he demonstrates by way of Abraham. And with this we have arrived at Golgotha and in sight of the Crucified.

Jesus is the one cast out by men. Nor is the apostle shy of applying to him the Old Testament verse that calls accursed whatever hangs on the cross. And Jesus seems abandoned by the Father, thus godless, and not by chance he cries, "My God, my God, why have you forsaken me?" He not only has become man but has descended into the hell that earth is not yet for us today but certainly is for most of its inhabitants, and in which we are complicit, since we live at the cost of these others. To believe means to hear that our God comes to us even in hell and thus will be called our Redeemer and Liberator. Indeed, who can believe this, especially when living in the shadow of darkness, suffering, and hell? Now it is clear why such faith as faith in the Crucified as its original is also bound to the Holy Spirit as its Leader, its Enlightener, and also as its Power. The Spirit makes of hell a place where there can still be faith, where even today millions cry to the Father and believe.

Our text requires one last step from us. It is no accident that Paul calls Abraham the father of the Gentiles. Wherever our God descends into hell for our sake and makes this known on the cross of Jesus, there he comes to those who have lived in godlessness. He breaks down the barriers that the pious have erected between him and his creatures and continually erect between themselves and the allegedly or actually impious. The profoundest and most powerful revolution has occurred where the pious no longer have the last word about themselves and earthly conditions, where they no longer set their criteria of basic values, virtues, performances, and merits at the entry ports of heaven and of the community of the respectable. It is entirely conceivable that the tidy burghers who are for justice and order will hear nothing of this. They do not know the God who breaks into hell and does not leave the godless alone as though they were abandoned by the God whom they no longer see. The pious everlastingly wear the cross as decoration, prefer to celebrate Easter rather than Good Friday, taking from Golgotha at most only that God has forgiven them, but having nothing more to do with other sinners. They edit the gospel and set up conditions — say, circumcision or the law or morality and middle-class convention. All this is most profoundly revolutionized and demythologized where the Spirit paves the way and wakens true faith. With the other God, the view of the world and of human existence is different. Golgotha upsets all recognized criteria. The Spirit does likewise, because he sets us beneath the cross and from there teaches us to see what is earthly.

Actually, the Bible no longer remains just what it was, and so Jews and Christians read it differently, though both find God's word in it. We have already seen this in the fact that they interpret the Abraham narrative differently. "By works alone" is the slogan of those who regard faith as a virtue and a good work. To this the apostle opposes "by faith alone." It is very important that we keep this in mind and radically reflect on it. Many members of congregations no longer do so, and mistrustful of the theologian (not totally without reason, and with considerable legitimacy!), they hold to the conviction that the Scripture is totally God's word, inerrant, and that criticism of it is sacrilegious. The fact that Paul and James contradict each other, that in his sayings and doings Jesus corrected Moses, that in Antioch not even apostles were in agreement and were irreconcilably estranged, that there is continual report of parties, even of deserters in Israel and earliest Christianity — all this makes no impression on those who simply will not have it so. Very often one reads only what one already believes, and the great poverty of Christianity stems not least from the fact that it always or mostly finds in the Bible what it already knew, thus actually intends self-confirmation. It is no longer known that the Gospels are collections with a thousandfold variety of tradition. There is refusal to hear that God does not say the same thing to the parents, children, and grandchildren, to the point that he might be replaced with a phonograph record. It is denied that the Spirit is critical and engages in criticism, because self-criticism is not allowed. Finally, many biblical utterances are not known at all because they are not understood or are skipped over. For each of us the Bible is and remains an unknown book in which something new is continually discovered.

It would be an uncommon enrichment of our own life as well as that of our congregations if we were to read Scripture again with the continual question, What is it that I have not yet known, considered, or understood? Then it would have to dawn on us that Christians must read and interpret the Old Testament from the New, not the other way around. Apart from the fact that for us, many laws of the Old Testament cultus and the Mosaic rules of purification no longer apply, that many stories of Israel are told only for the Jewish people, it makes a great deal of difference whether we set Golgotha or Sinai and the City of David at the center, whether we hear the gospel as a new law or Moses as herald of the coming kingdom, just as did John the Baptist. It makes a difference whether we live from the sacred tradition of which not one iota may be altered, or come from Pentecost where God tears down previous barriers between Zion and the Gentiles. We have no right to act as if the Old Testament were not also the Bible of the Jews, and we have no right to act as if the Jews were something like a preliminary stage of Christianity. But if the promise is what unites us, the message separates us to the effect that all promise has been fulfilled in Jesus alone, and thus the entire Old Testament is to be read from that point. We must decide where we want to stand. Paul made this decision for all time in his contrast between faith and works, between the God of the Gentiles and the God who demands circumcision.

Much more would have to be said about this than is possible here. On the basis of our text we have merely wanted to highlight the fact that the Spirit makes everything new and continually demythologizes, rescues us from the sphere of the flesh. He does this even with reference to the Bible, which is not to be interpreted merely on the basis of its letters, rendering us blind worshipers and slaves of past tradition. Christians are also free toward Scripture. They know that they do not have God's word clearly without it, thus must seek salvation in it ever anew, since God will speak to them through it. But they also know that not only Jews and Christians interpret the Bible differently, but that various churches and sects all appeal to it, that thousands of theologians argue over it en toto and in detail. So they must be told how to read the Bible correctly. On this point Paul asserts that every Christian message, thus also Holy Scripture, remains evangelical only when it points to Christ. A proclamation at whose center there are slogans of any kind is at least dubious and probably false, whether the slogans read order or liberation, reconciliation or piety. Ideologies almost always lurk behind them. We must let Zinzendorf tell us, "I have only one passion; it is he, only he." But since there are many different portraits of Jesus, Paul adds that he has intended to preach no one but the Crucified. With, from, and toward the Crucified the Bible is God's word, while otherwise it remains a document of past religiosity. Only with, from, and toward him does it lead to freedom, rather than leaving us to founder in the thicket of laws. Only there does the Spirit speak from it.

Finally, this concentration on the Crucified makes possible the unity of the community in the variety of believers. Beneath the cross are gathered those whom the world separates by origin, sex, estate, talent, and religious tradition, who in part find themselves in hostile camps, the most variegated host imaginable. This can occur only beneath the cross, since only the God who seeks out the godless and descends into the hell of earth has room for all around him. Schoolmasters and political parties continually seek to gather together groups of the like-minded and thus create human order. But Pentecost tells us that the Spirit does not intend uniformity, and all of church history proves that it cannot be confessionally, politically, or bureaucratically manipulated. Ever since earliest Christianity in harsh debate broke through the barrier of Mosaic law and could no longer be described as a Jewish-Christian sect, the church is ecumenical and ceases to be church if it is no longer such. The disciples of Jesus Christ are not summoned to deny or abandon their past and earthly position insofar as they can and would like to serve Christ there. Of course, Christian enthusiasts have often declared that such is necessary. They could do so because they no longer wanted to know anything of this world and felt, at least in a spiritual sense, that they had already been transported to heaven. So the watchword that Paul takes up at the end of our text ("There is no longer Jew or Greek, there is no longer slave or free, there is no longer male and female") may perhaps have its origin with the enthusiasts.

Today, we would say that the enthusiasts urged on the emancipation of women and slaves, in opposition to Jewish Christians even from Jerusalem, that they postulated the equality of all and radically regarded what is earthly as unimportant. First Corinthians shows best that there were such voices in the earliest community. If Paul actually referred to them, he nevertheless alters the thrust of their slogan. He no longer says, "All are the same," but instead, "All of you are one in Christ Jesus." This means, "naturally, as humans and on earth you are different, and that means sexually, socially, and even according to your cultural and religious tradition. But your difference no longer separates; it rather serves the advancement of each and is the presupposition for the universal priesthood of all believers, in which each is directed toward each and gives freedom to each for service." Thus it becomes possible that even today Christ penetrates every corner of earth in the most varied way and reveals himself there as liberator. He does so through those who have become members of his Body, who, as Paul says, have put him on in baptism and now with their body and all their powers can glorify him on earth as their Lord, can carry his lordship into the world around them.

Only those who no longer live for their own desires or by their own achievements can do this, who are no longer tortured by their own anxieties, who no longer seek refuge for themselves or desire to save themselves. Whoever truly came to Golgotha and found salvation there no longer needs to orbit about the self. Such a person lives and dies in service, thus in freedom from powers and forces, from one's own obstinate and despondent heart. Such a one has time and energy to be there for others, for those for whose sake the Lord lived and died, thus continuing Jesus' work, led by Jesus' Spirit. This is possible only when one discovers and uses one's own abilities, does not become an imitation of a common ideal or sectarian ideology, does not intend to represent a particular type of piety.

We have now come to the point of finally defining what it means to be a child of the Spirit and not of the law, a bearer of the promise to Abraham and, as a disciple of Jesus, a believer. In a word, it means to be open. Wherever heaven has been opened and blessed us because the Son became man and descended into the hell of earth, we need and ought no longer shut ourselves up in on ourselves, within the circle of the like-minded, in a traditional worldview or pious tradition. We can be open toward ourselves, no longer needing to put on makeup or pull the fool's cap of our vanities over our faces. We can and ought to be aware of our impotence respecting salvation, of our weaknesses and defects, our creatureliness. But equally we can and ought also recognize what we are in our deficiency, within our limits. Those who no longer need worry about their own salvation face an extraordinary number of possibilities for doing something for others around them, to think for them, pray, and intercede for them. The one to whom heaven is opened discovers that there are brothers and sisters nearby. A brother or sister is anyone who needs our help, and there are swarms of these if we are seeing properly. But to be open to others also means that I can know I am hidden in community, am carried along, just as I must do the carrying. To be open also means to continually find unknown, unexpected, perhaps even unwanted brothers and sisters. In these times we must open our eyes and hearts for ecumenical breadth and world-embracing service, something we would not have known about without the mass media. Our churches can be helped only when they are aware of the cry of the Third World poor and there bring freedom to the prisoners and the dying as children of the Spirit who receive and stand for freedom.

God's Image and Sinners

The topic assigned me is at the heart of biblical anthropology. Naturally, a single report cannot deal with it in any fundamental, comprehensive way, or in discussion with the extant literature. I cannot assume the place of the expert in Old Testament and Judaism and so content myself with discussing the motif of the image of God that prepares for the problem posed by the New Testament. In the main portion I will keep essentially to Paul, because only with him can we detect the beginnings of a systematically conceived anthropology. Elsewhere in the biblical texts we of course encounter traditions attributable to particular worldviews, but not to independent conceptions. This is most noteworthy as over against current tendencies. Just as only a few writings of the Bible — for example, Job, Ephesians, and Second Peter — circle exclusively about one topic, so they contain no fundamental doctrines about God or human existence. Such must rather be reconstructed by a reflection that abstracts from the largely narrative proclamation. Nor can we ignore the fact that almost throughout, New Testament ecclesiology, like the idea of the people of God in the Old, overshadows any explicit anthropology. And the nature of the case is such that treatment of our theme will be fragmentary.

1. *Genesis 1:26-27 and its interpretation.* A solemn and most uncommon decree in the court of heaven distances the creation of humankind, still seen collectively here, from the rest of the narrative. At the same time, a new beginning marks the highpoint of the creation narrative. The pair of con-

---

A lecture given on April 27, 1981, at the Kirchliche Hochschule in Bethel.

cepts "image and likeness," lacking further interpretation, forms something of a formula whose parts may not be isolated, since they are almost synonymous. That is, they describe a "model." We may recall those steles in the Orient that represent the king's ongoing effective and present power during his physical absence. Compared with the original, the model has only the character of a facsimile, but adding the word "parable" names it as expressly corresponding and belonging to the original. If we consider the snapshot of our text in Psalm 8:5, we may say that the one crowned by his Creator with glory and honor is "Elohim-like," "a little lower than God," but set next to the angels, an idea intimated by the plural "us/our" at the beginning of Genesis 1:26. God's uniqueness is not diminished. Yet he is not separated by a chasm from his creation, nor the earth from its Creator. Humankind as sign of the majesty and deputy of its Lord, as God's permanent vis-à-vis, is at the same time guarantor of the continuing presence and rule of God in the world.

Such a definition excludes false, idealistic interpretations. The quality of Godlikeness does not ignore humankind's corporeality as if only the "mental" conformed to it, a quality present also in animals, or independent personality or reason. It is said not only of the first Adam, but as the resumption of the key word in Genesis 5:3 and 9:6 indicates, it is said of every empirical person unaffected by the fall and the curse, and thus also characterizes human history. Perhaps we should make this more precise on the basis of our text. The quality of Godlikeness has come about through God's creative, promising, and summoning word, thus is not simply transmitted by procreation. God's counterparts and deputies will always be those addressed by the Lord and challenged by him; in remaining true to their call, they will be hearers who in prayer and throughout all of life will be answerers, responders. Here we need to note the contrast with the view characteristic of Israel's environs, according to which humanity proceeds from God's blood or seed or, as later in Greece, participates in the heavenly nature through the spirit. In the Bible, human existence and humanity itself are tied to the word from God and the answer to it. There is neither a God nor a human being in and for oneself.

Conversely, to the open heaven above corresponds an accessible earth below, in which, as Genesis 2:23 reads, Adam finds a partner and, according to our text, as a consequence and realization of his likeness, receives the task of *dominium terrae*, explained in just this way in Psalm 8. On this the narrator's interest unmistakably rests. His description now takes on detail. Whatever concerns Adam himself remains hidden, precisely when he appears as God's steward on earth. His destiny is broadly defined. The entire world is entrusted to him as living space and is to be filled by his posterity. His existence is never private but, as his function indicates, has a cosmic horizon. But that function is always reassigned him by God's word in the form of a blessing and thus cannot be a violent and egoistic exploitation of the earth. It is rather the responsibility of the one authorized by the Creator to preserve his good creation and its order in a way pleasing to God. But God is and remains Immanuel, the God for us and the world, not through ideas and ideologies, structures, organizations, and institutions, thus replaceable by an impersonal, neutral power, but by the service of living souls called to be personally effective by his word.

Hard by this report of the priestly narrative, which derives the earthly *ordo* from the *ordinatio* of the divine image, there is the other creation narrative, in 2:4b–3:24. This narrative sees the desert as living space and dust as human material, allows the human to fall from the grace of origin and to be driven from paradise, sees them handed over by the divine curse to trouble and servitude, guilt and death. We can scarcely say why the priestly narrative is not moved by all of this, not even by the flood narrative. We merely state that two different ways of observing are paradoxically maintained. Seen from the other side, the one made in the image of God is a sinner, but eternal goodness still holds heaven open to doubtful existence and readies earthly community for those who, like Adam and Cain, take flight in self-preservation. The "ruler of this world" tyrannizes and actually murders his brother. Clearly, this dialectic introduces a process of salvation history, if it is not to be meaningless and allow the world to be seen as impenetrable chaos. What salvation and ruin are must be described anthropologically.

2. *The Jewish understanding of being in the likeness of God.* Here I am following the traces of a book by Jacob Jervell, extraordinarily rich in material and entitled *Imago Dei*,[1] as well as his article, "Image of God," in the *Theologische Realenzyklopädie*.[2] Naturally, in doing so I am simplifying a more complex development, because I am interested in the Jewish view with which Paul disputes. In general, Judaism holds firmly to the human's being in the image of God. Sirach 17 illustrates this especially well. Here too, world order rests on the divine decree, by which each individual par-

---

1. J. Jervell, *Imago Dei. Gen. 1,26f. im Spätjudentum, in der Gnosis und in den paulinischen Briefen*, FRLANT 76 (Göttingen: Vandenhoeck & Ruprecht, 1960).
2. J. Jervell, "Bild Gottes I," *Theologische Realenzyklopädie* 6:491-98.

ticipates in a particular way, though otherwise remaining in subjection to a master. This assertion, in Sirach 16:24-30, is supported by reference to the two combined Genesis creation narratives. The human, of course, is mortal, yet this is not a curse but a limitation by the Creator's sovereign will and, among other things, a measure of divine world rule. It is, as it were, the shadow of the greatness and power that distinguish the likeness from its prototype. Here too what is human owes its likeness to the divine goodness, which continually views it as its vis-à-vis, gives to it as its steward the *dominium terrae,* concludes an eternal covenant with it, and calls it to respond to the law of life given it to share, addressing and commissioning it, to the praise of the Majesty on high. All the elements of Genesis 1:26 thus reappear.

But two things take us further. First of all, besides the gift of speech, the gift of eyes, ears, reason, and intelligent insight is most explicitly set forth. From this, according to Sirach 17:6-7, derives the possibility of choice between good and evil. The human can be disobedient, and according to Sirach 16:15, this means that it makes itself independent by assuming no one in heaven is inquiring after it. Correspondingly, by its fall into sin the human is not totally depraved but can comply with the reason given it, a reason enlightened from the law of life respecting God's work, respecting its own task toward heaven and earth, and the individual steps toward preserving order between the two. Here, then, reason most profoundly denotes knowledge of revelation. When the sage is described as the image of God, so also is the believer. Second, what results is that reference to establishing an eternal covenant with human beings climaxes in the statement "He appointed a ruler for every nation, but Israel is the Lord's own portion" (Sirach 17:17). In reality, then, the likeness is ultimately confirmed and preserved in Israel, though it may exist overshadowed elsewhere. Only among the people of the covenant and the law does it appear intact, more exactly among its believers who represent it, because they do not allow themselves to be seduced by the godless.

We find the same perspective in the Wisdom of Solomon 2:23-24: "For God created us for incorruption, and made us in the image of his own eternity, but through the devil's envy death entered the world, and those who belong to his company experience it." The context speaks of the dispute between the righteous and the godless, who appear here as deniers of immortality and as the devil's servants and his portion. The same problematic is mentioned in 2 Esdras 8:44 with reference to the seed often spoiled: "But people, who have been formed by your hands and are called your own image because they are made like you, and for whose sake you have formed all things — have you also made them like the farmer's seed?" The protest against it in verse 45 reads, "Surely not, O Lord above! But spare your people and have mercy on your inheritance, for you have mercy on your own creation." Finally, the situation is precisely the same in the Syrian Baruch Apocalypse 14:18-19, where the reference is to the counsel at the creation: "And you said that you would make a man for this world as a guardian over your works that it should be known that he was not created for the world, but the world for him. And now, I see that the world which was made for us, behold, it remains; but we, for whom it was made, depart." As Baruch makes complaint on behalf of believers, the righteous in Israel, so in 15:7, "with regard to the righteous ones, those whom you said the world has come on their account, yes, also that which is coming is on their account . . . a crown with great glory."

The texts cited denote a common situation. The believing community struggles to validate the law within its own ranks and, in so doing, sees itself forced to shift the promise of the likeness to God from anthropology to what is called in Christian theology ecclesiology. The image of God is in the succession of Adam, now singled out from his posterity as a lone individual, as Israel, and that only by way of reduction to the "righteous" as his true representatives. On the basis of Romans 2:23-24 we could formulate it thusly: The likeness is the true Jew marked by an obedient hearing of the law and thus by earthly suffering in the shape of the scorn and hatred of the godless and isolation in the heathen world. This finds sharpest expression in the later rabbinic view[3] that with the fall into sin not only the glory of the first man but also the likeness was lost, and only with the giving of the law was it returned to Israel.

Philo may be seen as taking a first step in this direction when he places Genesis 1:26-27 within his general anthropology but in addition describes the Logos as the real Eikon (image), which makes for itself earthly copies, thus is a bearer of a derived likeness. Both ideas can be united, since Philo, obviously indebted to Greek thinking, construes the spirit as a connecting link with the heavenly world and makes it the sign of likeness to God. On the other hand, for him the Logos is nothing but the Jewish Sophia, which in turn personifies the law. As a Jew, Philo sees in the spirit ultimately the human capacity for perceiving God's will and living according to it. When he describes the Logos as the true Eikon, he concretizes the likeness to God

3. See Jervell, *Imago Dei*, pp. 113ff.

as life from and under the law, whose true representative is the pious Jew, though it may be found shadowlike in the heathen because of their intellectual capacities — in fact, should actually be found there.

Now, likeness to God is all throughout the definition of the human being, not merely a characterization of a continuing relation to God, but the result of a journey in the struggle for virtue. We had better not speak of an ideal, so as not to jeopardize the realism of the view. By his creative word God has called humankind to a royal way, that is, continually to transcend self. By the aid of divine grace, among many errors and failures, concretized by the Spirit, thus led by the law, we realize the divine will and thus grow to the true human, who is at the same time the image of God. The Jewish law coincides with the concept of the spirit in Greek thought, insofar as it calls to self-perfection, achievable only in struggle with the earthly, especially with those who have foolishly and impiously forgotten their calling. Since the goal is never entirely realized in this world, perfection of the likeness must belong to eternal life. Then world domination becomes the promise of a future world marked by the self-mastery of the wise and pious, and by the struggle against pressing temptations and vices in the earthly realm. It makes good sense that the quality of likeness lost is regained with the giving of the law. Where the human even in community is defined by the division between good and evil, the Godlikeness must be something akin to a predisposition or to chance, to the capacity for obedient hearing of the divine will, unfolded on the way toward heaven under unavoidable temptations, and at its goal it arrives at perfection. In this way the law is leader of individual souls and redeemer of Israel, whereas on earth the likeness is present only in its shadow and by its imprint. The pious thus represent the law and evidence this with their insight and reason, their obedience, their virtuousness, and their praise of God. The fall into sin is taken seriously. From it proceeds corruption, which marks earthly relationships and drags members of the community into Gentile-like godlessness.

Contrariwise, the likeness to God may not be finally and totally lost. Otherwise the human could no longer be described as striving to fulfill the divine will, as resisting sin, as equipped with the freedom of decision between good and evil. This is what makes possible the doctrine of the likeness restored with the giving of the law. During their time on earth humans exist between God and evil; they are the objects and subjects of the dispute over fulfillment of the divine will. Of course, in view of the surging flood of sin, they can be such only under the direction of the law or in its shadow, actually or at least potentially belonging to the Israel of God and, though tempted, nearing the goal, since on earth they are both sinner and image. This is precisely the anthropology developed in the Qumran writings and that points to Paul.

3. *The Pauline view of sin.* Paul has unrestrictedly maintained the loss of the human's likeness to God after the fall and outside of Christ, and has not excluded the pious Jew from it. Here we first encounter in Christianity a theme later viewed under the heading "original sin." Indeed, the Gospels and Jesus assume the sinfulness of every person when they describe everyone as evil, when they unmask dubious piety, allow the sick and those plagued by demons to cry for help, and describe Jesus as Redeemer. Still, this is not theologically explained; it remains a presupposition of Jesus' activity. Only in James 3:9 is the human characterized in the true Jewish sense as "made in the likeness of God." Precisely this is what Paul basically disputes in Romans 3:23, where the Luther Bible makes mistaken reference to the failing, rather than the lost glory, of the creature. The apostle's statement is based on Romans 1:21ff., according to which the basic sin is idol worship, thus perverted religiosity. It hands the person over to vanity and transitoriness, and directs the flood of blasphemy over a world turned back to chaos. Romans 5 and Romans 7 contrast Adam and Christ as the old and new man, first under the cosmic, then under the anthropological aspect, but in either case in an eschatological, thus insurmountable, contrast. There is no other bridge from the one to the other than the grace that changes and creates anew. There is no more development than there is paradoxical simultaneity. Here, on the basis of the first commandment, it is reasoned and argued that humanity and the world exist only within the alternative of God or idol.

This explains why Romans 1:21ff. views idol worship as the essential sin. Moral failures follow from this sin, but they are not its core and essence. It exceeds the sphere of guilt in life with others or toward any other creature. Romans 1:24ff. helps us further when we inquire into the reason for such a view. These verses speak of the equality of requital that punishes each according to the evil done. Persons are responsible for their actions and by them reveal who they are at the core — more precisely, who their real lord is who moves them to act. Those who perversely set the earth under the lordship of idols by serving them instead of the true Lord, the Creator, become totally perverted, thus in all their relations with other creatures. We live, think, and act according to the god we have. Whoever abrogates obedience to the Creator from then on lives for idols. We may revert to Genesis 1:26-27 here. Even after the fall humankind remains the likeness of the Lord who obliges to service, makes it his representative on earth, the organ of his lordship within a worldwide radius. After the fall, identified by Paul with idol worship, humans are still merely caricatures of what God created them for, that is, manifestations and deputies of demonic powers, to which Adam delivered himself with the fall.

This leads to a second insight: Idol worship is original sin. Earth stands under the sign of the demonic powers reigning in it, perverting, violating, and ruining God's creation. In this situation individuals find ever anew what is present in their own existence. In the New Testament "original sin" is not yet oriented to sexuality or transmitted by it. True to its Jewish inheritance, New Testament anthropology does not revolve around the contrast between body and soul or spirit. All its terms denote the total person in a particular orientation, set not so much within the antithesis of matter and spirit but within that of God and the demonic, identified by the world to which one belongs and through whom it makes itself known on earth. Just as for Paul we are defined at any given time by the lord who rules over us, so also by the world whose member, part, and tool we are. Lordship always denotes a power that creates for itself space and recognition, and the dispute between God and the idols turns on the eschatological question of to whom the earth finally belongs. We are all drawn into this dispute, and in it, by our acting or not acting, we make a case for the demonic or the divine power. In such a context "original sin" does not denote the traditional preponderance of sensuality but the fact that one is always born and found in a world living in rebellion against its Creator and delivering itself up to demonic power in pride or despair. In Enlightenment terms, the human being is never an individuality but is always oneself *and* the world at any given time. The gospel thus proclaims the inbreaking of the divine Basileia (kingdom) when announcing salvation. Repentance means an exchange of lordship, rescue from the power of darkness and transference to the kingdom of his beloved Son, to speak with the baptismal liturgy of Colossians 1:13.

If we are clear about this, then we understand why Paul usually speaks of sin in the singular, indicating the demonic, world-entangling power. The Septuagint takes a first step toward this view, while, due to its casuistry, the rabbinate prefers to use the plural, emphasizing deeds and thus concrete guilt. We also learn that, according to the apostle, persons before or after Christ cannot create salvation for themselves with their own works, so that he must proclaim the justification of the godless. Human beings not only continually commit sin. They are sinners before they have done anything. They are sinners radically and totally because the might of sin that masters them not only seductively approaches them from outside but, according to Romans 7:14ff., dwells in them and takes possession of them. Only of the possessed can it be said that they do not do the good they would but the evil they would not, that they thus live schizophrenically in the profoundest sense. To this corresponds the function of conscience in Romans 2:14-15. It makes known to the heathen as well that they are never at home with themselves undisturbed but exist in the continual state of those accused before the court, even before the final judge appears. Just as in their actions they are their own enemy, so in their conscience they are always their own judge.

As we might possibly assume with respect to the Fourth Gospel and must maintain with respect to radical Gnosticism, Paul did not develop his anthropology from a metaphysical dualism. God and Satan are not opposed from the outset. It was the fall that first delivered humanity to the cosmic powers, but even then the Creator keeps faith with it by setting it ever anew in life, under promise and commandment. Thus Paul not only has in mind the irresponsible transgressor but the morally acting believer, even among the heathen. Because humanity cannot get free of its Creator, even as fallen it remains a creature and thus capable of life with other humans, of reason and responsibility, of good works. Even apart from the Sinai covenant, humanity is a law unto itself and thus in reality exists in a certain analogy to the pious Jew.[4] Paul never denied God's gifts but maintained that, since Adam, these gifts were continually isolated from the Giver and thus perverted.

Paul maintains this as well of the Mosaic law. We saw that after the exile Judaism assigns Godlikeness solely to those who, concerned with sanctification and righteousness, share in it under the leading of the heavenly Sophia and their spirituality, are climbing Jacob's ladder to perfection. Here the law is regarded as a guide toward a God-pleasing and God-glorifying life in virtue, moving toward perfection in the conquest of all hindrances and temptations. Paul branded this as an appeal to self-transcendence on the part of those who would save themselves with their pious performance, who understand God's gift merely as an aid to their own work, and who, in pride or despair, must come to ruin on that imagined "royal way." The law which was to make known God's will, was mis-

---

4. Käsemann alludes here to Romans 2:14.

used, made a means to pious self-exhibition. In actuality, it awakened the greed for taking one's affair into one's own hands and carrying it out on one's own. Romans 7:7ff. describes this venture not merely as hopeless, since, with all its performance, the human being never arrives at salvation in this way, but also as possession under the might of sin. This too is idol worship and against the first commandment. More dangerous than transgression is the delusion of satisfying God by one's own will and power. This takes from God the honor of creating from nothing, of justifying sinners, of being strength in weakness, and of raising the dead. The greed of those who make God the arbiter of good deeds and in fact set self at the center demonizes the law and no longer allows God to be the Redeemer. The fact that for Paul the human being is a sinner, a transgressor as well as an observer of the law, does not exclude the possibility and reality of moral behavior, responsible reason, and good deeds. Sin means to be autocratic, to want to be and remain as God because God may no longer uncover our radical need as creature, our continually being directed to his grace alone, because we prefer our freedom to his continually new deliverance and replace him with a religious ideology.

4. *The image of God according to Paul.* Paul gives concreteness to what was just said from the perspective of Christology. The apostle speaks from his own experience when he regards as God's true adversary the religious person who is concerned with perfection and understands the law as the guiding principle of behavior on the way toward it. Jesus was rejected by defenders of the law, and his cross appeared to Judaism as a scandal because it was incompatible with its image of God and not to be accommodated to its theology. The Pauline doctrine of the justification of the godless by faith alone in the Creator, who surrenders none of his creatures but wakens the dead and has mercy on sinners, was felt to be blasphemous. At the point of Christology the pious who rely on their morality are, along with Israel, separated from the New Testament gospel, and at that point God's will, since Sinai is just as visible as Adam's sin. Whoever does not yet see oneself totally lost in this world of rebellion does not see the Creator as the only salvation and thus supports the lordship of the demons continually projected into the world by human self-will. Such a person has forgotten self and God. Only with reference to Jesus Christ does a universal perversion make clear who God really is, our Deliverer toward creatureliness and, identical to it, toward humanity's becoming human. Here is also made clear when one returns from falling and perversion to likeness with God; when, after flight from the

Lord and from pious presumption, one stands again as a vis-à-vis "in the sight of God." And again is made clear when one is addressed by him in promise and called to serve in praise of God as an earthly sign of heavenly deliverance, though weak, unworthy, and yet an instrument in one's own living space, engaged to proclaim freedom to fellow humans and every creature as their destiny, and where able to contribute to their realization.

These are the essential contexts from which to learn why in Romans 8:29; 2 Corinthians 3:18; 4:4 Paul calls Christ and only him "the Image of God." This makes sense only when the title is no longer applicable in general anthropology. It is in fact no accident that it is never once explicitly applied to Christians. Obviously, the apostle is concerned to establish that, since Christ's appearing, likeness to God is once more encountered on earth and that Christians contribute to it. Yet he never says that the disciple of Jesus is "the image of God." According to 1 Corinthians 15:49, such is possible only in the heavenly world, and even then it still holds that Christ's image in us replaces that of Adam. We never are, and never will be, something in and of ourselves. We are and become something only "with Christ" or "in him," as members of his Body. This also applies when in Romans 8:29 there is liturgical reference to being "conformed to the image of his Son," or in 2 Corinthians 3:18 to "being transformed into the same image." What is perfected in heaven begins with the baptism on earth, to which we daily return. Colossians 3:9ff. describes the Christian life as a continual *reditus ad baptismum* (being returned to baptism), in which the old self with its practices is continually put off and Christ as the new self is put on according to the image of its Creator. The catalog of virtues that follows no longer describes the performances that the law requires of the believer, but rather the possibilities of the one who has received grace given with and through Christ, thus the charisms. It is not irrelevant that Paul does not apply the quality of Godlikeness to the Mediator of creation, as do Colossians 1:15 and Hebrews 1:3, but rather to the risen Lord. While primitive Christian hymns, indirectly, at least, allow the original state of creation to be restored through Christ, the apostle is concerned with the conquest of sin, death, law, and all demonic temptation in the power of the new world. The Christian remains tested, just as were the wilderness people according to 1 Corinthians 10:1-13, despite the sacramental blessing. In Galatians 5:16 the difference between Christian and non-Christian seems to be effaced; it is noted again only by reference to the Spirit which follows. Here the theme of the Christian in temptation would have to be explained in detail, at which point the later church separates itself from Paul.

I will content myself with stating that the apostle does not yet use the formula "image [of God] and sinner alike," and from his viewpoint could not. He lived in imminent expectation of Christ's coming and thus was certain that death and all the demonic with it are already yielding to the Victor, that Christian life must be seen under this aspect. For him, Christian life was not yet isolatable in its empirical form, since it was drawn into Christ's dying and rising. By itself, life is not the image of God but is such only in relation to its Lord as his member. On the other hand, this life can no longer be called "sinner" empirically, since its individual behavior does not constitute its true nature; rather, the Lord does, who has taken possession of it by his Spirit and conquers in and through it. Strictly speaking, Paul does not reflect on the immanent anthropological dialectic in the Christian life, and naturally also in the church, because he sees the Christian and the community basically as projections of Christ into the world.

For Paul, the dialectic of Christian life and the community consists in the fact that the image of God is not an anthropological construct but the epiphany of the Son in the demonized world. To this extent, setting up and preserving a divine world order is no longer the issue but the liberation of fallen and enslaved creatures. In addition, no ideology respecting human definition is offered, say, in idealistic terms. What is of sole concern is to hold fast the epiphany of the Son in a demonically perverted creation by confessing, believing, and serving. As exemplified by Christ, this can occur in the reality of this world only by suffering and dying. Participation in the likeness of the Son denotes the kinship of the tempted, the justification of the unworthy and of those incapable of their own salvation, and the rejection of idol worship, which, according to the first commandment, embraces both freedom and obedience. Standing under the first commandment, kin to the obedient Adam of Romans 5:19, one need no longer serve idols but lives from the one Lord and only for him. In earthly terms this means to move toward the cross with the Nazarene, but under the open heaven, it also means discovering and making known a new openness on earth. Christ holds the place of God and is heir to the promise of the *dominium terrae,* to which Christians may point.

The Sermon on the Mount — a Private Affair?

At the outset let me state as emphatically as I can that in this presentation I am treating only one section of the problematic presented by the Sermon on the Mount. The three long chapters would have to be dealt with word for word. A long tradition of exposition and the question of its application in the practical, especially in the political field (something passionately disputed today), would have to be carefully reflected on if, within the scope of my own possibilities and limitations, I wanted to be aware of or do justice to the entire problematic. The introduction to a discussion has the right to abbreviate perspectives, to allow subjectivity a considerable measure of freedom, that is, to accent the one and leave the other aside. I will speak in more strongly thetical and antithetical fashion than the exegete anxious to differentiate should do. And it is also my custom, where possible, to deal with basic questions more from the historical perspective than a systematician should or would do.

First of all, some information for nontheologians: Matthew writes after the destruction of Jerusalem, thus in the post-Pauline period, say, around A.D. 80, and for the community in Syria preparing for world mission. This means that he did not personally hear Jesus but is dependent on various types of tradition. The fact that Luke in 6:17ff. gives an obviously much briefer parallel to the sermon but also offers the same speech material scattered over his Gospel is best explained when we assume that both evangelists not only collected oral tradition but also possessed a common written exemplar. In such fashion, just as in the case of the Lord's Prayer or

---

A lecture given on April 20, 1982, at the Rabanus Maurus Academy in Frankfurt.

texts of the Lord's Supper, they use liturgical formulas in vogue in their communities and clearly distinguishable from each other. The Sermon on the Mount is thus not a speech of Jesus given in this form and context but a theological composition of the evangelist in which are deposited, along with genuine words of Jesus, post-Easter debates with the Jews and with fanatical prophets, and debates between strict Jewish-Christians and Gentile Christians. This is important for our theme insofar as it does not permit the sermon to be treated as a substantial unity at first hand but rather as a collection of speech material revised by Matthew at the end of the second early Christian generation, traced to Jesus and handed down in his name.

The question arises as to what our evangelist intended with this composition. Strikingly, he elsewhere strews a series of lengthy speeches of Jesus over his entire writing. Evidently he is especially concerned with the Master's teaching and, for his part, wants to impress it on the community. He is himself a teacher. Today we would say he is every bit a theologian who orients the tradition toward a specific goal. What is his goal in the Sermon on the Mount? It would be appropriate to begin answering by correcting the traditional, prevailing view. Just as non-Christians, Christians too, unfortunately, have often found in the sermon merely a sum of ethical instructions. But the introductory Beatitudes render that view unacceptable. They do not at all tell us what we should do and omit, do not list virtues and vices so as to attach a promise to them. Rather, they state where on the earth our God reveals himself and not only alters our relationships but stands them on their head.

When it repeats, "for theirs is the kingdom of heaven," it is declared first of all that the kingdom of heaven — which for the pious Jew means the kingly rule of God — is not where we are used to calling "heaven." Ever since creation, the kingly rule of God is manifest throughout the world of humans. It will be consummated only in the sphere we call "the beyond," when the resistance of demonic powers is removed, and thus is perfect. Second, from the speeches that take up the Greek word for "happy" with the meaning "blessed," "having been blessed," it is clear that God's activity is not conditional upon our own. Of course, the meek, the merciful, and the peacemakers are mentioned. But the focus is much more strongly on those who suffer than those who act. At issue here is not reward for the good and punishment for the wicked. It is said that, where heaven opens as at Pentecost, God is humanity's Advocate, Helper, and Savior. Third, he is such, since as Creator he creates from nothing. As Judge he wakens the dead, as Redeemer he justifies the godless who sought salvation on their own. He takes the side of the minorities, the deprived, those doomed to failure — those who need him for body and soul, since no one else gives them aid. This has nothing to do with ethical instruction. It is comfort, a promise of the almighty mercy superior to all other powers, which must be understood quite literally as the heart's turning to the poor — "merciful."

I would like to make a point respecting current political debate. In the Sermon on the Mount no so-called basic values are proclaimed. For the Christian there are absolutely no basic values if one takes the New Testament seriously. The Greek world knew of cardinal virtues, but Christ brings no new system of values, no particular worldview, no particular picture of human existence of an idealistic or materialistic stripe, no conservative or revolutionary norms and categories. He brings himself, thus the image of God, into a milieu in which God's as well as our image are perverted by pride or despair. His program, his promise and summons, his cardinal virtue, and his basic value are described by a single word: discipleship. A Christian is one who follows the Nazarene. This may be made concrete, protected on all sides against misunderstanding, but it is the only thing that obtains in God's royal rule and is necessary on earth. It is the human correspondence to the kingdom of heaven, the measure of the last day, the distinction between Jew and Gentile, believers and atheists. The Sermon on the Mount opens with Beatitudes because the Nazarene has appeared in the midst, has descended into the earthly inferno and takes to himself the victims of demons, takes those who protest and demonstrate against inhumanity, revealing mercy and salvation to the poor.

From what has been said, it follows that our text cannot be viewed as a Christian casuistic of virtues and vices in which every possible type of behavior in problematic situations is mentioned and regulated. We may see something here like a preliminary form of later community regulations. After all, in chapter 6, there is reference to giving alms, praying, and fasting, with the liturgical shape of the Lord's Prayer as Matthew knew it inserted into the theme on prayer. In chapter 7 judgment is first of all passed on fault-finding among believers, a practice already frequent then, then a summons to regular prayer, and finally a warning against prophets who tempt to faith without works, perhaps from out of a misunderstood Paulinism. At the end, the double parable of the two houses — one built on the rock, the other on the sand — would fairly suit a catechism-like introduction to Christian piety. But all this is merely an abstract from the speeches of the evangelist, which included four still longer compositions.

Evidently, in the Sermon on the Mount we have something like a foundation for all further teaching, for which reason its thematic differs from the later complexes. If we are aware of this, then we may in no case level everything out, give to each speech the same weight as to the others, or measure Christian existence by whether everything is observed.

We must rather search for the center of the Sermon on the Mount and from that point arrange each unit. This center is marked out by Matthew himself. He lets Jesus appear with the announcement that the kingdom of heaven has drawn near. Later, his parables will often begin with the words "The kingdom of heaven is like. . . ." His entire Gospel is the message of the kingdom. So, as early as from the Beatitudes, we have learned that the kingdom of God is the heart of the sermon, for which reason it gives a deliberate summary in 6:33: "Strive first for the kingdom of God and his righteousness, and all these things will be given to you as well." The Sermon on the Mount is an invitation to the royal rule of God and its order. With equal right we can say that it is the foundation for the discipleship of the disciples, since lordship and discipleship correspond, as was already established. But let this conclude the first part of my presentation. It is already clear that in this sermon there can be absolutely nothing at all of a private affair. The kingdom of heaven extends over all the earth, and the followers of the Nazarene penetrate it to its furthest corners as bearers of the promise.

Our second part concerns the so-called antitheses, in which Jesus opposes his commandment to that of Moses, at times actually abrogates the Jewish Torah. Two introductions precede in Matthew 5:13-16 and 5:17-20. In the first, the community is reminded of its responsibility to live a genuine discipleship before the world around it with good works. The two sayings "You are the salt of the earth" and "You are the light of the world" characterize an end-time task. Naturally as such, they are not "advice for success" but "statements of faith."[1] But this does not mean they were to be a Christian utopia or exaggerated figures applicable to a more or less small circle in family, neighborhood, or workplace. In any case, according to the text the Christian community does not trumpet its own self-understanding. So, there is a "statement of faith" here only in the sense that everything in the Bible is and intends to be such. We should more properly speak of "promise." If it is a mere matter of beautiful figures of speech here, as is customarily assumed today, then none of the beatitudes is to be taken seriously. Re-

---

1. Martin Hengel, "Die Stadt auf dem Berge," *Evangelische Kommentare* 15 (1982): 21.

ligious speakers like to express themselves in a grandiose way. The evil world or even visitors to worship tend to make of faith a pious hope or even the illusion of fanatics. But whoever judges our words in this fashion had best slam the New Testament shut.

Theologians say that the Bible offers "eschatology" on almost every page — in other words, that it sees our time and world as set within the breaking in of the end time, with Jesus as proclaimer and bringer of a new creation, a new earth, a new heaven. If this is not true, we need no longer concern ourselves with the Gospels, since religious figures and illusions are to be had on the cheap. But if it is true, then, as in the Beatitudes, it is said of the blessed community, which may not allow its blessing to become a buried talent. Its Master consecrates in order that something may occur among and through us. Most concretely Christians are urged (and that means each one as well as all together) to bring light into the confines of daily life as well as into the wide world.

To quote the Barmen Declaration of 1934,[2] despite the Nazis and cowardly citizens: like salt and sometimes like pepper, the Christian community should penetrate the fabrications of our theologians; that is, without the promise and claim of Jesus, it should cede no area to self or to one's own competence, to self-chosen or preordained rules of the game. The Nazarene himself referred to the fact that at times salt loses its power, is no longer of use. Unfortunately, this appears to be so much the case today that even theologians dare speak only of "statements of faith" rather than of "promises." The right to appeal to Jesus' word and will for our activity was disputed in the Third Reich. It will always be disputed where there is talk of the "autonomy" of politics and economics, of science and technology, of social and cultural relations, thus — in the name of liberalism — of the "free market economy," for example, or of an allegedly real socialism. Put briefly, those who could still help themselves, or at least thought they could, have never appreciated it when Christ attacked them through his disciples, broke through their worldview, or practiced the law of the kingdom of heaven on earth. There was always vexation right up to the cross. But in the end time, according to Matthew 10:27, what was once whispered in one's ear must be shouted from the housetops. "Light of the world" and

2. The reference is to the Magna Carta of the Confessing Church, with its six theses: (1) confession of Jesus Christ as sole Word of God and rejection of any other source, (2) acknowledgment of responsibility toward society, (3) refusal to yield to current ideological or political winds, (4) rejection of hierarchy, (5) embracing of the "two kingdoms" doctrine, and (6) emphasis on the church's task of announcing the free grace of God to the world.

"salt of the earth" apply either everywhere, every time, and radically — or not at all.

The second introduction to the antitheses of the sermon — 5:17-20 — continues the thought. What I have just called the "law of the kingdom of heaven" is now formulated in terms of strictest Jewish Christianity, which opposes certain Christian prophets and their adherents, perhaps within the circle of Stephen. In that circle, the mission to the Gentiles is established by the fact that the risen Christ may be more than the temple and law of Moses. Stephen is thus stoned to death by furious Jews. But the text may also be directed against those who understood Paul in such a way that only faith is decisive and that therefore good works were no longer required of the disciple of Jesus. The answer to them is that the Nazarene did not intend to do away with the Old Testament law and prophets, that heaven and earth would pass away before the smallest letter of the Torah. Only that disciple will be great in the kingdom of heaven who keeps the commandments of Moses and teaches others to do so. At this point two, as it were, Christian confessions collide. First, there were only Jewish Christians. Then more and more Gentiles were missionized. Should these be received into the church only after they had been taken up into the Sinai covenant through circumcision, had become proselytes, thus had subjected themselves to the Mosaic law? Paul had to deal with this debate in all his congregations because strict Jewish Christians followed him everywhere and opposed his "Christ alone" and "faith alone" with a Christ *and* Moses, faith *and* meritorious works. The dispute continues throughout all of church history.

Characteristically, Matthew has not suppressed the slogan of strictest Jewish Christian observance. But he interprets it from his view of the gospel and thus arrives at a mediating position. The Jewish Christian need not become an apostate respecting the tradition of his fathers. Nevertheless, Christian righteousness must be better than that of the scribes and the pietistic lay movement of the Pharisees. The law is not entirely kept when one blindly clings to its letters but where one allows oneself to be given eyes from the Holy Spirit for loving one's neighbor, even one's enemy. The radical commandment to love is the fulfillment of the law, the sum of all that deserves to be called "good works." It penetrates the previously separating walls of varying religiosity. Where the commandment is accepted, it makes a neighbor of one who once was a rival, even a friend, brother, or sister out of one who once was an enemy. The "incarnation of the human being," openness to creation and all creatures, liberation toward humanity

— this is the mark of the one who follows the Nazarene. He too came as a lover to serve.

This is the heading of the following antitheses, in which Jesus opposes his command to the commandments and prohibitions of Moses or Jewish tradition. Now we understand why Matthew allows the sermon to take place on a mountain. It is disputed whether in Judaism there was expectation of something like a law of the end time that should displace the law of Sinai. We can leave this historical question aside. In any event, Matthew appears to be of the opinion that Jesus brought the messianic Torah, extended the covenant with Israel at the end of time to all creation, and radicalized the Mosaic law by orienting it to the commandment to love. In this way electing and liberating grace places the renewed people of God under obligation, for which reason the Beatitudes precede the commandments. At issue in the commandments is the glorifying of God's rule on earth. This is expressed in the prodigious statement in Matthew 5:48: "Be perfect, therefore, as your heavenly Father is perfect." This is not[3] an *Imitatio Dei*, with imitation as the goal of its pedagogy. Still less is it a call to self-realization in a being directed toward the highest ideals. What is false is the perspective of a divine educative will that, in a process of sanctification, shapes one after its image. In that case, the term "blessed" with which the Beatitude opens is no longer Christologically oriented, no longer related to the Proclaimer of the gospel as the messianic Bringer of the kingdom of heaven. Rather, what the commandments contain is only a variety of religious ethic, soon to be discussed in more detail. In the quotation, "perfect" has the sense of "totally." The God who gives himself totally in Christ, who redeems us, demands truly incarnate persons who are totally and undividedly surrendered to the other creatures as a witness and reflection of the kingdom broken in. Perfection in this context is nothing like the formation of character up to its last possibilities and on the endless way of approximating the highest. Here, perfection (and this is constitutive) exists only in relation to the other, be it the neighbor or the enemy, and of course in the sense of radical service, undivided surrender.

In his essay "Das Ende aller Politik" (The Goal of All Politics),[4] my colleague Martin Hengel has so sharply accented this radicality that he first

3. Contra Pinchas E. Lapide, "Es geht um die Entfeindungsliebe," *Lutherische Monatshefte* 20 (1981): 505-8.

4. Martin Hengel, "Das Ende aller Politik," *Evangelische Kommentare* 14 (1981): 686-90. Subsequent references in the text are to this article.

thought he could respond to it only with the groan of the tax collector: "God, be merciful to me, a sinner!" (p. 690). In his opinion, the evangelist's Sermon on the Mount laid the cornerstone for a later two-stage ethic. According to Hengel, a small minority such as Francis of Assisi, "led by the spontaneity of grace," may have lived "totally with or in these words," and perhaps still do today (p. 690). The rest of us should be terrified by such a "high-altitude flight," by the "pitiless seeming lack of compromise that has resisted all attempts at domestication in the history of the church," and admit our inability, "which we as Christians should calmly call sin" (p. 687). So the summary drawn from this view reads, "The basic problem before which the Sermon on the Mount sets us is this superior force of our sin" (p. 687). This is suggestive of Luther's exposition that allows Jesus to preach a law here like a "Mosissimus Mose" (Moses to the nth power) so as to allow us to see our own sin.

I regard almost all the statements cited to be theologically incorrect, and must give the reason, since the political consequences of this view must also be incorrect. Hengel does not go so far as to maintain without further ado the impossibility of fulfilling Jesus' commandments construed as law. He knows that every pious Jew would have said it was blasphemous to call the law unfulfillable. God does not hand down unfulfillable commandments like some cruel despot. So it is stated that Matthew regards the requirements of his tradition as fulfillable, at least for a portion of the disciples. It is also correctly seen that, for the evangelist, "perfect" is opposed to "divided," thus means "undivided"(p. 687). Yet this is idealistically and pietistically related to the perfection of the isolated person, not at all to the self-forgetfulness of the one who in loving is more concerned with the other than with one's self. The error here is that the antitheses are not interpreted in throughgoing fashion from the viewpoint of the commandment of love. For this reason, counter to the entire New Testament, our human weakness is described as sin. There, however, "sin" is never seen as a human deficit but is always viewed in light of the pride or despair that would be something else than a needy creature, that is, would be godlike, would thus not let God be Creator and Giver, merciful to all the poor. Finally, it is correctly seen that Jesus is basically concerned with the royal rule of God and its righteousness. Perfectionism, however, feels its own pulse and investigates its own righteousness. In that case, we must set at center our incapacity, sin's superior might, and the petition "God, be merciful to me, a sinner!"

But in this way the reality of radical love is contested or reserved for a small group of the especially holy. If this were so, then a real question would arise, to which we may answer in an entirely different way. Christian faith is thoroughly aware of this question, and therefore it describes such love as a charism, a miracle worked by the Spirit. But it maintains the reality of that love as and because it witnesses to and represents on earth the reality of God and the total surrender of the Crucified. Where the royal rule of God, the discipleship of Jesus as glorification of the Creator and service to the creature, and the justice and the truth of the Beatitudes are proclaimed, human weakness does not render perfect and undivided surrender illusory. It is precisely the weak, in themselves imperfect and rejected by perfectionists, whom the Father of Jesus uses as his instruments. He does not leave them alone. He does not make them whole and strong and holy in isolation, but free in the discipleship of his Son to love and, in it, to conquer their own and alien hindrances. This goes beyond the mere domestic sphere. True surrender of the disciple is unbound, not a private affair, tends toward aid to the world, extends freedom everywhere.

For Pinchas Lapide, whose essay I cited earlier, this goes too far. For this reason he wants a "Realpolitik as the Sermon on the Mount actually intends." He subsumes this under a frightful term, but one that clearly describes his concern: *Entfeindungsliebe,* or "hostility-ending love." Jesus does not demand fanatical self-surrender, but a "robust reconcilability" as a "concrete strategy for lessening conflicts." So God's pedagogy calls us to nonviolence, because in reality the "sober alternative" applies, "make do or die." Lapide is obliged to interpret in this fashion, since as a Jew he cannot bring Christology into play. Otherwise, he would have had to say that Jesus himself scorned such realism and thus was crucified. As a matter of fact, in the moral realm a love oriented to pedagogy would deserve the name in only a limited sense. Without reason, it would be blind. Directed toward reason alone or primarily it would scarcely be self-surrender. Furthermore, parents and teachers know how problematic all "Realpolitik" is, and unfortunately politicians seldom have any confidence in "tough tolerance," preferring to relegate it to the private sphere.

There is a third aspect, which historical observation may simply not avoid. In his essay "Die Stadt auf dem Berge" (The City on the Hill), Hengel points to the fact that the situation of the church in Matthew's time was quite different from ours. In "Das Ende aller Politik" he maintains that the Sermon on the Mount cannot be formalized and adapted to changing historical situations (p. 688). As correct as the first statement is, so doubtful does the second appear. A text is not necessarily "formalized" when it is adapted to other circumstances. This is what every translation does. As a matter of fact, the Sermon on the Mount allows us to recognize the process of an ongoing adaptation and thus summons us to it. Jesus turned to all those who flocked to him. The exemplar used by the evangelist is directed toward the Christian community. Matthew himself no longer accepts the attitude of rigorous Jewish Christianity when he requires a better righteousness than that of the Pharisees and scribes and characterizes it by the commandment to love. And he also does so when, unlike Luke and probably also unlike Jesus, he no longer speaks of the poor in the material sense but of the poor *in spirit,* meaning the humble. He has brought both the Beatitudes and the antitheses to their completion, which I will not demonstrate now, and has set both within the framework of a small catechism. Ever since the early church, the Sermon on the Mount has been understood as instruction for the "perfect" — in other words, from the viewpoint of a two-stage ethic. In general, the blanket prohibition against oaths and the renunciation of force are strictly observed only by fanatical sects. This indicates that texts of a secular or religious sort must ever and anon be inquired into as to their meaning for the present and thereby unavoidably adapted to our given situation. No tradition remains unaltered, and it is entirely certain that the Bible — unlike the Qur'an — does not intend to be a book fallen from heaven, thus sacrosanct. It corrects the Old by the New Testament, James by Paul, Paul by the Pastoral Letters. Only adaptation to new situations keeps sacred and profane writings alive and generally intelligible. We have not only the right but the duty to inquire into their meaning for us.

So much for a brief disquisition on the theme of the renunciation of force,[5] though several lectures would be needed for it. Nothing at all should be said of nonviolence. Such is always ideology, since there never or nowhere is or has been a place free of violence. Furthermore, there is good, useful, and necessary violence, just as there is evil and tyrannical violence, and both in a hundred different shapes and grades. Violence in the singular is an abstraction and only through circumstance becomes concrete. Furthermore, circumstances determine whether one can and should submit to it willingly or, if one is not fit for martyrdom, should submit unwillingly, resist it in various ways, or voluntarily renounce all resistance. So the problem is complex, not to be simplified as is usual today when we merely pay attention to the wording. We may not forget that Jesus or the Christian

5. Hengel, "Stadt auf dem Berge," p. 20.

tradition interpreting him believed they fulfilled God's will in the law of Moses when in the antitheses of the sermon they deepened, radicalized or actually rejected the letter of the Old Testament. Just as, for example, our association with politics actually indicates, whoever persists in following only the strict letter of the law will at times totally miss the intention of a requirement. Not even earliest Christianity radically held to the prohibition against divorce. God and the Holy Spirit would be totally superfluous if the letter alone sufficed.

The Sermon on the Mount is no casuistry in which all human problems are solved once and for all. It must be understood from its center. So we must continually ask what is meant by the sentence "Do not resist an evildoer" (5:39). Not only church history but on many of its pages the New Testament itself calls to us, "Résistez!" Not for nothing is it incessantly impressed upon us that Christians must struggle. They must do so with their own evil lusts and base earthly desires, so also with flesh and blood that lure us from genuine discipleship or threaten us because of it, but above all with the powers and forces encroaching on all the world, forces that blind us, take from us our courage and freedom, and set themselves in place of our Lord. The Bible even contradicts itself when we pay attention only to its letters and play the one off against the other. In the context of our text, nonresistance is also illustrated by those who viciously attack us or force us to give service. In such instances we should recall that our God lets it rain on the good and the evil, the righteous and unrighteous, that he lets the sun shine on both. This clearly means: forgive those who vent their anger on you! Deal with those who demand from you what they have no right to demand! But it does not say to give in when *others* are struck on the check or are actually forced into slavery under a tyrannical power. For the lassitude of faith toward worldwide tyranny, about which evangelical bishops like to speak today, I find no support in the Bible. Of course, I find it in the Stoics, in mysticism, and in the modern psychology of tolerance. Wherever one boasts that God is to be obeyed more than men, and even takes the field with the obligation of conscience against authority, we cannot pretend as though "do not resist an evildoer" stood there isolated and universally applicable.

The central problem is posed with the question concerning the basic theme of the Sermon on the Mount, since every detail is to be interpreted from that point. I have paraphrased this theme by these key phrases: "the liberating kingdom of God" and "the discipleship of the crucified Nazarene in commitment to every creature." Resistance to human exploitation can in no wise be labeled as prohibited by referring to the renunciation of force toward others. Whoever deals with the Bible may not take from it only what suits, what corresponds to one's tradition or the trend of one's time. We must always pay heed to the constitutive either-or in, for example, this saying of the sermon: "No one can serve two masters. . . . You cannot serve God and wealth." God is nowhere else than on the idols' playing field. Idols are ever only at war against God's royal rule. With our action we witness to what lord we belong, and no beatitude is understood that does not subject us to the one Lord, Protector of the poor, Lord and Judge of the pious. No command has meaning in which we see only instruction for individual perfection or for a society. The first commandment is always decisive.

As historian, I have analyzed sections of the Sermon on the Mount; and as exegete, I have pointed to the presuppositions and implications of my analysis. Till now, I have not indicated the consequences for our time. They are to be dealt with during the discussion period. But by way of introduction to the debate, let me at least formulate a few theses that have occurred to me.

1. The Sermon on the Mount never was, is not, and never can be a private affair. Jesus spoke to all who would hear him. The Gospel regards our text as a basic introduction to the kingdom of God and to the discipleship of the Nazarene as its earthly response. The Christian community is taken to be the salt of the earth and the light of the world in the inbreaking messianic time. Therefore, it is sent into all areas of public life to witness to the promise, as well as to Jesus' claim to all his Father's creatures. There are no longer autonomies in the political, social, economic, cultural, national, and international spheres that at least would not have to be irritated by the gospel. The exposition of the Sermon on the Mount in terms of a private affair is the reaction of Enlightenment tolerance. It is actually a rejection of the gospel as God's reaching out for his world.

2. The Sermon on the Mount is no universally binding moral law, if such there ever was or can be. It intends to be the message of God's royal rule broken in on earth within a world in rebellion against its Creator. For this reason it is from the outset exposed to contradiction and must be responded to in such a way that an alternative between God and the idols results. By the way in which we react to it, we make known whom we have, and will have, as lord. This applies to the enlightened as well as the possessed, to believers as well as to atheists. What is assumed is an anthropology that defines one at any given time by one's lord.

3. The radicality of the Sermon on the Mount does not serve religious perfectionism in the life of the individual or in our everyday relationships. What is basic is that every person is viewed here as being in need, dependent on the Creator, as the Our Father makes clear with its audible petitions. Beatitude and individual summons point toward the one thing needful, but also toward what is possible for all, that is, God's kingdom on earth and discipleship in humaneness. An open heaven opens the eye to an earth to be opened.

4. The Sermon on the Mount has enormous political significance, and every Christian life has its political dimension. Of course, the gospel is not a set of traffic regulations for everyone's public life. Still, the either-or of God and the idols must force Jesus' disciples to take a position in the political, economic, and cultural areas, by doing which they can and will come into conflict with so-called inherent constraints, with parties, lobbies, and regulations. In any case, as free children of God, they will represent the rights of the weak; where able, they will resist the dance around the golden calf, the lordship of Mammon in the so-called free-market economy, as well as in state capitalism; and they will oppose the ruination of the creation. On the other hand, they will be intent on reconciliation between classes, races, and power groups because their Lord will have peace, and it is precisely on earth that they are open for the earth and in public service. They cannot commit themselves for any length of time because they are always and entirely bound by their Lord. In today's world, ruled by the white race, they will normally belong with the rebels, with the result that their passive or active resistance will often seem arbitrary, will not even exclude revolution, and will rather include martyrdom as a last recourse. On earth, God's royal rule as discipleship of the Nazarene and love for humankind and its dignity is always a political matter to which the powers of the world will variously react. In theory, in its practical shape, it is most often a scandal Christians must put up with. But we may not leave the earth to the powers and forces ruling in it.

The Gospel and the Devout

The way of the gospel throughout history reveals a moving drama, signaled in the parable of the sower. Good fruit grows unnoticed in all the world. But for two millennia the divine seed fell unnoticed on stony ground or among thorns, was choked and trampled. In the process, rather than being an instrument of the sower, Christianity too often associates with enemies of the seed. As creature of the Word, it should live from what it has heard, should reflect it as consecrated and blessed by it. But it shows itself to be greatly introverted, immovable, and deaf. It unfaithfully buries the talent given it; it discredits the gospel by quarreling, hereticizing, division, and ban; does not shrink from the spiritual; and fantasizes over the physical annihilation of those differently minded. The beginnings described in the New Testament do not merely set before us the first sowing and the harvest to follow. They also point to withered land laid waste, not by the brutality of adversaries, but at the hands of the devout.

Certainly, Jesus was executed by Pilate as a political agitator. But the gospel tradition makes clear that, before this, the religious leaders of Israel suspected him and, supported by the legalistic majority, especially by the Pharisaic lay movement, decisively contributed to the trial of the Nazarene. Unlike the so-called zealots, Jesus was scarcely active politically. But his behavior in the agitated years before the Jewish war occasioned public unrest and offered the authorities every reason for concern and misunderstanding. Put pointedly, and secured through research, we may say that from the out-

A lecture given on April 6, 1975, over Süddeutscher Rundfunk (South German Radio), or Südfunk 2, Stuttgart.

set the gospel has irritated in particular devout circles and unmistakably encountered harshest resistance precisely there. We dare not call this accidental, for all of church history can meaningfully be read under this aspect. In every period there has been considerable tension between gospel and piety, however surprising this assertion may be. Jews felt the Christian message to be blasphemous, and for centuries heathen felt it to be atheistic, a matter that engages us too little. When the gospel began its earthly course, the possibility that it would establish one religion among others was not at all a settled matter. In their pious convictions, conventions, and practices, its first hearers were most deeply shaken by it, plunged into a conflict with fathers, teachers, and communities, all of which, as with Jesus, could end in death and lead to exclusion from the community. Whoever is not aware of this conflict from the pages of the New Testament and personally drawn into it is no doubt wearing spectacles that conceal those beginnings.

Let us clarify this a bit from various aspects! We wonder that Jesus most often turned to the simple people. They were cursed by the Jewish rabbinate because, under everyday pressures, they could not intensively and continuously devote themselves to the study of Holy Scripture. Encounters with scribes and Pharisees who conformed to its prescriptions commonly came into hostile conflict with them, to the point that exceptions actually stand out. Unlike the religious world around him, Jesus did not take pains to sharpen the requirements of the law so that more room would be given the will of God to penetrate all of life. Rather, the Nazarene causes a stir by rejecting meticulously observed regulations when they hinder him from showing love. In the choice of his disciples he shocks the sensibilities of polite society and brings his mission into ill repute, not only through association with zealots and obvious sinners such as tax collectors and prostitutes, but in downright blasphemous fashion excuses it by saying he has been sent as physician to the sick. In a provocative way God and the godless are united. The sources preserved for us give no hint that Jesus methodically organized conventicles and communities as those around him were keen to do. If a greater circle of adherents does gather about him, strangely enough, he soon separates himself from it in order to bring the message to others. All along the way he does not at all behave like religious revivalists and teachers who want to make the pious ever more pious and remove them from the evil world. On the contrary, the Beatitudes, as well as the miracle stories, clearly show emphatically that for Jesus piety was not a condition for grace. Conflict speeches with the scribes mark it more as a hindrance to God's intervention.

We must guard against a radicalism that erects false fronts because it is oriented to slogans instead of to reality. The New Testament is aware of a genuine piety and gently describes it in the shape of Jesus' parents, of the Baptist, of Simeon and Anna, and of many others, all of which is worth compiling. What is characteristic of them is that they stand, as it were, in an Advent light. That is, they stretch hearts and hands toward the inbreaking salvation as the waiting and watching, as the poor, as those in need. The Our Father, not accidentally containing only petitions, is their prayer and the indication of their earthly state. From that point, then, we see clearly defined the kind of piety that Jesus provoked to harshest offense and actual hate. It seeks to impress God, whom it makes a kind of referee, and to escape his critical judgment. It refuses him the surrender owed by the creature or, as in the case of the prodigal son and his brother, that of the child, and in its place erects the tower of Babel — one of excuses, charges, claims, and privileges respecting self-justification and self-wrought deliverance.

There the Pharisee tallies up his merits, while the tax collector simply pleads for grace. There Samaritans help the attacked, where priests and Levites take to their heels; there one gives thanks for healing, while others remain mute. There the ritual prescriptions of the law are followed but love and mercy are neglected, and the Creator is isolated from his creature, as though there were a worship that did not call for consideration of one's neighbor, or that from the outset excluded enemies and the unsympathetic. Where piety thinks it can make a pact with God so as to claim him for itself, or draws limits to his freedom, thus shapes him and consequently fellow humans according to its own model and will, there the fall into sin is continually repeated. That it need not appear clearly amoral and asocial at first glance but is taken to be religiously motivated and even disguised as respectable makes it particularly dangerous. The gospel, of course, unmasks the nature of piety, and it alone can do so. Hunger for life and fear of death force us to self-assertion at any price. Not only the creature but also God bears the cost of this, being made to serve us by our selfishness and misused for our purposes.

Jesus broke through the arrogance of a religiosity orbiting around people. This is the reverse side of the redemption he wrought and the criterion of his freedom toward all earthly situations, as well as of the gospel, in which his work is continued. As the first word of the good news already indicates, at issue here is the conversion even of the pious, thus necessarily a reversal of thought that we may set under the rubric of demythologizing.

Said in all earnestness, with the Nazarene there breaks in the twilight of the gods, an event of worldwide consequence, but one that first and basically sets us and our ideas in the appropriate place — in the truth. No longer can the descendant of fallen Adam liken himself to Prometheus and, in illusion denying the creature in need of help and salvation, view himself as the superman on the way to Olympus. No longer do we construe God's omnipotence metaphysically from out of the wish-fulfillment dreams of pious fantasy, but we see it at work where heavenly grace anticipates the resurrection of the dead by giving itself to the lowly and condemned on earth to own, and so stands all the customarily held values on their head. God's great revolution began when the Nazarene inquired after those in need of salvation instead of the worthy, went in search of the lost and did not stay with those who wanted to prepare for or actually deserve grace with their pious intent and performance.

The sphere of revelation is no longer a spiritual sphere, but the rebellious world, abandoning itself to itself, delivered over to and hurrying after its demons, the world to which the Creator does not give up his claim. Here, then, unbelief is no longer the alternative to faith, and no longer is the absent or hidden God the central problem of religious humanity or even of Christian life. The real opponent of faith and the most widespread type of piety is superstition, which in its innumerable variations and disguises surrenders people to idols and avoids the sole rule of God. In face of the Nazarene and within the sphere of the gospel's operation, presumption and delusion end, masks fall, the deaf hear, the godless find their Lord, and the pious learn that the Father of Jesus is not their private idol but loves his world and will come to its aid. We must kill the Nazarene if we wish to resist this demythologizing of earth and humanity; we must not love him, allow him to work or rule because we want to make our own way, survive, remain the overt or covert measure of all things. Here his kingdom and ours, his salvation and our obduracy come to a parting of the ways, so that at the cross of Jesus the insipid view is destroyed that religiosity as such is pleasing to God and the highest human worth. Where the pious and heathen together erect Golgotha, it is no longer enough to be pious. We must become pious only as disciples of the Crucified, since it is at the cross that godless piety was unmasked.

What gave rise to the most bitter conflicts so very early in the first period continued throughout the history of Christianity and, soon after Easter, led to a division of the primitive community. One group pressed beyond the limits of Israel into the Gentile world. It was enough for it to awaken faith in the exalted Christ and, in so doing, as the Letter to the Hebrews will later broadly portray it, set the institutions and regulations of the religion handed down by the fathers in the shadow of the provisional. But alongside there was also a majority who wanted to see continuity preserved with the old people of God and the cultic law of Judaism as binding upon every Christian. Now the dilemma reads, Shall we free the gospel from religious tradition and especially Old Testament instruction, or must it remain in the context of this tradition, in fact be subordinated to it? No unequivocal decision is made, as is evidenced by Stephen's martyrdom and the exiling of his friends to Syria. In all of this, legalistic Jewish Christianity remains undisturbed and clearly did not retain solidarity with those who stood strictly for "Christ alone," thus "saved by faith alone," and who were persecuted as apostate.

For the majority of the community the way to such freedom was blocked precisely by its scripture-bound piety. Not even Christ could move them to leave the fathers' house and breach the traditional covenant regulations. Though others might lay claim to the Spirit and the biblical promises for the Gentile world, it saw its task as remaining true to the religious inheritance and forgot that Jesus himself, at least in exceptional cases, had broken through it when salvation was at issue. In the history of the church that follows, similar situations will continually put the Christian fellowship to the test, allow the words of Scripture to be played off against each other, will give birth to differing theologies, put the conservatives at enmity with the liberals, and make the community a battleground between subservience to tradition and discipleship in radical freedom. In this situation every disciple of Jesus as witness to the truth of the gospel must make confession in the trenches and in one's own way, in one's own time, wherever God's will and the earthly revelation of the eternal kingdom are encountered.

The question as to what criteria were then authoritative was, of course, raised by the first conflict. But it had to be thoroughly thought through, and with that dawned the epoch of Christian theology. Jesus' call to salvation was directed to all people, thus in fact, to every person. But his adherents set his gospel within the horizon of the church so that the way and goal of believers could be known from it. Experiences before and after Easter are now connected with the message of the Master and give it the impress of religious teaching and dogmatic weight. Here, then, false doctrine must be avoided and excluded. Theological emphases mark the given front and thrust.

This process is best reflected in the Gospel of John. In it Jesus' opponents characteristically barricade themselves behind Old Testament tradition to help them cast doubt on and contest the truth of his message. For this purpose they make use of the typical argument of professional theology: We all come from a past period of divine activity and are thus incessantly reminded in the Bible not to forget it. But when we seek to understand history, the world, and ourselves solely from our own experience, we hand ourselves over to the accident of the moment and lose direction; we do not learn of the faithfulness of God but of an arbitrary fate. True, without a spiritual and religious inheritance, no one has a home or refuge. On the other hand, the gospel retorts that patterns of education never replace the presence of the Spirit, as for example was given at Pentecost and, in the Johannine literature, is regarded as the mark of a genuine saying of Jesus. Many generations know of revelation only in preserved form and refuse to accept it in any other. Institutions, confessional movements, and entire denominations rancorously strive over religious canned goods. They seriously imagine God would lose his identity if he were not caught and rendered concrete in this way, if he were not committed to inviolable theological formulas and thus become a calculable object in pious interchange. With these efforts grave-watchers of the sacred past calculate who Jesus is and must be, that is, the one who fits the religious concept or traditional program. The Johannine Christ reveals that the guardian of tradition makes himself judge of his Lord and protects himself from a new intervention of God. He no longer need fear any surprises from heaven, and on earth he defends the status quo of his convictions, thus in effect is totally inaccessible.

The Fourth Gospel unmasks such an understanding of revelation as the caricature of a discipleship to which the Creator summons to service from out of that which was, thus continually to hear the Word as if for the first time and to surrender everything in order to remain with Jesus alone. Here, piety is given radical definition as discipleship. All tradition has meaning and value only insofar as it points us to Christ, and Christians are recognized solely by the Lord, who rules them and holds them in his love. In this way, cautiously but unmistakably, theological *Sachkritik* (content-criticism) touches base with the world of religions and the variety of their theories and practices. "There is need of only one thing" reads the watchword, by which the Spirit protests being bracketed by ideological and metaphysical systems. The sole decisive question is, Who is Jesus, and What does he bring us and require of us? Even the Bible is to be measured by this, interpreted on this basis. It is not the letter of the Bible but the One who is proclaimed by it that makes it a divine address to us, the bearer of all promise, the measure of genuine piety. Let rebels and reformers take care lest the explosive power of its summons be smothered by what is merely edifying, lest organizational atrophy and manipulation allow the great theme of Scripture as gospel to be forgotten — that is, the exodus of the once imprisoned into the freedom of the children of God, and the presence of the rule of God over our life and earth.

Here I am tempted to glance briefly at the problematic of the generally unknown Letter to the Colossians. Debate with false doctrine required a basic explanation of the relation between gospel and worldview. On the whole, the New Testament picked the most varied ideological fragments from its environment of Hellenistic syncretism. We may leave open the question whether another attitude was at all possible. In any case, primitive Christianity did not feel obliged to connect a particular worldview with its message. It could, though less often, be open to the enlightenment of its time and thereby manifest evangelical freedom. But all indifference ends in a trice when adherence to the one Lord and insofar the purity of the faith is endangered. When the false teachers of Colossae divide the universe hierarchically, conceding to the demonic powers a middle sphere of heaven, and set the community within a restricted service to angels, they encounter stubborn resistance.

The reason is given in 1 Corinthians 8:5-6: "though there may be so-called gods in heaven or on earth," Christians have only "one God . . . and one Lord." Every worldview is rejected that renders problematic the disciple's exclusive relationship to the kingdom of Christ. The object of faith is not a comprehensive structural arrangement of the All, a cosmic harmony anticipated symbolically in the church and realized on earth. The gospel is to be sharply separated from religious ideologies and utopias, though Christianity always remains prey to the temptation of wanting to mix them. Just as the Lord of the community may not be subordinated to pious tradition, to where the power of the past gains shape and voice in him, so he is not merely the Mediator of a new world-project, say, of a humanity united in paradise once more, or of a form of society with claim to monopoly. In his service each must work for peace and reconciliation at all levels, and the changes in societal structures are no less under the obligation of mutual love than diaconal care. Yet Christ may not be expropriated by any earthly order as its representative, by any social and political program as its guarantee, by any cosmic model as means to its enforcement.

His disciples are aware of the reality and power of what superstition equips with divine honor. But they do not take part in religious glorification of the world and, for the sake of their Master, do not allow themselves to be ideologically trapped or to ruin ready access to all camps.

No one has set this forth better or given it foundation than Paul, for whom the distinction between gospel and piety is plainly the midpoint of theology. To this very day he is the point at which spirits, groups, schools, and confessions divide. The fact that his portrait in Jewish Christian circles could be fused with that of the arch-heretic Simon Magus gives evidence of the immoderate hatred that can emerge even in intra-ecclesiastical debate. Not only rigorous legalists have accused, slandered, and persecuted him, but also Christian fanatics who, by fascination with the evangelical message of freedom, have been thrown from the path of reason, from morality, and from concern for their fellows. In miracles they experience the inbreaking of the kingdom of God and see themselves obliged to erect signs of it everywhere. Arbitrariness and chaos follow imagined autonomy and recklessly usurped emancipation. Now the gospel has the interchangeable signature of syncretistic religiosity. Thus we already see early Christianity entangled in a two-front war. If the scrupulous and fault-finders limit the freedom of grace, robust enthusiasts alter the gifts received to personal privilege and reduce the living space of the weak. Both regard the divine truth as a possession they are to manage, which allows them to bludgeon one another and measure the neighbor's view and behavior by their own persuasion. Here it most clearly appears that piety obscures the shape and word of the Lord, whom it imagines it represents, that it can become a particular weapon in the general battle of life. Performance, proven through works, and demonstrations of one's own right and freedom hold the field, as if the Nazarene did not die exactly by this means, stigmatizing the apostle with the wounds of the Crucified as the sure signs of his legitimate mission.

The abiding bequest of Pauline theology to Christianity is its proof of the absurdity of the illusions of pious performers and enthusiasts by confronting both with the image of the Crucified. We may confidently state that the first commandment is inflected and sharpened. At Golgotha, along with the idols and demons, our imaginings about ourselves are driven out. Where the heathen and pious are involved in the murder of Jesus, humanity as such is unmasked and given reality, and only forgiving grace can have the last word. At the same time it is there that the true God is at work, who does not rule unchallenged in glory according to our metaphysics but descends to the suffering, the outcast, and the damned. The depths now become the dwelling of God and his elect, of the festival of the redemption broken in, in which Beatitudes no longer invite the high, wise, and pious but the lost children, all in need of love and mercy. This alone is the salvation of the gospel, which throughout the course of history was continually despised and slandered by the heathen precisely from out of their religiosity, and by Christian theology and piety unabatedly obscured and betrayed. Every generation stands before the alternative of the first commandment. And after Golgotha this means standing before the choice between gospel and religious ideology disguising itself as Christian.

The Fourth Beatitude (Matthew 5:6)

Psalm 24:3 reads, "Who shall ascend the hill of the Lord? And who shall stand in his holy place?" Such a question not only threads through the entire Bible but can be heard in all religions. In it is expressed the fear of appearing before the face of God, in his presence, where we hear his voice and conversely lay our petitions or thanks before him. Who is worthy to let himself be seen by God, to hear him speak and answer him? When is it dangerous to submit to this sight and speech? What must we do carefully to prepare for such an encounter, and what must we omit in order not to experience the Judge instead of the Helper?

When the Old Testament contains a profusion of rules for purification, when the New Testament speaks of the one who appears at the feast without the wedding garment or of the one not reconciled with the neighbor who appears at the altar or takes part in the Eucharist, the questions just posed become biblically graphic. The Beatitudes of the Sermon on the Mount also refer to them. In them what previously applied to worship is, as it were, transferred to all of life in the kingdom of God, a kingdom that, with Jesus, has seized hold of the earth and summons disciples to follow. Whoever has to do with this following stands forever, daily until death, under an opened heaven, in God's presence, seen and addressed by him, forever responsible to him.

Since this is and remains the Christian's condition on earth, our speech begins with a beatitude. "Blessed" means more than what we call "happy." We would best render it "blest." The thought is of the condition

---

A lecture given on May 26, 1981, at the Dietrich-Bonhoeffer-Haus, Bad Urach.

of salvation, in which we no longer need to anxiously hide but have an open heaven above and need no longer fear persons or powers. Such blessedness moves through all difficulties and distresses, even through the grave, into the open air, into peace, into a life without horror and tears. "Blest" is thus not merely a promise for the future, although that is certainly included here. It is rather a promise for the present and our everyday life. The clause that follows better expresses what is central than any circumlocution we attempt: "For theirs is the kingdom of heaven." In Judaism one avoids uttering God's sacred name and thus speaks rather of heaven. What is meant here is the rule of God. In saying this, I have also set forth what is at the heart of New Testament concern when it speaks of the kingdom of God. This kingdom is not an area without a ruler. On the contrary, people encounter it only insofar as a lord encounters them — the First, who created them and set them on their way, and the Last, who calls them before his judgment seat when all other lords and judges have nothing more to say. But when we speak of his kingdom, we assert that our God appoints not only individuals and souls to his grace and service.

Our Western theological tradition has been too long determined by individualism and spiritualism. In a time when we are clearly confronted with the worldwide intermingling of persons and things, when the ecumenical movement must be recognized and affirmed as the most important ecclesiastical event of the twentieth century, we recall that the Creator and Judge lays claim to the whole earth. We make him a private idol when we allow him to be occupied first of all or, worse, exclusively with us, our families and friends, our societies, our territorial or national church organizations. When we navel-gaze religiously, allowing God to orbit about ourselves, we rob him of his honor and fail to understand the gospel, according to which all are to be helped, and for which reason his messengers are sent into all the world. He comes to us because the earth belongs to him and he will erect anew his contested lordship over it. Among us personally his universal work of salvation becomes concrete; it is shown that he forgets and excludes no one, calls each one to himself, and can use each as his instrument. We are not the privileged but the examples of his worldwide activity.

From this it also follows that his lordship has more than our inward life in view, that it is not only a rule over souls and spirits. Whoever says "world" has the corporeal in view. For centuries Greek inheritance allowed the rule of our God to become an invisible thing, hidden in hearts and perhaps at home in the prayer closet, something that produces pious intentions and ideas and at best strengthens Sunday customs such as church-going or middle-class respectability and the consciousness of obligation to family and the workplace. Still, the One who created us from earth and promises the world of resurrection reaches for our heart and conscience in such a way that he takes our bodies into his service, wishes to be glorified, witnessed to, and recognized in everyday existence as our true Lord, and thus he sets us in conflict with the idols, in resistance to all superstition. The first commandment is the reflection of the Beatitudes. Whoever hears, "I am the Lord your God" already hears from the Old Covenant the "blessed are you" of the New. There is no difference between "your God" and "yours is the kingdom of heaven," except that all are promised what first was said only to Israel. The kingdom of heaven is the God who comes to us, gives himself to be ours, sets us in his kingdom — the God who in, with, and through us seizes hold of the earth that belongs to him and snatches it from the idols.

Till now we have paid no attention to the middle section of our beatitude, where its real surprise lurks. It is absolutely uncommon and, when we investigate the promise thoroughly, it may even be scandalous that "those who hunger and thirst for righteousness" should be blessed. Everywhere else, that one is happy who has something to exhibit of internal or external possessions. Those who hunger and thirst have nothing but lack; in yearning, they stretch out empty hands like beggars; or in complaint, like rebels who feel defrauded of their rights. When they are called "blessed" and set off from all others, they are not at all the little flock we might suppose. Those who hunger and thirst for righteousness on our earth today, who wail in despair, rebellion, and hate against their fate and accuse their oppressors, are not merely millions, but the vast majority of the world's population. And there are enough of them among us who are denied what is theirs, who thus need an advocate if they are not to sink down in misery and bitterness all their life.

But are we merely to observe them as the dispersed of the Third and Fourth Worlds, as it were, where untold millions never reach their teenage years, who daily hunger and experience earth as a hell, who are tortured by tyrants, exploiters, and demons of all sorts, especially from the greed and wantonness of the white race? The holocaust of the concentration camps goes on and on, and whole continents are nothing but places of extermination for defenseless creatures who fall prey to the fearful god Mammon. Unfortunately, in our country now, just as in the Third Reich, we dig in behind an indifference that closes eyes and ears to the wailing of the miserable, behind the presumptuous advantages with which we justify and defend our presumed privileges, and in a provincialism that grows between the walls of our churches and at our worship.

The word "repentance" seldom falls from our lips. When it does, we seldom have more in mind than having to give alms again to persons unknown. In this way too the rich man of the parable allowed the crumbs from his table to be thrown to poor Lazarus and the dogs at his door without looking one or the other in the eye or knowing who would snap up the bites. Such charity is not a sign of goodness but of contempt and some day will leave us condemned at the last judgment. More yet, it indicates that today, without knowing it, we are living in damnation. To the hell of the hungering, despairing, tortured, and murdered corresponds the hell of the self-satisfied, of those intent on increasing their own wealth, of the hardened of heart and head who wish to pay off their debt to their neighbor with alms. Repentance means to return from one's own program and ideology to where God sees us and asks, "Where are you, Adam? Where is your brother Abel? Where were you when I went to the cross naked, hungry, derided, and trapped? Do you really love me?" Where God asks these questions it is a part of repentance to see and hear our exploited neighbor, get to smell him like Lazarus lying in the grave with his stench. Luther began his famous Ninety-five Theses with the assertion that the entire life of the Christian must be repentance. If this is really so and if it does not mean a woebegone face but a return to God and thus also a turning to the neighbor, then in our land today and wherever the white race sets the tone, we are, as it were, surrounded by thick fog. Technologically, we penetrate to the Milky Way; militarily, we manage to spend billions of dollars yearly for defense of the Western Hemisphere. Blind and devoid of fantasy, we have lost sight of the reality of those who over all the earth cry for deliverance from hell, who hunger and thirst that righteousness will finally pay them a visit.

Perhaps now we better understand Jesus' unheard-of word: "*Blessed are those who hunger and thirst for righteousness.*" The cry of the damned of this world is heard and is answered, "yours is the kingdom of heaven!" God has opened himself to the abandoned. He descends to their hell, as we can see at Golgotha. He intends help for those who can no longer help themselves. If we want to give what this means its proper name, we must use the horrifying word — "revolution." This surpasses the summons of the class struggle, "Workers of the world, unite!" Not the possessors, the sated, those preoccupied with themselves or sufficient unto themselves are called blessed, but those excluded from good fortune, from the rules of the game of the mighty ones, those overlooked and defrauded of their human rights. They lie like skeletons in the streets of Calcutta, bombarded in El Salvador by cronies of the junta, penned up in slums in Buenos Aires and São Paolo, exploited by the multinational firms that own an abundance of German firms, sold by politicians of all parties, and photographed by tourists like wild animals. God is in solidarity with them because the citizens of the white continents and actually most Christians from the most varied churches are not.

At the World Conference on World Mission and Evangelism, held in Melbourne in 1980, under the general theme "Your Kingdom Come," the following watchword was not casually chosen: "The Gospel Belongs to the Poor." In Luke 1:51-53 Mary's Magnificat deliberately underscores this message: "He has shown strength with his arm; he has scattered the proud in the thoughts of their hearts. He has brought down the powerful from their thrones, and lifted up the lowly; he has filled the hungry with good things, and sent the rich away empty." Whoever does not know where this is written will describe it as a subversive password of communism. Yet it is in the Bible and describes the promise of the gospel as the mother of God experiences it. In Mary's footsteps Christians should be more revolutionary than they think possible or necessary if, with Jesus' mother, they want to witness to the gospel and be worthy of it. Let none say this is pious exuberance, not to be taken too seriously. Whoever really knows the Bible will hear this sound not only among prophets of the Old Testament and on many pages but also in the huge song of praise in the Revelation of John over Babylon finally fallen. Revelation 18:11ff. contains one of the most magnificent scenes of Holy Writ. Besides the kings of the earth, the merchants of the earth weep and mourn since no one buys their cargo anymore, wares that, even down to the bodies and souls they bartered, made Babylon rich and alluring. The seer of Revelation was thinking of the hub of the ancient world at Rome, where Christians of his time were martyred. Is it really nonevangelical to wish that the consume-and-throw-away society of the white race, the costs of which the rest of the earth must bear, may come to an end so that the oppressed and exploited may finally gain access to their own lives? Are we no longer to pray, "He has brought down the powerful from their thrones, and lifted up the lowly; he has . . . sent the rich away empty"? Has our God become the heavenly model of the earthly bourgeois, as at least so often happens in our churches?

It is a dangerous thing to deal with the Bible, and especially with the

Beatitudes. For by doing so, we learn that our egoism cannot reduce God's will and kingdom to a single denominator. Whoever hears "your God" discovers the One who unmasks the idol worship of even the pious when they shape heaven after their desire. Can other than the pious practice idol worship, and should the demons be more powerfully at work anywhere else than where God will establish his rule? When he drives them out — and what else would his rule be than the demonic driven out, than liberation from demonic compulsion? — then he is never active without them, and our earth and heart are always the battleground between them. The Beatitudes apply precisely to those who are condemned on earth, and those are cursed who make of it privileges for the sated, the clever, the mighty, and self-satisfied — in short, for themselves and their cronies. This is the sum of all the Beatitudes, that God has mercy on those who are forsaken and need him. To be merciful means, literally, to turn attention and love to the poor. Our God intercedes for the weak; he works with material other builders despise. He always works in such fashion that the lame walk, the deaf hear, the dumb begin to speak, hard hearts and heads learn to feel, and the dead waken to eternal life, all of which begins here, today, with us, when the kingdom of heaven comes to us. The misery of Christianity is that we scarcely sense that the kingdom of heaven has come to its members and that the demons have had to retreat from them.

Some may regard these statements as too radical and assign them to a Marxist or at least to socialist thought that trifles with social-revolutionary ideologies. So it will be good to emphasize that the evangelists necessarily assume an understanding that links salvation to the poor. This understanding is embedded in their still more radical view that God associates with sinners and dies for the sake of the godless. This is what distinguishes the gospel from all the usual varieties of religion. These varieties allow salvation to depend on human worth, on a person's pious works, good intentions, and devotional practices, by which one hopes to make oneself pleasing to God. But the gospel sees our reality determined by sin, which comes to light not merely in evil deeds and omitting to do good. Above all, sin is entrapment in a worldwide rebellion against God and consequently a worldwide brutality in our relations with our fellow humans. Biblically, sin is most profoundly taking one's destiny into one's own hands without awareness of one's need. Even our reason is determined by desires and anxieties, with the result that we orbit about ourselves and look at the earth only with rose-colored or dark glasses. At bottom we think that we can and must manage without God because he leaves us in the lurch when we need him. The human in sin is the one dependent on self, trusting only in one's power, or in despair abandoning self to solitariness. But whoever is in this condition can no longer have final and enduring trust in the neighbor, must always be afraid of being abandoned and of having to manage alone. This is not only unbelief toward the One who has created us and will lead and bless us. It is also superstition, since no mortal being manages self and life alone. For this reason, the Bible states in Jeremiah 17:5: "Thus says the Lord: Cursed are those who trust in mere mortals and make mere flesh their strength, whose hearts turn away from the Lord." Living in sin and living under the curse are identical.

On the other hand, the prayer that Jesus teaches us contains only petitions. Its conclusion is the response of the Jewish Christian community, which in worship audibly adds its "Yes" to the petitions. Jesus sees the person as needy, as one who must ask, continually ask, that God may come, that God's will and rule may hold sway, that each day one be given what is needed for life, that there be protection from temptation to obstinacy and despair, and from demonic attacks. After body and soul there must be the plea for help, for grace, for the faithfulness of God and neighbor. It is sin not to recognize it, not to realize it afresh every time, or to hand oneself over to solitariness. Only those are helped who know their lack and cry to God from out of their need. For this reason, Jesus comes to sinners. Not the well but the sick long for him. And for this reason he heals and drives out the demons, since salvation and healing belong together. The rule of God on earth does not pass by our corporeality without a trace. Where sin is conquered, the poor are not left in the lurch. Not the imagined world of the mighty, the clever and pious, but the real earth that for the majority of its inhabitants is a hell shall come together with the gospel. God seeks out the rebels who want to manage without him or who no longer expect anything from him. He does not leave those who can no longer help themselves in darkness and death's shadow. The gospel of forgiveness and reconciliation is of necessity a gospel for the poor, a gospel for real live persons and for the whole world.

Till now, to put it figuratively, we have ticked off the meaning of the three parts of the fourth beatitude. In conclusion, it might be appropriate to consider what consequences are to be drawn for us who are Christians and churches of the white race. Usually, we do this quite naturally, as though we were the first to be addressed here, and at times we do not at all reflect on how others in the world of color must hear and understand the beatitude. If we do happen to learn of it, say, at ecumenical conferences or through our student young people, who snatch up slogans of the Third World, we are often shocked, and as evidenced by the German churches and especially Lutheranism in our country, we are so taken aback that we keep our distance from the *oecumene* and suspect it of false doctrine or, worse yet, of supporting revolutionary practice. We have reason to worry about our reaction. It could be that the others hear better than we and that our long Western tradition surrounds us like walls that hinder looking out into the open. Education not merely delivers from ignorance but often enough leads us to imagining. The person who for any length of time has been subject to educators or become an educator knows that custom stupefies, that unlearning something unnecessary or false is much more difficult than learning anything in the first place. At times, the most important process in the life of the disciple of Jesus is to break out of the beaten paths of our forerunners, to critically question their solutions to common problems, and to blaze a trail through an ever-present wilderness.

For a good 1,800 years the Western church has insisted that it is mother and mistress of the devout and, quite naturally, all the more of the heathen. We may object ever so much to critical theology, but to its credit, it has not recognized this arrogant assertion. Christ is our only teacher, alongside whom no religious authority may keep company with him as mother. The wet-nurse milk extended to us in all the churches has not always been nourishing. The wisdom we drew from tradition has often hindered us from putting our own questions; it has made us dependent and even drug addicted. In the Fourth Gospel we hear that every disciple must hear the voice of the Master, that discipleship of the Nazarene is not tied to uniformity — quite the contrary, to no uniforms at all. In any case, to sum up what was just said, the warranted Christianity in which we exist today as Protestants and Catholics is not the consummation of the kingdom of God. To great extent it is a ghetto that shuts us off from the larger world, in which the voice of Jesus is drowned out by a host of schoolmasters, managers and bureaucrats. A weight-loss regimen in the spiritual sense would be wholesome for us, since for the most part we no longer know what it is really like to "hunger and thirst."

In my youth there were poor boxes for the benighted heathen. We threw small change in it to indicate our sympathy with those who presumably ran around naked and were cannibals. After two world wars we could have seen that the cannibals among the occidentals have engaged more ferociously in cannibalism than all the wild men could do in many centuries, and that in our greed for power and lust we are exceeding Adam and Eve after the fall in our nakedness. It is high time to give up the conceit that we were required to bring to others the blessings of our culture and civilization. Christianity, at least, ought to realize that the white race must learn from the illustration of the world of color what it actually is, what misery it has brought over the whole earth, an enterprise that involved both theology and mission. It may be that we can properly hear and understand all of Jesus' Beatitudes again only when we bravely go from the bunkers of meritocracy and affluence into the no-man's-land in which our Lord died, when we sense something of the earthly hell in which our brothers and sisters in the Third World are dying. No theological statement is correct and worth preserving that has not been tested in this hell. No Christianity has the least merit that is not on the way toward Golgotha with the Master. Every church and religious society deals in opiates if it does not point beyond its walls to discipleship of the Nazarene and the fellowship of his suffering ones, so that rather than fancied demigods, we finally become real people, people in need of mercy, forgiveness, love, and support, who need to be given food and drink. The kingdom of heaven is never where one no longer hungers and thirsts for righteousness, for genuine life.

From this point we would have to begin studying the Bible again and to suspect what pastors and teachers, bishops and professors have not told us from the Bible because it did not suit their tradition or lifestyle. We would then discover how domesticated discipleship has become in the course of 2,000 years. Is it acceptable that almost all politicians and economists, in any event our bureaucracy and police force, for the most part are in agreement with the familiar form of Christianity, praise it, decorate it, and actually help to finance it? But those who hunger and thirst for righteousness have never been handled with kid gloves, reckoned among high society, or taken to be the voice of healthy national feeling and the model of middle-class virtue. They are not treated in this way in El Salvador and Chile, in the Philippines, in Russia, and in a hundred other states. Where is the Nazarene truly present among us? We must learn to ask in this way, since, besides all else, we have forgotten that according to 1 John 3:8 Jesus came to destroy the works of the devil, something of which the Gospels everlastingly tell us, but that he also came to commission the disciples to carry on this work to the end of the world. As we said earlier, the Beatitudes are in force only where the demonic is driven out. Why is it that in our time we still hear people say they are saved but no longer take much note of demons cast out?

The answer may be that the devil does not exist and that demons were merely part of the accoutrement of the ancient worldview. I agree. But this does not yet solve the decisive problem. For we cannot well deny that, to the degree the devil and demons disappeared from our thought, possession — not, say, in Africa or Asia but in Europe and America — grew ever greater. The twentieth century could not have taken a worse turn than if a couple thousand devils had had free rein in it. Whoever pays billions of dollars for defense, though at the end of a war nothing but desert and corpses are to be defended, would really have to be called insane rather than bringing order to the world. Those who imagine that they and their heirs will earn more and work less each year fancy they are living in a land of milk and honey. When the Crucified invites to his table all who hear his word, but when Anglicans, Protestants, and Catholics often will have nothing to do with each other at that very spot, they make their Lord the head of a sect and themselves a religious party. When church leaders continually glorify patriotic idealism, though untold millions die of hunger and the equitable distribution of material goods is the most important problem of our time, they are simply schizophrenic, blind, and dumb. They have learned nothing from the social struggles of the nineteenth century. When groups take offense at Native American women speaking of the great Manitou at the Women's World Day of Prayer, they become ridiculous. When husband and wife work like robots in order to reconnoiter the ends of the earth on vacation but their children are left to themselves and afterward, unhindered, wage their private war against the restrictions of their elders, we are guilty of fostering criminality. If any word of the Bible expresses a valid truth today, it is 1 John 5:19: "We know . . . that the whole world lies under the power of the evil one." What is meant here is the condition of demonic possession. Salvation and demons cast out may seldom be visible. More seldom yet does reason, repeatedly vaunted and everywhere laid claim to, appear to be at work. If we have become more enlightened over against the ancient worldview, we have scarcely become more clever. The word about original sin is more realistic than all the slogans about the mature man or woman in a mature world, assuming that we understand it as the power that hands one over in a frenzy to the earth and to oneself, to the romantic superstition of self-acquired emancipation and to the brutality of the struggle for a place in the sun. Repentance is salutary and indispensable for everyone.

The fourth beatitude places us where repentance is possible, namely, a return to the Father, without whom the child cannot live, to the Other, without whom we experience no love. The fourth beatitude calls us to humaneness. This is more than any dreamed-of heaven and frees from the dance around the golden calf. God intends that we become human, toward him and our neighbor. Many make demigods of themselves but are in reality despisers, murderers, and torturers of their brothers and sisters. But Jesus became poor and blessed the poor first of all. He teaches that hungering and thirsting for righteousness has promise on earth and in heaven. He dares to speak the colossal word that those who hear and receive his word shall not only be blessed but satisfied. Who can believe this in sight of the misery of this world? Who among us really believes that on our hellish earth, possessed by demons, God's rule will seize a place and be extended? Who of us lives from such a promise? To live from it means to wager on it, to take a stand by one's own work, to let oneself be called to discipleship of the One who destroys the work of the devil and all evil powers wherever he comes. Luther insisted that God's kingdom must also come to us, his will must also be done among and through us. All talk of God's kingdom would otherwise be nothing but pious prattle. If that is true, then we belong on the side of those who hunger and thirst for righteousness, then we must learn from them of our reality and our task. No one has an open heaven above who does not, as at Pentecost, become open to the world around by God's Spirit. The Beatitudes do not allow for closed societies. They open hearts and heads to a service that transcends earthly boundaries, perceives the neighbor in the most distant place, and never concedes to tyrants the right to the earth, which belongs to God. They make ready to follow the Crucified on the way to the poor, themselves hungering for righteousness.

PART TWO

CHURCH CONFLICTS

What "To Believe" Means
in the Evangelical Sense

What can be said or expected on the subject of "faith" that is new, when in and outside Christianity tons of paper have already been written about it and a hundred thousand debates have been carried on over it? With faith it is the same as with love and life. Books and debates on the subject help little or not at all. Risking is involved. I speak intentionally of "risking." Because a love that is assumed or even actual too often comes to grief, we ought not to say right after the wedding, "Thank God they have each other." But the Bible brings together faith, life, and death, along with the struggle on earth between the Father of Jesus Christ and the idols. Those who would summon up or create courage for faith should not forget they are calling to the fellowship of a people of God that journeys from Egypt into the wilderness, into the discipleship of the One who lays his cross on those who are his. So we must always distinguish between true and false faith; the courage of life belongs to that of death. Finally, notice that we have immediately arrived at the heart of our theme rather than having danced around it. According to the Bible, false faith is also infectious, but when faith is genuine, it becomes a blessing for others far and near. When we believe, and according to how we believe, we are destined to be either a blessing or curse for the world around us. So a risk is in fact connected with it. But in that case we will speak of it as simply as possible so that none can later claim they did not realize that it had to do with them, their life, their risks and dangers. Drugs are in ample supply, but our concern is with the ultimate truth, our salvation.

A lecture given on June 3, 1980, at the Schloss Mansfeld, Eisleben.

1. *First of all, faith as a verb!* We must make it clear that "faith" first of all and primarily is used as an action word, though we frequently make it into a noun. I believe, we believe — or we do not. This way of speaking must remain in the foreground if we are not to lose the proper orientation. Of course, it is sometimes said, "it is believed," but observers should never have the first word here, nor the last. Those in question are asked about the sum of their experiences and encounters and what they have learned in converse with Scripture. Too many prattle on about something they have not seriously thought about or understood in depth. We cannot treat faith as though it were a commodity to be bought and sold. Each must engage in it personally in everyday life, by name, in one's own way, to live, to suffer, to die. It is never settled once and for all what "believing" means in the here and now, or what it may not mean, not even for those called to it. We can make a slogan of it with which to beat the other over the head. We can use it to point to a worldview, though it is really questionable whether the Christian faith indissolubly belongs to any particular traditional or current worldview.

Not even religious convictions and the dogmatic traditions of churches or their separate fellowships unequivocally and ultimately define true faith. Too many of them passionately fight with each other, and there are thousands of theologians who live from the persuasion that they represent the claim of their confession and the problematic character of all others, who extol their own understanding of the way of salvation. We are on shaky ground when we flatly, perhaps even uncritically and without criteria, speak of faith as an occasion fixed for every time and place. Not even the Bible always speaks of it in the same way. If that were so, there would be no New Testament alongside the Old, no James and Hebrews alongside Paul, no four Gospels and the Revelation of John. They may all make contact, share issues and intentions. But this is what must first be discovered, and the particularities of each must be emphasized. If every Tom, Dick, and Harry knows from the outset what "believing" means, they no longer need read the Bible and meditate on it in detail.

The watchword disseminated in the Roman Catholic Church, that is, "believe with the church," is likewise truly problematic. Many Protestants, of course, have adopted this watchword without reflecting on its locale or origin. It makes good sense if one were to accept what Christian faith defined as truth. In a certain respect, we are all dependent on it. But we must not forget that the truth is not an ecclesiastical product but the judge of all churchly proclamation and theology. It thus allows doctrinal tenets and convictions of every Christian community to be continually tested for their legitimacy and to be frequently corrected or even rejected. Finally, even in Rome many parties and tendencies are at odds. In any case, "to believe with the church" should never mean that one is in harmony with the authorities in power or with the partisans, that one ignores the many living and dead heretics, does not take dissidents seriously, or overlooks the ever-present pluriformity of human existence.

Faith is not a religious possession one could have firmly in hand. It can be obscured, precisely by those called to be its bearers and witnesses. It can likewise be lost when despair or pride subdues the heart. Reformation insight allows faith to be a gift to be received daily anew, to be preserved in fear and trembling by the humble, and by which the gracious God opens to us the sight of heaven and the community of his creatures. It is the case with faith as with love, which also does not fall to our share like booty but is dependent on the fact that another takes us into his arms. So here we must begin modestly and cautiously, with what is writ small, as it were, because it is not given into our power, but rather describes the way of discipleship prescribed for us. I believe as I stand in the discipleship of the Nazarene. We believe, since community is linked to believing, without others' being able to take from us our responsibility for ourselves or for taking our place on the redoubt we are to hold.

2. *Faith as hearing.* Does what was just said deny the certainty of faith? Individuals who can create no substitute for their own responsibility are seduced and threatened from all sides. How can they fend off temptation, resist on the evil day? Who protects them from straying off onto a false faith, protects them from their own presumption? They cannot do it themselves if Luther's explanation of the Third Article is true, that "I cannot by my own understanding or strength believe in Jesus Christ my Lord or come to him." The community I enjoy at the moment helps me, but just as often it regards me as immature or hauls me into a ghetto, fanaticizes or deadens me. Theologies, dogmas, and catechisms are too varied, now and again too old or academic for me to live from them alone and get clear direction. We must learn from our Reformation forebears that, for the believer on earth, there is no security at all. If they are not calcified, believers can never take flight to a supposedly invulnerable fortress and live from their convictions as if they were on pension. Still, the disciple of Jesus as believer is neither truly alone nor without support and refuge. There are paths on which much may happen to us and nonetheless lead to the goal. Not security but

certainty is promised to true faith. No life is secure. Conversely, no life would be of use that did not possess a confidence with which it could stride into the uncertainty of the future.

The all-decisive question reads, Where does the certainty come from for the one who believes in Christ as Lord? To this there is only one answer: From hearing the divine word made known in the Bible. It was said to each of us at baptism, "I have called you by your name. You are mine!" From the Christian viewpoint, "believing" quite simply and irreversibly means to rely on this word when it comes to blows, to throw everything else to the winds that is offered to us as salvation or threatened as damnation. So it reads in Scripture, at first glance oddly enough, that we are "begotten" by the word, as though we were its creatures. But if we know where we find life and how it is daily renewed, we have as much certainty as we need. A fool wants more — for example, that evil will never befall him, that the sun will always illumine his path, and that God will fulfill all his desires. We fall from true faith if we cannot say with Isaiah 50:4, "Morning by morning he wakens — wakens my ear to listen as those who are taught." This too, of course, like everything else important, has its problems.

The Bible has many sides. As already stated, its books contain very different material, all written by human hand and even, when led by God's Spirit, sketched and reflected on by the human spirit. In a book fallen from heaven, everything would be equally important and unalterable. But, for example, we no longer keep strictly to the laws attributed to Moses; other than Catholics, we do not regard some writings as canonical. We know that Luther regarded the Epistle of James in a most derogatory manner and, like Calvin, found the Revelation of John more or less useless. Even a conservative theologian like Adolf Schlatter regarded Second Peter as nongenuine. So each of us has his or her own Bible with certain words preferred and others never really noticed. What, then, is God's word? Where is the evidence that it shines forth from other words in the Bible? The Jews already asked this question and then, as Jesus does, pointed to the dual commandment of love. Church history teaches that the heart of Scripture is viewed in quite different ways. Yet from all sides, grace shown the sinner is described as the chief subject. This at least is worth paying attention to when we inquire about the gospel that produces Christian faith. When we do so, two things result that cannot be overlooked. What is stated here is, first of all, who our God is; second, who we ourselves truly are, in sharpest contrast to all our illusions.

By ourselves and seen from our world's point of view we are sinners, creatures in rebellion against their Lord. It will be otherwise with us only when and so long as we let God's promise stand over us and we thus become his children. Conversely, according to this message, God is from eternity to eternity a God for humans, can never be isolated from them, or be thought of by himself alone. This allows him to become man with and for us till death in Jesus Christ. Whoever thinks of God merely as the highest essence enthroned in heaven, as omnipotent, omniscient, needing nothing, without his face turned toward us or without the Nazarene, is a theological speculator. Just so, no one knows what finally matters in life and death for humanity and the world who does not know our own, as well as the earth's, sin. We continually forget both truths, and not without reason. In their inmost heart, religious people too want a god other than the One who humbles himself in Jesus and descends into the inferno. They likewise take offense at the fact that they are not merely weak and erring but, in their thinking, willing, and doing, are rebels against this true God, thus fallen in sin. Throughout all of life, Christian faith most profoundly has to do with allowing ourselves to be told and to learn to spell ever and anon who God is and who we really are. In this the event of baptism is repeated, the old Adam drowned that the new creature may rise with the Lord. In this way faith becomes and remains alive.

3. *Faith as discipleship.* Together with Luther, we must understand the first commandment as the sum of Scripture. All other words, pages, and books in it form, as it were, a commentary on it, and in the New Testament this summary is repeated Christologically, unequivocally defined and made concrete: "I am the Lord your God . . . you shall have no other gods before me!" So speaks the One who leads his people out from slavery, the Liberator of those elected by his grace, who leads them through the wilderness into the promised land. This command, which in essence is a promise, is taken up in the Beatitudes of the Nazarene, which likewise speak of the God of the enslaved and promise his salvation to the poor, suffering, and damned of the earth. God's lost creatures are sought wherever the common, everyday life of this world shows itself undisguised. The light shines in the darkness, and whoever awaits the eternal kingdom is called to discipleship of the Crucified. Humanity's need is so great that we must experience our deliverance from outside ourselves and this earth.

Here too the Creator and creature are contrasted in their distinctive characteristics — on the one hand, of mercy; on the other, of deepest need. There is the world of principalities and powers, and there are those who in body and soul go down to ruin in it, misused, excluded, and damned. But to them the Lord reveals himself, the Lord who remains true to his creature enslaved by tyrants and demons even down to the inferno, so that they learn, "Your God brings you out of Egypt." To them the call to freedom applies, "You shall have no other gods before me!" The "you shall not!" is enjoined so that we no longer doubt we need no other God. There is obviously a tinge of atheism here. As early as in the second century the heathen branded the Christians as atheists, and for good reason, since they rid the world of its gods. Wherever only the Father of Jesus Christ is and gives salvation, idols topple, ideologies are unmasked, all great earthly powers have only penultimate significance, and we are no longer handed over body and soul, hopeless, to anyone. We no longer need to kneel to idols in order to achieve something, to claim their protection. But neither do we need to despair any longer in face of danger, suffering, and death, as though we were dependent on our power alone. We can face all the realities of life without fear, willingly accept them. We are held and led by the One who does not let us slip from his hand. Nothing and no one besides the one God need impress us.

If this is the situation with those who have heard the gospel and trust in it, then Christian faith has to do not only with the soul or merely with our head. Nor does it rest on our exalted feelings, our ideological insights, or on an inherited or personally appropriated dogmatic. All this may be connected with it, but it may never become the chief thing. Whoever has rightly heard the first commandment and the gospel lives as a member of the wandering people of God in discipleship. This means that we stand or fall with our Lord, that in relation to him we understand the whole world, both in its demonic possession and in its despair, and we recognize it as the area to which Jesus Christ in the name of his Father lays claim and which in its heights and depths he sets under his consolation. When we learned to believe, we became betrothed to the Nazarene as one in love is promised to another. False teachers make of the Christian faith something more or less than a daily renewed discipleship in the worldwide service of Jesus. However pious they may be, whatever dogmatic knowledge they possess and seek to broaden, is totally insignificant where the call of the first commandment and the gospel to salvation are abbreviated and replaced by religious tradition. "Follow me!" is the single theme of faith from which everything else results, no matter when or where. This commandment, which, unlike other laws, does not call us to come under a harsh yoke but to eternal life, indicates where the one Lord separates himself from the idols, and where we fall from his grace into alien hands. Like Peter at Easter, each of us is asked, "Do you love me?" And before everything else, each of us must hear, "I have called you by your name; you are mine!" Naturally, there are Christians and theologians who think they know better than the God who is partial to humanity what is and what is not godly. Those who do not derive faith solely from this root and who do not orient it to such a question and promise reduce the Almighty to a tool where they may least do so. They split Christianity up, render it unfit for service, a plaything of earthly powers and a laughingstock among the heathen. Christian faith is encountered in only one shape: "This one was with Jesus of Nazareth."

4. *Faith and confession.* Faith can denote both discipleship and confession. Naturally, we must ask and answer how the two relate to each other. At this point, churches, confessions, and Christian communities most often divide. Many persons pretend to be disciples or actually believe they are in the discipleship of Jesus without such being the case. Many pages of Scripture, as well as of church history, give evidence of this. Jesus himself turned against those who say, "Lord, Lord" but do not do God's will. And the saying that is handed down of him reads, "Everyone who acknowledges me before others, the Son of Man also will acknowledge before the angels of God." As certainly as faith and confession belong together and may not be played off against each other, just as certainly a problematic emerges from this attachment that is difficult to remove. To see in Jesus a model and thus to justify middle-class, ascetic, revolutionary ideals does not yet make one a "confessor" in the evangelical sense. Other heroes could be found for those ideals.

Where there is confession, the uniqueness of the Nazarene is set forth that distances him from all others. This is not a radical rejection of an idealistic attitude. Churches too should not renounce fellowship with those who are able to see in Jesus merely a human prototype, a teacher of genuine godliness. Their Lord rejected none who came to him, and today it is more important to come to see him for oneself and to desire to follow him than to have a thick dogmatics in the head and measure the world by its articles. For over 1,500 years the greatest atrocities have been committed and legitimized in the name of orthodoxy. In our time we learned in our struggle with the Nazis that the allegedly so-called intact Lutheran churches compromised with the enemy but left the oppressed in the lurch. Because we cannot forget that, we have become more patient toward alleged or real heretics and grown more critical toward those who call themselves religious, so as to mark themselves off from others. The Jews once cried, "This is the temple of the Lord!" yet their Lord withdrew from their temple. According to the parable of the wheat and the tares, pure doctrine exists nowhere else but where superstition and idol worship are mingled with it in the Christian community. Views of bygone eras and a welter of theological interpretations are always connected with the inheritance of the forebears, so that today there is an endless number of churches and communities with divergent doctrinal traditions.

This last aspect greatly worsens the problem. Those who do not see beyond their church tower and live in a religiously closed rather than an ecumenically open community do not perceive what we must unavoidably encounter in the near future. The confessions of the white race will be basically revised and pruned by Africans, Asians, and Latin Americans because too much of Western thought is reflected in them and cannot simply be taken over and continued by Christians of color. All theology is the response of a limited epoch and religion to the evangelical message, not to be held to for all time by any and all. Our forebears' dispute over the proper understanding of the Lord's Supper may no longer fundamentally separate Lutherans and Reformed. Infant Baptism is not necessary for salvation to the point that Baptists should be judged by us. Leading Catholics accept the Reformation doctrine of justification. The fronts are continually changing. Christianity does not live from canned goods, especially not from such as are no longer edible and digestible. If our parents rightly described the church of Christ as *semper reformanda,* as always in need of renewal, we must see to it that the world and members of our community are not fed with dogmatic formulas become unintelligible or useless. Our God and the Holy Spirit cannot be caged behind pious tradition. In any event, the confessions of the fathers are our guideposts, not live wires to keep the cows in the pasture or block the curious from entering the holy place. Since earliest Christianity, stupidity, ecclesiastical tyranny, and party strife have misused the confessions, as if they could replace the living voice of the gospel, the voice of the God who speaks to us today. In that case, the past of the religious world is made the sphere for a faith that no longer journeys into God's unknown future and there awaits the open heaven above.

Confessing belongs to believing, because living persons have experiences. They do not hoard them, but, as their life's yield, give them for reflection to friend and foe and, above all, to their children's children. That

God has not left them without a witness should lead others to ask whether or not they too have experienced something similar and must confess it. If the church supports such confessions, it will lift them out of the individual sphere and value them as an expression of the gospel. This can never mean that the formulations and theology expressed in them are sacrosanct. What applies to one particular generation is not without value in the next. The parents' inheritance is important as a gift, as well as a task, for children and grandchildren. Still, the lines of demarcation change with the times. New situations give rise to new experiences. New insights require new confessions and witnesses of fellowship, as well as delimitation, so that within the varying circumstances, the Christian message of the present uncovers the way, the danger, and the goal of discipleship. In changing relationships and experiences, however, continuity of the one thing central to Christianity must be retained: Jesus of Nazareth may not become unrecognizable, nor a model among others. He must remain the Crucified, the One who was exalted as Lord because he humanizes the earth wherever he appears and allows his disciples to be bearers of love. Otherwise, our confessions would not correspond to a Christian faith that must always be defined by its Lord and exists in discipleship. But because this Lord is sent to all the world, his way will urge his own to confess their faith that it may be heard and understood in every nook and cranny and in every time, may be accepted as the experience of God's goodness and the earth's salvation, awaking new faith, in service to the gospel.

5. *Faith and love.* Christian faith flourishes only in community. But in this community, existing under the sign of the One who, as crucified, lays claim to earthly lordship, there are not only pious souls and spirits half raptured to heaven. For good reason in Romans 12:1 Paul describes surrender of the body as the God-pleasing sacrifice and the daily worship of a Christian community. Faith must be confessed *on earth*. For this reason, love is its sign, which means that it may not be flight from the world or navel-gazing. At precisely this point we must let go all that appears edifying and that so easily and frequently treats the theme of love. It is a totally unedifying thing to go with Abraham from his father's house and away from friends into God's unknown future, for forty long years, thus for an entire life, or to wander with Israel through the wilderness or, with Luke 12:37, to see the mark of the victor in the apron of the slave, which the World Judge will put on again as he did on earth. No dreamed-of goals are named here. If affluent German society were to consider the way of the disciple in this manner,

it would probably turn away from it in horror. But if society does not take all this seriously, it is clear that the church has not thought or wished to be serious about it, for fear of losing its "sympathizers" inside and outside its fellowship, and still allows the message of the Crucified to be drowned out by hymns of its glory or withholds comfort from those tested by suffering.

Such behavior is, of course, avenged. It blurs the reality of the world before our eyes and in our heads. How deaf, dumb, and blind must we be to forget for just one day the atom bombs, the industrial exploitation of nature, the political polarization, beginning with the superpowers and reaching to nations, parties, and families, to forget the brutal methodology of a worldwide class war of the haves against the have-nots? With our children and grandchildren in view — more yet, in view of the hungering, the murdered, the oppressed, and the dishonored in all lands — Christianity would have to maintain its faith by making itself the voice of conscience and reason, thus to honor the Creator and Redeemer of his creatures, and to set forth humanity's becoming human as the will of God's kingdom and the saving deed of Jesus Christ. In our time love cannot possibly mean merely personal aid among individuals and groups. It must intend to alter and break structures, systems, and ideologies that foster inhumanity. It must offer defiance everywhere to tyrants and demons in order to create a place for the freedom of the gospel and ward off idol worship.

Christian love as bodily surrender and daily worship confesses what it believes when it regards the earth as the field of its Lord, thus in its ideas and in its arms embraces those most distant, as well as the brother, sister, or neighbor at the door. Only a love that extends worldwide, that does not merely give alms, corresponds to an ecumenically open faith. This assumes, first, that middle-class morality and tradition no longer serve as criteria for Christian behavior and, second, that risk, whether personal or in the church, is not to be avoided in service to God's creation. Genuine love does not remain with itself. Faith points beyond itself and to all who have fallen among robbers and murderers. Genuine love ties the imagination of the Good Samaritan to the reason of those who recognize in the other God's gift and their own task. Religious schizophrenia threatens us more and more. It separates Sunday from the everyday life of a meritocracy in which the whole creation groans and the Christ still dies among revolutionaries. In the school of Jesus we reflect on the fact that he preferred self-denying surrender to remaining in heaven and went as crossbearer into the embattled no-man's-land between interest groups and ideologies. Whoever cannot get free of all the entrenchments as he did will deny faith and love. Love is an export, and the cross its distinguishing sign. Christian faith is unfruitful where it does not bear this sign.

6. *On unbelief and superstition.* Remarkably enough, the Bible does not recognize the attitude we today customarily call "unbelief." But to the extent it seems to be referred to, it denotes either disobedience or little faith, when, for example, we doubt a concrete promise of God or yield it no resolute trust. Yet, there is no fundamental reflection on the possibility of remaining neutral in religious matters, of professing disinterest in them, banishing them as part of an ideological worldview to the sphere of private opinion. It must be said once and for all that the Bible denies such a possibility. According to the Bible, the first commandment is a confrontation, and this means confrontation with an unavoidable alternative that excludes neutrality. One trusts, loves, hearkens, is a disciple — or one lives in disobedience, mistrust, and hate and is an enemy of the truth. Mere things and situations are of no concern. But the Creator, no more than one's fellow human being, is such a thing. What is basic is the view that every living thing is dependent on the other, is bound to the other. In reality there is no isolated creature, nothing that can be preserved by its own hand and direction. Those who insist on their own right will not need the continual help of others or God's salvation, will live as rebels from illusion and self-deception, will live a lie, as may be the case even among the godly and then occurs in particularly characteristic fashion as hardening and hypocrisy.

Just so, according to the New Testament, one cannot follow Jesus as one savior among many others, as mystics prefer to treat with several deities. As Jesus gives himself undivided, he requires that his servants be undivided. Religion is thus never a private affair, never a mere ideological possibility, but rather existence either in grace or in possession. To our way of thinking, the Bible does not recognize atheism, according to which one may choose a god like anything else or may assert that God does not exist. According to the Bible, everyone, consciously or unconsciously, willingly or unwillingly, has a god. Thus, the Large Catechism states that the one on whom we hang our heart, on whom we most deeply rely, is our god. Here, no creature is taken to be capable of refusing its heart to any and all, of trusting nothing and no one, though it may call itself nihilistic and may live or appear to manage quite well alone in protest against every existing thing, perhaps even against its own inadequacy. To put it audaciously, religiosity determines the profoundest depth of human nature and cannot be effaced in anyone, since, according to the Bible, what is human cannot be defined when God is put aside. Because we as creatures are indigent and dependent on many things, we will always give ourselves to something, sell ourselves to it in a devil's pact, if necessary, just as Faust, prototype of the modern person. Atheism so-called is a logical consequence of the human's radical will to independence, an Enlightenment theory. In real life only superstition opposes faith. It is superstition to deny standing under the sign of the image of the Creator and to view everything under the sign of the image made of oneself, to try to mold the self and the world around it after the perspective of the gods, demons, and ideologies we have sketched.

It will not do to call piety as such Christian. The servants of Baal are also pious. Jesus' opponents, the adversaries of the apostles and prophets, were pious. One is pious even when dancing around the golden calf. The conflict between mere piety and so-called unbelief is an ideological argument that may not be identified or fused with the struggle of the gospel against superstition. The gospel is betrayed even where resurrection of the dead is understood as life beyond the grave. Here a pious worldview becomes the central concern of faith, and it is hardly by chance that the resurrection is separated from the last judgment, of which the middle-class person, imagining he or she is mature, wants to know nothing. To preserve the conservative tradition of our forebears does not yet witness to the Holy Spirit, who each morning intends to appear and radically reshape both hearts and the earth. Middle-class morality and Western culture are defended when a fractious generation and foreign races are denied access to the kingdom of heaven from the bastions of a religious ideology, such as occurs far and wide in Western Christianity. A repentance that is offered daily and required even of church communities puts old habits to the test. Conversion always means departure to another life, toward a new future; it means openness for everything about to be. Stupidity at peace with itself and the familiar is the normal form in which superstition appears, and from which the gospel sets free.

This leads to a final insight. There is a radicalized superstition of which only the consciously and intentionally pious are capable. Jesus came into a world and there suffered the death of a criminal where there was no lack of piety. It was precisely the pious, in solidarity with the heathen, who blasphemed him. Against all church practice since Christian beginnings, the work of the Nazarene is not to make the unbelieving pious and the pious more pious. Jesus was no schoolmaster. He did not institute the church as a society for the nursing of religion and orthodoxy, though that appears so today. Everywhere in it there is a stench that is much too human and unholy; realists would have to declare such an undertaking shipwrecked. Superstition in its radicalized, religiously perverted shape allows God to be concerned with the pious, only with them, and in this way isolates him from the evil world. The result is that he ceases to be truly a lover of humankind, a Father of all his creatures, and a Savior of the godless. No longer are his will and the reality of his kingdom the humanizing of the human in midst of an inhuman world. Christians everlastingly need to conquer the religious superstition that God exists only for a pious elite and leaves all others in the lurch. If that were so, faith that lives from grace alone without any merit or worthiness would die. Its ecumenical freedom would be transformed into the narrow-mindedness and slowness of heart of pious egoists. Its service would no longer be like that of its Lord, who excluded none from his loving devotion. Free of illusions, faith lives in the real world, but it is precisely this world that it calls God's world.

The Reformation Heritage Today

We will proceed cautiously toward our theme today. In some respects, notwithstanding all the Luther jubilees, it appears to have become outdated. Not even the word "heritage" suits many. They want nothing more to do with tradition. This is especially true of youth who, swept along by an exploding technology, behave without restraint. It is also true of all types of the elderly who look back with shame or at least with distaste at their past. For us all, the time is past in which historical and national formation were obviously blended. As those who avoided the destruction of Sodom and Gomorrah, we prefer not to look back where an abyss is yawning. For this reason we should understand that others see in tradition chiefly darkening shadows thrown on our day by earlier, alien life, ensnaring us ghostlike in its antiquated yearnings, anxieties, and customs. Of course, we cannot overlook those who avidly seek to hold to everything traditional because what they produce gives them the feeling of gaining support in an unsteady time. They must dig themselves in somewhere and take shelter, even if it closes them off from sight of the wider world or of the neighbor. A history lost or misused is more markedly peculiar to us Germans than to others. Fatal connections become visible when we inquire into our heritage, in order to enliven the past.

The key term "Reformation," however, gives us difficulty and embarrassment. It means "renewal" — and, obviously, of Christianity. But 500 years lie behind what was so confidently given this name, and scholars are

---

A lecture given on November 11, 1977, in Schwäbisch Hall and on November 30, 1977, in Hospitalhof, Stuttgart.

not at all agreed whether it belonged to the modern period or still to the Middle Ages. What do we as Protestants generally know of this Reformation? Too often we celebrate what we scarcely know, or at bottom do not at all understand. What do we think of when we hear that the renewal of the church is supposed to have begun with a dispute over whether or not good and pious works are necessary for salvation? Can we still seriously or even passionately participate in such a dispute? No doubt, our earth today is urgently in need of good and pious works, and each of us is obliged to do them. A flood of inhumanity and barbarity is washing over our world, allowing us to see that the apocalyptic horror scene in Romans 1:18ff. of God's wrathful power on a perverted earth is true and realistic. Resistance, then, is required of every Christian if the church's message of love and freedom is not to become idle talk. But how does this square with the Reformation heritage?

We must put the question in this way when we consider that Protestants contest the authority of pope and bishops over the Christian community if that authority is exercised as privilege. And we must do so if we want the organizational form of Christianity governed according to utility, depending on the situation, and not according to inviolable law. Still, today, in our country, what is for the most part a conservative or in part unmistakably reactionary Christianity might prefer powerful leadership to the so-called priesthood of believers. This latter watchword, championed at the Kirchentag and in base communities, smacks of the postulate "democracy in the church." But does it not give rise to an unsalutary splitting of confessions and denominations, which even the heathen mock? Do we not all need the motherly protection of a firm institution that is superior to individuals and their circles?

Least hard to understand is the Reformation struggle over the meaning of the Bible. At the same time, it cannot be denied that the number of those who live with and out from this book has shrunk mightily. Perhaps we should put it pointedly. While many Catholic Christians and, astonishingly, many of the youth are rediscovering the Bible, their message, seen from the Protestant viewpoint, has remained alive almost exclusively within the pietistic sector. There, certainly, legalistic understanding and an abridging of substance for the sake of "edifying" statements lead less to confessional conflict than to theological debates with critical interpretation. Here, within Protestantism, the problem of the Reformation heritage is at least as acute as in the ecumenical sphere, where it grows underground. Put figuratively, the explosive power of the gospel is felt more in other continents than in the realm of the white race, which to considerable extent sees in Holy Scripture only a support for its ideology and morality, and which has neglected genuine "Reformation" concern.

These last sentences already point to the worldwide shifts that are often not perceived here at home, not even by active Christians, and are often not grasped in their scope. Where they are not sufficiently noted, they obstruct access to our Protestant heritage, with the result that it is bound to be problematic or unintelligible as never before. It is necessary to recall that with us the link to Reformation tradition was for centuries most intimately connected with nationalism and patriarchal order. What is being avenged on the children now is their ancestors' failure to make any clear differentiation between what was Christian and what was nationalistic, between the gospel and humanistic idealism. For this reason, the admiration of heroic men, emancipation from traditional conventions of a religious and secular nature, the gaining of a German national language, and the consolidation of the middle class into wide layers of society could be the most important achievements of the Reformation.

It is not surprising that, after the collapse in the political arena, everything closely tied to the national idea lost its fascination. Long prepared for, a confessional heritage in a variety of Christian theologies emerged from that of the Reformation. In Anglo-Saxon lands knowledge and understanding, for example, of German Lutheranism is more an exception than a rule, to say nothing of the Orthodox churches. In our own house the same development can be seen. While in my youth the revival movement at least retained a modicum of Reformation insight, in the meantime German pietism has been caught in the undertow of an international fundamentalism that, despite protests to the contrary, is more concerned with the inerrancy of the entire Bible than with its center. If everything between the covers of the book is equally important, then the confessional tie is loosened, since each individual and even the tiniest fellowship must seek its own key to the exposition of the whole. In so doing, it falls prey to the magic of boldprint passages of a largely edifying sort, to an ideology extruding from the margin, to an institutionally recognized morality, or to time-bound regulations. Whatever can be proved from the Bible can now be made its midpoint, as is actually reflected in theological literature and all the more legible in the plethora of churches calling themselves Christian, in the welter of religious movements and groups cordoning themselves off from the world around.

From there we must recognize the problem posed to us by the

oecumene. On the one hand, in a world easily traversed through communication, solely as an ecumenical federation Christianity will no doubt resist the onrush of secular and religious forces and comply with the mission of its Lord. Theological reflection and church practice, which should always be looking ahead, ought to open themselves widely and decisively to this federation. We may no longer simply creep off into the shadows of our own church towers, into the safety of the like-minded, making our own history, the rules of the game of our tradition, or the peculiarities of our piety obligatory for others. A generation unwilling and unable to leave its father's house and kin with Abraham no longer follows the Nazarene on his wandering. It gorges itself and lets others starve, as happens only too often today in the countries of the white world, rendering us untrustworthy as Christians.

On the other hand, we may not ignore the fact that we cannot stand up for solidarity among the churches risk-free. It was not by chance that the Reformation led to what is frequently called the Western Schism.[1] It is characteristic of Protestantism that truth and purity of doctrine may not be sacrificed for external unity. The desire for ecumenicity is legitimized, but it is also limited by the gospel. In this respect also, we have put ourselves at considerable remove from the beginnings. Too often, academically trained theologians no longer know how to make themselves intelligible to the so-called laity. Perhaps they themselves have not rightly grasped the matter entrusted to them and must conceal it through sorties into the fields of psychology, sociology, and politics. The Reformation intended to stand or fall by stating loud and clear what is evangelical and what is not. In its wake, we can never omit doing that. Nor can we do so within the ecumenical movement, whatever else will be sacrificed for Christian unity. At issue here is not merely a theological doctrine or a particular confessional concern but whether and how we remain disciples of Jesus. On this everything else, and even church solidarity, finds its measure. By setting this forth as the chief thing, interpreting it ever anew, giving it precise definition, countering misunderstanding and false teaching, we as a confession make our specific contribution to the *oecumene*, both positively and critically. Our Reformation heritage can and must be both,

---

1. The reference is to the division between Roman Catholics and Protestants, beginning with the sixteenth-century Reformers, leading to the Counterreformation and to the "wars of faith," which ended with the Peace of Westphalia in 1648, a division that exists to the present day.

since genuine solidarity is never agreement with the other across the board, but it always places us critically alongside the other, drawing the other into the serious dialogue to be carried on in exactly the same way with ourselves and our friends. Fellowship, like life, must continually begin anew, an impossibility without mutual critical conversation. We are not at the goal but are still on the way. The *oecumene* has a future only if we do not avoid substantive debate. Well-intentioned attempts at papering over differences hinder rather than preserve solidarity, for the broader the union, the greater the number of differences.

In this sense the question as to what is and what is not evangelical is a genuine and never ultimately decided question on the personal and confessional, and all the more on the ecumenical, level. To speak of the Reformation heritage means to reflect on how we view this question and to enunciate it as precisely as possible for the present. If that is so, should we not begin with Luther's words from "A Mighty Fortress": "Das Wort sie sollen lassen stahn und kein(en) Dank dazu haben. Er ist bei uns wohl auf dem Plan mit seinem Geist und Gaben"? (The Word they shall allow to stand and have no thanks at all for it. He's surely near us on the scene with his Spirit and his gifts.) This was the beginning and foundation of the Reformation and the object of its intra-churchly strife. Toward this end the spirits are to be tested from the evangelical perspective. In Christianity as well there are many theologians, congregations, and societies that do not begin with the word but with their own ideas, programs, and utopias that continue and end with their good works instead of allowing Christ to do his work, entrusting themselves to his Spirit and further handing on his gifts. The foundation of all Christianity, the inviolable gospel, is that God has spoken to us, called us by name, and blessed us with his Spirit and gifts. It is also the limit to heresy and ideology of every stripe. Unbelief and superstition will not and cannot hear that God's people and the discipleship of the Nazarene remain what they should be only as *creatura verbi*, to speak with the Reformers — in other words, as created and held by the word.

Sometimes, for very pious reasons and intentions, they take the world's salvation, just as they take their destiny, into their own hands. Fanatics have the Spirit, which allows them to act from within themselves and thus hearken to their inner experience — say, to the voice of their blood, their race, the soil under their feet, or the stars over their heads. We have learned where this leads, and wherever we look, we witness the madness of a world possessed by yearnings and anxieties, near or far. We can just as well rely on the voice of our forebears respecting their worldview, morality, and conventions. In the church, for example, we can rely on their dogmatics or on the ideals of their conduct of life. If we do so, the past shapes us, and our concentration on it bars the ways, the possibilities, or the necessities of the future. This can be seen all around us, in that belief in progress that whips our technology forward, leaving it intent on a security that never existed on earth for humans or nations. Behind the alleged realism that politicians, economists, scientists, and, unfortunately, even church leaders imagine they represent, there is only too often hidden the romantic illusion of the nineteenth century, with its dream of self-realization, of a balanced social order, of a world most profoundly whole. It did not sense, would not see the impending catastrophes of our time.

Pardon this retrospective. This is the background for what is certainly the most scandalous thesis: that none of us should give up on the Bible, that we cannot do without it if we would hear the voice of the true God. As a book written by men that, in its writings, reflects the situation of many generations, it has a thoroughly earthly history that deserves critical research. A cloud of witnesses, as it were, has learned through the millennia that from it speaks the One who created us and who retrieves his lost children, frees us from our entanglements and the violence of tyrants and constraints. Where heaven remains mute and leaden above us, the earth becomes the place of despair, a playground of powers at war with each other and enslaving us. Where God speaks to us and appears among us in the Nazarene, earth does not cease to be an inferno, but we receive the promise and commission to be instruments of freedom. For this very reason we speak of the gospel in the Bible, of the Holy Spirit, who makes himself known from it and under an open heaven, sets us in a world no longer closed off, effects the humanizing of the human among and through us. Both belong together: Where God in his gospel steps out of his hiddenness and sets us before his face, as we perceive it in the Nazarene, there we also come to ourselves. The meaning of life is not fathomed from out of us but is promised to us from the outside. As Adam and Eve once were, we are called by name. This means that we are, as it were, "defined," no longer an enigma to ourselves and others. We are directed toward a firm place to stand, to a way to be taken, and to a clear goal. Distinctive gifts are given us for service. There, where we stand and where we go we are irreplaceable, not arbitrarily interchangeable, not puppets whose dance is directed backstage. When it calls us by name, God's word creates persons who are free. It is then that no one else has the right to command us. The people delivered out of Egypt confess only one Lord and resist all earth's idols.

As this example indicates, the "called" are always those "called out." To make it clearer by way of a Latin term, they are "provoked," addressed from outside themselves, drawn into continuing dialogue with their Lord, so that as hearers they become speakers, responders, entering the sphere of his freedom. This not only relates to the prayer closet. The one to whom God has turned his face becomes open to the neighbor and the stranger. It is a sign of immaturity or decay of soul, thus of God's word no longer heard, when the ability to speak with others, to be there for them in hearing and acting, is stunted or dies out. Humaneness is the mark of those in whom the Creator breathed his breath, so that they became human. Otherwise, we fall into a solitariness that precedes the many shapes of madness. The way to barbarism is made especially clear when, in our area of the civilized world, simple speech is overgrown with the brambles of slogans, the argot of the various professions and age-groups, with a manipulative propaganda in the technical, economic, and political fields. Then we flee from one another and perhaps from ourselves into the confusing tangle of things, schemes, and patterns, into the spectral world of masks and caricatures. In that world everything becomes more complicated except for us, who become more primitive. Everywhere functionaries and robots control existence. It cannot be otherwise. For where God no longer speaks to us, the demons rule, possession is spread and in unnumbered varieties. Without his voice we also lose our place on earth; we lose support and refuge and can stand up less and less in thanks and responsibility for what is eternal and what is temporal. The Reformation heritage says to us first of all that we receive and retain our humanity from and beneath God's word, or, Christianly translated, that we exist as an open church instead of as a ghetto or religious sect.

Discovering God and discovering what is human — it is of this that the history of religion tells in all its texts, pictures, and monuments. In its own way, philosophical tradition also does so when it inquires after the Supreme Being or Ultimate Value, after the unity of the world, the truth of history, or the ideal person. This takes place even when God is expressly denied, and our own responsibility — say, in the conquest of societal, national, racial barriers, and privileges — appears to be the meaning of life. Our Reformation heritage does not allow us superficially and abstractly to distinguish friend from foe according to whether the person calls himself or herself religious or atheistic. The human heart is enigmatic, perhaps most hidden from ourselves. In it faith and unbelief are mixed in peculiar fashion. Ideological slogans and contrasts, in any case mere pipe dreams, are not suited as criteria for theology. Luther's definition in the Large Catechism still has validity: "A 'god' is the term for that to which we look for all good and in which we are to find refuge in all need. Therefore, to have a god is nothing else than to trust and believe in that one with your whole heart. . . . Anything on which your heart relies and depends, I say, that is really your God." Perhaps only a few have really nothing on which to depend or to rely. The heart is not yet atheistic, though the head may be. To put it biblically, those in total despair, who regard life as absurd, may still be crying after the unknown God. Conversely, it is true and no less important, though seldom reflected on, that what we call piety does not necessarily reveal anything about one's condition in the face of the true God. The harshest dispute never occurred between alleged atheists and supposedly religious people, but between those who wanted to be religious and those who did not allow others to be so. The Old and New Testaments refer to this when they position us within the dispute between Yahweh and Baal, Christ and anti-Christ, true and false prophets, gospel and law, faith and superstition. God's people are always and at the same time the battleground of demons. For this reason, the entire Bible is a commentary on the first commandment: "I am the Lord your God . . . you shall have no other gods before me!" Even idols have their servants. One cannot simply say, as in Nazi times, that one believes in God. It is necessary to be precise about who our God is.

The Luther hymn gives the answer: "Fragst du, wer der ist? Er heißt Jesus Christ, der Herr Zebaoth, und ist kein anderer Gott. Das Feld muss er behalten." (You ask who this may be? He is called Jesus Christ, Lord of Sabaoth, and there is no other God. He must hold the field.) Christians are no longer permitted to speak of God without keeping the Man from Nazareth in view. Of him it is said, "There is salvation in no one else." The Gospel of John calls him the Word made flesh, God's sole exegete, thus his interpreter. The Reformation takes this up with its "Christ alone." This is not, as often supposed, devotional but polemical — more exactly, anti-speculative. To be evangelical means not to concern oneself with a God fabricated according to our needs, a representative of conservative, liberal, or revolutionary ideas and systems. Our worldviews, ideologies, and action programs are not the place of the true God, as scandalous as this may be in the concrete instance, even for Christians. The passion narrative demonstrates in radically demythologizing fashion that the strong, the wise, and the pious are irritated over such a message, can see in the Crucified only the one condemned. They often do so in the name of humanity.

Not by chance did the lustrous deities of Greece stand opposed to the One of whom the prophet said, "He had no form or majesty that we should look at him, nothing in his appearance that we should desire him. He was despised and rejected." This applies not only to the time of his earthly humiliation, overcome since Easter. According to Philippians 2:9, the obedient One is exalted. He would not be recognized and identified as risen Lord if he did not retain the marks of the cross. So the Revelation of John describes the judgment on his enemies: "Every eye will see him, even those who pierced him." Under this sign he is Lord and "Forerunner" of his disciples. Because of this sign he is blasphemed till this very day and in the same tune: "If you are the Son of God, come down from the cross!" Before they come to him, people have their fixed ideas about God, which do not allow the Nazarene to avoid their judgment, so that even apostles murmur. They also express a faith, one that lays bare their desires and anxieties, seeks meaningful life only among the mighty, plunges them into presumption and despair. This faith must come into conflict with the Christ who did not remain in heaven as an area beyond human need, as a condition of serene calm, but who descended to the depths of the distressed, the forsaken, those surrendered in body and soul to all the cosmic powers. His light, as promised in the Old Testament, lightens the darkness.

The gallows of Golgotha prove that God gives himself into our hands, not to make us supermen, but to let us find our salvation and that of the whole world in his mercy. The confession is revolutionary: "Jesu Christ, der Herr Zebaoth, und ist kein anderer Gott" (Jesus Christ, the Lord of Sabaoth, and there is no other God). With such a message even on earth a transvaluation of all values takes hold, and even believers must fear. They are called to discipleship of the Nazarene in order to be conformed to their Lord in mercy toward all creatures. They must learn that they are the likeness of God only as those who serve, who shoulder the cross with the Nazarene and descend into the inferno of this earth, free in love for the neighbor as well as the stranger, stigmatized by battle and suffering for the sake of the better righteousness, the truer humanity. Our God intends that in this world his people will not become more godly but more human, as he himself became. For this reason the Crucified is our Lord.

Just this was involved in the Reformation. The theology of the cross was set against the theology of human and churchly glory. Not by chance the first of Luther's Ninety-five Theses reads: "Our Lord and Master Jesus Christ, when he said 'repent,' willed that the whole life of believers should be repentance." As in the parable of the prodigal son and in the Old Testament, repentance denotes change, a return to the One from whom we have fallen away. For Luther everything depends on its occurring daily. But then the summons is not only to sinners but to all who would be devout, even to church fellowships — something hierarchies and bureaucrats do not want to hear at all and seldom practice. Rudolf Bultmann modernized this with his "demythologizing" formula, but at the same time he restricted it. He wanted to be a "translator" in the strict sense of the term, that is, beyond the flux of time to convey the gospel from its earlier shore to the present day. This is no doubt necessary and the task of all preachers and teachers, but it must be radicalized. For no one can hear the gospel without being summoned to the reality of earth from illusions about oneself, the world and especially God. Demythologizing must proceed to "de-demonizing." The God who was abased also topples the alleged enlightened person, who, for all the tools of his science and technology, still hungers for omnipotence. This God topples him from the throne of his arrogance and, contrariwise, proclaims to the victims of earthly constraints and possession the freedom to become something to the praise of his glory. He returns us to the place where we are nothing but creatures of his power and grace. Repentance means to allow oneself to be called daily to such a state and to preserve it in our everyday life. We must not lay hold of and defend our good fortune or whatever we take it to be on our own. The Father gives his children what they need as sufficient in joy and suffering. Our name need not appear over our house and, so as not to be forgotten, over our gravestone. The Lord knows his own and, for time and eternity, sets the seal of his faithfulness over all that belongs to him. It is not our image that is to disclose the traces of our path. He will mold us after the image of his Son, which bears the inscription "Humanity, Kinship."

This said, we arrive at the last point, a point never to be forgotten when discussing the theme "Reformation Heritage Today" — and that is, the priesthood of all believers. This bears most concretely on our church relationships. True, the little closet in which we meditate and pray belongs to Christian life, which would otherwise no longer concentrate on the one thing needful. Still, according to Scripture, everyone who has been baptized has at the same time been given Christ's Spirit, in a special way been made a member of the community sent by its Lord into all the lengths and depths of the world to carry on the salvation received from him. In the Body of Christ of which Paul speaks, there are no passive members, none can be regarded as pensioner no longer needing to work, none can be regarded as unable and thus superfluous or replaceable. God gives his Spirit so that his servants get in motion in a bodily and earthly way, not merely staring after their exalted Lord as did the first disciples on Ascension Day. They are now his deputies, each in place, with gifts and in weakness, but called out from the isolation of a private existence living only for itself, self-sustained and distanced from others. As Christ is our representative before his Father and ours, all we who bear his name and follow him are called to represent him. Whoever would bury his talent as did the unfaithful steward becomes unfruitful and lacking in imagination, has only empty hands to show his neighbor, becomes blind to the Lazarus before his door and deaf to the groaning of a creation crying for help and freedom worldwide.

Today, in a period of ecumenical movement toward solidarity, Christianity may no longer be viewed under the aspect of a hierarchical order and even less as a bureaucracy by virtue of its functionaries and administrative tasks. The times are finally past when church officials could be distinguished from the so-called laity in any fundamental way or *jure divino*, by divine right. There have always been fanatics who separated themselves and their conventicles from the rest of the community, who proclaimed emancipation in the name of Christ and arrogated to themselves privileges that degraded their brothers and sisters. It was expedient and it stood the test when a community order took care that the church did not become a playground of arbitrariness. When creating, God made nothing totally like the other. In the Body of Christ we would only be bored if everyone had the same capacities or had to do the same thing. Christ intends to penetrate every corner of earth. He can do so only if his disciples are sufficiently different, so that in representing the entire community, they too may penetrate these corners, thus creating a hearing for the gospel and a space for love. God does not will the uniformity of his people. Still less does he intend that there be classes cut off from each other, with various grades and prerogatives among his people. Just as he sends out each of the baptized, endowed with the Spirit and with everything needed for the given task, so each in his or her place is officeholder of the Lord, to be respected by all others as such. Conversely, together with him all are "laity," a term denoting members of the people of God, not a lower grade but a distinction and obligation.

Finally in Protestantism, which — unfortunately with many of its theologians, on principle, and, with most of its administrators, in actual practice — leers hungrily at hierarchical order, we should recognize that the so-called laity and base communities recently recruited from them have become the churches' most significant pioneers. From the evangelical perspective what we usually call "office" is legitimate only when it furthers and preserves but does not limit the freedom of the children of God. This applies to our relationships. It is decisive when we view the future of Christianity ecumenically through congregations that are not shaped after the model of the white race or Western history. With John the Baptist, we must learn to decrease so that the Christ may increase worldwide, and we must entrust his kingdom to the people of color. On the whole, without making a flat judgment, this development is more hindered than helped by representatives of the white race. At issue is the assigning of authority to the gospel alone, thus everywhere dismantling privileges that are inadmissible, at least at the foot of the Crucified.

The key-word "universal priesthood of believers," however, assumes that we do not separate service to the gospel from the social diaconate, as foolishly occurs in German church societies. Those who are tied to the bureaucracy, and evidently cannot do without shelves and drawers, have hung out shingles advertising vertical and horizontal service. From the viewpoint of the Reformation heritage, we can only be ashamed of this sectarian theology. The Sermon on the Mount indicates that we may not isolate the Creator from his creature. The fact that we serve God is serious and true only where we are open and in readiness for our fellow humans. Whoever creates a separation here becomes schizophrenic, and God no longer remains the Father of the One who became man and descended into the earthly inferno for the sake of his brothers and sisters. He does not remain so when we relativize our ecumenical responsibility, allow our own edification to be the decisive thing and are ready to sweep only before our own door. Today and in an affluent society the call to repentance must let us see mirrored the conditions of the Third World, so that we get eyes and measures for our pious egotism, for the hypocrisy of capitalistically infected churches, for our participation in exploitation of the earth and non-Western peoples. The priesthood of all believers assumes a gospel that is lived, in which there is healing of the body alongside sanctification, a gospel in which mission to all the world is not misconstrued as mission to the old world, and in which, based on the justification of the godless, we strive for righteousness and justice of a new heaven and earth. Meanwhile, pagans actually think that Christians have to do primarily with the soul's salvation, with the beyond, and with middle-class morality and preservation of social order because we have taken this to be uppermost, have preached and lived it. It is time for the message of the resurrection of the dead as the act and will of our God to determine our activity and, by disruption, to break through the contentedness of the haves and the edifying empty promises to the suffering. The resurrection of the dead reverses what applies and obtains on earth. It revolutionizes our thinking and the conditions around us. Christians must rid themselves worldwide from the encirclement of a power-hungry and murderous meritocracy that serves Mammon alone.

Let me just allude to one last thing: The priesthood of all believers does not revolve about pious works, by which we strive for God's recognition of our self-sanctification. It is rather expressed in godly labors, by which, as representatives of our Lord on earth, we celebrate kinship with the least and are in solidarity with those who cry after the freedom of the children of God. Faith calls to love, not for cronies, but for the outcast, for those despairing of God and the world. Only then is faith valid, only then do rank and privilege no longer play a role in the church. Only then has every disciple a share in the mission of the Lord, in his authority and his cross. Today the Reformation heritage should set us in the discipleship of the Nazarene. It should allow us to hear and accept the word of the gospel, shape us after the likeness of the humiliated and Crucified as the true and only image of God, and make us members of Christ's Body, priests of the One who claims not merely our souls, and not merely the pious, but the whole world. In this way he also lays claim to the unworthy, the godless and the lost, as his children, and with them establishes his kingdom on this earth. The inheritance is not yet spent. We are asked whether we will receive it.

The Righteousness of God
in an Unrighteous World

Two preliminary remarks may make clear my present concern. The antithesis in my theme does not intend a theodicy, a defense of God's existence and world rule in view of an abundance of earthly injustice. "Righteousness" in my context does not, as in Greek, denote the action of a higher court in settling grievances among contending parties. According to the Bible, righteousness is the saving action of the Creator toward his creature in which he retains his right to a fallen world and, by doing so, transfers us to the place that befits him and the earth, sets us in the "right" that is our due.

Second, I will not speak primarily of the justification of the Christian, though this belongs inseparably to God's righteousness. In justification the divine righteousness is actualized, proves to be true toward the creature and as such "righteous." On the other hand, in the New Testament the two ideas do not simply coincide. "Justification" is often closely connected with baptism. It is an end-time event with God's righteousness as foundation and goal. A cosmic dimension adheres to the event, but it occurs in the context of struggle with rebels. It separates God's people and all its members from the servants of unrighteousness fallen prey to the powers of this eon. There is no reference to a justification of the world as a whole. We should be wary of such exuberance, at times expressed in the church's hymnody. Otherwise, we lose real ground beneath our feet and end in speculation and ideology. Both things are true: God rules over his enemies

---

A lecture given on May 17, 1983, to the Catholic Student Organization at the University of Bamberg.

and thus justifies the godless. But on earth he has not yet finally conquered. If that were so, we would have no problem. God's righteousness is contentious and contested.

In what follows I have as little as possible to do with specific questions of the academic guild. I will not avoid exegetical and systematic statements, but where they are discussed, it shall be to serve actual practice, which, incidentally, applies to all theology. So then, only crucial points will be noted on which a conversation can turn. Precisely put, God's righteousness is referred to first as the relation of God who remains true to his covenant with all creation, second, as the victory over possession, and third as the foundation for discipleship of the Crucified. The fact that we live in an unjust world would have to be clear to anyone who does not dreamily miss the reality of our earth. Whoever does not take note of the experiences of daily existence is in any case not authorized to discourse on the problem of the divine righteousness. All biblical promises have meaning only when the discipleship of Jesus is lived in attack and resistance to the demonic forces pressing in upon us. Now to the theme itself!

1. *God's righteousness as his faithfulness to the covenant with all creation.* We cannot avoid pointing to a few of the results from the scientific debate underlying what will be stated below. Of course, there is never consensus among exegetes without contradiction and readiness for later correction. For all that, occasionally something appears airtight. So it is everywhere recognized that in the Bible righteousness assumes a relation between partners obliged to mutual faithfulness. In Greece, at least of the classical period, the term has another meaning. There Dikē appears as an impartial judge in a heavenly sanctioned ordering of justice over the behavior of gods and humans. Furthermore, at the core of the Bible the divine righteousness is not the special instance of a more comprehensive justice to which God is also subject. Just as in similar genitive constructions that speak of God's power, love, grace, wrath, and truth, the emphasis is on the genitive. For this reason there is no thought of an attribute detachable from God or only partially defining his nature. God is in action wherever such predicates are assigned him. He is such from varied perspectives, but always in his total Godhead and personally. He thus manifests himself to be Creator and Judge, thus always as a God in relation to the world and humans. Wherever he makes himself known, we do not merely get metaphysical insights about him and us. What we rather encounter is the ultimate splendor of salvation or ruin. Thus, even where partnership with us is ex-

pressly accented, the motif of lordship is always in play. This One intervenes in our life who has established it, lays claim to it, takes it into his service. Justification thus means that he sets us in his right.

This being the case, it is first of all incomprehensible why God's righteousness is described primarily as creating salvation and not in parallel as meting out justice. The answer lies in the basic conception of the Old Testament: that God is Israel's covenant partner and remains such even when punitive. His righteousness is expressed precisely in the fact that he keeps covenant with his people, continually enforces it, and correspondingly requires that the partner shall not behave in any other way. If Israel breaches the covenant, punishment ensues that still reveals God's faithfulness. It is even renewed in the worst case by its being limited to a remnant, as some prophets, but also Qumran and earliest Christianity, make clear. So, to be righteous means to be a covenant partner and obliged to remain such beyond human dereliction. Justification accordingly means that, obligated in his freedom, God holds to his partnership even with those who have been unfaithful, and that he returns them to it. God's righteousness is under the sign of an irrevocable promise, even though in the concrete instance it may punish and judge. As grace, justification stigmatizes for time and eternity. It is thus not a neutral justice, to be put to the test by the indifferent. On the contrary, it reveals that the creature is never rid of its Creator.

With the last sentence I have tacitly extended what the Old Testament describes as covenant faithfulness toward Israel to faithfulness toward God's creation. But such a move is already indicated in the Old Testament. It does not regard the sum of individual believers as covenant partners, but rather Israel with its members, and not in a primarily national or sociological respect, but as the chosen representative of creation. So, at least in legend, the Sinai event has a cosmic dimension. The New Testament radicalizes this aspect. Since Easter, early Christianity can think less and less of itself as a Jewish sect. If reference to the covenant people is initially still held to, with Paul it occurs metaphorically, that is, as including Gentile Christians. The Jewish believer cannot sanction this metaphorical occurrence, since for him the covenant involves keeping the ritual law, so that Gentiles must first be circumcised. The Jewish-Christian view still glimmers in the liturgical fragment of Romans 3:25: The covenant of Sinai was renewed with Christ, and through the forgiveness of trespasses, God's righteousness has confirmed the former election. Characteristically, Paul corrects his exemplar, from the perspective of the beginning world mission. As God brings the dead out of nothing and does this most profoundly in all his activity, so he took to himself the Gentiles as representatives of the nonexistent. In just this way the hymn in Colossians 1:15ff. allows the worldwide creation to be the antipode and model of the cosmic resurrection, in which Gentile Christians participate. Since Christ, the promise is universal. God acts justifying toward his whole creation insofar as it recognizes him in faith as Creator and Lord. The new covenant displaces the old, though Israel retains preeminence as firstborn. And it is not by chance that Israel first opened itself to the gospel among the disciples of the earthly Jesus. I would at least like to hint at the fact that such a universalizing of the covenant also entails a previously unheard-of individualization. Where the promise is tied to faith rather than to the law, the Creator calls each individual to the new covenant; each is justified, not alone, yet individually.

God cannot reveal himself more clearly than he has done here, that is, in his nature as "Immanuel," as a God related to humankind, holding fast to his creature. This needs to be preached. It is foundational that the Father of Jesus is, as has been formulated, "pro-existence." Thus he requires witnesses to his gracious will and activity who, in view of the universal fall of sinful creation, proclaim his righteousness as the power to redeem the godless. This also means that protest is raised against inhumanity in any form as a consequence of godlessness. Where Christ dies for the godless and therein reveals the Father's faithfulness toward his lost children, all inhumanity is a denial of God. It is actually the only form of atheism that may truly be called enmity toward God, is thus not merely at home in ideology or leveled against religion in general. Christians too are continually tempted to relapse into this atheism. They only too often deny radical fellowship with all creatures of their Lord and his righteousness. Yet believers have no privileges that exempt them from earthly society. The world is delivered over to demonic forces when we ignore the justification of the godless occurring in Christ, when we measure the neighbor or stranger by our worldview and morality instead of by God's mercy, when we reserve the Crucified for ourselves. God's righteousness applies to enemies.

2. *God's righteousness as conquest of possession.* The first part has laid the basis for the second. The exegete is furnished the theme of demonic forces and human possession by the Synoptic healing narratives and by extant fragments of primitive Christian liturgy. The oldest material is there, though overgrown with legend. The historian will be allowed to say that the conceptuality and activity of the earthly Jesus are reflected here. There

is no doubt he legitimized his heavenly mission by his power to drive out the demons. His enemies could only contest it by tracing his acknowledged ability to satanic activity. We must proceed still further. Not only an earliest stratum of Christian documentation is being uncovered here, for in a certain sense we are dealing with the midpoint of the New Testament message. The post-Easter church conceives its own driving out of the demons as a sign that the divine lordship has finally broken into the world and now moves toward fulfillment. God's righteousness must be seen in the perspective of the demonic as conquered and expelled. A new world breaks in where, in midst of a world possessed, God retains the right due him and creates salvation even in midst of the profane.

Today's theologians will not be altogether happy about such statements and will take up the demythologizing program against them. Wherever exegesis would carry over the primitive Christian message into our time, insights gained in the Enlightenment respecting biblical mythology should not be contested. For centuries, people suffered from a superstition that reckoned with evil spirits everywhere and churches felt duty-bound to persecute witches. Wherever reason uncovers reality, illusion barring the way to the gospel should retreat. It is thoughtless and hazardous in the extreme when Christians withdraw from the reality of their world and everyday life. Churches should vigorously resist when, to great extent and by no means only in the religious sphere, people shut themselves off from the call of reason, indulge in astrology, imagine amulets are necessary, and in all manner of sects are subject to visionary delusion. At times even Christianity serves to keep others blind, deaf, dumb, and dependent, though the gospel reports that, in encounter with Jesus, people become seeing, hearing, speaking, and walking, and the possessed are returned to the community. The disciples received from the exalted Lord the commission to carry on his work, to make whole, to be open to existing prospects and tasks, and to lighten the darkness where the suffering are tormented. To the extent the Enlightenment and Christianity are in service to humankind, they belong together.

On the other hand, it cannot be denied that the Enlightenment, which once intended to liberate, has to large extent become a tool of the white race for subjecting the rest of the world. Just as every gift of the Creator, so also reason can be misused. It can lead to the hubris of a maturity in which God appears superfluous and the earth becomes the domain of the superior, in which alien existence falls victim to technological progress. Where reason no longer allows us to serve, but rather to exploit the power given with it, a modern and worse possession occurs. It can totally estrange us from earthly necessities, as occurs, for example, when we consider only our own interests and the requirements of our society, without reflecting on the worldwide consequences of our actions. In this respect a second and more radical Enlightenment is necessary today. This Enlightenment must be less optimistic than the first and may not lay aside the mirror of the underdeveloped countries, in which the brutality of tyrannical pride is reflected back to it as the reality of its supposed maturity. Everywhere among us there is the insane ideology that the future belongs to a ratio that masters the earth instead of preserving it in reasonable service.

But it is a monstrous possession when billions are spent yearly for military armament, when one everlastingly asserts one's will to peace yet supports military dictatorships through the delivery of weapons, weakens freedom movements, and apart from this keeps the hungering alive merely to be able to exploit them. Demonic specters need no longer haunt where official and private hypocrisy has assumed such proportions. Perhaps without knowing it and against our better intentions, under the heading "quality of life" we spin the net of deception and violence in which we ourselves are tangled. "Basic values" are preached to us from all sides. Few find in themselves any guilt for the fact that the youth in particular are often trapped in identity crises, no longer find meaning in life, and cannot get through the day without drugs and gurus. In the affluent society political, societal, even religious propaganda gobbles up critical sense or drives to anarchy. Words no longer have the same meaning when used by different parties. Everything and everyone is there to be manipulated. God becomes a cipher either for murky yearnings or for moral self-assertion. Beyond that, the human is defined as a rational being, though one dances unembarrassed around the altar of the golden calf. The jungle of violence grows thicker and thicker, and barbarism has become the mark of the twentieth century.

We have breezily sketched just one detail in the picture of Western "culture." But it is enough to characterize the demonic that rules over us and the possession that rages among us. The demythologization of the Bible was only a beginning, beyond which it is necessary to go. Originally, it was chiefly to serve the existential interpretation of ancient documents. But it should have been more widely applied to the needed de-demonizing of humanity, society, and the world. Possession precedes mythology. The powers and forces of which the New Testament speaks rule before ever ideologies appear in the literature. Now, of course, the real nature of possession must be precisely and theologically defined. I should like to describe it as the condition in which the first commandment is no longer heard or taken seriously, thus in which the earth is inevitably handed over to idols. There is absolutely no genuine human being or true God "in and for himself." Our Lord is a God who is *for* human beings. We, on the other hand, are always within reach of the radiation of that power we overconfidently chose as the final arbiter of our life, or that in violating fettered us. Whoever does not serve the Father of Jesus unavoidably carries on the business of idols. Where idols rule, not only human heads and hearts but wide spaces of earth are demonized.

In the Bible, phenomena that occupy psychiatrists today exemplify an evil power that reaches beyond individuality and limited groups of the physically or psychically ill and ensnares the whole earth. This power is not merely reflected in pathologies and in any case cannot be chiefly gotten at in any rational way. In the world of everyday, the *civitas Dei* and the *civitas terrena* collide. They use each of us as their tool wherever we are, with our capacities and weaknesses. According to the New Testament, if we see differently, we do not perceive the reality. According to the New Testament, we are never our own masters, and only possession tempts us to desire mastery over others far and near. For this reason, the first commandment forbids us to submit to the antigodly powers in our dreams, anxieties, and actions. When we pose as God's rivals and arbitrarily wish to be in control of ourselves, there are consequences for the world around us. Our true freedom is not expressed in being able to do or to omit whatever we please. We are thus not entitled on the basis of our ideals or ideologies to shape the creation around us as we please to demonstrate our power. The One who must determine our path and goals is the One who called us into life, preserves us by his grace, and bursts the fetters in which we continually enchain ourselves. His rule over us is the kingdom of freedom, which marks the children of God and is practiced by them. For this reason, exorcism is unavoidably connected with the gospel. Since Adam's fall we need liberation from the power of darkness. There, according to Romans 1:18, the truth is held down demonically, so that we no longer know to whom we alone and forever belong. To sum up, healing of the possessed determines the history of salvation. Under the promise and summons of the first commandment, it actualizes the humanization of fallen humanity, and in midst of the inferno of our world, founds the kingdom of the beloved Son.

As already stated, not only the Synoptic healing narratives speak of this, but more fundamentally, so do the primitive Christian confessions.

Formulated in hymns, they celebrate the disarming of the cosmic powers as the salvation event of the end time. In that event, Christ's exaltation is likewise manifest as God's will to raise the dead, for baptism has snatched us from the constraint of the old eon and assigned us to the new creation that announces the coming world. Paul speaks in a theologically more reflective way. He knows and naturally shares the popular views of his time concerning demonic powers. Yet he has radicalized the conventional view. What makes this especially striking is that his pupils, say, in Colossians and Ephesians, fall behind the master into the usual approach. Paul himself gave concreteness to the message of de-demonizing the earth begun in the church, that is, he anchored it constitutively in his anthropology. Perhaps we may actually state that he rationalized it. According to him law, sin, and death represent the lordship of calamity over the world, thus the possession of the individual person, as well as the entire cosmos. It would be worth pursuing the question as to what led the apostle to this variation and basically distanced him from the naive superstition of his surroundings. In any case, this example makes clear that reflective faith also sublimates thought. In the debate with Judaism, criticism of traditional piety became unavoidable, the gospel was defined as justification of the godless and even as the election of the Gentiles. This means that the demonic as encountered everywhere in the world has its origin and superhuman force in the passion of human hearts. Where we wish to cope on our own, we forget the Creator. Then idols are necessarily produced, which first of all are projections of our yearnings and anxieties, but are gradually objectified as "compulsions" and become despots. In his dispute with the Jewish law, it dawned on Paul that the most profoundly tempted, imperiled, and dangerous person is the one who takes salvation into his or her own hands.

With this insight the apostle's theology stands or falls, and the controversy over it accompanies all of church history from its very beginnings, as the New Testament makes clear. When we think of pangs of conscience, we think primarily of our moral imperfections. More than half of all the sermons dealing with repentance would lose their content, interest, and the approval of their hearers if they were not oriented to what we lack and makes us liable to evil. In glaring contrast, Paul scarcely concerns himself in any crucial way with people who are aware of their imperfections. Almost throughout he deals with the strong. For him, their representatives are the devout, whether in the shape of those concerned with their own sanctification, or in the shape of fanatics who boast of their election and imagine they are already more at home in heaven than on earth. The Reformation took up this theme by describing despair as the primal sin behind all pious busyness or the presumption that imagines it has already arrived at the goal. In either case there is no true reckoning with God as Creator and Redeemer. In either case we orbit about ourselves, feeling our pulse, navel-gazing, and regard others merely as accomplices or opponents.

It is altogether conceivable that such theology provokes criticism and protest. There is an "established" piety that, as in the secular realm, perches on security and views salvation as diminished if it is to be a mere matter of candidature on earth. The warning against imaginings in 1 Corinthians 10:12 should also be reflected on theologically: "So if you think you are standing, watch out that you do not fall." More than striking at individual Christians, this word strikes at churches of the white race, which enforces its will in them. But we must also call to mind those revolutionary liberation movements that are certain of victory by their own power and see in Christ only the model on the way toward independence. No one is justified before God on the basis of what was received from one's parents, what was acquired or gotten by fighting on one's own. Clear distinction must be drawn between God's righteousness and our rights. Where God does not actually remain God but his name becomes the logo of a conservative or revolutionary program, one loses oneself. A perverted piety stands this rule on its head, insisting that one must transcend oneself and, by one's own effort, force God to allow room with him. This is the basic sin and at the same time the fate of Adam's children, the mark of their being possessed in thought, will, and deed. They make God their vassal, at their beck and call. Unfaithful creatures, defined by earthly powers even in the religious sphere, they form God according to their imaginings, thus in fact according to their own image. Basically, it holds true that the God who is imagined reflects the person imagined and vice versa. Illusion hinders the Creator, who inclines to earth and its creatures, from creating our salvation by justifying us. It does not arrive at the proper place before his countenance, under his gracious lordship, the place toward which we are directed, where abundant life is at issue here on earth and forever. A salvation achieved on our own is in fact our profoundest calamity. In many ways a lasting and immeasurable guilt emerges from such a cosmic fall into the sin of wanting to come to terms with self and the earth. But sin and death are indissolubly connected. The destiny of death is announced wherever true life with the true God is absent. According to the Gospel healing narratives, it is not by chance that the demoniacs make their homes among the graves.

Most unfortunately, church tradition describes the interrelation of one's own greed and doom as "original sin." What is meant cannot be surrendered but in our time is less and less reflected on or precisely set forth. Human beings belong to a world that preexists and shapes them; they are always only a reflection of Adam and dependent on cosmic forces. At bottom, they do not see through their immaturity as much as they may suffer under it and, in concert with others or alone, struggle to be rid of it. As Greek tragedy has it, they run blindly toward their fate and at the same time against it. It should not be forgotten that Romans 7:7ff. views human misery as founded on the illusion worked by demonic attraction. The apostle's anthropology and the cosmology of the Revelation of John agree in speaking of the self-estrangement of the creation, which succumbs to the fascination of powers immanent in the world. This is expressed with a radicality we do not meet elsewhere in the New Testament when Paul makes the law the cause of the enchantment and misery of the religious person. As such and originally, the law is not demonic. The apostle rejects this idea as blasphemy. It is a helpful guide toward a life according to the will of God, but as all other gifts, it is misused when one's own piety is made the meaning and goal of the divine mercy. The law kindles the desire in the ever-finite creature autonomously to break its chains, to arrive at the good (that is, at the freedom of the children of God), to allow earth to become the theater of one's efficiency. Such a will disdains humble service as an instrument of grace in a world continually and everywhere in need of service. It covets an independence that sees in the divine mercy something like the initial igniting of one's own righteousness and that credits a service performed to its personal account. The one possessed misunderstands self and task, as well as God's goodness and claim. In the Bible, godlessness is the stupidity of the one who objectively lives from illusory deception. This is clearer in the pious will to perform than anywhere else. The law misused is the sting of sin and the destiny of death. Together they characterize the demonic reality since Adam's fall, as well as the possession from which God's righteousness must set us free. Where we no longer revere and fear them, we are conquerors.

3. *God's righteousness as foundation for discipleship of the Crucified.* I would like to begin this part with a polemic. It is appropriate. We cannot speak non-polemically of God's righteousness when it sets us in the arena of struggle for the first commandment. Serious dialogue is being critically carried on because we are conformable only as a herd and because all sci-

ence receives the spur for its research from the debate between different opinions. Where God's lordship and the discipleship of Jesus are at issue, the cross of Golgotha, just as the first commandment, distinguishes and separates the children of Adam from the members of Christ. It is no accident that in all of Scripture the Holy Spirit appears as a polemicist. If he were not, there would be no Christian pedagogy. Still among us, though often in pale form, is that German idealism which hands on the ancient heritage of humanistic thought. For this reason youth will still be preoccupied with self-realization, whether the formula reads, "Become what you are!" or "Become what you should be!" The search for what today is called "identity," or earlier, "personality" is always tied to growth and now may have become more tense and confused. For this reason, in contrast to an earlier generation, there is widespread hunger for credible experience, for what proved true in the past and can steer a clear course. Even distant cultures are supposed to yield models, to say nothing of the various ideologies or methods that might burst through the limits of the "I."

This problematic should not be summarily dismissed. Still, according to my conviction, the Christian is not to be shaped by it. Each person has individuality, because the Creator does not copy, and among Christians it may be particularly pronounced. The talents given us may not be buried. God will be glorified through them, and they are to be of use to the neighbor. The word "self-realization" is dubious. We are not obliged to shape and exhibit ourselves but to point to our Lord or, if you will, make him real. This can occur in such thorough fashion as is shown by the almost bewildered face of Rembrandt in his last self-portrait, or by the corpse of the Crucified in Grünewald's altar painting,[1] that is, to the point of self-dissolution. In contrast to ancient and modern idealism, the Old and New Testaments do not proclaim earthly harmony or the development of human character. They speak, rather, of a God who uses up his instruments in time, who, according to Isaiah 53 or Jeremiah's lamentations and Paul's catalog of sufferings, reduces them to the most detested and unworthy, to an absurd spectacle and a curse. Churches have no right to keep this a secret, least of all when they look toward an imminent future. For the youth, and not only for them, it is a bitter lesson that Christian identity is found beneath the cross, that God's righteousness is accepted only in faith. We are not urging anyone toward nihilism who is searching for meaning and a goal, for a promise and a task. The Beatitudes of the Sermon on the Mount

---

1. See note 1 on p. 8 above.

apply to the hungry and thirsty. Yet the One who spoke them goes to Golgotha and characterizes discipleship with the word, "Those who will save their life will lose it, and those who lose their life for my sake will find it." This is the price of justification, which otherwise becomes a utopia.

A second critical point is a variation on the first but projects it into the political sphere. It cannot be denied that in many places today the message of Christian freedom is illustrated by the Old Testament story of Israel's exodus from Egypt. On the contrary, it was a great gain when we learned to relate this freedom no longer solely or at least preeminently to our inward life but to make it the predicate of the wandering people of God. Mission always means that one is summoned from out of one's own existence. This no longer concerns merely the private sphere or, as the Reformation discovered, one's daily calling. Today, more of those areas still exist in which tyrants keep other persons in chains, torture them, and murder them, while even the religious bourgeoisie often closes its eyes to it or shamefully declares it to be unavoidable and unalterable. A condition in which a white minority gorges itself at the cost of an overwhelming majority and scandalously forces its own rules of play on the exploited is incompatible with the righteousness of God. Nowhere does glorification of the status quo in the societal sphere have support in the Bible. The first commandment is also directed against the dance around the golden calf in the capitalistic economy, against its defense through an armament that scorns God and the earth. Simplest reason would have to see that, as a society of the white race, we do not prepare for peace by what we do and propagate but rather prepare our own ruin, and see that Christians do not deserve the name when they do not resolutely resist such a trend. The disciples of Jesus must also be able to rebel.

At the same time, we should be wary of ideologizing the exodus that promises liberation movements an earthly victory as the unavoidable result of their struggle. Solidarity with the oppressed may not incite in us illusions about earthly realities. Christology preserves us from anthropological utopias. We know from experience that revolutionaries once come to power have seldom become the avant-garde of humaneness. But in no case may the scandal of Golgotha be rendered harmless by fanatics. The cross of Jesus is not merely a stage on the way toward ultimate liberation, though church people for the most part think so and theologians or entire confessions give it support. Christ is not a means to our goals and the fulfillment of our longings. He remains our Lord, who may not be demoted to a model, however gratifying. He commands, "Follow me!" We must obey for his sake, even though we do not know how it will turn out on earth. On Easter morning his disciples still complain, "But we thought. . . ." His kingdom is not a playground for our postulates, and God's righteousness is not a guarantee of our actual or imagined rights. This insight distinguishes Christians from their most serious rival in the worldwide, ultimate religious conflict — that is, from Marxism. It also distinguishes us from the various nationalisms whose tides have borne us along in our own history to the point where we can scarcely protect the oppressed. Yet what we must tolerate out of love and understanding is not at all a fixed component of our faith as it once was under the rubric of a theology of the orders of creation.

The Old Testament must be interpreted on the basis of the New. Of course, Israel's exodus is a model for our discipleship, but it is not the main key to God's kingdom. To what extent, then, is it the cross that the Nazarene bore and beneath which he calls his followers on earth? What has this cross to do with the righteousness of God? This may be the central question among all those put to Christianity today, and also the problem that even churches least recognize as decisive. There is no use to engaging in apologetics as though God too would have to pay tribute to what is earthly, or in taking up a pedagogy already familiar to the Greeks. The wisdom of antiquity that calls us to "learn through suffering!" and in Goethe's *Dichtung und Wahrheit* is prefixed as the motto of his biography is inflected Christologically in Hebrews 5:8, "Although he was a Son, he learned obedience through what he suffered." This occurs for the purpose of describing him as our model and guide unto salvation. We too must learn obedience in order to arrive at perfection. This is no doubt correct and yet does not suffice to answer the question of the connection between the righteousness of God and the discipleship of the cross. If we isolate the statement, it remains a directive as to how character is formed or a stout heart achieved. But with this reading we remain in the nineteenth century, when Christianity and idealism worked hand in hand for the education of the individual, when God and the soul were the dominant theme of church work.

The challenge to our century is that if we merely wish to, we can survey the entire earth and descry its reality. A gospel that still revolves about human individuality and is not oriented ecumenically or world-related becomes religious first aid. It should be such, but not primarily. In summary, 1 John 3:8 emphasizes that "the Son of God was revealed for this purpose, to destroy the works of the devil." This takes up what Luke 13:32 reveals as the meaning of Jesus' earthly life and the presupposition for his death: "Listen, I am casting out demons and performing cures today and tomorrow, and on the third day I finish my work." The bearer of salvation must not only become man, as usually stands at the center of our Christology. At Golgotha it becomes clear that his way leads to hell as the kingdom of God-forsakenness, and that Christmas must be understood on the basis of Good Friday. But no one goes to hell without paying for it with his or her life. So 1 Corinthians 2:8 states that the demons were the cause of Jesus' cross. The righteousness of God, by which he temporally enforces his right to earth in saving way, must break fresh ground among the possessed by suffering and dying. The first commandment, which as promise and beatitude begins with the words "I am the Lord your God," calls to resist idols and demons and makes of the church a resistance. This does not begin without the experience of the cross.

God's righteousness makes itself manifest in an unrighteous world. This will become evident to the disciples as it did to their Lord. At this point criticism of bourgeoisie Western Christianity catches fire. In it everything turns on one's own salvation and, most of all, on one's own wellness. To the poor, described by the Beatitudes as recipients of the divine mercy, we merely give alms from our superfluity. We did not set out to unmask the real forces of this earth and destroy its works of rape and exploitation. What we call love does not bring freedom to the possessed, though love always assumes deliverance from possession. God's righteousness, however, cannot be linked with worldwide inhumanity. So we must daily anew, and today as never before, allow ourselves to be summoned to be witnesses and servants of that righteousness in which God on earth exercises his gracious right toward his fallen creature, for which reason it lives in pride or despair.

Healing the Possessed

It may be that the theme assigned me is seldom meditated upon in the great churches of the white race. If, due to the assigned lectionary, the theme is preached, the healing as such should always be accented. Jesus helps the blind to see, the deaf to hear, the lame to walk, and together with the senses, opens hearts and at times the understanding. In this way he returns the possessed from the desert of outer and inner ruin to the fellowship of everyday life. He no longer lets them house among the graves, where the solitariness of death fogs hearts and heads, and where humaneness must atrophy. This message is absolutely essential, and we will have to take it up. But first of all, we must reflect thematically on the fact that *possession* actually exists and that, with the greatest impartiality, the New Testament, more or less in all its writings, assumes such a state of affairs.

Still, we must formulate more objectively what should concern us. Possession is known to us in many forms, from depression to an insane terrorism become evident worldwide in our time. In addition, we see individuals or groups whose sufferings drive them to despair or cause explosions of brutal violence. But the New Testament treats possession in a cosmic context, that is, it confronts us with supra-individual and supra-human beings. It may be stated historically and without restriction that the New Testament, just as Judaism, shares the worldview of its time, according to which demons rule everywhere on earth, in the air, and under

A lecture given on October 1, 1987, at the Missionsärztliches Kolloquium (Medical Mission Colloquy) of the Deutsche Institut für Ärztliche Mission (German Institute for Medical Mission), in Tübingen.

the earth. Antigodly powers and forces with Satan as their head devastate the creation, hinder divine salvation, and, with visible success, assert their claim on humans. The Enlightenment has generally freed us from the nightmares of the ancient and medieval worldview, though horoscopes are still being consulted, secret magical practices performed, and a considerable portion of Christianity believes that faith in God is endangered if we do not believe in a personal devil and in demons spiritedly lurking about. We must demythologize. Among theologians this has occurred in such thoroughgoing fashion to the point where the theme of possession is relegated to the practice of the psychiatrist and at best discussed from the perspective of mental illness — that is, if the relevant New Testament texts and their meaning are not resolutely ignored or their significance disregarded. Of course, it may be assumed as obvious that physicians accept and approve such an approach.

For a long time I swam in this stream. Secular insights may have first allowed me to think more critically theologically, or at least brought me to restrict my school tradition. For me, demythologizing the ancient and medieval worldview remains an indispensable requirement, in any event, in the theological sphere. But what needs to be more radically demythologized is especially that optimistic Enlightenment faith, not merely in economic, but also in mental and moral universal progress — and, further, the myth of humanity's essentially good core and the possibility and duty of self-liberation. In the New Testament "possession" is not at all, as our German term suggests, a merely anthropological condition; rather, it is a cosmic condition that gains power over individuals. As such, it has significance for theology as a whole and in any case may not simply be left to psychologists and physicians. Sociologists and politicians must at least be involved in the discussion, and the alleged rationality of our economics and technology would be rendered more suspect if we were to replace the somewhat extenuating aspect of "possession" with the problem of the demonic in the world and in history. Possession would then be understood as the concrete sign and product among individuals and groups. In addition, the particular condition would be targeted that the Christian history of dogma most unfortunately and erroneously describes as "original sin."

Now an excursus is necessary, though it may try the patience of hearers who, given the objectivity of their fraternity, aim at the concrete. Sometimes we arrive at the concrete only by way of detours and systematic reflection. I think I should make a few observations, at least in a compressed way, beginning with the correctness or incorrectness of the term "original sin." Naturally, we should dismiss the view that conceived it in terms of human sensuality transmitted from generations past, and particularly in terms of sexuality. Conversely, it is neither biblical nor required by our knowledge of human nature to break up the complex of "sin" into a variety of individual transgressions. As surely as we may not ignore such factors as the accumulation of guilt and everyone's responsibility, even less can we reduce "sin" to such factors. In that case, the aspect of rebellious attack against the holy will of God is obscured, and a purely moral approach too easily obtrudes. Sin is primarily the rebellious desire of the creature to maintain itself over against its Creator, whether in thought, word, or deed.

What the church calls "original sin," however, no longer has individual offenses in view but a common, potentially worldwide destiny in which the individual is willingly or unwillingly implicated. There is a guilt that, as fate, is thrust upon us by the world around or by our forebears, a fate we cannot avoid but continues to work as a curse and constantly begets evil deeds. We are never just "we ourselves" but always ourselves as a part of our world. The expression "possession" describes this condition much more precisely than "original sin," in any case where individual life is involved. Correspondingly, the Bible views sin at least as often as a "power" as it does an individual transgression. As a theologian, I do best to proceed from the first commandment, "I am the Lord your God. . . . You shall have no other gods before me." Here it is said that no one ever exists "in and for oneself," can never really "emancipate" oneself. Always and everywhere we are subject to rule. There is only the alternative between God and the idols. This alternative, however, does not merely define the life of individuals and groups, but confronts everything called human, thus the entire world. The world is sinful insofar as it always emerges historically from revolt against its Creator and enters into fresh rebellion against him. With their deeds, individuals participate in such a fate. By it they give evidence that they never and nowhere can truly be their own master, but always and everywhere they are claimed, co-opted, "possessed" by powers and forces and become sinners.

The first commandment not only shows us this fateful and universally valid alternative. It is first of all a promise, not a commandment. It is spoken of the One who redeems his people from Egypt and leads them to freedom from slavery. "You shall not" at bottom means "you need not serve other gods. You already have a Lord to fear and love, whom you are called to trust. You should know that you have a Lord who blesses and sets free, that you reject blessing and freedom when you place yourself under the yoke of other lords and do not entrust yourself alone to your Creator." Sin is always grace rejected, a despising of the redeeming Creator, an exchange of the loving Lord for ravishing and enslaving powers. The world and individuals are hopelessly ensnared in this sin if its true and only Lord does not prove himself to be mightier and, according to Colossians 1:13, rescue them from the power of darkness and transfer them into the kingdom of his beloved Son. Only a change of lordship puts an end to sin. Redemption means nothing else but a change of lordship — indeed, a return from slavery to supra-earthly and earthly powers to the Father who awaits his children and in promise says to each, "I am your God because I remain your Creator, and as Creator, I must be and remain *for* and *not against* humankind." Contrariwise, from now on those whom he has brought home and set free are not left to themselves. To be free of idols does not mean to be free for oneself. Transferred into the kingdom of his beloved Son, we belong to a world that likewise has its lord and king. Naturally, freedom in this new world no longer violates, but remains service. It is documented and preserved in the evangelical sense only in love for the neighbor; it seeks to remove from the neighbor the tyrant's yoke and heals the possessed.

After this excursus on the first commandment, we are at the place where we recognize our theme as a call and a promise for all who are possessed. Jesus healed the possessed. If anything in gospel history is as historically guaranteed as Jesus' baptism by John and the cross on Golgotha, then it is, as primitive Christianity formulated it, that he fought with demons and drove them out, freed the possessed from their darkness, and transferred them into his kingdom. In his narrative portion prior to the passion story, Mark, first among biblical authors to write a Gospel, heaps up the deeds of Jesus, giving special emphasis to the healing of the possessed. We could assign this to the artistry of the evangelist, who in such fashion effectively contrasts Jesus' suffering and dying. The One who with heavenly power brought God's mercy to human misery is paradoxically delivered up to humans and earthly powers. Yet, there is a series of data that forces us back to the history of the earthly Jesus himself. Mark 3:22 allows scribes to come from Jerusalem on official mission to declare that Jesus is possessed. "He has Beelzebul, and by the ruler of the demons he casts out demons." This statement makes sense only if by his deeds Jesus has created unrest in the Jewish community and finds adherents. The realities cannot be contested, but they are debunked as a demonic conjuring. The devil uses his messengers to blind the people. Magic feigns divine salvation and leads believers astray. Matthew 12:46 reports that Jesus' mother and siblings thought he was possessed and wanted to dissuade him from his path and fetch him home. The result is a breach between Jesus and his family. He proclaims solemnly that only the one who hears God's will and does it is related to him. This is how he resists the accusation of the scribes. They have no objection to other Jewish exorcists, since they do not threaten their authority. If their accusation against Jesus were correct, the result would be that Satan is at war with himself and is thus destroying his own kingdom. The opponents thus commit an unforgivable blasphemy against the Holy Spirit, whom Jesus reveals as benign toward humans, as healing, and as gathering God's people even among the possessed.

What Jesus understood as the gift given him and the task assigned him may be more evident here than anywhere else in the Gospels. With him the end time of our old aeon heralded by John the Baptist is breaking in. God no longer remains in a closed heaven but prepares for Pentecost, the festival of a heaven opened above us and to all the world, thus of a world in which the message of salvation can no longer be hindered by powers and forces or human tyrants. Luke 11:20 triumphantly states, "If it is by the finger of God that I cast out the demons, then the kingdom of God has come to you." Satan's armor, the text continues, is taken from him and can now be distributed as booty. He has nothing more on which to rely. The two last verses of Luther's "A Mighty Fortress" are anticipated here. Finally, to this context also belongs the enigmatic word in Luke 13:32, reported as a message to Herod: "Listen, I am casting out demons and performing cures today and tomorrow, and on the third day I finish my work." According to Mark 6:7 and the appendix in 16:17-18, the disciples must continue this work of their Lord and in all time to come document the inbreaking of the kingdom of heaven within the earthly present. From the epistles of the New Testament we know that there actually were Christian exorcists. The Apocalypse of John is a powerful hymn for the day when the hellish power is finally annihilated.

The historical results seem unequivocal to me and may absolutely not be overlooked in church and theology. This is why I acknowledge the demand for demythologizing. The ancient worldview, which lived on in the Middle Ages and in our time openly or subliminally still haunts us, has no claim on us. Contrariwise, a demythologizing carried on and given legitimation theologically should not toll for a burial already conducted 200 years ago by rationalists inside and outside the church. Nor should it be used as springboard for a Christian existentialism that no longer needs theological heralds to remain up to date. Today, demythologizing must be more radical than in the days of the Enlightenment, more critical toward its faith in progress and science and toward the postulate of human maturity in the modern era. Not merely texts are to be demythologized respecting their ideological wrappings. In the evangelical sense demythologizing occurs as a battle and resistance against superstition. And superstition, at least according to Luther's explanation of the first commandment, is everything that does not allow us most deeply and without compromise to fear, love, and trust God "above all things." Thus demythologizing, evangelically conceived and rooted, denotes ridding humanity and the earth of the demonic.

The devils, of course, no longer run about in the witching hours with tails and cloven hooves or masked in the light of day. Rather, according to 2 Corinthians 11:14, they change their shape according to place, situation, and audience, and at times they prefer to represent what we imagine to be "angels of light." Goethe knew: "The crowd never senses the devil, even if he had it by the throat." Today, of course, his chief domain is no longer the seduction of young maidens. It was not at all pessimistic but soberly realistic when 1 John 5:19 declared, "We know that the whole world lies under the power of the evil one." We have no reason to contradict this. We come from the most barbaric century, to the extent we can survey history. It is part of possession to be blinded, and stupidity may be the most common feature of original sin. Whoever lived through our eventful century wide awake, a century in which all the extremes of human passion burst open and every abyss of suffering was endured worldwide, would have had to encounter stupidity and blindness without end and, in thought and action, been ensnared in both. My generation, at least, went body, mind, and soul through the inferno and, if it survived at all, is not rid of the scars of torture endured and the pain of an accusing conscience. The frenetic character of our existence has its explanation in the fact that we would like to leave the past behind and justify and entrench ourselves in Towers of Babel feverishly thrown up and proving seemingly unbroken power. Once more we have a need to erect a political, economic, scientific, and technological monument to the grandeur of the white race. The surf of a future we can no longer manipulate is rolling irresistibly toward us. From their ecumenical experiences Christians at least must see that the driving downpour with which Luther compared God's gracious work is passing us by. In church and confession, in theology and piety, the wasteland is growing wherever we speak rhetorically of the national church, the charismatic community, and the deepened fellowship of separated churches, thus papering over the reality of obsessed claims to power and weak compromises.

Still, this is only one side of the matter. More than ever before we are compelled to hear the cries of a humanity for centuries exploited by the white race, herded into the misery of slums and starved there, plagued by epidemic, and for the most part treated worse than cattle. To the extent it resists its tyrants and by doing so at least claims human rights for itself, it is hypocritically charged with violence and terror. In this respect the colonial powers were only in advance of the people of color and today still practice violence and terror in a neocolonialism that hides behind the mask of an alleged free market.

Looking concretely to our own German situation, and limiting ourselves to one single aspect, we see that the affluent society from which we come and in which to great extent we still live began in the period of the Korean War and profited from North America's needing our economic expansion. Since then we live from the export of our industrial products. The dangerous rise in unemployment among us coincides not only with the development of computer technology but also with the fact that the possibilities of export are partly dried up and partly limited by competition. But to great degree the Third World stands open to us, precisely because it needs our help. We furnish its dictators weapons of every sort and size for their wars and equip them with nuclear power plants, even though they could get their energy more cheaply from amply available water sources. We supply them with chemicals we in part no longer dare to handle, establish among them branches of firms that eliminate their small and medium operations, buy their raw materials at starvation wages, and to top it all, under the heading of "development aid," prevent the further increase of unemployment among us. That we still dare to speak of human rights without having ratified the U.N. Convention against Torture[1] simply completes the picture of our having gone to ruin on Mammon, on a capitalistic egotism that sustains itself at the cost of the poor, and on a shameless deception in the political and economic spheres. Christians and churches are also at work here, profiteering, tolerating, or actually agitating.

Criticism of the theology of liberation in underdeveloped lands is in no way practiced merely by the Roman curia. It fits the middle-class worldview in Protestantism as well. Academically, of course, much can be raised in objection to it, especially when we keep in mind that in its own way it implies a Catholic ecclesiology. No more than we can deny the heri-

---

1. Not until October 1, 1990, did Germany ratify this convention, exactly three years after this lecture.

tage of classical idealism and the Enlightenment can we avoid its dependence on syncretism and Marxism in politics. On the other hand, a respectable theology has always been a theology of liberation and must remain so. Freedom and the *parrēsia* (boldness, confidence) with which Paul and John describe the joyful courage of the redeemed are God's will for his creatures and the mark of a genuinely evangelical life. Whoever opposes it sees the splinter in the neighbor's eye but not the beam in one's own eye.

This was the intent of my argument and is, I hope, its agreed-upon resume. We need no longer defend ancient and medieval mythology. At their most varied levels, demonic possession, superstition, and idolatry, worldwide in operation and taking each one of us captive, absolutely cannot be disputed as the powers and forces holding sway in our own time. Rebellion against the promise and requirement of the first commandment is our cosmic reality, and its result is an inferno from which we no doubt would like to flee into that middle-class private sphere where we seal off eyes, ears, hearts, and heads from alien distress and feel at home in illusion and utopia. There is no private existence. The human being, as the Greeks already made clear, is a *zōon politikon*, destined for fellowship, in need of it, and corporeally incapable of avoiding it. What we are we are always in a quite concrete relation to the world around us. To be unworldly always spells loss of existence, creatureliness in a deficient state. Our own reality is at stake where we do not perceive the realities of our world. Unwillingness to perceive them expresses not only a lack of intelligence but ideological possession.

If this is the case, then the healing of the possessed is far more than a mere biblical theme too often unjustly repressed in church and theology. It has acute significance not only for psychiatrists, sociologists, or politicians. The demons have to do with all of us, and no life is protected from them. In a certain respect, our theme thrusts us at the center of all theology because it raises the question of the humanity of the person, *every* person. It is too easily spiritualized when, according to good Christian tradition, one regards the forgiveness of sins and the hallowing of personal life as the chief concerns of evangelical proclamation. For Jesus, healing the possessed was the sign that the kingdom of God had broken in. Do we exaggerate in pious fanaticism when we insist that exorcism is still the criterion of the earthly reality of God's rule, and precisely because we can no longer overlook the inferno in our world, seeing that we are trapped in it? In the course of time, private piety and the restriction of edification to conservative groups became the hiding places of religious delusion of a middle-class that was once the support of the Reformation and the Enlightenment and now, at least from the Christian and churchly point of view, threatens to close itself off in a ghetto from the evil world and fresh air. Today, Western theology must summon to a breakout from every sort of blind alley. As evangelical promise and as the task of personal as well as of collective hallowing, it must proclaim that the possessed shall be free and to that end must mobilize all existing energies and possibilities in the church.

How can this be realized? We must at least put the question to ourselves before we enter into a discussion that by no means may end here and now. Let me start with the word in Ephesians 6:12: "Our struggle is not against enemies of blood and flesh, but against the rulers, against the authorities, against the cosmic powers of this present darkness, against the spiritual forces of evil in the heavenly places." Such a robust and grandly graphic admonition deserves intensive meditation but, in keeping with the train of my argument, must first of all be demythologized as to its wording. Naturally, that world of spirits between heaven and earth of which ancient mythology speaks does not exist. But again, first of all, we must roundly oppose the assertion that we do not have to contend with "blood and flesh." Right at this point I am ready and able to submit an entire list of names at home and worldwide from politics, economics, technology, and science whose positions Christians must not only refuse but also energetically resist. After all, the demonic does not emerge in those airy or even higher strata in which astronauts can encounter them today. It always and everywhere emerges in human heads and hearts that disavow their Creator with their knowledge or ideologies. Because human discoveries and fantasies are at issue, then, as happens with Goethe's sorcerer's apprentice, what is most important is beyond our control and becomes demonic, that is, inhuman. The rebellious student generation of 1968 spoke of "constraints" that lead to the point of no return. In the history we are able to survey, persons who imagine they are autonomous and emancipate themselves are always the creators of idols. In self-assertion or despair toward their true Lord, they create their own gods that fittingly obligate and enslave them and the world around them. This is the genesis of the evil masters and spirits who are at home in the darkness of our world and represent it. These evil masters and spirits actually exist, and it is not ideological pessimism but a reason-illuminating revelation that allows them to be recognized.

Against this, Christianity must be urged on toward struggle and resistance. In this way it must be shown and proved that the gospel rids of demons, that it deserves to be called mother of the Enlightenment and, in league with the Enlightenment, unmasks idols. The Gospel narratives report all kinds of strange practices that Jesus used in healing the possessed. To imitate them would scarcely be of use to us. They signal the appearance of exorcists in earliest Christianity. The only thing to be learned from this is that, wherever we have to do with possession, we may apply all the means and experiences at our disposal that have proved helpful. There are no taboos as long as humaneness is in the lead and there is a striving toward ending possession. It would be presumptuous if the theologian were to meddle in the affairs of the physician or psychologist. The theologian can only summon us to avoid no experiment born of humaneness and that leads to the human's becoming human. In just this way we remain in the discipleship of Jesus and his mission.

Let me conclude by pointing out once more with emphasis that to which I already alluded. Possession denotes precisely what in the history of dogma is called "original sin," that is, an addiction to earthly powers and forces. All individual sins have their root in it; they are, as it were, its projections and concretions. The world will not acknowledge its true Lord and of necessity creates its own lords. The creature is always only under one lord and in the service of his kingdom. Consequently, there is no healing of the possessed as long as we have only individual, allegedly private existence in mind. Here, for us, healing occurs as liberation from fixed ties and relations infringing on the individual, the symptoms of which may be expressed in various types of guilt. In just this way, we who would help and heal must be aware that we too will never get free of a worldwide fate if we do not live every day from grace and in service to the promise of the first commandment. We are in solidarity with all the threatened, with those who suffer, and with sinners. There is possession even among the religious. The Bible does not primarily have to do with atheists, but rather with the religious who are possessed. Christians do not forget that justification of the godless and it alone spells salvation and healing, that only by the side of, and in the fellowship of, the godless do we find salvation and healing. We are not removed from the earth when we have been transferred into the kingdom of his beloved Son. This is what only fanatics think who despise the body and, at best, see brothers and sisters merely as objects of their own superiority and swerve from the path of the Crucified. The healing of the possessed is a perilous undertaking. It brings us inevitably into conflict with the morality and illusions of the world around us, especially of the middle-class world. To serve Christ as sole Lord and to bring him as such to others has its cost. Tyrants can persist only as long as the possessed are not healed.

Now this as a final word. Healing of the possessed as redemption in body, mind, and spirit spells the glorious freedom of the children of God for which all creation groans and, as the Old Testament formulates it, changes all tyrants from earthly idols to nothing. The one who is possessed is the person whom Luther called *incurvatus in se ipsum,* thus, whether lovestruck or frightened off, turned in upon the self, concerned only with the self. To such a one neither heaven nor earth is open. According to Mark 5:2ff., even while alive, such a one is at home among the graves. Just as his comrade in Matthew 9:32, he is mute, incapable of communication. God, who has called each of us by name, fetches us from anonymity, from the status of the mere consumer in the uniform of the meritocracy. From whatever tradition or party we come, he makes a display of us who are, as it were, members of his triumphal procession, as envisaged in 2 Corinthians 2:14ff. Behold, what a person! We can no longer be made to conform. We are witnesses to his truth and go forth under an opened heaven toward the victims of idols in every nook and cranny of earth. Freed from isolation, we go in courage and power toward a common life, giving and sharing.

The One and the Many

At your request I will conduct a seminar in which to discuss the question how unity and diversity can come together in the Christian community. It is not my task to hold a detailed lecture. Rather, I must set forth as precisely as possible theses that provoke conversation, perhaps also debate, and do it briefly enough so that we keep much time for discussion. I will thus limit myself to an introduction.

In all of Scripture the issue is unity and uniqueness. Three times daily every devout Israelite prays in the words of Deuteronomy 6:4: "Hear, O Israel: The Lord is our God, the Lord alone." To this corresponds concentration on the one commandment in the following verse: "You shall love the Lord your God with all your heart, and with all your soul, and with all your might!" The first commandment says nothing else. In a certain sense it is to be taken as the sum of the whole Bible, of all Christian devotion, and is given Christological concretion in the New Testament. This is how simple the content of our faith and our preaching is. Its content can be summarized in a single sentence and thus be made intelligible to a child. All theology can and ought to do nothing else than make clear this simple thing. That is, in midst of the changes in time and place, of generations and individual life, it ought to function like a ferryman, carrying someone across to another shore. It would be useful to trace such simplicity not only of speech but of message throughout the Bible, and by it to comfort and encourage all who despair at a complicated theology. I will give at least two

---

A lecture given on October 25, 1977, at the theological seminar of the Evangelical Methodist Church in the German Democratic Republic, Bad Klosterlausnitz.

examples from the Old Testament. Micah 6:8 reads, "He has told you, O mortal, what is good; and what does the Lord require of you but to do justice, and to love kindness, and to walk humbly with your God?" The old covenant closes with the promise from Malachi 4:6 that, in the divine future, the hearts of the parents will be turned to the children, and the hearts of the children to their parents. Whoever has to do with parents or children will recognize the magnitude of this quite simple word involving everyday life on earth. Unity, worked from heaven, and among the families of the hearing and believing community!

The New Testament directly connects with this when in John 10:16 there is promise of one flock and one shepherd, or when, in an invocation arguably against heresy at the worship, Ephesians 4:5 confesses that there is one Lord, one faith, one baptism. To cite further passages is superfluous. It should have become clear that what is expressed here is a central motif of the entire Bible. To the one God, who alone led his people out of Egypt and by that act is known as sole Creator of heaven and earth, there corresponds the people who, in a miracle of the end time, shall be gathered from dispersion. To him likewise corresponds the Christian flock, which sees this event begun in Jesus, must demonstrate it in worldwide service, and, despite all conflict and division, exhorts its members to hold fast the unity in the Spirit, loving, believing, hoping, and reflecting the unity of Father and Son. Where this admonition is not heard and not realized, Christianity has betrayed its Lord and its task and becomes a religious sect among others, a divided Body of Christ.

With these last words I am reminded not only of an extremely important theme that, from the Pauline viewpoint, emphasizes Christian unity and the necessity of a universal priesthood but that, for the first time in Christian history, deals in a basic way with the problem of the plurality of groups and the diversity of members in this Body of Christ. Early on and painfully, Paul learned that the unity of Jesus' disciples does not denote uniformity of opinion and behavior. In all his congregations differences and antagonisms erupt that are given classic illustration in the various parties at Corinth and anticipate later intrachurch quarrels, disparate confessions and denominations. The message and confession of Scripture are simple and summon to a oneness and unity that they also promise and see modeled in the relation of the Father to the Son. But if we look to the earthly reality little of this can be detected. Of course, it is continually emphasized that we have the same God and the one Master, to whom we pray in common and whom we serve in common. But is this true when we take a careful look?

As early as in the ancient church, were there not controversies over Christology that led to a division in faith and to various attitudes toward the law, baptism, and the Lord's Supper? Is not theology from the outset more than a critical and not rather also a polemical affair, since one must continually contend with other views? Under God, is it impossible to think in a totally different way according to whether one comes from ancient or modern philosophy, from a particular Western tradition, or from a tradition being formed today in Africa, Asia, or Latin America? Is there not an Old and a New Testament that cannot simply be reduced to a common denominator, however feebly Jews and Christians believe it? Are there not four Gospels, and why does not one suffice if all witness the same thing? And afterward is there not an abundance of apocryphal books, whose importance is not unanimously evaluated in the confessions? Must not the *oecumene* suffer from the fact that we desire worldwide fellowship but only seldom can leap over our own shadow in matters of truth and love? In Germany, do we not come from a Christianity in which our forebears could not agree and in which religious parties once more make war on each other? These examples suffice to ask whether or not beautiful words and postulates mask the grim reality that confession of the "one holy, catholic church," believing, praying, and serving in common, is no utopia. No one will deny that, in the individual realm, as well as in that of the family, groups, and congregations, we continually have difficulties with one another and still retain them, though we would like to be Christians. The Body of Christ is still Grünewald's Crucified.

Now Paul has been able to wrest a positive view from diversity. How was this possible? First of all, we must reject an erroneous interpretation, or at least an unfortunate formulation, precisely because it is everywhere assumed. The apostle does not affirm pluralism as he is represented to be doing, in which different parties and ideologies exist alongside each other, and where we must put up with others' views and modes of behavior. Here, the needs of society are made the norm, whereas Paul makes express appeal to Christology when he speaks of the Body of Christ. Where Christ rules, diversity arises and persists, as is already shown by the conduct of the earthly Jesus, who deliberately gathered about him the religious and sinners, zealots and tax collectors, men and women of all levels. He was in dead earnest that all should be helped, and the missionaries who after Easter went into all the world, thus beyond the limits of Israel to the Gentiles, rightly appealed to his will. In 1 Corinthians 12:12ff. Paul gives theological weight to what we can read from the Gospel narratives. For him, the body is the essence of the person, capable of contact and liable to attack, and willingly or unwillingly, in desire or suffering, gathers with others and with everything earthly. The earthly Body of the exalted Christ is the means of his communication with our world. Christianity is commissioned and empowered to make known his presence in each new day and in every place, by word, deed, and suffering.

But if this is actually to happen, there may be no uniformity in Christianity, as often as this has not been recognized but actually been inverted. This connects with what we traditionally call original sin but today may be better described by the term "possession," that is, our continual attempt to shape after our image persons formed after the image of God. This means that we do not allow them to be creatures, thus manipulate them at the core, make of them our tools. Just as this occurs in our personal contacts, so also in the family, whether by parents or children, man or wife, in profession and society, among nations and continents. By this means, even if we do it in the name of human rights, the rights of God are violated.

From the beginning God created people differently, for example, brought man and woman together, gave us various skin colors, ways of thinking, capabilities, and limitations along our way. We are born into various circumstances and, with pride or pain, bear the heritage of our ancestors. We cannot choose whether to be large or small, powerful or weak, clever or childish, whether to die early or late. We all have different fingerprints, of which especially the police make use. None is like the other, each has his or her own peculiarity. Naturally, we can allow ourselves to develop through education, or we can be ruined and stunted through bad company. And, of course, we cannot deny changes and interruptions that at times lead to self-alienation or make it impossible for others to recognize us. By no means do we remain just as we are in every phase of life. The world exists in coming and going, and each shares in it in one's own way. But we are not uniform. We are what one customarily calls conformist, only through violent intervention. If that were not so, the individual would no longer be unique, no longer that one and not the other. In society we would only be bored, since all would be made superfluous. There would be no help for one another because we would not be able to complement each other. There would no longer be any genuine task, since all could, would, and would have to do the same thing. By virtue of its personal and never-ending need, the human being is so situated that in marriage and family, profession, society, and nation, it has need of and in turn is of use to the other. Otherwise, earth would be a hell and an isolation ward.

When he calls disciples, Jesus excludes no one, because everyone is God's creature. For this reason, a new creation is visible in him, seen once more as creation, brought into the light from human and demonic darkness, and summoned to service to it. The Spirit brings the new day by returning to the beginning, renewing each day toward the place where God is Creator and is at work, where we as his children may work together with him so that the creation becomes visible and is preserved. Since, with heaven open above us, Jesus brings about a new earth and returns us to the place from which we fell, he also establishes his lordship among us. He is the Mediator between God and humanity and remains such even after his exaltation. Through his Body, that is, through the Christian community and all its members, he reaches out toward each creature of his Father in every place and time, beyond every grave and separate camp, as once did the Nazarene.

But this is the crucial point: As Paul holds fast to the diversity of the creative activity and will not have it compromised by us, especially not by the churches, it is doubly important to him, for only through it can the Christ be everywhere and always present on earth. Since Easter, he is present through his disciples. But his disciples can only fulfill their task when they are not uniformly equipped, when they not merely speak the same language or know how to sing a single song, share the same cultural presuppositions, stem from one class or race. The figures of the Bible are not only heroes and martyrs. They are seldom geniuses, for the most part poor and humble people who can stoop to enter every door, laugh with those who laugh and weep with those who weep, not at all simply congenial, not even especially moral. A motley crew, they fit almost everywhere, least in the circle of the mighty, rich and satisfied, though on occasion an Elijah or a John the Baptist may be there. So it is that, together with his people, Christ penetrates the earth to its every nook and cranny, comes even to those who live in the inferno as violated and dying. Without the variety of disciples, their gifts and lacks, there would be no lordship reaching out to the whole world and every creature. Variety makes it possible that no space remains outside his comfort and claim, and earth is continually confronted by him.

In 1 Corinthians 12:4ff. it is said of the Spirit of God that he distributes talents and energies differently so that in each place an ensign of the eternal kingdom can be raised, and none must be deaf to the gospel call or refuse to answer it. Diversity is precisely the path and means to that unity of which the Bible speaks. This unity, which has variety for its obverse side and which allows for tensions within it and requires mutual replenishing and aid, thus love, is what we call solidarity. Not uniformity but solidarity, in which all members intercede for each other and the world about them, is what is demanded of the Body of Christ, allows Christ to be present. There was a reason why the theme of this introduction read "The One and the Many." It would have been much more abstract to speak of Christian unity and diversity. Then the thought could have been of pluriformity from a sociological perspective, as is reflected in the formation of political parties. But what is at issue for us is the one Lord, the one faith that holds to his word and persists in discipleship, the one mission into the universal priesthood following Easter. At issue is the first commandment, its realization on earth, and salvation for all in need. The one Lord cannot do without the many if he is to be served everywhere, and his name glorified at all times and under all circumstances.

If this is so, then, as 1 Corinthians 12:12ff. once more concludes, no member of the Body of Christ can say to the other, "You are superfluous; I don't need you." But also no member may say to himself or herself, "I am superfluous, not unconditionally claimed, because I am really of no use." Here, resignation is forbidden, just as is pride that overestimates self. Paul answers to both responses and types of behavior with the categorical statement, *"God arranged."* Whoever opposes this comes into conflict with the Almighty, which cannot possibly be of benefit. Not by chance is it emphasized that precisely the weak, the less imposing, and even the despised must be taken into the fellowship. This is in conformity with the Lord, who, according to Isaiah 53, was the most despised and had no beauty. It is in conformity with the Nazarene, who gathered about him a host of the miserable, the outcasts, and sinners, and who was decried as demonic. Through its emphasis on doctrine, Christianity, at least in the sphere of the Western middle class, has largely forgotten this. Of course, it saw the poor and carried on the diaconate that involved individual sacrifice, but for the most part the majority merely gave alms from its superfluity, as though it were dealing with dogs. What was forgotten and has remained so is that we are all beggars before God and have no credit with him that could be based on our piety and good works.

Respectable society, at least over the course of time, withdrew more and more into the churches and rendered them middle class, with the result that the proletariat was just as excluded as any other group measured by his or her ideals and morals, then branded as a heretic. It is clear that this type of Christianity is undergoing basic revision today, and since we did not effect it on our own, it is occurring from the outside. Our children and grandchildren will perhaps learn that, together with the might of Europe and America, the influence and privileges of all the Western churches are disappearing. God returns to his people the exploited, whom we have too long put out with the garbage. He brings down what is religiously exalted and conceited, and even in Christianity raises the humble out of the dust of Africa, Asia, and Latin America. Those who understand the signs of the time must hear the admonition of Romans 14–15: "Welcome one another!" They will no longer make their own confession and tradition the keys to the kingdom of heaven, but as hard as it is and with so many thorns and stones not yet removed from this path, they will think and act ecumenically and, in so doing, reap a gain, be it only a farsightedness and a turning away from longing for a warm nest and quiet within their walls, among their friends, in the familiar heritage.

No one is superfluous. But I must also hear this for myself. It is true that my powers are too weak to master every situation, that my eyes and ears observe things only at limited range, that I continually experience my limits. This is the obverse side of our need for God, for our brothers and sisters, of our inability to avoid community. In 2 Corinthians 3 Paul expressly states that the Father of Christ, even where he calls apostles, works with useless material. He is always the One who wakens the dead and gives proof of it when he takes us into his service. So, conversely, we are not allowed to bury our talent and become the unfaithful servant. Each person has something with which to serve. None went away empty when the world was created. Before everyone's door a Lazarus is waiting, even when each of us is lying sick unto death. In the past we too often trusted that others with an office and regularly called should act for us. We must break with this habit and are taught to do so when we cannot do it by ourselves. Each one who is a disciple on Jesus' way is sent, and each must direct eyes, ears, and all the senses and all of reason toward where he or she can serve. What need not be treated in detail is that this must happen today, particularly in view of the Third and Fourth Worlds, which for 500 years or more the white race exploited, and whose goods we still devour. Only when we have taken our criteria from there will we learn again to evaluate our own situation properly. Christian faith and the world belong together. No one person is to do, reflect, or program everything, but there is always something at our feet needing to be raised. No one can manage self and what is temporal on one's own. For this reason, mutual replenishing is needed. No one is more than an instrument that one day will break down. But each must confirm his or her faith by working with others.

We come to the final question. There is solidarity only where the many work together, each in his or her own way and not necessarily without tension. But now we learn daily that solidarity is not self-evidently exercised in Christianity. It is too often lacking in families, groups, and communities, to say nothing of the great churches. We must keep in mind that sin has not disappeared, even among believers, that it always means God's gifts to us are not used or are misused. None stands trial here over what he or she did not have. The judgment on each one is levied according to what was given. The solidarity of Jesus' disciples is open to all because heaven was opened and remains open over all creatures. We must emphasize this personally in thinking and acting. The church can never be too open. It is rather always in danger of becoming a closed society. But where are the limits of unity and diversity? This topic would naturally have to be discussed in detail. I will content myself with naming three marks of Christian service that also indicate where our service ceases to be Christian. These are the marks of love, reason, and the cross.

No doubt so much has been said about love that most of the time we are unable to say exactly what is meant by it and think merely of sentiment. In the Bible it means life for others, and here the New Testament characteristically includes strangers and enemies together with the neighbor. This has sense only when the lover, as Jesus, goes out from self and accepts the other where nature and tradition, inclination and our professional goals do not lead us. The cry of those who are foundering and the word of the gospel must open our eyes and ears, readying us for surrender. Where it is genuine, love will have something of the exodus about it, something of dying, since it assumes self-denial. Just this, according to 1 Corinthians 13, holds all the charisms together — thus all our God-given capabilities and energies — and creates solidarity out of diversity, directs the many who on earth are positioned differently toward the One who is their Lord. It is just this that fulfills the first commandment in a twofold sense. Here we see that the human remains a needy creature and is oriented to the grace of the Creator and toward the care of the earthly community. Thus, genuine love as service for God and his creation wrests us from the grip of demonic powers that drive us to isolation and, out of pride and despair, ruin the world and allow it to be changed to an inferno. Just as faith hears, "I am the Lord your God," so love hears, "You shall have no other gods before me." For wherever it is selflessly active, love brings with it the breath of freedom that also surrounded the activity of Jesus. It recognizes no differences that are man-made or caused by fate, sets no conditions for its work, puts no questions concerning right or worth or standing or confession. For love, it is enough that a child of its Lord is shown to it. This frees one from constraints and proves to be an aid toward humanizing the human.

Reason has often been opposed in the name of faith. Many think they must still oppose reason when it encounters them in critical shape. We need not treat this theme in its entirety. What is important first of all is that faith and reason must not at all be in conflict, that faith slips off into ideology or merely holding something to be true if — and precisely on the basis of the first commandment! — it does not become and remain supremely critical. In Romans 12:2-3, Paul calls all Christians to a renewal of mind that, in testing, retrieves the will of God from ideology and absurdity. Second, love remains blind when not given definition by reason that opens our eyes, hears the cries of those fallen among robbers, and soberly and purposefully does what is needed. Just so, faith must know what is and is not uppermost so as not to suffocate in scruples but to live from the freedom of the children of God. We must recognize that our world is tormented as much by anxieties as by longings. We learn to our misfortune that reason alone does not rescue us from them, but we also learn that a Christianity that thinks, acts, and lives unreasonably buries its gifts and no longer does justice to its tasks. It loses its relevance in dealing with neighbors and relationships. It no longer perceives that the white race must look at itself in the mirror of the Third World to recognize its true face, its greed and self-righteousness, to see that our children and grandchildren must pay for what we have done and omitted to do in the present. These are only a few examples from the wealth of what needs to be held before Christians in defense of reason. If I were to reduce it to a common denominator, I would say that the renewal of the mind to which Paul calls is indispensable where it is a matter of fending off a possession that in many shapes and disguises ensnares humanity worldwide and allows humanness to die out. Christian freedom consists in the fact that, since heaven has been opened, we allow earth and access to the other to be more open without preference for the warm nest of a closed society.

Let none be deceived that, on the way of Jesus' disciple, one is continually led beneath the cross and from there indelibly marked. Neither faith nor love, neither reason nor freedom, neither grace nor the hope of Christ are to be had cheaply. The servant is stamped with the image of his master. Resurrection from the dead, which always occurs where God is at work, occurs by way of the graves and through judgment of the old Adam. It begins each day when we are always waiting for it. Christianity is not a religion of martyrs, certainly not of self-chosen and reckless martyrdom, though since Ignatius of Antioch such has existed till most recently. The Revelation of John sets forth in a clearly biblical way, and church history proves, that the witnesses must enjoy a certain relationship to the martyrs. In a certain way, every Christian is affected by it. Whoever does not gain theological understanding from this point more likely belongs to the religious author or a spokesperson of a particular ideology. The young Luther correctly formulated it: *crux est theologia nostra* — the cross is our theology — something to be related not merely to doctrine but to life as well.

More than hints were not given here. My concern is to point out that the disciples of Jesus are stigmatized, as Paul says of himself in Galatians 6:17. We will give careful attention to the fact that this stigma can never be entirely unequivocal, since only God knows the truth of our heart and our way. Nonetheless, there are traces of truth in bodily-earthly reality that we should at least see and consider to be signs. In the concrete instance, love and reason are quite open to suspicion, and the suffering we bear may not be ordained by God but a self-flagellation. But where these three marks unite and point to the Nazarene, and where they waken offense among the religious and sinners, there the limits to the diversity of members in the Body of Christ, as well as the basis for its unity, become visible. The many must remain in discipleship of the One if they are to achieve solidarity and are not concerned with displaying their own image for the present and future, and instead of his image forcing their own on others. He is our measure and our limit, our freedom and our bond — he alone.

God's "Yes" to All

First Timothy 2:4 reads, "God our Savior . . . desires everyone to be saved and to come to the knowledge of the truth." This sentence sounds as though it were obvious. Almost always the Bible speaks so simply and downright childishly. But it becomes dangerous when we begin to deal with it and take it into our everyday life. It may happen to us as to Christopher in the old melancholy legend. The child on his shoulders became heavier and heavier when he waded through the river. The Christ whom he had wanted to carry finally had to carry the stumbling Christopher to the other shore. If God's word has once seized hold of us so as to penetrate our everyday life, and thus intends to be lived there, then, rather than mere hearers, we become those who ask, learn, and pray. Then inwardly and outwardly we move toward a goal we did not choose, perhaps even toward roads where heaven and earth appear otherwise than usual. In this fashion we will carefully consider each of the words of our text.

"God desires." Christian faith maintains that the entire world began with this desire, that all of history should stand beneath this watchword, and with it our own life from its first to its last breath. When we hear it, perhaps it should sound as unearthly to us as it once did to the disciples at Easter, when first of all not joy but fear of the resurrected One overcame them. What does "God desires" mean? We can only answer that we are no more left alone to our wishes and anxieties than we are left to others, to known or unknown powers. An almighty hand stretches toward us and overshadows everything we desire, do, and fear. Easter occurs with us daily

A lecture given on June 27 and 28, 1980, at the Kirchentag in Schwerin and Neustrelitz.

till the hour of our death. One continually appears to us whom we so easily forget, whom we take to be dead or a phantasm. Now Psalm 139:5ff. applies: "You hem me in, behind and before, and lay your hand upon me. . . . Where can I go from your spirit? Or where can I flee from your presence? If I ascend to heaven, you are there; if I make my bed in Sheol, you are there." Just as the Risen One at Easter, so in every moment the living God enters into the present when we hear, "God desires." He seeks us as the lover the beloved, as the one abandoned seeks what he has lost, as the hunter his prey. He continually goes before us to show us a way we learn to know only by taking it, a way we will probably often resist and that ends in such fashion that our Creator alone still holds and can help us. Just as the people of Israel on Sinai once heard "God desires," so we are named by this word in baptism and remain for time and eternity under the first commandment, "I am the Lord your God. . . . You shall have no other gods before me!" This is the sum of Holy Scripture, merely commented on by all its other statements. In Jesus Christ it takes on bodily, human shape. Each of us finds existence, measure, support, limit, task, and goal when addressed with these words, "I am the Lord your God. I will have you." This is God's grasp of his creature, following which we are all addressable, whatever else happens to us and whatever we make of ourselves or others in love and hate, entirely apart from whether we know and want it or not. By it we first become truly human, and when we accept it, we remain human in midst of worldwide inhumanity.

God has willed us and called us by name. There is no disputing that others also reach for us, persons near to us or who await us from afar, relations that oppress us or in which we have made a permanent home, powers of good and evil that demand our service or submission. Claims are incessantly laid to us. Someone seeks to bring us under alien rule with promises or threats. Above all, our own heart never leaves us in peace. There is always something it wants to have, something that seems necessary to it, of which it is frightened or for which it cares. Many voices in and around us drown out the first commandment, so that we begin to ask and doubt what God's will really is. No one is spared times of suffering in which head and heart turn dark. We must all gradually get used to dying or are thrust unawares at the grave of our dear ones. Then believers lament and unbelievers scoff, "Where is now your God?" Finally, there are those shocks in which we perceive with horror that we have created disaster for others, can no longer make good what we omitted, are most deeply enmeshed in earth's great rebellion against its Lord, and must confess with David, "I have sinned against the Lord." With good reason Hebrews 13:9 states, "It is well for the heart to be strengthened by grace." We agree with the premise. A firm heart goes its way unerring through the unrest of the day, through the dreams and horrors of the night. It keeps faith that will belong only to One where others totter, fall, and turn away to others. But the verse reads that we achieve it only by grace; we cannot gain it by our own strength or understanding but must allow it to be given to us. Only love allows our heart to be fixed when we hear its voice, affirm it, respond to it. We have need of another to whom we can hold and who can speak to us when we flounder.

Plainly put, we should open the Bible daily and from it hear the voice of love addressed personally to us. Grace makes use of the divine word to bring us out of earthly confusion before the face of the eternal Lord, to set us in the kinship of the disciples and urge us to mutual love, which prays, "Keep my heart to the one thing, that I fear your name!" In this way the first commandment is kept. It is not, as only heathen assume, a heavenly command that penalizes disobedience and omission. In reality it is the great promise as it comes to us at Christmas, once more at Pentecost, and to all the world: "I am your God; you need no longer follow other idols and saviors." The true God — that is, the Father of Jesus Christ — frees us from imagining that we take our destiny and that of our children under our own control, submit unrestrictedly to the war of competition, or must flee to the protective shadows of alien powers. Just as he redeemed Israel from Egypt, so God gives his people whatever they need for confident life and death. So Luther's Large Catechism explains the first commandment in this way: "A 'god' is the term for that to which we are to look for all good and in which we are to find refuge in all need. Therefore, to have a god is nothing else than to trust and believe in that one with your whole heart." Now it is clear why the watchword "God desires" is followed by "everyone to be saved." The way in which the first commandment distinguishes the Father of Jesus Christ from all other lords and powers is that, from eternity to eternity, he is a God for, among, and together with humans. We know of no god who exists in and for himself. About such a god philosophers and heathen may speculate. As Creator and Judge, he lives and rules for humans' sake, for which reason we need not stare into heaven as if he were to be found only there. Our God has come to earth, become human like us, and died on the cross; he was blasphemed by believers and unbelievers, was excluded from the community of the church, as well as from political authority, and was numbered among criminals. Our faith is directed toward him. He is our help.

We do not say this in advertising, as so often happens where help is promised. Naturally, there are Christians who take themselves to be God's propagandists and render him and themselves unbelievable. Churches become complicit when their preaching aims at binding the number of their adherents more firmly to themselves or at increasing their number. We use God's name in vain when we take him to market like a ware. He is no quack who by sleight of hand cures everyone of actual or imagined worries. Experience has taught us that we can knock on his door without having to get from him what we expected or actually asked for. Many are not healed and, like the rich young ruler, have gone away sorrowful. Frequently, our hopes collapse over graves, as occurred with the sisters of Lazarus or the Emmaus disciples, who did not recognize the Risen One. We should never forget that this very day thousands are hungering, being exploited, tortured, and murdered. For the majority of its inhabitants this earth of ours has become a hell. Of all living creatures, only humans can close their eyes, ears, and hearts to what they do not want to see, hear, or feel. Christians have no right to distance themselves from the suffering of their brothers and sisters, to be silent about cruelty, to remain neutral where the future of our earth and the annihilation of life are at issue.

Under the cross of Golgotha we learn two things: God does not give himself into our hands so that, with his name as a magic formula, we could solve all the problems of our life and all the conflicts of the world, could shield ourselves from evil, violence, tribulation, and death. He gives himself into our hands with the Man from Nazareth, who would not save himself but would serve others and render his disciples human. So we sing, "Fragst du, wer der ist? Er heißt Jesus Christ, der Herr Zebaoth, und ist kein anderer Gott. Das Feld muss er behalten" (Do you ask who he is? His name is Jesus Christ, Lord of Sebaoth. There is no other God. He must hold the field). Here and only here we stand at the place where we may speak openly, confidently, and to everyone of God's help. It exists only in the name and under the sign of Christ.

This leads us to the next step in reflecting on our watchword: "God our Savior, who desires everyone to be saved." The message of divine help is in no way to be limited or rendered problematic by what was just emphasized. Nevertheless, we must always resist a false faith if we are to create space and understanding for the true faith. For this reason, Christianity includes the guild and trade of professional theologians. Too many Christians have not learned the first commandment by heart or have forgotten it again. Not even religious people are aware that our God always enters an earth possessed by alien powers and rebels. Faith in him does not flourish in empty space. It is rather always something like resurrection from the graves, for it prays with Jesus in Gethsemane, "Your will be done!" Right here we should have Luther's explanation in mind, which sets forth as rigorously as possible when and how this prayer is answered. "Whenever God breaks and hinders every evil scheme and will — as are present in the will of the devil, the world, and our flesh — that would not allow us to hallow God's name and would prevent the coming of his kingdom, and instead whenever God strengthens us and keeps us steadfast in his word and in faith until the end of our lives. This is his gracious and good will." This is not easy to swallow, and it makes discipleship of Jesus for us and others annoying.

The New Testament is full of stories about the exorcising of demons and of conversion from false faith. Both belong closely together. Through all our life there is the old Adam or Eve, who are content with God only when he attends to their wishes and anxieties, who would like to prescribe for him how he must rule. Conversion means to take leave of this old Adam, this old Eve each day, and, as it were, to repeat one's baptism. We may gladly and truly hear it as gospel that God intends to help all and thus create a new heaven and earth. But the new world begins with the fact that in Jesus Christ the new self appears and delivers the second creation from earthly chaos, that he begins to shape his disciples according to his image. The Gospels speak of this, and whoever has to do with Christian existence, has to do with this New Man, who sets them in discipleship from out of demonic blindness, egotism, sloth, and resignation, and compels them to rethink inwardly and outwardly, to turn about, to become a reflection of their Lord. It is not enough to have pious convictions, as did the Pharisees and heathenish fanatics.

There are very few who have nothing at all on which to hang their heart, on which to build, something to fear and love above all things, and thus allow to be their god. Whoever was baptized is seldom asked, Who is your God? How much are you ready to risk or lose for him? Where is the limit at which he may no longer disturb you with his burdens and tasks, at which you give notice to obedience, when he leads you on arduous, sorrowful, perilous paths, leads you like Abraham out of the familiar nest of the inherited tradition of the fathers, out of your previous society and companionship into one unknown, into his future? What price are you able to pay for your faith? At sometime or other, each must give an answer. We all must die, and then at the latest the decision must be made whether the life we lived was worth living, whether we followed the true Lord or will-o'-the-wisps, demons, and illusions. Since this is so, our watchword closes with the words, "and to come to the knowledge of the truth." This is not an edifying appendix but the foundational characteristic of the divine aid. This aid does not exist where truth is not visible, experienced by us, and spread through us as its reflection.

Now, we may be inclined to repeat the old question of Pilate, "What is truth?" Is this a question that should concern only those who are not tied to the everyday, to family and business, to the dangers and possibilities of success in the world around them, while the rest of us have neither the time nor the requisite conditions for theories and speculations? Is it not enough that we deal with the reality of life halfway? Viewed from the Bible, at least, these objections are evasions. The Bible does not speak of truth as a sum of individual truths or, as we are used to saying today, of basic values or norms that dogmaticians, jurists, and perhaps science in general must reconcile. "Truth" for Christians has entirely human, personal features and shapes, for it is the face of God that he turns to his creation. Psalm 80:3 clamors for it: "Let your face shine, that we may be saved." At the conclusion of every worship service the congregation is blessed with the words from Numbers 6:24-26: "The Lord bless you and keep you; the Lord make his face to shine upon you, and be gracious to you; the Lord lift up his countenance upon you, and give you peace."

This face of God turned toward us became flesh and went over the earth in the One who, according to John 14:6, says of himself, "I am the way, and the truth, and the life. No one comes to the Father except through me." He alone and in a way that cannot be misunderstood shows us the One who gave the first commandment and his promise. Together with the true God he also shows us the true Man, so that we recognize ourselves and earthly relationships in his light, without prejudice. He opens heaven above and the earth around by calling us to the succession of his disciples. As long as we remain there, continually allow ourselves to be included there, we stand before the countenance of God, in the truth. Then Jesus becomes the way for us, as the Easter hymn choruses: "Wo mein Haupt ist durchgegangen, da nimmet es mich auch mit. Er reißet durch den Tod, durch Welt, durch Sünd und Not. Er reißet durch die Höll. Ich bin stets sein Gesell" (Where my Head has gone, I too am borne along. He bursts through death, through the world, through sin and misery. He bursts through hell. I am forever his ally). In this way we at last become truly alive. Where the path leads through world, sin, need, death, and even hell, without ever coming to an end, there breaks into earth's daily routine the reflection of eternal life. There heaven begins on earth because God is for us, because we are his children.

This truth is not the personal privilege of individuals or groups. Not even churches possess it so as to control it. The Nazarene came to all in need of help, and the Holy Spirit blows where he will. Even today he clearly empties out the entrenchments erected by confessions and fellowships against each other and against the non-Christian world. In these days Germany has celebrated the 450th anniversary of the recitation in 1530 of the Augsburg Confession. We have reason for remembering this date on which Lutheranism found unity in faith and doctrine. But today we may perhaps be permitted to state critically that it is no longer enough to see the true church only where God's word is clearly and purely proclaimed and the sacraments rightly administered. At least we must realize that no proclamation of the gospel can be clear and pure that does not point expressly to the Beatitudes. Wherever the white race still represents Christianity, the middle class dominates in the church. Its worldview and morality have become determinative, and we, at least for the most part, live in a closed society of religious people. It is no longer evident that Jesus, himself excluded by the good and the religious, blessed the poor, those who mourn and hunger for righteousness, blessed the persecuted and exploited, since in the end it was for them, the helpless and damned of the earth, that a helper had arisen. He took whores and tax collectors and radical zealots into his retinue and did not prevent women from becoming his servants. He accepted a host of slaves into his discipleship and admonished all not to strive for power, success, or esteem but to become like children, who, confident as the needy, continually petition their Father for his gifts.

In Germany we are only slowly coming to realize that in our time Christianity has become ecumenical, but that it is still provincial and middle class within the shadow of its own church towers and the private circle of the like-minded. In this way we obstruct the great help of our God, which applies to all, but especially to all the excluded who cry for liberation from earthly fetters. We cannot reproach ourselves often enough over the fact that everywhere Christians are only a minority and at best work as leaven in the world. If we are becoming ecumenical today, the issue is not majority rule and defense of our traditional rights and imagined privileges. We hear rather that God's Yes will be realized worldwide, will penetrate to every abyss, every nook and cranny. This is possible only when Christianity seriously and resolutely reflects on the commissioning of the Risen One, who teaches it to look out from the haze of a pious circle and see the whole earth as the realm of our Lord's rule. Our God is not a private idol whom we can contain in our heart or in a confession. He will have worldwide fellowship, as the description of the last judgment in Matthew 25:31ff. makes clear. None may object that the Son of Man did not stop by, did not call to service, call to be the instrument of his help. "Just as you did not do it to one of the least of these, you did not do it to me." The Body of Christ on earth has no tolerance for inactive members who do not have their most distant brothers and sisters in mind and heart and, as the church of the One who for our sakes became poor, do not apply the salvation and help of our God to the miserable, the dying, the forgotten, and the despised of the earth.

Now, of course, there will always be those who feel too weak or unable to share in this work. They will often have reason for such a fiction as is left to mere imagining in order to shift their burden to others. Whatever the case, both groups are unmistakably summoned by the apostle in 1 Corinthians 12:12ff. None is superfluous or useless in God's service. Each one has gifts, possibilities, and chances, however insignificant or taken for worthless. The Man from Golgotha makes clear to us all that God does not build his kingdom from the top down but rather sets the lowly on their feet and to their work. There are always those hopeless cases from which he creates his elect. He rejects the proud who stride through life on their own strength and understanding and want to come to terms with death on their own. Second Corinthians 12:9 reads, "My grace is sufficient for you, for power is made perfect in weakness." This is not just spoken to the wind. Paul must hear it when he feels attacked by Satan's angel and, close to despair, prays to be set free. The effect of God's omnipotence is not that it allows us to fold our hands in our laps or makes supermen of us. It is shown in the fact that it enlists in its service what is nothing and smallest, equips it to hand on love and grace to others. It does not give freedom so that we have nothing more to learn of anxiety, pain, and death, but that from out of our own distresses we become more human in contact with others. We are God's seed in the stony and thorny ground of the earth, destined to ripen from the depths and bring forth fruit for our Lord and neighbor. Whoever will not be and become such is thrown aside. God's salvation ends where God's will is not resolutely seized, where discipleship of the suffering Servant of God and service to God's needy creation are refused. Only those who could die can rise again, and in their everyday life Jesus' disciples must continually go a step further toward death in order to be signs and witnesses of that power which brings Lazarus forth from the grave and conquers death. Where God assumed responsibility for us, he also carries us toward the goal.

Naturally, we will not cease to ask how this should and can occur with us, and in a way all can experience. When do people stop asking in this way? They should not, for whoever does not ask gets no answer. It would be good for us to hear from Scripture that God appears to us with questions. "Adam, where are you?" — so the first man is asked after his fall. "Where is your brother, Abel?" — so it continues with Cain. When he became an adulterer and murderer, David hears, "Why have you despised the word of the Lord?" Job's complaints are struck down with, "Shall a faultfinder contend with the Almighty?" To Isaiah comes the call, "Whom shall I send, and who will go for us?" In John 6:67 Jesus asks his disciples, "Do you also wish to go away?" and in John 21:16 to Peter, "Do you love me?" or in Luke 22:48 to Judas, "Is it with a kiss that you are betraying the Son of Man?" We should study the Bible for all the questions God puts to us. His questions summon us from our illusions to the reality of our life. Truly abiding and comprehensive help begins with our seeing, hearing, and experiencing where we stand, what we are about. All the calamity of this world roots in a possession in which we no longer see ourselves, others, our relationships and the earth as they really are, but as we wish them to be.

It is not the errors we make or the weaknesses that cling to us that are truly dangerous. We are not angels and need not become saints. Jesus teaches to pray the Our Father, which contains only petitions, thus always assumes needy and guilt-laden people. As God is and remains our Creator, he wills to give us what we need. Because he is our Father for Jesus' sake, he will continually open his arms even to lost children if only we come to him. To forgive, however, is more than merely to excuse and let bygones be bygones. According to the old baptismal hymn in Colossians 1:13, to forgive means to be rescued from the power of darkness and transferred into the kingdom of his beloved Son. What is really perilous is to live and die as though the kingdom of Jesus Christ began only in heaven, as though we did not already belong to his kingdom today and in the body. Mussels close up when one takes hold of them. When the Nazarene came to us, heaven opened over us, and it remains open over us because, as at Pentecost, God's Spirit continually allows us to hear that the Father says "Yes" to his children, to me and to all he created and calls to himself. There is only one life-threatening sin, that is, to refuse to be totally open to the One who speaks his "Yes" to us and allows us as members and witnesses of his kingdom on earth to become something to the praise of his glory.

Let us look back and summarize. Second Corinthians 1:19 reduces everything Paul and his companions have to proclaim to a single denominator: God has said "Yes" to us. Jesus Christ is this "Yes" of our God in the flesh, that is, the One who for our salvation became man, died, and rose again. The chief thing in life and death consists in allowing oneself to be set under this great "Yes." It means to recognize in God our Creator, Father, and only Judge; to be transferred into the kingdom of Jesus Christ already on earth. And so that we do not stray even when threatened by powers and suffering, God's Spirit speaks to us through the word of Scripture, that is, consoles us ever anew with this "Yes." To live from it and become productive, we must hand it on to all for whom we are responsible and, in so doing, may never forget that God loves and seeks the humble, the lost, and the mistreated. Each of us then becomes a sign of the open heaven above. Each comes to experience his or her own gospel and thus gives witness that "God our Savior . . . desires everyone to be saved and to come to the knowledge of the truth."

Justice for the Unjust

My theme is a variant of the Pauline formula of the justification of the godless in Romans 4:5. This is how the characteristic uniqueness of Paul's view of divine and human righteousness is from the outset marked off from other views. My theme assumes that the formula, though found only once in this terse form, reflects the apostle's theology as a whole and may absolutely not be relativized. Admittedly, this formula has become strange even to Christians and churches, in part seems quite unintelligible, and is usually regarded in edifying fashion as a rhetorical paradox. Paul is assumed to be boasting of the power of grace to the extent that he actually allows it to extend to the godless. But one takes great pains never to contest the justification of the godly. Almost everywhere in Christendom all are convinced that, of course, God must always deal with human imperfection, error, and weakness but that still he answers to the longing of our heart and the impulses of a will to the true and the good. If this never occurs without grace, on the other hand care is taken as to whether we were on our way toward God in despair or childlike trust, and thus at the deepest level were not entirely ungodly. The Pauline formula is relativized in another way when understood exclusively on the basis of its context — thus related to Abraham and Old Testament history, but no longer allowed to characterize the story of the new covenant. If this were the correct approach, support for my variation on the apostle's statement would be eliminated. We can only speak of justice for those who are without it if

---

A lecture given on June 22, 1976, at the Ecumenical Institute at Château de Bossey, Switzerland.

Abraham's story describes God's activity for every time and place, if God is never experienced other than in just this way, as justifying the godless.

At this juncture, faith and superstition, the Father of Jesus Christ and the gods of human invention, are distinguished and separated. No psychology may obscure the fact that, with his formula, Paul most precisely summarizes his teaching regarding God and our salvation, that he derives from it his rights as well as the necessity of being a missionary to the Gentiles, and thus in unexcelled clarity interprets the message and work of the Man of the cross. The Nazarene knew he was not sent to those who are well but to those who are sick, that his Beatitudes applied to those who were despised by Pharisees and scribes, that he died for sinners. From the Christian perspective, we cannot treat the divine and human righteousness if we do not proceed *from that point* and recognize that Paul points in precisely that direction.

Not accidentally even in Christianity, the attempt is made to take the edge from this theology. Let it be noted that it originated beneath the cross of Golgotha and is thus unavoidably opposed to our judgments and prejudices. In the reality of the world around us there must be a claim to justice if it is to be achieved. Only those authorized may demand it for themselves or can actually sue for it. Paul is aware of this idea and has allowed it to be expressed in the context of Romans 4:5. In earthly society reward is linked to prior achievement. Religious people apply this to their relation to God. He becomes their referee between good and evil and requites all according to their works. Where sins and merits are more or less in balance, his everneeded mercy tips the scale to our advantage. In any case, none can approach God and please him without pious deeds. When Paul contradicts this it sounds blasphemous.

Debate with the apostle not only occurs in the religious sphere. We have to keep in mind that, in modern democracy since the Enlightenment and the resultant French and American Revolutions, basic human rights are postulated that pertain to all and are to be observed and defended, especially respecting the weak. Can this still be supported and acknowledged from the Christian point of view, where, in the context of Pauline theology, we can speak of justice only for those who are without it? The question is difficult and not to be answered in a simple sentence. The Enlightenment watchword does not merely appeal to ancient tradition, say, to the late Stoics. No doubt, in its own way it intends to hand on the biblical teaching of creation. Whatever else happens, every person is and remains a creature of God and insofar is to be respected. So Paul explicitly took up the slogan "to each his own" and made it the basis for his teaching on the charisms. This does not exclude the fact that he counsels each to remain in his or her social position, does not advocate the emancipation of slaves, commands women to be silent at worship, and clearly assumes a thoroughly patriarchal order in and outside the congregation. In any event, he did not and probably could not speak of basic rights. He was concerned with a mutual and universal service that claims may not limit or obscure.

So, as regards the subject itself, if the Enlightenment slogan can be interpreted and accepted in Christian fashion, its formulation has resulted more from the ancient worldview than from biblical proclamation. From that perspective it has a certain ideological tinge leading to particular consequences that cannot be justified from the Christian point of view. Proof of this would be, for example, the demand for emancipation at all possible levels of societal life, so current and varied today. But we only need a critical eye for earthly reality in which, say, basic democratic rights are proclaimed, to be aware of the problematic of this proclamation. Have liberty, equality, and fraternity ever existed empirically, even in a democratic order? Do these not express mere wish-fulfillment dreams about the dignity of the individual and the proper condition of various societies? If the ideals aimed at were anywhere approximated, such always occurred within narrow limits, as in the contest between nationalities in a concurrent oppression of others who had to pay the price. If one tried to apportion welfare justly in any country, a bureaucracy would immediately arise, persons would be dominated by it, and no doubt, the few areas of wealth and superabundance would be set against the wide world of the exploited.

It is no accident that in the twentieth century the mantra of "revolution" canceled out that of "evolution" from our grandparents' time. Even in the democracies there exist privileged and authoritative strata, classes, and races. There need only be greater unemployment, and immediately tolerance toward the evicted and immigrant workers retreats. To wide extent, the greater part of humanity remains without freedom or the chances of realizing their so-called basic rights. If one attempts it by force, his or her place in the sun is displaced. Others who are favored now use their possibilities, create new dependencies, and perhaps also practice new tyranny. To see and put it precisely, in surveying more than 200 years of modern democracy, only those can glory in it who have profited by it. For the rest, power always trumps justice. It keeps justice penned up or violates and replaces it. Theologians at least should fearlessly demythologize the ideals of the white race, since here too much blindness and hypocrisy are in play. This, then, is the result as regards our theme: The principle of performance and competition commended to the underdeveloped at current world conferences serves the egotism of the privileged who defend their status quo. No reason — to say nothing of the gospel — can be seen in this.

Religious and secular objections to the Pauline theology need not impress us to the point where we would cease to ask for the apostle's opinion respecting divine and human righteousness. Further, it is clear that Paul thinks of the relation between the two in a different way than we. We proceed from the *concept* (ideal) of justice and by it measure the concrete behavior of God or of humans. Justice for us is a value that we can describe without first keeping in mind the one who practices or neglects it. Justice is ranked by us on a scale of values, over the sequence of which we can argue. If we may describe this as an objectifying approach, we must state that the Bible is scarcely aware of it. Perhaps we may formulate it like this: The Bible thinks in personal terms, even when speaking of powers and forces. According to the Bible, what we term worthy and unworthy is decided by the relation to the Lord in heaven. He determines what being human involves. On the other hand, one recognizes one's self, thus one's humanity, the meaning of life, and the truth of the world only in recognition of one's lord. There is no scale of values that, say, as virtues or characteristics could be connected with or viewed in isolation from the kingdom of God.

For Paul, the righteousness of God is not an attitude that measures out gifts and tasks on the basis of human merit or weakness. Conformity in terms of the *do ut des,* quid pro quo, is not its criterion, and it is not what jurists call *aequitas,* equity. At bottom, righteousness is the revelation of God in his nature and truth, and in a particular relation, soon to be described. Righteousness means that God is at work and makes known before all the world what he is and what is according to his will. With this view the apostle roots firmly in Old Testament tradition and its Jewish environment. What makes this particularly clear is that for him the righteousness of God does not have the features of judicial requital but remains a gracious activity even in judgment. Israel described God's righteousness from out of the relation of fidelity to the covenant, thus from its central experience of Sinai and wilderness journey. God who established the covenant with his people watches like a protective power to see to it that his covenant partner remains within the space of the fidelity promised him and, from all lapses, is returned to it again.

Perhaps I should linger briefly over the fact that I am speaking emphatically and consciously of "power," and must do so even over against the Pauline view. This is appropriate, seeing that God is epiphany-like in righteousness and covenant faithfulness, thus proves himself to be Lord and draws one into the sphere of his lordship or preserves one in it. At issue here is not a once-for-all act but a continual event in no sense to be privatized, that is, limited to individual persons and groups, but rather occurs within a worldwide horizon. God cannot and may not be conceived of apart from the sphere and presence of his lordship as expressed in his concrete activity. From this point it also becomes clear that the divine faithfulness is described precisely as righteousness, while at least *for us* the key words "grace," "love," and "mercy" appear to be more appropriate, and many exegetes quite obviously substitute them for "righteousness." Where it is a matter of God's kingdom in relation to his people, within an earthly space and a global horizon, where his power is asserted in protecting and demanding, grace is the making known of the divine right to rule, not a merely inscrutable or arbitrary love. God manifests himself, majestically creating and preserving his kingdom when he brings righteousness and allows it to prevail.

Paul needs to alter the structure of this traditional context at only one point but, in so doing, gives to the whole another direction. His experience before Damascus, his understanding of the cross of Jesus, and his mission into the world of the Gentiles lead him out of the area of Israel in a theological way as well. They allow him to use the motif of the people of God in a merely historical or metaphorical sense. Justification of the godless is the central theme of his proclamation. The fact that he can appropriate traditions in which God's righteousness still passes for covenant faithfulness has remained a problem unnoticed till now. It can be cleared up if we assume that Paul has transferred the idea of the covenant from the story of Israel's exodus to the creation — incidentally, a move already prepared for by the Old Testament. The Creator's faithfulness toward his creature, irrevocably fixed in his promise, is made known at the end of time in Christ's graciously returning to God's rule what was created for it, but which had lost and forgotten its calling in godless surrender to the world. The human as such is now the covenant partner. Everyone united to the One who died for sinners is certain of election. Justification of the godless is justification by faith alone. If one is altogether retrieved from one's own works, performance, and merit, but also from prior obligations; if one is made entirely dependent on the action and promise of Another; and if this Other unmasks us as sinners and only in dying for us can be our Lord, the result is that God's righteousness is justice for the unjust. We no longer have any privilege or claim, thus no righteousness of our own. Only hypocrites or the blind do not see it. Our own justice could only be judgment on us.

Before God and at the deepest truth of our humanity, we are unjust. Nonetheless, the One who created and called us retains a right to us, laying claim to it in a forgiveness that he otherwise could not award us. Only he can forgive who is our Lord and Judge, who can lodge complaint against our guilts. In view of the dying Christ, who goes into death for us, we may flee from our own unrighteousness to our Creator's right to us, to God's righteousness and the shelter of his kingdom. Justice for the unjust is not a beautiful paradox but a precise description of what Paul means by salvation. So, both aspects are to be emphasized. Here, the righteousness of God is not a value, one legal opinion among others, an object, but personally the "God for us" who with his gracious will and all-conquering power of his love reaches out to his lost children. It is not a state of ownership one could own as a permanent or even inheritable asset but a gift continually in peril and preserved only by the fact that our Lord remains true to himself and us. This righteousness appears *sub contrario,* under the sign of its opposite, insofar as we cannot exhibit it, develop it by our own strength or understanding, perhaps make it the mark of our character. It is hidden in Christ as our Lord. But it is also *sub contrario* because this Lord is the Crucified, as such, the mockery and nuisance of the world, One in whom only believers put their trust.

In saying this, we have turned to what for Paul denotes the righteousness of God among the basically and factually unjust, that is, God's right to us, a right recognized by us as that for which humanity is ultimately destined, erected among us in the dying Christ as the power and sphere even of earthly lordship, and witnessed to in our service to all the world. It should have become clear that we are not dealing with a moral norm or the principle of a worldview, but experience with the Man from Golgotha. Otherwise, it would be a matter of an absurd religious ideology. There is no independent human righteousness alongside God's, only a standing and persevering in his righteousness. This means that righteousness exists only when we are continually hearers and keepers of the word of promise and of the claim on us in which our Lord assures us of his faithfulness, from out of which he summons us to live. This must now be removed from the abstraction of professional theological language and related to the actual situation. This may be best arrived at when we begin with an outdated aspect still central to the New Testament. Where the righteousness of God effectively directs us to our place on earth within the justice and realm of our Lord, we stand under the sign of a twilight of the gods. An old world with its acknowledged demonic forces is sentenced to death so that the truth of Christ's resurrection as the rule of the Crucified may come into view on earth. In the Bible, resurrection is not first of all anthropologically viewed as life from the grave but, in the cosmic sense, as the beginning of a new eon and the signal for breaking out of the sacred and secular encampments of idols into the freedom of the discipleship of Jesus. The righteousness that justifies the godless is polemic and aggressive because it allows God's justice to light up against an earth rebelliously yielding itself to demons and their ideologies. It sets one in the struggle against a presumed, illusory justice, so that the first commandment appears as the truth of the Old and New Testaments.

Christianity has unjustly forgotten or at least diminished the theologically non-rescindable, though haplessly described, doctrine of original sin. In the right place, demythologizing is appropriate and necessary, that is, when traditional forms of speech and points of view become barriers to understanding. But it does not at all justify surrendering oneself to the worldview of the Enlightenment. There are not only believers and unbelievers. There are also superstition, obduracy, sluggishness of heart, and stupidity of head that no education or revolution can overcome. These exist worldwide as projections of death's power. There is the evil will of the saints and the unsaintly that erected Jesus' cross and incessantly surrounds it with new crosses past counting; lays waste to the earth for the sake of egotism, vanity, and the lust for power; enslaves the lowly; and everywhere practices exploitation, all of it under the sign of the white race and its dominance. For the sake of the realities of our time, we cannot afford to look away or be silent about the fact that, for most people, earth is a hell. To want to demythologize this fact is a crime by which God's rule is necessarily spiritualized and shifted to the infinite distance of the beyond. It is undeniable that our Western tradition and the heritage of the Enlightenment have long obscured our view of the world ruled by demons. What kind of piety is it that maintains it lives from the word of God and the victory of Christ but stops its ears to the cries of fellow humans, soothes itself with the resurrection and life of the world to come, but leaves the Crucified alone on Golgotha?

Justice for the unjust should mark the Christian's status on this earth. But then it must be just as much the criterion for our mission and service. According to the Fourth Gospel, our Lord sends us as he himself was sent from the Father. According to the Synoptists, he does so as the sheep among wolves. How should the truth given our life from God not have further effect from and by us? We surely cannot keep life hidden, even when lived in a corner, in prison, or between the crypts of the dead and among the dying. Life that proceeds from us and draws its circle about us is not a special something added to what occurs within us. All life takes on expression, whether in truth or deception. If justice for the unjust is the avowal of the divine power toward us and the gift accepted by us, it must also become our work and service. We may, if you will, call this sanctification, which is the emergence of justification. Obviously, it does not denote a refined type of self-realization or achievement attributable to our effort as merit. Faith, on the other hand, is not holding something to be true, nor is it merely such that one can be fed like a tiny child. Faith is the mission of bearing the truth of the Crucified and the lordship of the Risen One to the earthly realm of demons and ideologies, a mission by the fact that one quite simply lives from it. Because it has become grace for us, justice for the unjust becomes the worldwide service of Christ, a gift to be handed on to the nearest and furthest. Clearly, this must provoke all the privileged who imagine they themselves are in the right and enforce it at others' cost.

At this juncture, we absolutely cannot avoid showing our colors, making crystal clear who our God is and is not, or to what extent the risen Lord remains the Crucified. Nor can we avoid making clear what we think of others, or of the fact that the gospel has a social and political, even an ecumenical and cosmic, dimension. In our time at least we can no longer be content with defining the nature of the church as the Reformers did, that is, in terms of word and sacrament. The church exists as the Body of Christ only where there are also the poor, those who mourn, and the despised of the Beatitudes. Where these have no part in defining the social portrait of Christianity, there is no church but a religious club falsely gathered in the name of Christ. Whatever the objection to the black theology, represented, for example, by James Cone,[1] at this point he must be unconditionally given his due. He writes, "Our Lord is the God of the oppressed," not to be found outside their fellowship. This also means that God is an enemy of all the mighty and those who sit in judgment, who maintain their own rights and the resultant status quo. The preaching of John the Baptist, as well as of the Johannine Apocalypse, has not been invalidated, that is, that every-

---

1. See James Cone, *Black Theology and Black Power* (New York: Seabury Press, 1969; repr., Maryknoll, N.Y.: Orbis Books, 1997), also his *God of the Oppressed* (Maryknoll, N.Y.: Orbis Books, 1997).

thing exalted is brought low, and everything low exalted when our God is abroad on the earth. An idealistic Christianity that cares only for the soul and eternal life is a mockery of the Man who went from the stall to the gallows, attracted the wrath of the believers of his time, and, if not exclusively, in any event continually, spent time in bad society.

If this appears too radical today in Christian middle-class society, our response is that there is neither Nazarene nor grace other than the radical kind. If this is understood by white politicians in the East and West as a preparation for, and primary support of, revolution in the Third World, and in fact not only there, then they understand the Christian message better than the conservative and reactionary circles in all the churches who do not see the face of their Master in their exploited brothers and sisters. That according to Ephesians 6:12 "our struggle is not against enemies of blood and flesh, but against the rulers, against the authorities, against the cosmic powers of this present darkness" applies to all those ideologies and demonic practices developed by the white race to its advantage and by which it seeks to force its law on the rest of the earth. The gospel does not proclaim and bring justice to the unjust from heaven, but on earth. It points us as the disciples of Jesus to the place where we must stand, and all the other places where we dare not stand. We know that we cannot overturn the world on our own, but we also know that our God will overturn it, and for this we must set up visible signs. It is an absurd perversion of the gospel to separate salvation into the vertical and horizontal, as if it were directed at angels and not at the damned of the earth, at salvation for the hopeless, the healing of the sick, and victory over the demonic. It is not necessary to explain this further and in detail. What is needed here is simply to oppose the stupidity and hypocrisy that confess and extol God's righteousness for sinners but all the while do not leave the camp of the privileged — unlike the Nazarene — or do not award justice to the brother (or sister), to everyone. This would mean that we know of a Liberator in edifying fashion but nothing of freedom and dare not anticipate the resurrection of the dead in Christian freedom.

What Does 1 Corinthians 12:12-27 Mean by "Solidarity"?

"For just as the body is one and has many members, and all the members of the body, though many, are one body, so it is with Christ. For in the one Spirit we were all baptized into one body — Jews or Greeks, slaves or free — and we were all made to drink of one Spirit. Indeed, the body does not consist of one member but of many. If the foot would say, 'Because I am not a hand, I do not belong to the body,' that would not make it any less a part of the body. And if the ear would say, 'Because I am not an eye, I do not belong to the body,' that would not make it any less a part of the body. If the whole body were an eye, where would the hearing be? If the whole body were hearing, where would the sense of smell be? But as it is, God arranged the members in the body, each one of them, as he chose. If all were a single member, where would the body be? As it is, there are many members, yet one body. The eye cannot say to the hand, 'I have no need of you,' nor again the head to the feet, 'I have no need of you.' On the contrary, the members of the body that seem to be weaker are indispensable, and those members of the body that we think less honorable we clothe with greater honor, and our less respectable members are treated with greater respect; whereas our more respectable members do not need this. But God has so arranged the body, giving the greater honor to the inferior member, that there may be no dissension within the body, but the members may have the same care for one another. If one member suffers, all suffer together with it; if one member is honored, all rejoice together with it. Now you are the body of Christ and individually members of it."

A paper given on May 21, 1978, at the Kirchentag in Sessenheim, Alsace-Lorraine.

I was asked in writing if I might speak here about solidarity. I note from the program that others will do so too, but that a Bible study is expected of me. For this purpose the text we have just heard is better suited than others and has the advantage of setting us in solidarity with last year's great German Kirchentag in Berlin. Whatever else separates us we are listening to the word of the Bible together. Now, perhaps, I may and actually must leap right into the matter at hand and state that by "solidarity," different people understand different things. From the Christian point of view, deep and abiding solidarity comes only from listening to the Bible. Listening to it together makes for solidarity, even before we know precisely what it means or to what it leads us. God's word intends and always does create solidarity; it never allows for the isolated person. Our text says that it does not leave us in isolation but sets us within a common and mutual membership. It erects the Body of Christ on earth.

For a beginning, these statements are probably too high-flown. So let us try to see simply and clearly what is involved. In the Sermon on the Mount Jesus warned his disciples not to lapse into the solidarity of the tax collectors who are friendly only toward their kin and who make love dependent on their being loved. In a certain respect we hear the heart of the gospel beating here. It receives tax collectors and sinners and yet condemns their ethics oriented to mutual giving and receiving, or, to put it more succinctly, to business. The tax collectors collect taxes and tolls. Is it surprising when they make what they live on the norm of their private behavior? Only the one who is able to pay is recognized. The gospel resists this because it is not God's world but the world of the godless. God does not inquire after the one who is able to pay. If that were so, there would no longer be any connection between him and his creation. Before him none is able to pay, though many believers refuse to believe it, regard themselves as willing to pay, and actually seek to bribe him with their merits. God is a business partner for none of us. To hear this is the obverse side of the gospel and the basis for salvation.

The gospel does not tire of telling us this. Jesus appears on the scene to bless the poor, the suffering, and those who hunger and thirst after righteousness because salvation has come near to them. He calls to those who labor and are heavy laden, calls himself the physician of the sick, and dies with terrorists. John the Baptist describes the work of the Messiah: "The blind receive their sight, the lame walk, the lepers are cleansed, the deaf hear, the dead are raised, the poor have good news brought to them." The narrative of the prodigal son is not only our story when the gospel illumines it, but also the ultimate question to us wherever it is a matter of the one genuine truth, the one abiding task, and the only promise at the last judgment. The matter for discussion then will be who was or was not a disciple of the Crucified. Everything else will no longer be of interest. Then it will be decided whether or not we sought our Lord among the least of his own. To formulate it brutally, at the last judgment the rules of the capitalistic society, which give credit only to those who can pay, no longer count. All churches and Christians sin against the Father of Jesus Christ and against persons awaiting salvation on this earth if they do not audibly and unequivocally confess, in Europe today and everywhere, that their God cannot be a God of the capitalistic society. Whoever calls Jesus his Lord speaks of the God of those who cannot pay, who forgives trespasses rather than tallying them up, a God who has taken the side of the abandoned and is continually occupied with making the lame walk, the deaf hear, and the dead live. Again, to put it drastically, everyone is deceived about the Father of Jesus Christ who knows him only as throned in heaven. The Greeks dreamed of the gods of Olympus and did so in a quite earthy way. Our God does not celebrate festivals on Olympus. We confess that "he descended into hell." Christians have nothing to do with the Olympians. Their God came to the cross and had to do so, since for more than 80 percent of the people alive today the earth is a hell in which one hungers and dies and is exploited by demons and their servants, then thrown on the garbage heap. This and only this is the reality of earth according to the biblical gospel.

Now, if someone asks what this has to do with the gospel and solidarity, I answer that it does so because the gospel does not invade our dreams but the reality of human life. It proclaims the message of grace, love, and freedom for the lost, the helpless, the imprisoned, and the possessed. In a certain respect the gospel is more Marxist than Marx because it does not believe that we ourselves can break our chains, and thus it involves God Almighty in our worldly game and makes this hell on earth the place of his revelation. The crucified God — this is promise in a world of suffering and sinners. And if this is so, then this also describes the locale of solidarity in the Christian sense. God became solidly united with us through Jesus and at Golgotha. We are thus disciples only when we are in solidarity with each other — naturally, not in our dreams, but in that earthly reality he chose, not as the tax collectors, who anticipated the rules of modern society and risked friendliness and love only if they received it in return.

Now our Bible text is beginning to speak. It states that two things are impossible and actually forbidden in Christianity. Paul would not be able to say this if what was forbidden by God did not play a role in his congregations. There are people who measure themselves by others, concluding that they are superfluous and meaningless. These are the ones who, according to Jesus' parable, bury the talent received. But there are others who measure the world around them by themselves, then assert they have no need of many around them; and if they do not manage alone, then at least with their playmates and like-minded friends. These are the representatives of the meritocracy who despise the least among Jesus' own. If the first are in despair, the second certainly are, and both are godless. To both the apostle must call, "God has appointed and joined together what you have torn asunder, both strong and weak." God did so for the express purpose that none should call oneself or others superfluous, unworthy of life or regard, exempt from or incapable of service. Today perhaps, not even Christians are able to understand much in their Bible any longer, and no longer believe that our God brings down the proud and, as is also said in our text, accepts the lowly and gives them his special love. Perhaps all of us no longer hear the revolutionary voices from Holy Scripture announcing that the world as we know it is passing away, that the new creation has begun, and that the rule of the demonic kingdom is already being shaken and supplanted by the love of Christ as the area of his earthly rule. But none can forget or deny that the gospel calls each to service and accepts none who will not serve whether from despondency or spite. The earthly sphere of the rule of the Body of Christ recognizes only members who serve, who are active. Here, the decisive criterion reads that only the one who serves him in his brothers and sisters serves the common Lord.

There can be no debate over such an obligation or the criterion that underlies it. Whoever excludes oneself or others from it is no longer a disciple but a parasite on the Body of Christ. Sadly, that Body has innumerable parasites and thus can be ridiculed by its enemies. The many buried talents are the disgrace and misfortune of Christianity in all confessions, groups, and individual lives, when what is often buried is what bishops, theologians, and believers no longer thought they could respect, sanction, or use. The official representatives of Christianity, to say nothing of their bureaucracy, continually dig graves for the hidden or misunderstood talents of the so-called laity, though in the people of God there are only priests — or, the other way around, there is only laity. Whoever no longer calls the office and officials in the churches to repentance should not speak of repentance at all. Today we suffer much from those who make themselves God's representatives on earth and are at best its vigilantes or shysters. If they allowed the Spirit more freedom, resurrection of the dead would be more credible, since the graves of hidden talents could be opened that today are often enough bureaucratically sealed by church authority. Taking control of all authorities and removing all the halos belong to the marks of the Spirit of Christ and his genuine Body.

Since it may yet be suitable, permit a further remark. For the most part, Christianity is viewed as especially sustaining the state and stabilizing society because it far too seldom behaves critically and too often makes lazy compromises with the mighty and the majorities. At the same time, God's Spirit is acting critically as can be learned from every page of Scripture which persistently describes the struggle between God and the idols and their worshippers. To be critical, however, means to test and choose what is right, useful, and even reasonable, to be subject to the will of God and rebellious toward all who erect a human image in Christ's place.

Everything depends on giving room for, or awarding the prize to, the image of Christ everywhere among us. Everyone can do this who bears the name of this Lord. None is too weak, old, or sick to participate. None is too great, strong, or clever to be obliged to ask where responsibility lies, to be engaged with one's gifts and powers. Here obstacles must be critically put aside, new possibilities discovered, and others encouraged to the common work. Christ's image bears the inscription: "He lived and died for us." Wherever, as Paul has it, one cares for the other instead of for oneself and one's associates and, in the wake of the Crucified, serves the least, there it is shown that Christ has risen and become Lord, that on earth he possesses a Body as the sphere of his presence, that he has disciples who reflect his image. In this context solidarity means to prepare the way for the Crucified so that all the tortured and helpless creatures of his Father may know they are not abandoned. Through our service God reaches out for his children, in all directions throughout all the earth, through every social standing and camp.

We cannot speak of solidarity without considering how widely it should be extended. Only among tax collectors is that clear beforehand. They can answer jauntily, "As far as we can do business." We may not overlook the weight this answer has today. Almost everywhere those beautiful sentiments that moved us after the war and allowed us to vote for a united Europe have long since fled. Of course, in all the countries of our continent politicians still make use of these feelings when they demand sacrifices of us. Actually, the Western European community lives from the fact that we can and must do business with each other. This becomes clear each time a new partner is to be taken on, whether from Spain, Greece, or Turkey, because then there must be haggling over the benefits and disadvantages for economy and trade. It is the same with the so-called development aid for the underdeveloped world. Till now people invest almost exclusively where they get their capital back with interest or bring lands that have incurred debts into their own sphere of influence. The fact that under such circumstances development aid also involves weapons, warships, and planes, or even atomic energy plants surprises only the one who imagines that development aid is given for peace instead of for business. The one world about which there is so much prattle today has naturally been shrunk and can be easily traversed. This world, with every possible hindrance, is united merely by the fact that it dances around the golden calf. We should not use the word "solidarity" to describe this. It would be a fig leaf for the war of survival and the greed for profit.

And we should no longer use the word idealistically as was done earlier, perhaps in good faith, when one spoke of the infinite worth of every human soul and was fascinated by slogans calling for "liberty, equality, and fraternity." Christianity, at least in our region, has long since sacrificed its sense for reality on the altar of pretty slogans and ideals. Even wars, revolutions, and the alteration of the entire world in our time have by no means made us Christians as realistic as we would have to be on the path of the Crucified. In a century more bestial than any other for almost 1,000 years, in which more people have been murdered, exploited, and violated than we can imagine, do we actually live because we belong to the tiny minority in the lee of the wind? The Bible calls to us that it is now the moment to wake from sleep. Solidarity is not a matter of dreams, any more than it is to be misused as a business label. In every circumstance Christians must be agitators, asking what is really meant by solidarity, how one arrives at it, and how far it must be extended. They can do that only when they unmask deception.

Much is gained when we learn and adhere to the fact that solidarity has something to do with humanity and is nowhere found where others are treated inhumanely. It does not flourish in lockstep. This also applies to churches and Christian groups that too often yield to the temptation of training their members as though each had to do, think, and say just as the other, or at least as one's pastor, teacher, or union leader. God has created us different from each other, and according to the Gospels Christ has gathered about himself a varicolored and most contradictory fellowship. If only brave, pure, and successful people sit at worship and others must remain in the forecourt to receive charity, we have become a religious and ideological group. When we all utter the same pious words and confessions, have the same edifying feelings, and run through the daily routine in our Sunday best, we belong in a museum. Persons who are alive have their own heart and head, and they must speak with each other to be understood. They are different, come together, and remain with each other only when they love one another. Solidarity is humane because the partners may remain different so that they can really help and love each other. Identical creatures have nothing more to say to each other, can do nothing for each other but be bored, since each is the reflection of the other and only learns from the other what one already knows. With solidarity in the Christian sense, freedom comes into play, allowing others room for their personal approach, conviction, and development; more still, it encourages them to find their own way behind the Nazarene and then, with their own possibilities, gifts and weaknesses, to enter into the service of the One who calls, accepts, and can use each one.

Let us begin with this in our own family! When we hear the sermon or receive the Lord's Supper together, for the most part everything is in order with husband, wife, and children. Difficulties first arise when we are at home again and in our daily routine, when we chafe at the differences we found so endearing when we were in love but now suddenly irritate us. Others in the family make clear to us that things no longer go as we wish, that if need be we must not only show tolerance but actually give in and submit. In their own families all are taught that they never have justice and rights by themselves, that they must daily be converted, not only toward God, which is difficult enough, but also toward husband or wife, toward parents, and, as promised in the last verse of the Old Testament, even toward their own children. Solidarity means to say "Yes" to others who are not simply of my opinion and whom I obviously cannot commandeer. This is what love does. But love cannot do this if it is not proper love, which guarantees liberty and lets reason prevail, practices forgiveness, and allows oneself to be forgiven. Solidarity must be learned in the school of life and wherever barbed-wire fences are to be eliminated. This does not occur without wounds. But it is not to be had more cheaply.

This one example from our most intimate daily experience may suffice, since it is bound to be widely discussed. My purpose was merely to show that Christians may not roam about in the distance when, in the most intimate circle of their life, they must keep eyes and hearts open. Of course, there is conversely a shortsightedness that does not look beyond the shadow of one's own church tower, though the newspaper, radio, and television bring the wide world into everyone's home, by which Christians ought to be reminded of their obligation toward the whole earth. I am saying this only to emphasize two things. Our text speaks of the Body of Christ that embraces all Jesus' disciples, which must thus be called ecumenical. It seems to me that in the church history of the twentieth century nothing was more important than the coming together of many hundreds of confessions and Christian organizations in the ecumenical movement. A congregation that today exists merely within the confines of its provincial church necessarily becomes narrow chested and short of breath. It remains within the framework of a sect and hears neither the summons to mission in Matthew 28 that sends us into all the world, nor the cry for unity over against those powers that threaten Christianity globally. It suffers the fate of all individuals and groups occupied with themselves, so that it is stunted in body and spirit and, in its tiny everyday life, loses hold of reality in order rather to cling to edifying feelings and egotistical dreams. Wherever they are, Christians belong in the draft of the world. Their Lord is not content with our hearts but lays claim to everything that is called creation and belongs to God. When we allow the sphere of Christ's lordship, the worldwide Body, to be limited and shrunk to our range of sight, he becomes a religious ideal and once more the wandering preacher from Galilee. Then Easter becomes a private affair of those who yearn for something beyond the grave. Our opponents have always supposed that Christianity is a private affair. Whoever accepts and practices this notion denies Jesus' discipleship and is inwardly stunted.

Solidarity with the ecumenical movement is not only our obligation. It is much more a promise for us that we come out of our own circle of haze and the warmth of a self-contained society into the open and ourselves become open, human. At the moment, the prospect for the *oecumene* is not good. Everywhere reaction is raising its head; everywhere in Europe we tend to return to outdated traditions. Precisely for this reason the *oecumene* must receive new impulse from below, from the congregations. Christian solidarity is a questionable catchword as long as the disciples of the one Lord are not found together under the word of proclamation and at the table of the Lord and from there call their church authorities to repentance and to a braver move forward.

Participation in the ecumenical movement is thus especially important, since without it we probably would not become aware of the second great task of contemporary Christianity. We still think and act from within the context of the white race. In the church this generally means from the context of middle-class society. Perhaps I am startling some when I maintain without hesitation that, along with white supremacy, middle-class society is also coming to an end, that, in light of it, Christians at least may not stick their heads in the sand. A significant auxiliary effect of the ecumenical movement is that it opens our eyes and hearts to this fact, while otherwise we will not admit it. There are always those who, after two horrific world wars and all their results, do not see that the old and familiar is sinking and that we are moving into a dark future with our children. There are always those who arrogantly place their trust in the possibilities of our technology and imagine they are invulnerable. There are also those who read the Bible but do not hear from it that everything has its time, that for a given generation fiery letters at times appear on the wall: "You have been weighed on the scales and found wanting." After all the experiences of the twentieth century, we should no longer allow ourselves to be dulled but be prepared to break camp, an act that has often led God's people from the fleshpots of Egypt into the wilderness. Solidarity at the end of the twentieth century is limited to the defense of group interests and the privileges of an affluent society — if it does not continually keep in mind the conditions of the Third World.

Christians may not forget that the citizenry and unfortunately also the churches in our grandfathers' time either paid no mind to the distress of the host of proletarian millions or fed them with alms and thus shared the guilt for the revolutions in our century. But this was merely prelude to those worldwide changes in motion today. Whoever uses television to be politically educated and allows it to show the pictures of misery, exploitation, and brutality in Africa, Asia, and Latin America can see what is in store for us who, aside from all our problems, still hold the riches of the earth in our hands and for the sake of our economic growth enslave entire continents. I repeat, 80 percent of all people are hungry and experience the world as a hell. When Christ asks us about the least among those who are his, he looks first at those left in the lurch by the white race, at those who are tyrannized and extorted. Our entire relation to life would have to change if we did not close our eyes, ears, and hearts to those crying and dying. We would be aware that there are not only ugly Americans, Germans, or Russians. Our own ugliness would drive us to despair. As Christians, we would at least have to associate with those who do not merely egotistically preserve their own status quo or actually make it the sole criterion for friend and foe.

It seems to me that a Christian in our days can only be a nonconformist, someone who resists the dominant powers in state, society, and economy and declares oneself in solidarity with the damned of the earth. I do not know how we all can help and do it together. But I know that we must revise our thinking, our habits, our conduct of life if our children and grandchildren, to say nothing of the crucified Nazarene, are not one day to judge us as fellow travelers and as guilty. Today, everyone must declare for solidarity, voluntarily and consciously or not. The only thing up for debate is which side we are on. The entire Bible and all of Christianity become unintelligible to me if I do not hear the call with Abraham, the people of the wilderness, and Jesus' first disciples to move into an unknown future under the command and promise of our God. Currently, it is assumed to be realistic when we sue for and increase our own rights and privileges. Whether or not by doing so we have chased after illusions and idols is a question we may scarcely put or discuss if we do not want to be suspected as subversive and revolutionary. Christians dare not allow themselves to be intimidated by this. At least, to put this question loudly and sharply is their present duty and the expression of their solidarity with those who are weary and are carrying heavy burdens, whom their Lord has sought and consoled.

We would have needed to explain this further and give further consideration to much else, but what we have said is enough to be aware of what is ultimate and decisive. It has become clear that Christians must exercise solidarity near and far, must be self-critical and resist the tendencies that dominate us. It cannot possibly have been ignored that this first of all involves each one of us, that none is exempt, since each received a special talent and must use and hand it on, with the result that the despised, who usually come off badly and are misused, take center stage. In conclusion, what constrains us all to such solidarity should perhaps be made quite clear. Paul did so when he spoke of the body and its members with the word "So it is with Christ." Our Lord became solidly united with his Father's creatures, and was so up to the cross. He descended from the glory given him into what had to appear to him and all the abandoned as a hell and thus became light and truth in midst of earthly darkness, the Savior of the lost, the Liberator of the oppressed, the Revealer of the divine love. He says to us, "Follow me." Solidarity with all who need help is only another word for discipleship. We cannot be disciples of Jesus if we are not on the way to the other as the Master before us. If we are not, this Lord would no longer come to earth and there build his Body and his kingdom. After Easter he does so through those whom our text calls his members. He needs us for his service and through us will be glorified. He is at work, and as he once did, he conquers demons and possession when we remain in his work and care for one another. No one who belongs to him lives and dies only for self. Because we belong to him, we belong to the others thrown at our feet that we might lift them up. In Christian terms solidarity means to be free for humanity, since God came to us in Jesus Christ in the solidarity of grace.

Sacrifice and Accommodation

Our life is continually determined by conflicts. Only if this is true can sacrifice and accommodation be spoken of as possibilities always open to us. They denote paths in the event of, and out from, conflict. Of course, we must immediately ask, Are they the most likely, or actually the only, possibilities? Why is there no mention of such types of behavior as stubborn resistance or readiness for battle? Does this express a Christian conviction that, for the sake of peace, our own interests are to be surrendered and good-humored agreement to be striven after? Here too caution is in order. Dare we speak of peace in general? Can we do so other than in the concrete? Are "sacrifice" and "accommodation" specifically Christian key words? To what extent can present conflicts actually be addressed and solved on the basis of these words? My questions intend to make clear that we may not simply deal in clichés. We must first locate the context in which they can be integrated, as well as the perspective from which we can measure their importance and interpret them.

1. Humanistic tradition offers us the theme of the meaning of life by which to deal with core human problems. Earlier generations were forced to broach the theme, partly from the personal experience of suffering, injustice, and violence, and partly from the distance of philosophical inquiry. We can understand this perfectly and respect it. But the problem arises when we are to find a suitable response to this theme. On the hunt for the

---

A lecture given on October 20, 1976, at a retreat of the Evangelische Kirche der Union (EKU).

meaning of life we rapidly move into the jungle of speculative fantasy or crippling despair, so that imaginings and feelings orient our thinking and acting. In any case, we cannot argue objectively here. Within the horizon of this theme either believers must make personal confession, or ideological theoreticians must give shape to their wish-fulfillment dreams or night visions. There is always the danger that this will lift us beyond the earth, which must remain our place and our limit. I confess I am not happy about dealing with the Western tradition here, a tradition that can hardly be smoothly integrated within Christian theology. According to my understanding, the Christian is limited to speaking of promise and service.

In any event, we should give concreteness to the question in view, so that it is not projected beyond space and time or can only be dogmatically answered. From the outset, the question must emerge from out of our own time and in it provoke individuals, groups, and societies. This, then, would be the desired perspective, in order to speak meaningfully of sacrifice and accommodation, and as Christians. It seems to me that our present day, faced with a crisis we cannot deny, is marked by a barbarity that is breaking out everywhere and is on the increase. Then the decisive question is, How can we preserve humanity, defend and increase it? This question is put to each and every one, must be reflected on, and cannot remain theory or dogma. Christians who would close themselves off at this point will scarcely keep company with the Man from Nazareth. Here, earthly responsibility and discipleship of Jesus are not to be separated. I would actually hazard the thesis that all of Christian theology must be drawn in. Whatever does not contribute to it is, I dare say, outdated and superfluous. It is scarcely necessary to support such a view in detail. Two world wars, national and international upheavals, and economic and scientific changes whose scope cannot yet be seen gave to the world a new face and other emphases. We have fallen with breathtaking speed into the undertow of a technology that makes of its inventors and managers functionaries and even threatens to get out of our control. If humanity has been able to increase numerically in a way undreamed of, it nonetheless is threatened worldwide and as never before by the pressure of having to continue on the path it took, and of being unable to stop without undergoing economic collapse. So, it can be manipulated, and the area of freedom, not only of individuals and groups, but even of nations and continents, is more and more greatly limited.

Outside of the margin left open for private life, more than any others, two questions are decisive: How does one come to power and preserve it?

and How can prosperity be achieved and increased? Clearly, these questions lead to igniting and mercilessly waging the war of all against all, however much we may conceal it. The methods of modern warfare, the exhausting of natural resources and the plaguing of the environment, the exploitation of the weak and dependent, the wildness at all levels of society — these all indicate that we have long since abandoned the Enlightenment ideals. When we appeal to reason, it is most like conjuring. Judged from the human point of view, the desert around us is spreading wider and wider, and barbarism — no longer primitive but all the more horrible — is on the increase. What the Bible says of demonic forces will have to be interpreted today on the basis of such a reality, and, as in the stories of the healing of the possessed, at issue is rescuing what is human. What was earlier called the meaning of life must be explained and answered from this perspective. For us, more is neither possible nor necessary, but less would mean nihilistically to surrender responsibility and promise. The foolish chatter that distances the gospel from the area of the social only proves how little we have grasped Jesus' debate with the believers of his time. They set healing and rescue in the shadow of obedience and religiosity and, with their worship, erected barriers between the Creator and the creature, surrendered earth and locked themselves away in a self-chosen ghetto. There is still too much of that idealism lurking about that ties God's Spirit to our own spirituality and inwardness, denies the real person in its world, and thus no longer recognizes the true God who descended into the hell of humanity. Yet it is a part of our own way toward humanity when we encounter others humanely and, of course, within the horizon of an indivisible corporeality that alone enables communication.

Finally, on this path we are bound to encounter the hatred of powers hostile to humanity, and all our lives will be at war, will be prey to the temptation to retreat or capitulate. If the gospel truly speaks of God's becoming man that we may become his image, then society and the entire world has been made the sphere of salvation that only fanatics transfer to heaven. Then also, sanctification is the process of becoming human in faith and love. Here there is nothing else to do than be seized by the Lord and stretch out to receive promise and service anew. At the same time, the spirits and powers are to be continually tested. What is necessary and good are to be learned, and we must diagnose the moment for its opportunity and danger. We must not fear being often alone. For if humanity is not merely the object of theory and discussion but is to be practiced, it is not at all popular. At least one can no longer howl with the wolves and bray with the asses, which is more strenuous and at times more painful than rationalists assume.

We are faced here with the issue from which Jesus speaks in John 14:6: "I am the way, and the truth, and the life." It is conceivable that the Revealer calls himself the truth and the life because he brings the Father's will and thus salvation to earth. But why does he call himself the way first of all and with emphasis? This makes sense only if we assume that the promised truth and life are to be won in a movement of onward progression. Precisely put, till eternity we are on the way with Jesus. The disciple is truly a follower and, as such, accompanies the Master on his errand. If we stand still, we soon lose the Lord from sight, and thus the truth and life that are united to him are never a possession at our disposal. This is the peril of all Christians who no longer engage in experiment, who make their way to settled camps, then pay homage to the status quo. Their Master goes further on ahead, as once from Galilee to Jerusalem. He does not stand still. If we take to the trenches and, despite the deeper insights, lovelier memories, and religious feelings, remain behind in the area of the church and its traditions, we are no longer disciples of the One who still strides toward the cross and the resurrection. He will draw us daily onto his path with his call and command, in power and love. Whatever others may say of humanity, Christians — who praise their Lord as the way, the truth, and the life — confess with Pontius Pilate, *Ecce homo.* If we call him the way, this means that we are preserved from inhumanity only within his light and shadow, that we ourselves can become human and further hand on humaneness as his gift.

The meaning of this last sentence is that, for us, true humanity is tied to having a God and serving him. More precisely, humanity arises and is preserved when the Father of Jesus is our God and Father. This accords with biblical teaching. If the word of the Creator called us into life and we became human by hearing it, then only the hearing and preserving of this word can allow us to be human. Humanity, of course, is not merely the affair of Christians, who have been fairly frequently outdone by non-Christians. The problem noted here is too broad to be discussed now. It is enough to state that our confession does not establish a monopoly and that our God does not appoint us his managers on whom he is dependent. This is the insight at issue, that whoever truly encounters Jesus must forswear inhumanity within oneself and one's environment. Not by chance does church dogmatics, illustrated for us in the Gospels, revolve around the theme of the incarnation. Our Lord is solely the One who came to the outcasts in the depths, became the friend of sinners, freed the possessed for community, was thus open to distress, brought healing to body and soul, taught us to believe, love, and pray and wait patiently and confidently for his mercy, and, precisely because of this activity, came into irreconcilable conflict with church and political power. He dies a death on the gallows because he did not erect principles, law, and order but unmasked the inhumanity of our earth by accepting its damned and oppressed. There are many gods whose preoccupation with self, self-will, and violation of life in the world are not disturbed, unlike the God in whose name Jesus came and to whom we cry that finally his will and his kingdom might increase in and around us. The disciples of the Crucified are set beneath the first commandment by their Lord in such a way that, along with the alternative between God and the idols, the abyss between humaneness and demonic perversion of the creation comes to light. On the other hand, grace is revealed as the judge of earthly brutality by its resistance to the creature's self-glorification and by its solidarity with those in need of aid.

The message of the gospel is most profoundly clear and simple — perhaps we could even say, simple-minded. We can make no mystery of it for scholars or Gnostics. Problems first arise when one accepts and practices the good news. In the reality of our world every event and whatever exists or is to be seen has two sides, often a wealth of varying aspects. Even on earth Christ stood in the twilight. The Crucified is both salvation and scandal. As our Pentecost hymns emphasize, only the Holy Spirit teaches us rightly to know and own him as Lord. So it is with the way of Jesus' disciples. Their faith cannot be unequivocally read off from their deeds. In the changing situations, partners, and opponents, not even the disciple is able ultimately to define his or her position but is captive to what is provisional, where there is a change in fronts, error, breakdown, and defeat. The one on the way with the Lord cannot be oriented to the world's ideals. Though this may be desirous for a time, or even required given the circumstances, the disciple is dialectically linked to what is provisional and limited. The disciple is in no way the measure or object of self-realization, intent, say, on sound character, equilibrium, on representing an idea, value, or worldview. For the disciple, everything depends on remaining in the discipleship of Jesus, evidence of which must be given in life and action, in suffering in the world. All this is done out of weakness, foolishness, temptation, and the mortality of an earthly creature whose concentration on discipleship the non-Christian environment will misunderstand.

There is a profound dialectic wherever Christian existence is to be realized. Paul gave expression to it in 2 Corinthians 4:7ff., with his image of the heavenly treasure in earthen vessels, and illustrated it from his own experience. Where discipleship of the Crucified is determinative, death and life collide and struggle with each other for lordship. One must suffer to be able to help others, or else one can probably never be a theologian. Whoever transmits salvation is stigmatized by Christ's resurrection for the purpose of carrying the cross a little way after the Master. The proclamation of God's kingdom in our time and world renders the witness contradictory, both inwardly and outwardly. From the Christian point of view our proclamation is credible when it emerges from weakness and transitoriness, when it sets us in conflict with earthly powers and in demonic hostility. This is the horizon within which, according to my conviction, our theme must be approached. The various and perhaps alternative watchwords "sacrifice" and "accommodation," at least if they are to be useful in a Christian sense, do not denote a worldview, an idea of the human, the ethos of a moment or of a society, but the reality of the discipleship of Jesus. The real problem, however, is seen in the extent to which the Christian can effect humaneness with sacrifice and accommodation and oppose barbarity.

2. Criticism of Christianity and its history is historically based. It is also theologically necessary because it hinders the religious glorification of our past. Naturally, a criticism that continually and exclusively emphasized the negative would be ideologically conditioned. At issue now, however, are not the undeniable infamies committed in the name of Christ. We are inquiring, rather, into the appropriateness and meaning of the summons to sacrifice in the Christian community. What first of all applies, in opposition to current trends, is that we would have to be blind and deaf no longer to see or hear, with Hebrews 11, the cloud of witnesses that went before and is surrounding us. Thanks to our forebears and out of reverence for the history of salvation we share with them and did not receive without them, we are obliged to speak of the divine seed and its fruit throughout the series of generations on earth. There is still that host of Romans 11:4 which has not bowed its knee to Baal, that company of Revelation 7:14 which endured the great tribulation in persecution, torture, murder, and tyranny, and defied the demons.

The community that does not remember this and lacks imagination, when it does not see the table of its Lord in the midst of his enemies, has forgotten itself. It abridges the gospel when it concentrates on the worship of believers but does not take into its everyday life the Beatitudes, uttered over the outcasts and plagued, does not hear God's praise from those who even in prison witnessed to freedom and over graves saw heaven open. Such a community would no longer live under the kingdom of Christ but in a religious ghetto. Sated and craven, it could no longer manifest the stubborn patience, the joyful bravery, or provocative power of the Conqueror, would be unwilling and incapable of disputing with the forces and ideologies around it. To put it pointedly, we have no objection to a calendar of the saints when posted and used intelligently, that is, if it includes representations of the untold anonymous disciples of the Crucified as the true apostolic succession. With them lie multifaceted before our eyes the great themes appropriate for our meditation, the themes of grace, faith, love, hope, service, and patience, and with the others of Christian temptation and defeat. Where conversation with our forebears is broken off childish stuttering grows like weeds, heart and head become narrow, and we fall prey to boredom and sadness, which render Christianity intolerable.

The other side, of course, may not be concealed or trivialized. Within the context of a worldview, hero worship may appear indispensable. In the discipleship of the Crucified there is no place for it. In fact, here too and no less seldom than anywhere else there exists what we usually call heroic. But it breathes a spirit to which secular categories poorly apply. In the community of Jesus we know of no anthropology according to which the human being is the midpoint and truth of history. Rather, the New Testament defines our nature from the perspective of creation and Christology. There is nothing heroic about the creature in rebellion and lostness, which must be sought by its Lord and drawn into his love, nor about the creature called under the lordship of grace to obedience and service and equipped for it. We are not totally sovereign or, in the wake of Prometheus, on the way toward Olympus, but we are a battlefield between God and the idols, organs of the Holy Spirit or the unholy spirit. The sinner has no tragic greatness. Whoever has received grace has no intrinsic value. Humans are never their own representatives. They are stewards of that power to which they belong and that sends them out as servants of a Lord to whom they are loyal or whom they deny, mirroring a world to which all sorts of claims are raised, and whose future is everywhere determined by the lordship that defines them.

Now we cannot ignore the fact that in the New Testament Jesus and his disciples can be described as models. But in saying this, what was already said still stands. At issue here are not strong personalities but Christian service, which, according to Paul, God makes possible for those who in themselves are unfit and which is carried out in weakness. In the Gospels the apostles', and especially Peter's, lack of faith and betrayal are deliberately set forth. Jesus' messengers are a demonstration of human capacities and limits, of temptation, falling, and overcoming. According to John's Gospel, Christians are like the figures of Rembrandt, struck by light in midst of darkness. They have and can do nothing by their own rights. For this reason they cannot compare themselves with each other, then assign the place due each in a series of virtues or a scale of values. Such would be possible only in an immanent moral world-order in which each must justify his or her own place, compete with others, and condemn all who do not recognize and pursue the achievement principle. We should beware of sacralizing the earthly. It is grotesque and impious in view of the cross of Golgotha, which throws the fallen creature solely on mercy and in doing so demythologizes humans and the world more harshly than all the Enlightenment. History is no longer the theater on which we act as tragic or comic actors, perish heroically, or play a trick on fate and defiantly make our way against hostile forces. Where the Son of God, rejected by Jews and Gentiles, by believers and cynics, by tyrants and the masses, dies on the gallows, nothing like an elite with values and privileges can any longer exist.

The consequence is that in Christianity the idea of sacrifice has no value as long as it is intended to describe an ideal, establish differences in rank and value, and in some fashion transcend human reality. All this is heathenish, godless. The reverse applies. We all live from others' making sacrifices for us, as mothers for their children, lovers for each other, or as in society all must make sacrifice for the well-being of individuals and the whole. Just so, we ourselves must continually make sacrifices for others we love and for whom we are responsible. Otherwise we would lose our human face and become parasitic. Community exists only where vicarious substitution is practiced and solidarity exercised in a way that leads necessarily to the waiver of our rights and desires. Otherwise, the desert increases where each is the other's enemy, robber, and murderer. Where we no longer can or will make sacrifices, hecatombs of victims surround us, and every day on earth becomes a hell. The same occurs in an elitist society where the motif of sacrifice is raised to a principle so as to subject oneself and others to abstract goals. One obvious example of such dialectic may not be forgotten. We once heard the slogan "The individual is nothing, the nation everything." This slogan founded a racism that misused all Germans as instruments of a single person's power and worldview, exterminated opponents by the millions, and made slaves of neighbors. Here "sacrifice" became the seductive catchword of an unscrupulous and barbaric ideology. But if people are manipulated into being a means toward earthly goals and thus dehumanized, if the law is hung about their neck, and if their lives must be an unceasing sacrificing in the service of an idea, then the Father of Jesus is excluded, as occurred under the National Socialists. There idols rule that promise equality with God and engage in bestiality. They still have power today. Out of impotence, a sense of duty, or unfettered fanaticism, extorted and twisted sacrifices are offered. But they only reveal the stony face of fate and the norm of the white race, which measures everything by performance and success and, through their agents, have taken world history, even world judgment, into their own hands.

Where the limits of reason and conscience are overstepped in such a way, the New Testament calls us to soberness. It does not describe our relation to our environment by the one word "sacrifice," but by the union of love and freedom. In this way it also fends off despair. We must not search for our identity and self-realization, for in creation and with the first commandment, God has already promised us such identity and rendered it concrete in Jesus' cross and resurrection. As his creatures, we are his children and his servants. We need not erect the kingdom of tyrants that is being continually destroyed by our God. He constantly bursts bloated ideals. In his kingdom we learn to become human and to behave humanely with others. Each sacrifice that serves this goal is fruitful and necessary. From the Christian perspective, sacrifice for other purposes cannot be justified. On this basis the idealistic traditions of our culture are to be put to the test because they have too often sketched the portrait of the superman and in actuality have fostered the reality of the gangster. In any event, they have been too concerned with heaven and too little with earth, in which God through Jesus will be Lord. The egotism of the strong screens a strong ideology. The Crucified teaches that we serve God, our neighbor, and our world only with humaneness.

3. After bitter experience, our generation is generally aloof toward, or actually dismissive of, the heroic. This in no way quenches our appetite for playing roles and pushing ourselves to center stage. According to the paradise narrative, no temptation is stronger than to want to be like God, and it is not merely expressed in the madness of tyrants who seek to bring everything in subjection. In everyday life we can enforce our own will and allow ourselves to be driven by the urge for recognition, wealth, and power, and by the will to great performance. One variation of this is our continual en-

gaging in opposition, incessantly demonstrating, protesting, drafting programs and resolutions, adopting an ascetic posture, turning morality and
religiosity into a business or a weapon in the struggle for life. Who is
stranger to the desire to want to be or appear more than one actually is and
thus betray humaneness? The other possibility only seems to be opposed
to it, that is, to be and appear less than one is and ought to be. One can also
attempt rescue through cunning and cowardice, by ducking, withdrawing
into an imagined neutral corner, keeping one's mouth shut in the face of
inhumanity, or, if need be, like a chameleon changing color depending on
the circumstances, attaching oneself to the persuasion of the majority. For
the most part, this is the way in which humanity is being betrayed today.
There are several reasons for it. First of all, in the twentieth century, in the
Western world at least, we are worn down by great ideas, words, and horrific events, thus skeptical toward authorities and cautious toward the
powerful. More important, at least in our region, the middle class has lost
its once considerable power to shape public life. It surrendered civil courage and preparedness for sacrifice, resigned in the face of newly ascendant
powers and was content when it could defend the status quo as well as possible and satisfy its ever-increasing needs. We know well enough how seductive this attitude is.

One of the greatest problems of Western Christianity is that, for better
or worse, it is interlaced with middle-class society. Everywhere, we try to offer new and useful insights to the church but overlook the fact that, for the
most part, our work benefits a bourgeois middle class and neglects other
levels of society. It is doubtful whether the upheavals of our time have altered anything of the fact that the middle class is still the object, limit, and,
as a result, decidedly also the norm of our practice. But then morality and
the religious, as well as political ideology of a particular social stratum, restrict the gospel. Actually, in the church of the white race the Beatitudes,
which have to do with the poor, the outcast, and the exploited, have largely
become alien. It is the same with the doctrine of the God who descends to
the lost, to sinners, who justifies the godless, or with the call to the no-
man's-land in which Jesus ends on the gallows with the miserable of the
earth. Where there is universal defense of the right to possess, in matters of
religion there will be no swerving from tolerating the contrary as at best an
edifying exaggeration. If the message of the raising of the dead was the primary witness to Christ's kingdom as broken in, in middle-class hope it has
been more or less reduced to survival after death. This no longer marks specifically Christian expectation, but simply religious introversion.

My statements here do not aim at a societal restructuring of our congregations. On the contrary, the gospel still falls victim to the prejudices of a sociological majority when it is not sharply differentiated from our worldview and morality. Established tradition may not be the decisive feature of interpretation. The risk of shocking characterizes the message of the new heaven and earth promised to us and for which we must raise the standard. It contradicts every status quo, even that of believers. Christ's kingdom cannot be controlled. It is the work of divine revolution that sets earthly reforms and upheavals in the shadows and creates the new heart with the will to obey and suffer along with Jesus' poorest brothers and sisters. Otherwise, we live from a utopia. Busied with our own religiosity, we can no longer, as the priest and Levite, pass by those who have fallen among thieves and succumb to the unjust structures of a white meritocracy. Humanity is not measured by ideals that move us, nor by the profit we derive from them. It is necessary to continue on the path of Jesus, and in doing so, we certainly cannot simply be partners of the like-minded. A citizenry that regards the gospel as its possession and allows it to extend beyond its church towers solely in the shape of charity hinders the lordship of Jesus and renders it incredible to all the world. It shares guilt in the spread of barbarity. For where love and solidarity are reserved for the so-called respectable society, the door to inhumanity lies open. This furnishes us the transition to our second keyword, "accommodation."

4. I admit that I find "accommodation" poorly expressed. It means that we take prior relationships into account by putting on the appropriate clothing and adjusting our face, our moods, and our words so as not to be out of step or make trouble. It does not foster the inner sympathy that moves us to rejoice with those who rejoice and weep with those who weep. Ultimately at issue is the purposeful behavior to which reason counsels us. Now, let it be happily conceded that there is no humanity without reason, that Christians must give it succor against stupidity, egotism, and violence wherever they can, and that they must be indifferent to whatever they risk by doing so. They need a rationality that is realistic sense and the capacity for critical testing and deciding. This sense is so important that in Romans 12:2 the apostolic admonition opens with it. For good reason, the reference there is to a renewed, thus radicalized, reason. We too seldom consider that our thinking is steered along by our desires and anxieties, that not even a science striving for objectivity can totally free itself of them, a condition still reflected in the various theologies. It is characteristic of human nature

that it can close its eyes and ears to unpleasant things and afterward can aver with a clear conscience of having seen and heard nothing. In our history till now we have learned again and again that in this way inhumanity and impenitence are hidden and excused. The question to us all is how our reason is freed from secret selfishness, our conscience from the pressure of the situation and convention, and our will from contradiction of Jesus' cross and lordship.

Again we are faced with the fact that everything has two sides, for which reason it can be variously interpreted, judged, and applied. What is always at issue is the sign under which a thing is viewed. This also applies to the use of our reason. No one is an isolated being. Christians would not even admit that of the dead. Each exists in various forms of society given beforehand or chosen. Nowhere may anyone demand uniformity in all others. Nowhere may an idea or program rule unchecked so that individuals and various groups no longer matter and one is oriented to abstract goals instead. In every community a truly human reason is needed with which one understands the other and concedes the neighbor a place in the sun, air to breathe, and freedom for personal growth, even at the price of one's own renunciation and sacrifice. But where does this truly humane reason gain access among us so that it is not thwarted by the egotism of our hearts? Where can it be maintained against the pressure of the forces ensnaring us? In such a context, what sense does the keyword "accommodation" have, besides its being really unclear? Must we not assert that it stems from resignation in the face of existing situations, recommends the way of least resistance, and actually urges conscious deception and hypocrisy? We never know whether the persons pursuing it are really behind it. They are always camouflaged by their ability to hide in the world round about, by appealing to the majority. They do not need to disclose their opinion or conviction, are not led by love or responsibility. Their attitude is of use when they want to avoid threatening conflicts. But is it enough to invest our reason in what is useful? The world around us proves that in such cases our interests rule the field and gracelessly exploit the impotence of the weak. What is factual or practicable is taken to be the answer to our problems, leaving the future to unfettered technology. The underdeveloped countries and our grandchildren do not agree. They will endure what we called useful and will have to suffer for what only satisfied our greed.

What is dangerous about all this is that such activity is in reality directed by managers and tailored to the horizon customarily called normal. But "normal" is a category with no existence at all in life. It appears only in statistics and is used by the bureaucracy. It helps the mediocre to become the determinative factor of the population, which means the layer that can be most easily manipulated and dehumanized. Modern mass society with its standardization, its idea of performance as the ideology of producers and consumers, oriented primarily to success and profit, reveals what is regarded as useful and reasonable and to which the appeal to accommodation necessarily leads. Christians should manifest more reason here, not less, since they are concerned with human society in a radical sense, that is, under the sign of the crucified Jesus. In this way life becomes both simpler and more complex. It becomes simpler because it need regard no catalog of virtues and values as normative. Wherever such catalogs are set up and recognized, one is trapped by the rules and ideologies of a particular society and its groups. Then it is necessary to distinguish friend and foe, young and old, conservative and liberal, the religious and the godless, the moral and the nihilists — to orient good and evil to it and to hand oneself over to a particular party.

The renewed mind to which Paul summons is not regulated by abstract principles and their given ideological interpretation. Their norm is a concrete and historical person who may not be taken for a cipher of a religious ideology. He is actually the hanged Nazarene. So the criterion of their thinking and acting reads that everything is permitted that agrees with Jesus' cross, and everything is forbidden that finds no place there. The Gospels and Christian history prove that at the cross everything comes together that on earth is usually separated and unalterably opposed. This reflects the freedom of Jesus, who without pause broke through the taboos of his contemporaries, their traditions and conventions, when help and love were needed. We could almost call him irreverent, since the morality, the politics, and even the religiosity of his environment, while not directly attacked by him, had no final authority for him. He lived from out of the coming kingdom of God and thus had one single passion, which also marked his mission. It is told of Diogenes that he went about the market in daylight with a lamp. When asked about the meaning of his odd behavior, he answered, "I am looking for men." Jesus too sought and found men. But he did not care about the wise who are able on their own to concentrate on what is needed. He made his way where the world is most human, in the depths of distress and perdition. He taught us to see where we all truly stand and must discover one another and thus gave us the Our Father, that prayer that demythologizes the piety and wisdom of the earth. It contains only petitions and allows us to stretch empty hands toward God, whether it be for daily bread, for a forgiveness that cannot be deferred, for liberation from the worldwide power of evil, or for the imminent future of the eternal rule and realization of the divine will.

This cannot be called accommodation. And it is not the motto of the hymn in Philippians 2:5ff., in which Jesus' deed is described as a self-emptying and self-humiliation. It is not even possible from this point to speak of compromise. Among us Germans, unlike among Anglo-Saxons, the term "compromise" has never really been at home. We have often accommodated ourselves when necessity forced us to it, but we have neglected the art of compromise, though it is indispensable in all social life. Compromise does not spell disguise, but readiness from the outset to make concessions on behalf of the neighbor or community, without surrendering what was received and must be preserved as gift and task. From a specifically sociological approach, we should contrast compromise and sacrifice and let them supplement each other. But here again it is evident that secular categories do not fittingly describe what is peculiarly Christian. Emptying and humiliation have a radicality that has nothing to do with compromise.

The nature of love cannot be more rationally characterized than when it is said, "Love your neighbor as yourself." This means, do nothing to the other you would not have done to you. This seems to be nothing but common wisdom, coherent with the fact that the Gospels often describe Jesus as a wisdom teacher. Yet, the word has an impenetrable depth. Whoever loves himself is so busy about it that everything must serve him. Paradoxically, whoever loves the neighbor as oneself no longer has time or energy for the self but must be occupied with the other, totally and without reservation. This is what is at issue: Jesus was occupied with persons, with everyone who came his way, even his enemies. He was by no means friendly toward them. He did not accommodate himself to them. He struck no compromises with them. But he was totally for them and gave himself to them with everything he had. Nothing else can be the watchword for the disciple, called the "pupil" of Jesus in the Gospels. Paul illustrates this in 1 Corinthians 9:19ff. Christian freedom does not consist in demonstrating arbitrariness and enforcing one's own rights, in realizing principles and living from a particular worldview. It intends and effects fraternity and solidarity with as many as possible and is thus the companion of Jews and Gentiles, of those under the law and those without it — the companion of everyone. The decisive catchword is repeated again and again: "Welcome one another."

Baptism does not introduce a heroic but a radical attitude. For the disciple the horizons widen, and earthly limits furnish no insurmountable barriers. All the outposts of advocacy groups are broken through. A renewed mind transports the disciple from dreams and anxieties to reality, binds conscience to the one Lord and to the invisible host needing to be discovered as neighbors. It gives insight and courage for distinguishing the spirits, and it resists cowardice and shortsightedness, greed for life, and fear of death. It does not strike a pact with the mighty and cannot be awed by them, and thus is not quiet about unrighteousness and cannot be seduced by the propagandists of modern barbarism. But this means that there is no contradiction between what we first meant by sacrifice and accommodation when both are no longer construed in a secular but a Christian sense. Whoever has to do with human beings in all their possibilities and achievements learns that such does not occur without readiness for sacrifice and self-denial. Here the obverse sides of the same subject are named as occurs in the Gospel: Whoever will preserve life will surely lose it, in time and eternity. One must risk and surrender one's own life to win it eternally, to be blessed and a bearer of salvation here on earth.

On this earth humanity is not to be had more cheaply if, for its sake, God himself had to go to Golgotha and into hell. Since this is the way things are, accommodation and compromise are terms that do not appropriately describe our task. Nor will rationality alone be able precisely to describe what is good and necessary. As Christians, the first commandment gives us the promise and the commission. Where God goes before us and gives himself to us, earth and heaven open, and we are blessed, living or dying. There is also no doubt concerning our task, about the difficulties and dangers of which none should be deceived. The Old Testament motif of the exodus is often taken up in the New Testament, as is shown when, in John, Jesus is called the way, and his disciples, followers. God's people are continually pulling up stakes from the old and familiar for a new world and unknown future. This applies not only with respect to heaven but first of all to earth. Here is no status quo for Christianity, no place at which we might come to a halt and rest, as happens only with the fleshpots of Egypt. The New Testament also states this with reference to our neighbor, who, according to the gospel, can also be furthest from us and certainly is always dependent on our service.

We must leave our own atmosphere to find our neighbor and may not merely, as German provincialism suggests, look about in the shadow of our church towers. When theology and church do not orient their thinking, speaking, and acting toward what occurs outside Western culture and in this way unmask our inhumanity, we are not searching for the neighbor but for our companions and, at best, for the recipients of our charity. It is true that not everyone can take part equally in the exodus toward what lies before us as future. But each can fling the heart on ahead, and what is more, we do not so much lack ideas, money, and organization, or even persons who can be sent. What is always lacking are hearts that do not cleave to the known or repristinate the past with all their might, who willingly allow themselves to be taken by their Lord on a new way and into a new day. Since Abraham, this is not merely the summons to our life. It is also and above all the promise that will be retained and preserved in the summons. God has put on our humanity to seek and find the lost. In the discipleship of Jesus we are called to be human and encounter others humanely. When we set out to do this, we will not only resist the barbarity around us, but we will find more than persons. We will find brothers and sisters, the children of our God.

"Where the Spirit of the Lord is, there is Liberty." What Is Due in the Church?

To begin with the question put to me, but also to include the sentence from 2 Corinthians 3:17 I have proposed for it, let me first state that what is "due" in the church is always and more than anything else "the Spirit of the Lord." This is not an assertion generally understood today. Further, it must be set within a context dealing with the contrast between the old and new covenants intending to disengage Christians from obedience to the Mosaic law. The Spirit of the Lord is opposed to this law insofar as he resists the misconception that God's will is set down in writing for all time and unequivocally set forth through official exposition of Holy Scripture, so that believers would have to follow it without further reflection, thus in blind obedience to the letter and official tradition. Let us not forget that it is assumed that God has in fact made known his will in the old covenant and its Holy Scriptures. Thus, as liberal Protestantism often supposed, it is not a matter of taking from the Bible its dignity and value as mediator of the divine word, or of taking from Israel its dignity and value as recipient and protector of this word, and in their place obligating persons to the traditions peculiar to them, their nation, their culture, or even to their personal feelings, insights, experiences and ideological ties. Here no one is left to one's own discretion, to self-chosen responsibility, to the independence of one's reason and conscience. God has spoken, and his witnesses must hold to his will in the Old Testament. This cannot be shaken. Further, everything is to be measured by it that elsewhere encounters us as promise and command. Setting the reve-

A lecture given on December 12, 1977, at Hohenbrunn, near Munich, at the Arbeitskreis für Evangelische Erneuerung (Task Force for Evangelical Renewal).

lation down in writing is not against the Spirit of the Lord but an aid against arbitrariness. And we do not repudiate the heritage of our forebears that meets us in the tradition of Scripture exposition.

The Spirit of the Lord is not only ours to share but is at work since the beginning of creation, since Pentecost is the power of the gospel for all the world. For our text, every fanatical enthusiasm that ignores the earthly and the enfleshed, that ignores what once occurred and is transmitted through time, intending to be merely intellectual and spiritual, has no part to play. At issue is God's being beyond our control, his not becoming superfluous for the future when he gives himself up to earth in his word or in his Son. There is and has always been the pious company that thumped the cover of the Bible and, with the devil in Jesus' temptation story, boasts, "It is written." Naturally, we should and are allowed to say, "It is written," but we ought to know that when it is a matter of ultimate decisions, the devil and his servants can speak in exactly this way, have always derived their own right from it. That God is beyond our control means that he may not be made the prisoner of his own revelation, that we are not masters of his word who at our pleasure pen him in or release him from the prison of the Bible's covers. It likewise means that no confession may claim him for itself, as though its tradition replaced its Lord and all other Christians had to be subject to it. We know that even in the ecumenical era such claims are still being raised and are not seen as in bad taste, even in Protestantism. When this occurs, the Christian community necessarily becomes a closed society that treats with the rest of the world only in the religious and political war of competition. Individual believers will mirror this attitude by seeing themselves set at rivalry, thus by feeling obliged to pious performance. If we infringe on God's being beyond our control, then grace loses its supportive and reconciling power, and since we no longer acknowledge grace alone, we are individually and collectively forced — but also desire — to have control over ourselves.

Only the Christian who is not in control of self, who is not to be manipulated by persons and forces, corresponds to the God beyond our control. God, humankind, and the world are at issue when the decision is between law and gospel. This holds true even for everyday life. In midst of continuous and progressive secularization, religious disputes still mark the currents of our time, acting on the surface of our life from the deeps. Where we have put God under our control and as a result regarded the creature as at our disposal or under our control, someone to be valued by performance and shaped from the setting of earthly goals, we have arrived at the hour of the managers, of exploitative and brutal ideologies, of a managed earth. Here the Spirit of the Lord breaks in to overturn everything. With the God beyond our control, he brings the neighbor beyond our control. Opposed to what is feasible he brings responsible service to the creation. He breaks through all forms of closed society, dispatches us from ownership of an arrived-at status quo and from obsession with programs and ideologies, sending us into the whole earth, into the great mission of discipleship being revealed ever anew.

A second assertion is needed to understand our saying. Paul opposed the Spirit to the law in order to describe the displacement of the old covenant by the new. Till now, I have only stated in a totally abstract way that this Spirit brings us before the God who is beyond our control, who cannot be taken captive by our wishes or anxieties, and whom we cannot misuse in the struggle for existence. But our text speaks of the Spirit of the *Lord*, and as the context indicates, it is obviously speaking of Christ. He is the One who raises the lid over the Mosaic Torah and leads to clarity and freedom. Thus, as in the farewell discourses of John's Gospel, he can be identified with the Spirit. He is at work in the Spirit, who is sent by him, who represents him on earth; conversely, the Spirit allows him to remain, to be known and recognized as present on earth. Luther's explanation of the Third Article puts it in just this way: "I believe that by my own understanding or strength I cannot believe in Jesus Christ my Lord or come to him, but instead the Holy Spirit. . . ." Note the sharp polemic linked to this sentence. There are no theological explanations without polemical delimitations and distinctions. Objectively put, the Holy Spirit is not only but also always a polemicist and critic. It is precisely his work to bring God and humanity together, as well as to distinguish the one from the other. Thus only critical theology deserves the name theology, in any event as long as and wherever, to the extent of historical effort, it is oriented to this distinction and separation. We will now draw conclusions from this assumption.

First, as surely as we cannot separate Christology from anthropology, cosmology and eschatology, just as surely is Christology the measure and center of all theology in all its parts. The Spirit teaches us to know and recognize Christ and thus establishes the right teaching about God, human existence, the world, time and eternity. Whether in practice we may have another point of departure remains to be seen. It strictly applies that theology is ultimately Christology and must remain such in its consequences for ethics. Second, we can scarcely ignore the fact that in our context Paul is speaking of the risen Christ. He is the Kyrios who sends his Spirit into the world and gives to the new covenant that glory that far exceeds that of Moses. Still, for Paul the Risen and the Crucified belong inseparably together. More precisely, they are identical. Whoever speaks of the Risen One has in mind the Crucified, who has conquered and as exalted raises God's claim to the earth. The Risen One would have no face if it were not that of the Nazarene, and his lordship is unique only so long as it sets us beneath the cross of Golgotha. If this is correct, then we should speak clearly of the "Spirit of the Lord" as the presence of the Crucified and connect it with the promise of our sentence from 2 Corinthians, thus with freedom.

I prefer this interpretation because it allows me to highlight in a polemical way something that might be helpful, at least today. Our theological thinking is too strongly determined by the ancient church, so that the cross is too often set in the shadow of the incarnation, while with Paul and the Reformation the incarnation should be interpreted as beginning the way of the cross. Early Christianity was induced by Greek ontology to think in terms of the contrasts between time and eternity, being and becoming or dying away, and thus understood the incarnation as the entrance of the Eternal into the earthly in terms of a transition from one mode of existence to the other, and correspondingly understood the exaltation as a return to heavenly status. On this view, the cross was the low and turning point. Not much objection is likely to be raised against such a Christology when viewed in isolation. Its dangers become apparent from the anthropology connected with it. The result is that the way of the disciple corresponds to that of his Lord by its leading through earth to heaven, from the human to the divine nature and mode of existence. This is an anthropology under the sign of the *per aspera ad astra,* the laborious ascent up Jacob's ladder, or, idealistically expressed, of the sanctifying and perfecting of one's own life, of inner growth, of character formation, and whatever in this connection may be taught in formulas.

If, on the other hand, Christian anthropology is determined by the cross, it necessarily results that discipleship is not directed at another status for human beings but intends a way and a discipleship that most certainly does not lead out of the world into a deepened inwardness and more ideal humanity but rather to earth, where its distress and torture are most visible. We must go out of ourselves, just as Christ, according to Philippians 2:6ff., went out from what was his, not merely to attain the heavenly goal and achieve his own sanctification but for service in no-man's-land. This way leads to the depths and continually allows for stumbling over the nearest or furthest who need help. From the Christian perspective we must be able to lose ourselves rather than wanting to win ourselves. We must be conformed to the One who was most despised and worthless and may not long for reward. Here, promise means to live in the traces of the Master. As stated, incarnation and cross should not be separated. There are consequences, however, depending on the emphasis. There are also consequences for the word in our saying that we have not yet discussed, the word "freedom." I will now point out these consequences in a third preliminary remark.

In the New Testament liberty is a concept taken from Greek political life. Most characteristically, the term combines a number of various meanings that, in my opinion, are best made intelligible from the status of the full citizen in the Greek polis. This citizen may appear in public, speak with candor, and on questions relevant and applicable to all — thus political questions — and, in so doing, evidence personal independence. Freedom is also freedom of the responsible person, appearance in the open air, the possibility of expressing oneself and behaving toward others without timidity. *Exousia* (authority) and *parrēsia* (established and confident openness) are the genuine equivalents of freedom. Perhaps this may all be summarized in the periphrase "state of outspokenness."

The concept in the New Testament is deepened eschatologically, that is, it denotes the standing of the children of God who are called by Christ to follow him and thus are loosed from the powers of the world. Here too, the public element is decisive. What we would describe as private Christianity does not exist. Naturally, each one enjoys an area of life that shields against curiosity and obtrusiveness, as well as a narrower or wider circle in marriage, family, profession, and culture. One must beware of becoming a Christian demonstrator and manager, of which, unfortunately, there are far too many. Still, the Christian is never really alone. The New Testament states that the Christian always stands before the presence of the Lord, and as other passages expressly add, this means that the Christian lives within the sphere of demonic temptation. We cannot be often enough reminded of Luther's answer to Cardinal Cajetan, who asked where he would be if, together with the Roman Church, he also lost the *corpus christianum,* what then was in fact the *oecumene.* "Sub coelo" (under heaven) was his reply: We remain under the open heaven even if everything else were to vanish. Admittedly, we may not forget that following the Nazarene *sub coelo* can mean, and in the Third World does mean, living in earth's inferno. Eschatological openness under the lordship of Christ and in contest with the demons has worldwide dimensions, even when we ourselves do not notice it. In the eminent sense it involves the entire earth, though we perhaps do not suspect it, or wish to do so only occasionally and partially. One of the decisive experiences of the twentieth century may be that German Christianity could or had to learn to understand the discipleship of Jesus as penetrating every aspect of daily life, as penetrating earth's spaces, though many or even most of us have not yet grasped this at its roots and others actually polemicize against it.

This closes the ring that began with the description of freedom as a word from Greek political language and with highlighting openness as the specific mark of Christian freedom. It is enough to ward off the misconception that we had to participate persistently and eagerly in the business of party politics, or were continually to pose as critics of professional politicians. Both may be necessary, given the time and person. Yet, at best it is a reflection of the fact that the Spirit of the Lord does not urge us to throw up fortresses, to be surrounded with ever thicker walls, even though our churches for the most part appear to be such, and though after the last war we have everywhere gone on the defensive. The Spirit speaks of the opened heaven and thus sets us on earth in an open field. The less the world around us knows or loves the draft, the more Christians, wherever they are, should let it in to drive out the stale air heaped up everywhere. Freedom means to be able to breathe and to enable others to breathe.

As any exposition must, so we have rounded out our saying and researched its separate words for their orientation and scope. Now we move over into the practical sphere, which means into the sphere of our own life and present world. The somewhat rakish question as to what is due in the church may be of use. "Due" denotes what is possible and necessary, perhaps not unconditionally for everyone, but in any case for the here and now. At the risk of taking an edifying approach, I will begin with what would have had to be obvious, but is not at all obvious in daily life. The Spirit of the Lord does not come or create freedom in us, through us, around us, and in the incalculable distance, without our hearing the word of the Scripture. We were already reminded that the devil and a great part of his entourage also know the word of Scripture. But there is a difference between such knowledge and listening to it as a disciple, for which, according to Isaiah 50:4, the ear must be wakened. Too many know what is in the Bible and thus use it as a cudgel against their neighbors, just as in other areas knowledge usually helps one to gain power and is used in the general war of competition. If I cannot by my own strength or understanding believe in Jesus Christ my Lord or come to him, then I also cannot by my own strength or understanding remain with him.

The Gospel of John graphically describes how we can hedge ourselves in against the Nazarene striding toward his cross, and precisely with the aid of the Bible. John records the self-confident reply of Jesus' opponents, who say, in effect, "We know what Moses said and what is in Scripture." We need only note that this attitude applies no less with regard to our religious tradition — say, to the Reformation heritage — and that it can separate us from Christ as well as from the neighbor and the earth. Appeal to the Bible and church tradition as arguably the most dangerous weapon against God and humanity would be worth a long treatise. What was said in the beginning about God as beyond our control now takes on concrete shape. Smothered with information, we live in a world in which we hear less and less, though becoming human began with hearing God's word of creation and is not continued without continually hearing it. The very fact that the misused Bible can hinder our humanity, our becoming human, signalizes most painfully what threatens us even in the secular realm. The Spirit of the Lord opens us to the Scripture, over which, as 2 Corinthians 3:15 reads, a veil lies when we treat it in our own way by rendering it sacrosanct or by merely taking from it what suits us, no longer dealing with it humanely, no longer asking, puzzling, spelling it out, ready to allow ourselves to be addressed for comfort, admonition, and judgment, in the freedom of the child who looks around in the father's house and bumps into one surprise after another. Christian freedom, getting free of self and being open to heaven and earth, begins with learning to listen like a disciple and ends wherever we are already in the know and no longer want to learn.

Let me jump from the personal to the universal and anticipate my concern directly in a thesis. Present-day Christianity neither can correctly see itself now nor can correctly see its past or future except in the mirror of the Third and Fourth Worlds. The Spirit of the Lord is certainly not at work where eyes and ears are closed to this earth of ours, whatever they may say who only navel-gaze, who continually feel their religious pulse and that of the world around them. We must get used to the fact that the world has shrunk in the last decades and that almost all can see, if only they would, how things are with it, how it was violated by the dominance of the white race for 500 years. Besides the Bible, everyone whom the Spirit of the Lord would lead into the open has title not only to the largely conformist German press or to the television, as instructive as it is, but also to such books as Eduardo Galeano's *Venas abiertas de América Latina* (1971), banned, of course, in the schools of Württemberg, or Reinhard Brückner's

Südafrikas schwarze Zukunft.[1] We need not call true everything that we read here. But there is enough to let us shudder at the thought of what our children and grandchildren will be reproached for down the road. We must be open here and listen because only then does our past take on a perspective appropriate today.

For example, only then does it become clear how nationalistic idealism hindered us worldwide from perceiving reality in Asia and Africa. In school and university — after school, the military, and considerations of status had taught us to march in step — we were encouraged to develop our own personality, to mistrust current democracy as a product of revolutions, and, where necessary, to die with God for the fatherland. To what extent this was supported by the churches is clear from the reading of the devotional literature and sermons of that period. The classical past since the battle of Salamis, as well as German history since the Cimbrians and Teutons, was familiar to us well-nigh after decades, but the earth about us was as alien as other planets. What was more alien to us was not technological development but the workers' movement connected with it. In 1918 we were immediately confronted with a proletariat of which we scarcely had any notion, even in the Ruhr. Today, disregard for political reality, again with the exception of technical and economic interconnections, persists with the average citizen, who intellectually is still living in the nineteenth century. The German church has every reason for confessing its complicity and repenting for it. From a lack of contact with reality toward the earth, barbarism sprang up in the Third Reich, and without our noticing it, a particular national idealism became the culture for inhumanity. What have we learned from it? It is not that we should simply overlook all the faithful work performed from generation to generation in church and school, which stretched a net of charity over our entire country.

On the other hand, we cannot deny that where the service of churches is concerned we think first of pedagogical and diaconal tasks, and most often connect them with very conservative ideas. The enormous alteration of our world has scarcely registered with our congregations, despite their use of all the technological changes, or they take note of the change as the mission to the heathen once did, and for which funds were gathered now and

---

1. Eduardo Galeano, *Open Veins of Latin America: Five Centuries of the Pillage of a Continent,* trans. Cedric Belfrage (New York: Monthly Review Press, 1973); Reinhard Brückner, *Südafrikas Schwarze Zukunft. Die Jugendunruhen seit 1976, ihre Ursachen und Folgen* (Frankfurt: Otto Lembeck, 1977).

then. But this means we are unaware of the hideous dance around the golden calf, into whose undertow we in West Germany have without exception been drawn more powerfully than in the rest of the West, or we are unaware of the innumerable victims that our idol worship gorges on worldwide. Edification, diakonia, and pedagogy should not cease. But if nothing more impels and moves us, we are and remain a closed religious society under Christian auspices. The Spirit of the Lord cannot do his real work with us as long as we make of the church a mere collection of schools, places for edification, and nursing homes. He leads us into the open and never lets us rest when we try to allay the secret anxieties of an avaricious, pleasure-seeking, power-mad society, and merely soothe it over individual distresses and unavoidable graves. He summons Christianity from pre-programmed service in a middle-class environment with religious needs and calls us to prepare the way of the unknown future of our God throughout the world. Christian freedom today must be tested ecumenically, in order that the Babylonian Captivity of the churches of the white race is put an end to, and the Body of Christ no longer goes into decline. What is urgent, then, is not the conflation of church organizations, though that should not be neglected, but the awakening of ecumenical thought and compassion in individual congregations. Every expert knows how difficult this is because the old Adam resists seeing his neighbors outside his own hazy circle who may have fallen among thieves. We become provincial, narrow-minded, and trapped in selfishness and self-righteousness, and aside from all our worship, we blaspheme the Crucified if we do not thrust through here. Here is the most important front for us today. We must stress this all the more as our environment increasingly closes its eyes to it and defends its own status against the victims of its affluence.

More acutely than our forebears, we live in a situation of transition. This is the third assertion of our saying that is of interest to me. Can we, at least for a moment, try to imagine the world into which our children and grandchildren are growing? The depleted resources on which our country has been living till now, the hazardous creation of alternative energy, a continually growing arms competition that clearly cannot forever promise the balance among the great powers, the rationalizing, and the increasing unemployment, the shrinking economic growth, and, finally, the displacement of the center of gravity to the Third and Fourth Worlds — all ghost-like shapes for the white man, who still behaves as if he were totally invulnerable, but whose conceit is bound to collapse like a house of cards. In view of these visions, hardly dreams, how can we live from the nineteenth century without a break and defend the status quo established there with all our means, as South Africa did most spectacularly and most perversely? The great trek is announced, though in the interim there is a circling of wagons everywhere. This should have an effect on ecclesiology, which no more than any other doctrine can be timeless. Even outside Roman Christianity there stubbornly persists that old church view of the divinely instituted institution as continuing the incarnation of Jesus, to which predicates such as "Mother" or "Teacher of the faithful" (naturally also of unbelievers!) are applied. All this may suit the Roman doctrine of faith. Protestants, particularly in Germany, are called to demythologize concepts and ideas that have crept in among them since Romanticism and the antirevolutionary Lutheran orthodoxy of the nineteenth century. To put it roughly: for us "incarnation" is a word to be used in an exclusively Christological way. For this reason we cannot speak of any ecclesiastical continuation of the incarnation of Jesus. Next to the Father and the Son, we have no heavenly Mother and no hierarchy of offices reaching to heaven, unjustly derived from the motif of the Body of Christ. Even the title "Teacher," if used to describe the archetype, as it were, belongs only to Christ, since he alone is the Word become flesh and world Judge.

A second critical point should be made about speaking of the church in the singular, however biblical and meaningful. With the Roman or Greek-Russian Church and particular sects, it is consistently oriented to a spatially existing organization, in my opinion, in an entirely illegitimate way. As early as in the New Testament period there are extremely different congregations, not at all connected with each other. Clearly and demonstrably there has never been "one holy and catholic church" identifiable with any earthly phenomenal form. Where this was asserted, homage was paid to ideology. On earth, Christianity has always crumbled into a plurality of church structures. On earth, unity has been present only in the conciliar sense. In Africa today there are said to be 5,500 churches and church groups. The *oecumene* outside Rome numbers many hundreds. But imagine what a black Christianity, dominant in fifty or a hundred years, will jettison of theological doctrines that appear inalienable to us, being the patrimony of the white race.

And imagine what shaking of the head the 400-year tradition of German provincial churches will then evoke. Founded by princes and imperial cities to give the gospel free rein, then used for its domestication, managed bureaucratically, privatized for nurturing religious life, intent on organizational independence, a battleground between orthodox, liberals, and pietists, tolerated in modern secular society since morality and general tranquility are useful, all the while passing as a national church — these are the characteristics of our German provincial churches. Let us not elaborate on the fact that, since the Treysa Synod of 1945,[2] these churches succumbed to the Restoration, just as did the political society in the 1950s, that in fact the union of Lutherans and Reformed was to be reversed, that the object has been one Lutheran Church, with a primate in the high church sense. My statements do not aim at rejecting provincial church institutions. Wherever a single wall still stands that gives shade, protection, and support, things should not be pulled down. Every vacuum has its effect, and on the weak most of all. On the other hand, we will recognize the provincial churches as the makeshifts they always were. We can neither display them as peculiarly appropriate models of Christian organization in the ecumenical age, nor can we accept their historical claim as justified theologically and in practice, above all because they tend more and more in the direction of private societies, which they conceal by aid of the fiction of the national church.

There is no Christian society without corporeality and embodiment. But the embodiment of Christian society is not guaranteed by an apparatus of authorities, and today it is no longer tied to synods, especially when they facilitate the habit of making majorities of minorities. The embodiment of discipleship through institutions as corporations of public right, with all the privileges and obligations appertaining, had its original roots in the national church, its mythology in the *corpus christianum*. Since the Reformation the mythology became fragile. Among us, provincial churches appeared in place of the national church, each with a confession regarded as its spiritual basis. Such a construct was already relativized by the free churches and Christian dissenters. In view of the ecumenical movement, the range of their effectiveness has become so restricted that we can speak of them only as marking particular territories, excepting the sphere of the Roman Church.

It is no accident that what is coming to be more and more dominant, from Finland and Lapland as far as Provence, is the preserving of religious tradition and thus a substitute for the task of earlier confessionalism. It is no accident that even in the Catholic Church there are Christian communes everywhere, underground congregations, Bible groups, movements such as at Taizé, which can no longer be reduced to a common confes-

2. On the Treysa Synod, see n. 12 in Käsemann's retrospective (p. xix).

sional denominator but represent modern ecumenical Christianity. Whoever studies the Bible and is aware of church history knows that from earliest times there have been wandering preachers, communities that did not belong to the Great Church, whose peculiar embodiment on earth of Christ's lordship we cannot deny. It seems as though we are returning to such times in inverse ratio to the reduction of the mastery of the white race. Be that as it may, we must recognize that we are in an upheaval that, at one rate or another, will dissolve the forms of Christian organization familiar to us and replace them with others. To speak of national and provincial churches today is a juridical fiction, no longer connected with reality. And as for pietism — its extent, its founders, and its developments — it is too diffuse and too closed off not to confirm the collapse of the old order or actually to hasten it. We are moving into an unknown future when we use the word *oecumene,* and we are standing today amid the rubble of earlier forms of organization, however much those involved refuse to see or believe it. What is due now is to use what is at hand without overestimating it, to destroy nothing without having a substitute for it, but to be ready to be forced to leave the old houses. Others in the centuries before us had to do so. This too belongs to Christian freedom.

I would gladly have said a word about Christian responsibility for democracy and for bridge-building between West and East, since in midst of progressive global and national polarization, we face a task I believe we dare not evade, since we must work for peace. Still, I have already exceeded the amount of time given me. In conclusion, then, I will state that what is due today from us is openness of heart and mind for God's word and his creation, vicarious service to the neighbor in the Third and Fourth Worlds, the insight that a church exists and remains only where Christ appears and finds disciples with him on the way to the cross, that we thus need not worry about ourselves or the church as long as we remain in his calling. Then the freedom of the Christian will always emerge. For where he truly appears and is at work, the Spirit of Christ always creates human freedom.

Freeing the Prisoners (Ephesians 4:7-10)

"Each of us was given grace according to the measure of Christ's gift. Therefore it is said, 'When he ascended on high he made captivity itself a captive; he gave gifts to his people.' (When it says, 'He ascended,' what does it mean but that he had also descended into the lower parts of the earth? He who descended is the same one who ascended far above all the heavens, so that he might fill all things.)"

Dear congregation! Freeing the prisoners: According to our text, *that* and nothing else is the Easter message. This should surprise us, since at Easter we are used to speaking and hearing of Christian hope beyond our own death and grave. Our Bible passage does not reject that. But it healthfully corrects our expectations, which always view how we fare as ultimately decisive, which we want confirmed in our worship so that, just as in daily life, everything, even after this life is over, revolves about our person, its problems and desires. It would be good if we sometimes left church wiser than we entered, if we allowed our Christianity to be surprised by the Bible and were led to thought and learning.

It was not a real Easter at which none got to hear what Paul in 1 Corinthians 15:25 made the theme of his great chapter on the resurrection: "For he must reign until he has put all his enemies under his feet!" Every day is lost about which it is not said, "Christ must reign!" The meaning, power, and comfort of our life do not depend on what *we* wish, do, or think. Someone has called us to his service so that, in and through us, his name

---

A sermon preached on the Sunday after Easter 1981 on Ephesians 4:7-10 at Rotthausen, Käsemann's former parish. See pp. xvii-xx above.

may be hallowed, his kingdom come, his will be done also on earth. For this reason, the Easter message of our text reads, "Freeing the Prisoners." Too often religion is nothing but an insurance agency with an imagined God to whom I cling so that he in turn keeps harm far from me. Yet every faith suffers shipwreck that is preoccupied with earthly well-being and, after death, a place in Abraham's bosom. At Easter we sing: "Ich hang und bleib auch hangen an Christus als ein Glied. Wo mein Haupt durch ist gangen, da nimmt es mich auch mit. Er reißet durch den Tod, durch Welt, durch Sünd, durch Not. Er reißet durch die Höll. Ich bin stets sein Gesell." (I cling and ever cling to Christ as does a limb. Where my Head has gone, I too am borne along. He bursts through death, the world, sin, and misery. He bursts through hell. I am ever and always his ally.) He forgets none who submits to him, but all are deceived who claim him for themselves alone and do not allow his work to be worldwide, thus also for themselves a personal freeing of prisoners.

Important insights seldom come when one does not proceed cautiously. First of all, then, we will take a second look at our text. Surprisingly, it does not merely speak of Christ's ascent to heaven, as we expect at Easter. Rather, his ascent is emphatically tied to his descent into the lowest parts of the earth. These two events may not be separated. If they are, then it is no longer the same Lord who is involved, characterized by the one as well as by the other event. This is a new danger into which we dare not fall, and precisely at Easter. The earthly Jesus and the exalted Christ belong together. We understand nothing of the risen Lord if we do not have the Nazarene in view, and we understand what is said of his exaltation only if we do not ignore the Crucified, who descended into the lowest parts of the earth. We may ask whether this last little phrase has the realm of the dead in mind or regions where people feel abandoned by God and all the world. In fact, the difference is immaterial. The entire weight rests on the fact that we hear what separates our God from all the idols of the heathen. He does not remain beyond our earth among the blessed spirits. He is a God *for us* and thus descends from his heights to our depths toward the cross reserved by the Romans for those convicted of high treason, such as, for example, for the 6,000 rebellious slaves nailed to the wood on the Via Appia. Our affluent Christian society knows nothing more of the fact that we have a God who not only associated with two zealots on Golgotha, hence with rebels against political tyranny. The Bible is full of rebellious shouting, which we most often miss, since we are no longer interested in the radical change of our situation. But the Father of Jesus Christ not merely promises the new heaven but, with it and precisely because of it, promises a new earth in which righteousness dwells. The Beatitudes of the Sermon on the Mount apply to the condemned, the outcasts, the hungering, and the dying in our murderous world, then to all who are not ashamed of these their poorest fellows.

There is no more revolutionary book than the Bible, if only we read it with open eyes and alert minds. It proclaims as Lord the One who was most despised and died among criminals, derided by religious and respectable society. We must search for our God in earth's inferno before we meet him in his glory. It is not by accident that the Gospels report that he frightens off the demons and breaks into their kingdom to free their victims from their violence. How little we know of him who shapes his creation from out of chaos, promises resurrection to those who come from and return to dust, and descends to the lowest parts of the earth so that once and for all the humiliated and crushed see light in midst of the darkness daily surrounding them! Whoever does not begin to study with the Nazarene what salvation means will never learn it. He will rather dance around the golden calf, be occupied with desire, greed, and the despising of neighbor, though wanting to be pious and to belong to respectable society. The history of Christianity, as our generation has experienced it here in Rotthausen and often elsewhere, has been defined by an exodus from Egypt that ended with dancing around the golden calf, imagining it serves our God, though all the devils rejoice over it. The Nazarene breaks into this bustle. He sets the enslaved and possessed free.

Now we are prepared for the third step into our text. It states most strangely of Christ that he ascended on high and took captivity itself captive. We must be clear that Christians continually drag around with them remnants at least of the worldview of their day. At times they have also shared a belief widespread in the ancient world that the stars are the dwelling of evil spirits, from which they hunt for souls freed from their earthly bodies in order to imprison them and thus hinder their ascent to heaven. Now our text glorifies Christ as the One who bursts all bonds. As he brought redemption on earth to those who had become prisoners of their own greed or of an alien tyranny, so by his ascension he has broken through the demonic blockade obstructing access to the Father's throne. His resurrection does not merely occur for his own sake. It creates a new order of the world and, as Pentecost proclaims, sets us under an open heaven. Not even death has the last word. It too must give its prisoners back to their Creator. But wherever death's prisons are no longer closed, all other wielders of power must envision the end of their power. It was not only to Herod that the star of Bethlehem announced the arrival of One stronger. It signals the shaking of the foundations of *all* the kingdoms of this world. To those who feel given over to tyrants, to their systems and ideologies, who thus live in fear and horror, 1 John 3:8 states clearly, "The Son of God was revealed for this purpose, to destroy the works of the devil." Prisoners of anxiety are to become conquerors because the first commandment gives them the promise to accompany them on their way: "You need no longer have other gods besides me. I alone am your true Lord, and I make of you a people to offer resistance on the evil day, to preserve the patience and hope of the saints."

To put it as clearly as possible, what the church of Jesus Christ should be in our world today is a resistance movement of the exalted Lord against all who make God's creation a prison for anyone, near or far, a playground for their selfishness, vanity, and lust for rule. Those with whom we must live each day are entrusted to us and are more important than anything we possess, respect, or wish for. We are asked not only about what we called our own, but even more about whether we created breathing space for the others' bodies and souls, urged them on to independent thought and action, were their pioneers for Christian freedom, and drew them with us under God's open heaven and into a way of life not simply fenced in by legal prescriptions, prejudices, and arbitrariness. For too long the pious have been the most conservative stratum of society. In the twentieth century, at long last, they should have heard the call to exercise civil courage and, for the sake of righteousness, rebelliously to represent God's affairs in a political, social, and truly quite special way toward ecclesiastical convention and bureaucracy. Cowardice and stupidity prepare the way for demons. One may pray in one's closet. But discipleship of the Nazarene is never a private affair, hidden in nooks and crannies, making church walls a pious ghetto in daily life on earth. It is sent into the world, which belongs to its Lord.

This is the last word we hear from our text. The exalted Lord who earlier descended to the lowest parts of the earth will fill all things. For this purpose he has given grace to each of us, and, of course, in differing measure, according as it corresponds to his service in the given instance, and makes us instruments of his glory in a particular place. He can fill all things only when after his ascension he does not leave the world to itself but remains present on earth with his Spirit and gifts. For this purpose he needs disciples who bear his image and reflect it in the world around them. But then they may not all say, think, intend and do the same thing, as if they were machines of identical make instead of human beings with their idiosyncrasies. The One who wills to penetrate and fill all things must give shape to what is different, to what suits all relationships, finds its way everywhere, even in the alien space of language, culture, or race. This is something not known by wearing the same uniform but in the ability to understand others, to live with them, and to suffer among them as the discipleship of Christ requires. Only in this way is none superfluous, none comes off badly, the one does not disturb the other, is not bored with the other — and continual surprises are in store for the observer. Christ has given each of his servants a particular share, a particular gift, a strength or weakness, a distinctive living and dying, so that in his members he may fill the whole earth with his presence.

His disciples are not the same as to their gifts, but the work entrusted to them is the same — it makes them his servants and plunders the demons. At this point we must take up what was said in the first part of the sermon. While he wandered through Palestine, the Nazarene was at work freeing the prisoners and the possessed. According to our text, freeing all those imprisoned by demons was the concern of the One who ascended from the lowest parts of the earth to the Father, and thus created a breach in the realms of power that separate creatures from their Creator and allow them to entrench themselves against each other. As Pentecost makes clear, the One who since Easter thrones in glory gives the gifts of his Spirit to *all* who receive him. He blesses each one in a special way, even those who suppose they are useless. Those who do not brush his word aside will note where *their* place, *their* chance, and the meaning of *their* life and suffering await them. With all the others, they are called to witness to the open heaven above them, and in such a way that they contribute much or little to making possible more openness on earth. Each of us, in the family, in the workplace, and in the neighborhood, has to do with prisoners and the possessed, if only we would open our eyes and not close our hearts to the stranger's distress. Each of us drags chains that limit thinking, feeling, and acting and that hinder us from risking freedom and love.

Finally, none of us can avoid recognizing the shame of the white race in the misery of the Third World and our own complicity in it, perhaps hidden till now, nor can we avoid fighting against it with a clear and persistent protest, with helping and praying. The pious egotism that does not see beyond its own church tower falsifies the word that God's kingdom reaches out for the whole earth. Only when we grasp the inconceivable measure of human despair, torture, exploitation, and murder — when we understand that the twentieth century was the most inhumane period of world history — will we see Lazarus at our own door and all the possibilities of being servants of God for greater earthly freedom. We often do not understand what we are doing until we see its effects. What should prevent our children and grandchildren from growing in the greed for pleasure and immediate gratification when they learn from the example of their parents that possession and the gratification of desire are determinative for our entire society? The same brutality that allows millions to die of hunger in the Third World defrauds the poor of their rightful wages, shoves our aged into nursing homes, and treats the youth as though we had to mold them after our image and will, leaving those repulsed by our notions of success to their solitariness, to drugs or a commune, like applying a Band-Aid. Foreigners whom we once summoned and whose labor we have exploited suddenly appear as rivals and, as such, are despised or hated. Like the world as a whole we too are polarized in our communities, and whether from East or West, the Left or the Right, each is labeled sympathizer or conformist. No one should maintain that the class struggle has ceased! It has become worldwide, and we are mostly in agreement with it because our own society profits from it.

We have reason to look daily into the mirror the Third World holds before white churches and their members to see that we have been possessed, to understand that the Nazarene must free us from prison and set us in the service of his liberating love. The resurrection of the dead never occurs if it does not already begin on earth as an awaking from sleep, as a freedom that sees an open heaven above and draws those nearest and furthest into its light. The measure of the gift of Christ of which our text speaks spells *surrender* to the power of that freedom the Nazarene bore to the lowest parts of the earth and by which he imprints his image on the world. Easter grace calls each of us to share in this Easter service. Freeing the prisoners is the true message of Easter. Preserve us in truth! Give eternal freedom to praise your name! Through Jesus Christ. Amen.

National Church and Body of Christ

In treating this theme we must consider the sequence of the key words in the title. The sequence I have chosen allows their discrepancy to appear more clearly and is better suited to initiate critical discussion. At the outset I would like to state that the term "national church" embarrasses me. I am not certain as to when it begins playing a role in theological debate or what substantive issues it envisions. There is little reflection on its origin, and as to its meaning we seem less and less in agreement the more we use the term, especially in the last decade. What is actually clear is only a style used technically in South America today. There, chiefly within the framework of so-called liberation theology, *iglesia popular* ("popular church") denotes a more or less revolutionary Christian lay movement that, in hearing the message of the Gospels and discussing it with reference to its own plight, turns away from the institution of the official church and its dogmatic tradition, at best still respects it in worship, but in everyday life is less able to do anything with it. I am told that something similar occurred in Norway when a type of national church came into existence there. Contrariwise, in present-day Germany, at least in its western part, the official institution as represented by its leadership, emphasizes its character as "national church." This claim is somewhat confusing. It has more the appearance of something threatened and needing to be defended, or that has actually disappeared, than of something whose reality and necessity are beyond doubt. Are only pious wishes and illusions at issue here?

A lecture given on May 7, 1988, at the Evangelisches-Lutherisches Missionswerk Niedersachsen (Evangelical-Lutheran Workshop, Lower Saxony) in Hermannsburg.

The term cannot denote earlier national churches that geographically and for the most part politically conformed to particular national territories in which they enjoyed certain privileges. Such scarcely exists in a time when boundaries no longer separate cultures. Neither can it denote institutions that represent a particular confession dominant in an area and that, at best, still allow for religious minorities. We live in a world of religious syncretism in which confessional links may represent majorities, but not nations, and former conditions give us no title to current demands. Today, we often hear the national church defended by the argument that Christians must be open to the world around them to the fullest extent. Apart from a few sects that rigorously close their doors to the outside world and remain secret associations, all religious communions want to work at missionizing and winning their environment. It would be a swindle if this intention led to conferring on oneself a title that set other religious groups in the shade. I fear that actually, but I hope unconsciously, swindling is going on when church authorities label their organizations national churches. Such labeling totally ignores that, in our time and its relations, all religious associations represent only minorities in their countries, and that, in order to survive, our Christian churches — even in regions of the white race, or, more correctly, there most of all — must carry on mission as did early Christianity. In this the pietists are without doubt the most realistic.

However I try to establish any right to the title "national church," to which we so often lay claim, I can nowhere establish it. I see that I am forced to call the claim presumptuous and totally unrealistic. Here, like children in a dark wood, we muster up our courage and, to put it crudely, trick our hearers, especially believers. Naturally, there are traditions that allow us to understand the claim to a national church. I have gradually come to think it most probable that, in using the term, one is harking back to hopes and goals from the period following the German Wars of Liberation.[1] At that time Romanticism, under the influence of but also in antithesis to the French Revolution, discovered the ideal of national character and, with Ernst Moritz Arndt,[2] for example, identified nationality together with traditional Protestantism as divinely ordained. In conservative and

1. The German portion (1813) of the struggles of Prussia, Austria, and Russia (1806-13) to get free of Napoleon's tyranny.

2. Ernst Moritz Arndt (1769-1860), professor of history and philosophy at the University of Greifswald, exiled to Sweden because of his literary attacks on Napoleon; following Napoleon's defeat, appointed professor of history at the newly founded Bonn University.

liberal circles the nineteenth century was most deeply stamped by this ideology. We were able to learn this in our youth, even from such a brilliant theologian as Schlatter. Sermons from both world wars give evidence of it. For this reason, the evangelical church in the so-called Third Reich was able to treat with the Nazis. A name such as Eugen Gerstenmaier's[3] is a reminder that, even after the last war, the Christian Union Party remained loyal to the tradition that the nation is a gift of creation, that the state is an order of creation, from which the rigorously monarchical Bishop Dibelius,[4] one of the most significant and bravest figures of the church struggle, excluded the Marxist states. Since the end of the 1920s we were lured by the propaganda of national missionary tasks and possibilities, solemnly invoked by the Nazi party program in its last paragraph as a confession of "positive Christianity." Later, the leadership of the Rauhen Haus in Hamburg[5] and the Tübingen theologians enthroned Reichsbischof Müller[6] before knowledge of the murders of handicapped and communists, and finally Stalingrad, painfully demythologized us. But even then we were not able to take it in, as was all the more true of Lutheran bishops. In view of this history should we not speak of a swamp that, like the shibboleth "national church," produces bubbles, fogs over the realities, and allows Christians along with their synods to be fanaticized and possessed? The Bible does not at all lead to this view.

If once in Judaism the nation and synagogue — or, better, the religious community — should have been identical, a notion historically problematic in view of Israel's tribes, the history of Judaism as early as in the Old Testament period, and all the more in the epoch of the Maccabean wars and Qumran literature, was a continual process of distinguishing and separating believers and lawbreakers. Today, Israel is still defined by Zionists, Hassidim and the religiously indifferent. For the outside observer it is not a unity of people and church, though propaganda maintains that is so, and

---

3. Eugen Gerstenmaier (1906-86), early member of the Confessing Church (Die Bekennende Kirche); involved in the July 20, 1944, plot against Hitler and later president of the German Parliament (Bundestag).

4. Otto Dibelius (1880-1967), bishop of the Evangelical Church of Berlin-Brandenburg-Silesian Upper Lusatia and staunch opponent of Nazism.

5. A rescue home for homeless urban children, founded in 1833 by J. H. Wichern (1808-81).

6. Ludwig Müller (1883-1945), awarded the highest offices in German Protestantism because of his personal connection with Hitler. His collaboration with Nazism led to the formation of the Confessing Church.

we largely accept it. (Of course, none of us will contest the fact that the New Testament knows nothing of a national church, that the church in the Diaspora can know nothing of it and thus, in a markedly different way, must speak of the family or people of God and the Body of Christ.) In a church whose leaders and conservative members are forever warning against transgressing political boundaries, advocacy of the term "national church" by tradition and current tendencies is a politically impermissible infiltration of theology. The consequences of such a blurring of boundaries are obvious and, as appears to me, disastrous.

1. *The theological problem of the national church in the current context.* If Christians allow themselves to be defined by the idea of the national church, they need not but, almost unavoidably, at least inwardly, in fact distance themselves from the ecumenical movement as well as from the Catholic Church, which already in name claims worldwide authority. Lately, however, in the twentieth century, the ecumenical character of the gospel and of evangelical communities has become theologically constitutive. Fellowship with Catholics, happily grown very close on an ecclesiastical basis, should be tended and furthered wherever possible, despite all the still insuperable differences with its hierarchy and dogmatism. At any rate, threatened worldwide by the assault of other religions and ideologies, Christianity can no longer encapsulate the confessions from each other. In West Germany, of course, it is so strongly defined by the middle class that its evidences of decay clearly encroach, not only on family and society, but also on the church. In the political arena polarization is manifest in a persistent anticommunism, in economic life totally dominated by capitalism, in society and family through conflicts with the youth and emancipatory groups, in the Protestant church with the strife between conservative evangelical theology and liberal opposition, in Catholicism with the strife between the official church and the theology of liberation, to great extent also with the so-called laity. The churches are involved in such polarization. In them the dispute is often so radicalized that opponents accuse each other of betraying the gospel. Where self-understanding as a national church orients the theory and practice of Christian fellowship, not only will the tradition and convention of the middle class dominate, and not only will polarization persist at all levels of society. There also will be failure to recognize that today the Christian church should be measured only by predicates that point to the gospel and the discipleship of Jesus.

It appears to me to be a sign of a dangerous secularization when

Protestant houses of God are named after significant figures of ancient and modern church history. As Protestants, we have no saints or heroes. Nor is reference to nationality a category of Evangelical-Protestant usage. Where we take up such categories we in fact still live from the heritage of the nineteenth century, or, to put it so as not to be misunderstood, from the period of the worldwide colonialism of the white race. I hope it is not pedantry or fanatical iconoclasm that allows me to judge in this way. To do justice to the reality of our world today, we need to understand that the cosmic centers of gravity have shifted. Europe is no longer the center of world history, and the Atlantic area is such only provisionally, at most militarily and economically. More rapidly than others, we Christians should get used to seeing the North-South conflict as more important for the earth's future than the still dominant West-East perspective. The underdeveloped world of color is beginning to break free of the West and its modern bridgehead. What is becoming crystal clear, in ecumenical encounters at least, is what many regional upheavals at the political level are signaling. In general, the West German citizen still views the Third and Fourth Worlds as the object of the exploitation of raw material and manpower, or as the recipient of the charity of erstwhile colonial lords. This is disastrous not only for the other side but for ourselves and our children and grandchildren. When Protestantism of middle-class white provenience views itself principally from the perspective of the national church, it not only pays homage to the spirits of an outdated past but gives false signals for the future. Naturally, one may reply that this takes relatively harmless slogans too seriously and sees ghosts where there are simply mere links to tradition. My generation, however, has learned through experience how swiftly underlying currents are forging ahead, and slogans become battle cries, especially when tied to national feelings. At best, national feelings support and legitimize the term "national church." It is a questionable care of souls that will not renounce the term. Theologically, the concept is a changeling susceptible to religious demagoguery.

2. *Theological problems and biblical perspectives.* Without further ado we turn to the Pauline understanding of the church as the Body of Christ. This term also can be misused. It was misused when Romanticism understood it to be something of an organism reaching from earth to heaven, or when mysticism conceived of it as a metaphysical reality in which the exalted Christ united with his own and drew them into the heavenly world. For Paul, the first in recorded history to define the church as the Body of

Christ, corporeality *is* the mark of creatures exposed to a particular power in a particular world — creatures that are pressed into its service as its tools, as members within the sphere of its rule. Idols as well as the true God lay claim to creation. Both are visibly and publicly at war to make creation their kingdom. Christ calls his disciples to become witnesses of his rule on earth and thus of God's expanding rule, and to do so bodily, thus publicly and visibly to resist the demons of this world. They are members of his rule in their corporeality; in their totality they are the Body of Christ, the community in which, following his exaltation, he still reveals himself on earth with his Spirit and will, reveals the new world under God's command and promise.

This means that the church is no more autonomous than the individual person will ever be. Corporeality is never come of age; it is always in position to serve. The church, therefore, never replaces its Lord. It can never appropriate his authority unrestricted, never in the name of the exalted Jesus carry on its earthly work according to its own discretion and without control. His Spirit may not be domesticated or, for example, hierarchically managed. Precisely as the Body of Christ, it is and remains nothing else than a world that is sovereignly ruled by him, hears his voice, is chosen and continually directed by him. Its sole characteristic is the acceptance of his word in daily obedience and willingness to suffer. Power and glory, therefore, are not its distinguishing mark. It must be continually reminded, heard by, and ingrained in each of its members that its Lord is the Crucified, who spares none of his followers the way of the cross. The *signum crucis* marks the Christian in a world with its fascinating heights, depths, breadths, miracles, talents, and glories everywhere; it advertises them and at times even offers them to us. The task of the members of Christ's kingdom is not to promise those who, by virtue of position, possessions, opportunities, and capabilities, securely feel that they will have heaven besides. Jesus' example and his Beatitudes prove that they must help the poor, oppressed, despairing, and dying; they must proclaim to all the world the glorious freedom of the children of God and must demonstrate it by resisting constraints and tyrants. They should not doubt that in the course of time, in any event in white Christianity, the superstition took root that the Body of Christ must be a site of harmony and subjective balance, the objective equalizing of extremes. It would be good if the church were more often an asylum for the persecuted. All the same, on earth it has always been a battleground. Where God and Mammon encounter each other everywhere as they do today, where avarice and possession spread unchecked over corpses, where the insanity of military preparedness poses as reason and religious people are often entrenched behind walls of self-satisfaction and indifference toward the neighbor and a tortured earth, there may be no neutrality in the Christian community — each must take sides. One cannot secretly belong to and serve two lords or take the side of those who think they can remain anonymous. There are no anonymous Christians whom God in baptism has called by his name and by it made himself known.

The message of the resurrection of the dead becomes credible only where it is witnessed to and anticipated in following the Crucified. As if embarrassed, Paul said of himself, "It is no longer I who live, but it is Christ who lives in me." This word from Galatians 2:20 is interpreted in Philippians 3:10-11, where it is said, "I want to know Christ and the power of his resurrection and the sharing of his sufferings by becoming like him in his death, if somehow I may attain the resurrection from the dead." The apostle is taking to the street on which Jesus went to Golgotha, toward the conquering Victor, to join his triumphal procession. This gives in precise and gripping fashion the summary of what constitutes discipleship. The same is exactly true of the Body of Christ. This word draws no edifying picture by which the church is glorified. Rather, it describes the communication of the exalted Lord with his community on earth. This community is the realm of his lordship on earth, identified as witness to the resurrection by the fact that its members, in midst of the inferno of a creation terrorized by ideologies and despots, demonically disfigured by hunger, exploitation, torture, and murder, go to meet the One who alone allows the creature to become human and the human to become a creature once again. At issue here are rebirth into a new creation and the human's finally becoming human.

From this context is to be heard and understood what is detailed in 1 Corinthians 12:12ff. on the theme of the Body of Christ. I will follow the structure and logic of the chapter. It is necessary to state first that, according to the Pauline view, and other than in classical Greece, no one "has" a body. One "is" a body, and in all its parts, thus heart, head, and soul. Existence is only given bodily, even among plants, beasts, stars, angels, and demons. I can never distance myself from the body, and when death separates me from it, it must wait for a new one. All its organs, its "members," as we term them, are possibilities and capabilities given me to use. This even applies to Christ after his exaltation. He is and lives in his earthly body and its members and needs them for his service in the world. The church as his earthly body is the realm of his lordship, in which, together with his Spirit, he makes known his will and is present among us, communicates with us in blessing and judging, battles with his adversaries, and suffers under them. Every illness, every lack, every damage done his Body and his members affects him. This sounds mystical, but in fact it denotes his rank and title. The Lord is attacked, his lordship is stunted and suffers where the church disavows him by its activity or is humiliated or violated by its opponents. According to Paul, ecclesiology is Christology. Only as such is it of significance — though of cosmic significance. Only the Lord is its measure as well as its limit. Other aspects, say that of sociology, may never impair the primacy of Christology. Naturally, we can see, acknowledge, or evaluate it from many sides, insofar as it is temporal. But what is alone determinative is whether it manifests its Lord or obscures him, as happens when it obstructs his way, puts on airs with its own understanding, strength, and importance, when it wishes to impress the world or, by its weakness, denies him.

Second, Christ's lordship is the kingdom of grace. For this reason at the beginning of 1 Corinthians 12 Paul enumerated the abundance of gifts with which the exalted Lord equipped his earthly body. We are inclined to think little of the church and to be ashamed of it. From its very beginning it is derided, blasphemed, and cornered as long as it serves One who is crucified. It is betrayed by its own members when it is misused by them to satisfy their religious needs, in this way finding its measure and limit by what is human. Since it has been split into hundreds of confessions, denominations, and sects that war against and hereticize each other, and cannot even gather at the table of Jesus, it is easy for the world to despise and manipulate it, as everlastingly occurs in white society. It is true that Paul suffered from the congregations he founded and forever had to call them back from egotism and superstition to the kingdom of grace. We intend to hide or keep nothing secret, no more than we intend to make of our Lord a miser. He has given, and he gives, without end. He blesses his people so that at his table it must celebrate the Eucharist, which literally means "thanksgiving." And joy and rejoicing over God's great deeds echo throughout the pages of the Bible. If we would less anxiously feel our own pulse and gaze enviously at our neighbors, if today above all we were more interested in what is happening in the upheaval of the world of color, if the misery there gave us eyes for our wealth in so many respects, then we would whine less, would give thanks and praise more, would go our way courageously. From the cross the kingdom of grace is opened to us, and the Body of Christ becomes the site of the charisms enumerated by Paul, of graced and gifted persons. Many a person suffers more from discontent than from any actual lack. More than from its adversaries and despisers, the church suffers from those buried talents of which Jesus' parable tells. If we do not use what God gives us but put it under our pillow or in our savings account, we never know how much we can begin, how far we can go, can overcome, or can give.

In Christ's lordship those categories of "being" and "having" do not apply that everywhere else on earth determine life. God's Spirit leaves none at an ancestral place but sets in motion. Our task is not self-realization; no urge is released in us to make others dependent on us. "To partake" and "to impart" are the decisive criteria of a Christian life that in this way becomes adventurous and suspenseful day by day. Categories of the end time and the resurrection from the dead seize hold, so that "being" and "having" must be replaced by "partaking" and "imparting." This is so, since at Pentecost heaven has been opened over the arid earth, has opened our eyes, hearts, and even our reason to grace, to its gifts and tasks, and it calls rebels to become servants of a new opened heaven and a new earth awaiting its freedom, to share in the divine revolution within the realm of darkness. As not all believers are aware, rebirth means revolution, the beginning of a march toward freedom, and a genuine, credible humanity.

Now, third, this allows Paul to compare the Body of Christ with an organism in which all members mutually help and supplement each other. And at precisely this point "to partake" and "to impart" is the highest divine law. Christ will have no introverted servants. The church is not a society in which there are passive alongside active members. Here, to put it provocatively, all are militant or they cease to be members. In this text, the apostle is speaking in a very critical way. He knows there is no perfect harmony and concord in the Body of Christ, that balance is continually lost, that the way toward humanizing the children of God is a process. Fanatics and the scrupulous are also romping about on this meadow. The new creature is always the one often tempted, always inclined to exchange the image of Christ for Adam's image, for earthly reason, strength, and metaphysic.

In religious groups, in theological rough drafts, and in some church administrations, the solidarity of those who differ is replaced by an enforced conformity in thought, action, and intent. But uniformity reduces all service to senselessness, just as, conversely, the privileges of those with greater talent even in so-called charismatic communities make the flock of the Good Shepherd hypnotized sheep in the train of a wether. The silliest polemic hereticizes pluralism in congregation and *oecumene,* though life is differentiated even to the fingertips. The New Testament speaks of differences in heaven itself. The creation thrives only where various possibilities and capabilities are manifest in the alternation of becoming, maturing, and decaying, where gifts and defects in individual existence and community are united, where customs and traditions change slowly or in crises overnight. We are not speaking here of political, moral, or social polarization or the splintering of forces. Yet, ideological fanaticism allows the earth to become a wasteland. In the church at least, each must be permitted to retain one's own features. If there is a religious leveling out, love dies, boredom spreads, and only navel-gazing is left. Jesus trafficked with variegated figures. The men and women in the Bible are not signaled out for their high moral tone. Not even the apostles were altogether in agreement. We poach on God's preserve when we measure his creatures by home-made or purely traditional norms and conventions.

The Christian community is no less endangered, however, when the weak wish to be less than God believed them capable, when they lazily, cravenly or resignedly bury their talents, dispiritedly fold their hands in their laps, leave thinking to others and feign death. Before dying, none should voluntarily take to the isolation ward. The one who is solitary already experiences hell on earth and passes it on when refusing to participate actively in life. The Body of Christ has no superfluous members. Nominal members are not desired, even when the inventory of persons and reserves shrinks. Those who dig their graves before they die will live like monads under a closed heaven; they deny the Holy Spirit, who calls to work and into community. Whoever does not foster caring communication on earth robs the communion of the perfect in God's future kingdom of its basis. There is no heavenly continuation of what was not already begun on earth. Whoever was not physically engaged on behalf of the nearest and furthest was not there for Christ, whatever was believed, prayed, or sacrificed, and Christ will not be there for that one in all eternity. First Corinthians 6:13 clearly proclaims that the Lord is present for the sake of corporeality. And this means, for the earth. For this reason he became man. First Corinthians 15:25ff. defines the Easter message as meaning that Christ must reign and the world be subject to him. This makes clear that we must not be concerned about heaven but for service to the Exalted One on earth and be used by it.

This brings us to the last thing we need to see and hear from our text. We are not to forget that the Body of Christ is spoken of here within the framework of an admonition, and to the Corinthian community. This means that this Body is no more an affair that is over and done with than is the humanizing of the believer. In either instance a process is involved in which growth, relapses, and risks always occur. Corinth is a precedent for the path toward *oecumene,* and the community lives within the severest tensions and at the margin of perilous division. The community is the Body of Christ in promise and under temptation, in a daily becoming new, and with the possibility of falling, as is true of all human situations. We cannot live from out of ourselves. We must be supported by the community's continual aid. Each needs the fellowship of mutual support and suffering, through whose members the liberating work of Christ is kept in motion. Conversely, each in turn must accept the weak, the burdened, the sick, and the despised. Mutual service may not be limited by the various confessions and denominations. The diversity of members makes it possible that help and liberation occur in all kinds of ways and penetrate to all corners of the earth. So the church becomes the arena of the ubiquity and omnipotence of the Nazarene in midst of a fallen world beset by demons. Here, from the perspective of the end time and beyond the whole earth, the promise and claim of the first commandment are proclaimed and realized. The gospel lived is and becomes an explosive and revolutionizing power able to burst all human barriers. In such a process all must recognize the gift given them to share, in service make use of their opportunities, turn to the one lying at their feet and in need of them. Each must keep watch over the other and appeal to all to think and act worthy of the gospel, not to bury their talents or abandon that host moving toward ultimate liberation. Finally, each one must never forget that the Lord does not intend the ghetto or the asylum, even less a national church, but rather the new earth under a new heaven; according to Matthew 28, he intends that his servants carry his lordship to the whole world. In Christ's Body we are the firstfruits of a new creation.

Prophetic Task and National Church ("Volkskirche")

The theme of prophetic task and national church hides a very concrete, but possibly unanswerable, question. According to the Pentecost narrative, no congregation can be called *Christian* in which prophecy has no place. In that case, it would not contain the activity of the Holy Spirit, who, according to the New Testament message, cannot be conceived of apart from prophecy. There is a profusion of tasks and talents wherever Christ has called men and women to glorify him in his service. According to 1 Corinthians 12:12ff., every Christian has a part in that service, thus a talent, which, according to Jesus' parable, must not be hidden but must be shown, must bring forth fruit. Whoever does not increase it, regards it merely as a private treasure or hides it; whoever does not experience any discomfort at being a disciple, at introducing discipleship to the community's life, is an unfaithful servant. Such a person denies the Lord who gives, denies the brother or sister in need, and denies the gospel — which may never remain in the closet but in the world around us, in explosive, contagious, repellent, saving, and awesome fashion, reveals God's rule presently breaking in on earth. According to Ephesians 2:20, the Body of Christ, his earthly kingdom, his way of communicating with the world after his exaltation, is built upon the foundation of the apostles and prophets. According to 1 Corinthians 13, prophecy too comes to an end, remains piecework, a fragment of the perfect. This alters nothing of the fact that, according to the apostle, it is indispensable for the community, a visible mark and stigma of true community. As if they were synonyms, 1 Thessalonians 5:19-20 sets "do not

---

A lecture given on June 25, 1983, at the Munich pastors' conference in Innsbruck.

quench the Spirit" alongside "do not despise the words of prophets!"
Where there is no prophecy, there is no Spirit of God and, according to
Romans 8:9, no Christ or discipleship. To summarize: There is no true
church without prophecy, and none can shirk from its commonality, distance oneself from it with the excuse that he or she is no prophet.

I have heard this excuse too often to tolerate it silently. Naturally, I understand the one who talks this way and actually prefer such a person to all
those who have no inhibitions. Jeremiah beautifully declares, "I am of no
use." Moses and Elijah rebelled when they were to be sent. Those who set
themselves too quickly and wantonly in the circle of the prophets may not
have considered that ecstasy is also demonically inspired, that not only on
Mount Carmel were false prophets in the majority. The same applies to the
one who has sensed in his or her own body and life that it is a fearful thing
to fall into the hands of the living God. "Woe to me if I do not proclaim the
gospel!" There is simply no gospel and no message where one avoids the
task of prophecy. With this we have let fall a key word that may not be mis-
appropriated, that is, the word "task." We live in a time of specialists and
are inclined to rank everything according to performance. It is important
to keep in mind that our God does not use or create uniform models. He
acts in manifold ways. Only institutions organized in his name prepare the
ground for functionaries. Prophecy is assigned the Christian community,
is never the privilege of particular members of the Body of Christ. More
than elsewhere, we should be cautious of speaking of a prophetic "office."
For the most part, prophets afflict church bureaucracy and administration,
to say nothing of the community's secular surroundings. Prophets have no
mandate for life, but only a task within a concrete situation, after fulfilling
which they can return to the rank and file. The Spirit is not bound to persons and positions when uniting himself with and revealing himself
through the community.

On the other hand, in the Old Testament as in the New, persons and
something akin to groups are regarded as representatives of prophecy, are
respected and, if need be, function as wandering prophets beyond the individual congregation. The Spirit cannot be pressed into neat systems, and
the prophetic task may actually claim and consume an entire life. We can
see that the subject we have in view is complex. It denotes no privilege, no
fixed office tied to temporal order, and yet it is a task that obliges particular
persons to a specific proclamation for a shorter or longer period, lifts them
from the rest of the community as instruments of the Spirit in a particular
mission. Their recognition is required of other members of the commu-

nity and, at times, even beyond this is required of church groups. They have a special service as well as a special authority. Naturally, a limit must again be drawn. Like every service in the Body of Christ, so also the prophetic task is subject to continual critical testing in the community. If that were not so, it would be a privilege. Other than among fanatics inside and outside the church, ecstasy is still not a sufficient Christian legitimation. There are false prophets who insist they have an inalienable mandate, construe their ecstatic experiences and avowals as signs of their authority, and demand to be recognized. By contrast, we must distinguish between the spirits, since discerning the spirits is the gift of the Holy Spirit, which is to accompany all prophecy. Matthew 7:15ff. names as its criterion the obedient one who does God's will rather than merely speaking of it. In 1 Corinthians 13, Paul calls the love that embraces the nearest and furthest the mark of every Christian service, thus also of prophecy. Romans 12:6 requires that all prophecy be according to faith, which means the gospel accepted by the community. In summary: True prophecy is confrontation with the power of the Holy Spirit and is itself under the control of this Spirit, who is alive in the community.

After these general statements that furnish the basis for my presentation, I take up again what I stated in my first sentence. The theme assigned me hides a concrete, actually unanswerable, question. We cannot make sweeping statements about prophetic authority without regard to the relationships in which that authority is to manifest itself. Nor can we level out dogmatic, ethical, economic, and political problems and everywhere assign the same responsibility to the prophet or the Christian community. There must always be a concrete test to determine whether the prophet is assuming too much, whether the community that intervenes in such cases is dominated by prejudice or whether it is ready to accept information, admonition, and criticism, and to determine which arguments are best suited for evoking the unrest and change necessarily connected with prophecy. At this point there are new barriers. Many, of course, are prepared for service but would prefer not to cause unrest.

Here we should consider that, according to current scientific insight, the Old Testament prophets emerged from the ranks of oracular priests, who generally had to announce a happy outcome. Since Amos, however, they are described as torn from this role. Their task now is to be political mischief-makers and heralds of the imminent, at times universal, judgment on community and nation. During the exile this situation is changed again for a time but very soon finds continuation leading up to the Baptist.

Normally, the classic prophet of the Old Testament is a messenger of catastrophe or, in extreme cases, of collapse. As such, he is at war with the prophets of salvation, who accommodate themselves to the yearnings and anxieties of the nation, the government, or the believers. Struggling with his own desires, as Jeremiah demonstrates, he is subject to earthly judgment and death. What is especially important here is that there is no separation of religion and politics. Contrariwise, a self-secure religion and morality that violate God's commandments in everyday life compel the prophets to political appearance, to determined criticism of government and community. It is equally important that they make use of the tradition of the fathers, but do not merely repeat it. Their task is the new, surprising word of God, who never remains the same, whose word works horror and hatred alongside obedience. Trust in pious canned goods is shattered by their message of the God who breaks into our moment of time. The listening community must respect the freedom of its Lord, which for the most part it does not know, do, or want to do. The prophet is witness that God, as free Lord, is on the way to his people. We may actually say that the prophet has neither regard for himself nor for the people that takes itself to be devout. He has regard only for the Lord, whom neither his people nor his enemies can domesticate.

I cannot deal with the New Testament as a whole or in any sweeping fashion. But in any case, no one will dare to contest or forget that prophecy, just as the gospel itself, has a political dimension. The Baptist and the Revelation of John witness to it. Wherever God's imminent rule is proclaimed and the Christian community appears as the breaking in, or at least as the seed, of the kingdom of heaven, all the world is summoned to its limits, and every form of piety, however private it may appear, takes on exemplary weight. There, as at Pentecost, preaching is directed to all the people, the open heaven shouts to an earth in which the demons retreat, barriers between people fall, and everywhere the first commandment visibly and unmistakably separates the spirits. This is also the background of 1 Corinthians 14, where Paul most emphatically sets the prophets against the glossolalics. The one with an ecstatic seizure is free to use the language of the angels in the prayer closet, but in the congregation there is to be intelligible speech. Reason is to govern rapture, perhaps in such fashion that the glossolalic has an interpreter nearby so that no more than two or three may speak ecstatically, each giving space to the other when the other is seized by the Spirit. Above all, the other prophets present at the worship are to mutually test and review the legitimacy of their words. It is too often overlooked that the same apostle who forbids quenching the Spirit, who recognizes each baptized person as endowed with the Spirit and as an official "officeholder" in the community, resists unbridled ecstasy in the name of reason. In addition, the Spirit mighty in the prophet must remain subject to its bearer, since the bearer must allow being measured against the gospel and must strive to build up the community, that is, to equip it for the present hour and the coming daily routine.

Again and again the community must learn what is needed today. Christ must reign on earth, his kingdom increase among, through, and around us. Yet the whole world, including the heathen who may be sitting as candidates for baptism at the worship, should be able to understand what is occurring in this congregation when Christ reigns in and grows through it. God is not a God of disorder, where everyone shrieks in confusion and acts on one's own. He is a God of peace. This does not spell middle-class tranquility and solemnity but the revealing of his lordship on the earth that is his, its breaking into the concrete moment and daily routine. Heathen participants in the worship, just as the wise men from the east at Christmas, are to kneel and, overcome by the Spirit, confess, "God is really among you!" Precisely for this purpose the service of the prophet is needed. In this way his authority is demonstrated, not by his ability to put a crowd into a trance, plunge it into sentimentality, or produce a hearer who remains passive. There are times when the theme that the Lord is at hand will have to be explained as an interpretation of the future, thus as prophecy. But that can only be the lengthening of an event already broken in. And not merely the great deeds of God may be recalled. The ancestors must be regarded as witnesses, not primarily as models of faith. What is proclaimed is, "Today, if you hear [my] voice." The prophet serves the present as the arena of the promised rule of God, while the teacher recalls past history. The prophet whose hour strikes speaks publicly and intelligibly, without equivocation, like the trumpet, while the pastor is concerned for the individual. As a matter of fact, Luther thought that the prophet thus described is the biblical model of the evangelical preacher — the public, audible, intelligible voice of the Spirit, who conveys the gospel to the present.

If what has been said applies, then reference to the prophet in the Old and New Testaments can only have one thing in view, that is, that it be "according to the Lord"! The prophet is to deliver the message of the first commandment, a message that in reality is the promise that we no longer need serve idols. We belong to the one Lord, who leads us out of Egypt and has freed us for earthly glory in the freedom of children. Now the real problem to be addressed is, *how does this prophetic task cohere with the affairs and concerns of the national church that beset us?* At the outset I stated that this question cannot be answered in general. It may have become clear in the meantime why I did so. It cannot be answered in sweeping fashion or as valid for all time. The prophet is given a task we may not simply leer at from above or below, though the Spirit desires that God's will in the actual moment be clearly and loudly proclaimed in the openness of our daily life. In any event, we must diagnose the situation in which we find ourselves. To what I just referred someone might reply, as did the Old Testament prophet, "This is too much for me. I neither wanted to be, nor can I ever be, a prophet."

No doubt such a comment is to be taken seriously. At times harsh consequences should be drawn from it. Too many are preaching who should not be let loose on others, who should keep silent rather than prattle piously. On the other hand, the entire Christian community is sent by its Lord, so that none may be excluded from the mission. According to the Pentecost narrative, the entire Christian community has the Spirit, who proclaims God's will today and himself mobilizes our reason. We should consider whether we ought to look at the mission committed to us and the gifts given us rather than to stare at our weaknesses, make excuses to our Lord, and quit the field. This may be allowed and practicable in a so-called national church. Actually, the question hidden in our theme is really unanswerable only when we bring into play what we currently call a "national church." This term allows us to retreat from heavenly and earthly reality to pious ideology. By itself, it is unclear and creates confusion wherever used. Personally, I have consciously and radically stricken it from my theological vocabulary and fear I will not come to an understanding or to solidarity with anyone who will not surrender the term or thinks it unnecessary to do so.

How did this changeling of theological phraseology come about, which enjoys such popularity in German Protestantism, and with such deleterious effect? For many, and unmistakably for church leaders, it has long been rated as the norm and criterion for the most important decisions. I assume that Romanticism may not have birthed it, but in any case it nursed and nourished it. There have always been national churches that differed from others geographically, culturally, even politically, churches that displayed theological particularity. There is no objection to this, since God does not equip our fellowships with uniforms. There have just as often been national churches, and there are still such even today, though for the most part with clay feet, seeing that state and church mutually weaken each other. Is what we call "national church" a substitute, say, for a state church, since with this term we can traditionally lay claim to as many citizens in our nation as possible, and for it demand support on the part of the representatives of a state that once allowed the *summus episcopus* to the Protestants?[1] A national church is then the bequest and surrogate of a past in which religion contributed toward keeping unnumbered territorial dominions in Germany alive and thus enjoyed the requisite privileges. Romanticism transfigured this inheritance. When Schleiermacher demanded that the sermon must "fit the congregation," what surely led him to it was the motif of the universal priesthood of all believers as stewards of evangelical truth. But in addition, the form of religious organization represented at the worship was supposed to remind the preacher of its needs and give actuality to his preaching in that direction. When Wichern[2] asked for a national church diaconate, he wanted to penetrate the slums of the proletariat in Christian fashion. But clearly connected with it was the attempt to work against imminent revolution and to prevent the nation from being newly constituted in a democratic way, as was clearly the case with Stoecker.[3] Who, then, is surprised that such a "national church" became more and more conservative and nationalistic and in the world wars announced that it preferred the union of throne and altar, national tradition and provincial church, an appetite for hierarchy and bureaucratic administration over the reality that, as a religious minority and a church of mission, it would have been obliged to recognize?

Today, the face of the national church is characterized by the fact that the majority of its members no longer comes to worship but supports it financially and officially allows it to be recognized as a political power. In this church an extremely conservative minority, stamped by a worship according to church tradition, determines its management, as well as the picture the public has of it. Its spiritual life is oriented primarily to the care of the individual soul who wishes to be preached to in an edifying and consoling way that retains the tradition and inculcates middle-class morality.

1. In the Middle Ages the territorial state was self-sufficient, and its ruler was the "highest bishop" *(summus episcopus)*, with total administrative control. In the nineteenth century the emperor of Protestant Prussia was so regarded.

2. See n. 5 in the previous chapter (p. 282).

3. Adolf Stoecker (1835-1909), court chaplain to Kaiser Wilhelm, founder of the Christian Social Party, one of the first anti-Semitic parties in Germany.

The needs of this active minority necessarily become the horizon, frequently also the central content, of the gospel accepted in only this reduced form. Unavoidably, those remain away who no longer share these needs of the minority, or at least are passive though they still participate in celebrations and continue their support. This opens the door to a polarization that, as early as a century ago, allowed the proletariat and, to great extent, the intellectuals to separate from the churches, which divided conservatives and liberals, pietists and critical theology, and today in the wake of party politics has increasingly made the churches a chief battleground of ideological, ethical, cultural, and world-political debates.

What was addressed in thematic way under the heading of "What Is Needed in the Area of the So-Called National Church" must now be given an accent without which what was said is not sharply enough contoured. At bottom, the plurality of provincial churches, or a glance at the competition between Lutherans, Reformed, united, and free churches together with Christian sects, above all at the Catholicism now dominant in West Germany, would force us to be suspicious of speaking of a national church. This is what all the others want to be and actually are, with the same right as we have. The term "national church" makes sense only when we bear in mind that a great majority among the citizens of our country, socially at least, is tolerant or open toward Christianity, though from this most draw no practical consequences for themselves personally. The national church, precisely formulated, is the Christian organizational form of middle-class society, to which, meanwhile, as political parties and trade unions indicate, all our people belong, with the exception of those at the margin. The mere fact that middle-class society to great extent sanctions Christianity "publicly and legally," does not allow speaking of the national church in terms of a pure utopia or propaganda formula. In this issue lies its reality but also its real problematic.

We may never forget what we in the church owe to the middle class, which for many centuries was the main pillar of Christianity. Our domes and hospitals, our worldview, our pictorial art, and our music grew out from it. The Reformation was in essence borne along by it. Pietism still leaves its mark on the actively worshipping community, and the Enlightenment was determined by Christian morality and made possible a critical theology that rendered the biblical message more intelligible to a world that had changed. It would be stupid not to treat all this carefully as a heritage owing chiefly to the middle class. On the other hand, from the very beginning it was no doubt the mark of this class that earthly possessions were treasured and increased. For this reason one took to the shadows of fortresses and behind walls of cities, in which trade and commerce were exposed to fewer dangers. The urge to secure life and possession remained the leading motif and, despite all the bad experiences, led looking to the government to guarantee justice and order. Of course, the reverse side is just as clear. A society ultimately determined by possession falls into clearly contrasting layers in which the stronger always establish and protect the rules of social behavior. Here the settled arrangements of power and education limit Christian freedom. I cannot forget an angry word I once read in a Catholic magazine to the effect that the Reformation doctrine of the freedom of the Christian was in fact realized in the emancipation of the middle class and, in addition, was reduced to it. This, of course, is exaggerated, but it contains a kernel of truth that must be swallowed whether we like it or not.

Our heritage, the advantages of which we do not dispute, is a burden weighing more and more heavily on our shoulders and conscience. I will only quote slogans. The property owner naturally inclines to preserving the status quo and, after losses, to restoring the status quo ante. He will become conservative or even reactionary rather than break out of antiquated schemes of thinking and acting, even though in business he grasps at every money-making scheme. He will perhaps sigh under the arbitrariness of a power making its own political and bureaucratic way, but will remain subordinate rather than resist, even when the determining factor is not Romans 13 but anxiety before the fickleness of the crowd. Democracy always grows out of revolution, which the citizen accepts only when societal relationships have become unbearable, or when it serves and increases privilege and advantage. The proletariat, which scarcely exists in our country now (though it did in my youth), sustains the cost of development toward middle-class democracy. So it was and is in Europe and in the supposedly "new" world. So it is, above all, in the underdeveloped countries. Where the slogan of the redistribution of power is heard, all are indignant who have something to lose, including the majority of an EKD synod,[4] though this slogan was used much earlier in a church memorandum and in frequent discussions of church boards. It was most clearly touted as an unavoidable requirement by the *oecumene,* such as the Brandt Report on

---

4. The Evangelische Kirche in Deutschland (EKD), or German Protestant Church Federation, founded during the postwar period (1945-48) for the purpose of representing the Protestant churches to the occupying powers, as well as to the ecumenical movement.

the North-South divide.[5] There, together with conservatives, so-called evangelicals led by radical Württembergers still captive to chiliasm, voted it down. What we call "national church" may never have been more nakedly represented than in the twentieth century, and as a form of Christianity under the yoke and dictates of middle-class, affluent society. True, it is ready and willing to make great sacrifices where charity is concerned, but it interprets the gospel as a guarantee of wealth and directs its hope in the resurrection of the dead toward persisting beyond the grave, thus toward its own permanence. Obviously, the national church must come into conflict with the *oecumene* as advocate of the underdeveloped world and with its watchword respecting the redistribution of power. Against this background the theme of prophetic authority and concern for the national church is to be seen and discussed. I at least can understand it only against this background.

Now we are standing where we not only understand the question at least indirectly put to me but can and must give an answer, to the extent the analysis given till now was correct. Whoever has stricken the term "national church" from the vocabulary and in the last analysis regards the church structure it envisions as a pipe dream will certainly not dismiss pastors' considerations for their congregations. But such a person will absolutely not be led, legitimized, or defined by a relation to the so-called national church. In that case, there could be only accommodation, tolerance, and normalizing that measure church and gospel by our traditional bourgeois perspective, remain provincial, and lead to false rather than to genuine prophecy.

We simply may not treat the two motifs of our theme as equivalent or of like importance. At least in church practice as regulated by the middle class, we see too little of Paul's description of the gospel as foolishness and a scandal to the world around us, of Jesus' blessing whoever is not offended by him, as if that were a miracle, or of his calling his disciples beneath the cross and to the place where one must lose life to gain it. The term "balance," so favored in our churches today, suits none of this, but rather obscures the rigor of the first commandment, as well as of the gospel. Just as our life must be a battleground between God and the idols, so, according

---

5. A report produced by the so-called Independent Commissions, first chaired by former German chancellor Willy Brandt in 1980, for the purpose of reviewing economic development in the Northern and Southern Hemispheres, noting the chasm in standards of living along the North-South divide.

to the New Testament, we must fight not only with flesh and blood but with demonic powers if our faith is to be preserved. Here, tranquility does not suit the concept. It is rather avoidance of the place assigned us in everyday, bodily worship and toward an inwardness highly prized by mysticism, idealism, and liberalism. It cripples our Christian faith and renders it past belief.

Here, perhaps, we should inquire behind the statement that Christianity is the religion of love, something that appears almost obvious and yet, based on history and reality, is more the description of an ideal or represents a pious lie. No doubt Matthew meant exactly that when he spoke of the better righteousness. But we should strictly inquire whether this interpretation of the gospel as a religion of love is possible and requisite only as the consequence of the rule of the Crucified, while the gospel itself as a message of deliverance (such as in Jesus' so-called inaugural sermon at Nazareth, and in conformity with the Old Testament credo), proclaims the freeing of the prisoners and the possessed, with the result that Christian mercy becomes a reflection on earth of the divine. At all events, it cannot consist primarily in nonviolence if it is really to be a love that liberates rather than tolerates. In sum, the Western churches have allowed the ethic of middle-class Enlightenment to shape their preaching and the believers' self-understanding, to reduce their radicality and more and more to assign the fellowship of the crucified and risen One to the sphere of private piety.

On the other hand, there is a new, increased enlightenment in the churches today, uncompromisingly oriented to the gospel and through it to the requirement of the hour — concretely, to the task of Christian prophecy. The repentance to be daily undergone by the Christian, the continual *reditus ad baptismum,* and the evidence for the authority of the disciple are beginning to show themselves theologically and must be marked off from false theology. The task of a genuine theology in every age, thus also today, is so to actualize the gospel that it can no longer appear as the canned goods of pious tradition from the past of our forebears and ancestors. The prophet's authority, as both Testaments describe it, proves to be thoroughly discordant and totally ruthless in its polemical antithesis to pious ideology, whether of Israel's earthly security divinely guaranteed or of an ecstasy and glossolalia that proclaims and anticipates heavenly conditions. If my analysis till now has been at all correct, prophetic authority in present-day West Germany is concretized by its dispute with the middle-class mentality that has taken on more and more weight in the churches of the white race and, together with technology, unavoidably belongs to the instrumentation of its politics. Just as at Sinai, and according to Luke 4 just as at Nazareth, there must be brought home to us in a prophetic way that the church is Jesus' freedom movement to proclaim, bring, and defend the humanization of the human in the freedom of the Christian and the priesthood of all believers, not in the pious ghetto but worldwide.

More concretely and probably most irritating for many, such assumptions logically lead to our taking up the genuinely prophetic and upbuilding sentence of Franz Alt with which he begins his superb little book *Frieden ist möglich*, written in 1983: "Our religious, private, and political existence is a unity. . . . The most momentous schism of Christianity is not Luther's division of the church but the separation of religion and politics."[6] Of course, we must interpret this dangerous sentence since prophecy and gospel always speak in dangerous fashion and must be interpreted ever anew. What is in mind is not engagement on behalf of a party, of questionable "basic values" and propagandistic programs. What is in mind is what in Paul and John is called *parrēsia*, the right of the ancient citizen to be allowed to appear in public, make known an opinion, and follow personal conviction. Authority and freedom are identical here and have their locale, perhaps also their field of battle, not in the prayer closet, but under God's open heaven. This is where Luther wanted to be in answer to Cajetan's question,[7] that is, in full view of the powers and authorities, who look on Paul's running in the arena and yet crucified Christ. To believe does not mean to have a religious conviction but, together with the cloud of witnesses, to confess the Crucified alone as Lord and fearlessly to serve him, doing so, of course, on this earth. It means that in midst of our own and alien corporeality, we give resistance to idols. Without such *parrēsia* there are only Christians of little faith and churches that renounce it.

Again, with catchwords in view, in an affluent society Christian churches are answerable to their Lord and the world for denouncing the dance around Mammon, for pillorying success and pleasure as a plague that ruins souls and bodies, with whomever they may come into conflict or drive away from worship. They can no longer remain protectors of religious individualism, in which no Christian can live and grow, where brothers and sisters no longer are seen in the Lazarus at our door and in the thousands of children who die daily in the underdeveloped countries,

6. Franz Alt, *Peace Is Possible: The Politics of the Sermon on the Mount*, trans. Joachim Neugroschel (New York: Schocken Books, 1985), p. 3.

7. See p. 266 above.

but only in like-minded friends. Before their Lord and all the world, Christians and churches can no longer afford to leave postponed till St. Never's Day the long-overdue redistribution of power among whites and people of color, among profiteers and the exploited, tyrants and their victims. The poor, primarily, are the promise-bearers of the Beatitudes. Christians and churches obscure and betray this fact if they do not take sides with these Jesus chose but limit themselves to merely making contributions. And, as happened nationally in the nineteenth century and is only too rapidly becoming the international mode again today, they can no longer regard law and order as basic values, in respect of which even the Sermon on the Mount finds its limits. Where scandals of such proportion as we experienced in the last year are possible and actual among parties, courts, and state organs,[8] as well as in the media, law and order as the bases of society become problematic, for they too often become instruments in the hands of the powerful. This may not hinder churches from interceding for them wherever necessary. But they should take care that it becomes loud, clear, and necessary when authorities and majorities go beyond what they solidly maintain is inviolable where others are concerned. Today, more among us experience injustice and arbitrariness than the most liberal German constitution thought possible. Even human rights are continually violated. Christians and churches should then be the mouthpiece for the weak, as was clearly the case with the Old Testament prophets.

In the book named earlier, Franz Alt states that, for the first time since the division in 1945, the idea and reality of a unified Germany is to be taken seriously, that is, in the peace movement that is uniting people West and East.[9] We cannot maintain that the West German churches up to the Tagung (congress) in Hamburg have been pacesetters of this movement, though the gospel and Protestant groups contributed materially to it. Now we face an autumn in which the harshest political dispute regarding the positioning of atomic rockets threatens, and it may be that force will seize a place in our democracy as never before. Can a Christian remain neutral in such a situation or be content with official pronouncements that do not unequivocally condemn all atomic armament as endangering the whole earth, every human, animal, and plant? Must not German churches speak

---

8. Here Käsemann evidently refers to the so-called Flick Affair, in which a major German conglomerate gave millions of German marks to members of the German parliament, among them Chancellor Helmut Kohl, for the purpose of influencing legislation.

9. Alt, *Peace Is Possible*, pp. 97-98.

unreservedly against all the prattling about security, deterrence, and parity and declare clearly to one and all that, in the case of emergency, nothing can be defended because nothing will be left alive? Along with ecumenical advocacy of the hungering and oppressed in the developing countries, this would be a word of the gospel made actual in our current situation. It would be that admonishing, warning, judging, and edifying prophecy of which Paul speaks in 1 Corinthians 14 and takes to be the duty of a Christian community. Here freedom would be exercised, not merely preached. It would be something we in our practice owe the whole world and that looses us from our traditional entanglements and the propaganda slogans of a society in which power, business, and privilege determine life. This would render discipleship of the Nazarene credible, since the cross he bore would unavoidably have to be our particular feature. Then genuine prophecy in our country would resist the idols and the prophets of weal.

Did what was said overplay the question about concerns? Is there any room still left for them? It should be obvious that striking out with the whip of a fanatic is not prophetic speaking. Today and in our country is this the real danger? Obviously, each one has his or her own method and must deal with very different relationships and persons who may not be violated in the name of Christ and the gospel. But in view of the task, a disciple of Jesus will still retain the rod so as to remain rational, to speak and act humanely, where able even pedagogically, and not without the subtlety the gospel assigns to serpents. Love is not expressed in silencing the truth. It develops an imagination in order in every conceivable way to show itself to others ready for service. It also has the courage, skill, and selflessness necessary for compromise, so long as the first commandment, the gospel, and a life in conformity to Christ are not at risk. This "so long as," however, inexorably marks the limit that may not be overstepped and at which, with Galatians 1:10, it is said, "If I were still pleasing people, I would not be a servant of Christ."

Let me summarize. According to both Testaments the prophet, as no other messenger of God, is tempted to lead astray to idol worship. The gospel must be made actual. Otherwise it becomes a religious worldview or a rigid dogmatic. Only the Spirit who makes alive can actualize it. But there is also the inspiration of the Anti-Christ. The task of the Christian, especially the theologian, is thus to discern the spirits. We see in this something impossible and presumptuous, to which Paul replies in Romans 8:9: "Anyone who does not have the Spirit of Christ does not belong to him." Saying this, he actualizes the first commandment, which summons each member of the people of God to distinguish between God and the idols, to decide for one or the other. Discerning the spirits is an especially prophetic task, as can be inferred from 1 Corinthians 14:29, 37. If it were not, it would not actualize the gospel. In any case, the criterion for distinguishing cannot be the national church, which demands consideration for its existence and needs. This was once the aim of those prophets who felt justified in prophesying political salvation to Israel and its rulers. It was also the aim of primitive Christian fanatics who expropriated the kingdom of heaven for themselves. Just as they separated themselves from anything earthly, so from their brothers and sisters at the Eucharist. Concerns of the national church type are common to every religious fellowship with fixed organizational forms. The main concern must always be that the members stick together and that sympathizers are not frightened off. To this the word from the Sermon on the Mount applies: "Strive first for the kingdom of God and his righteousness, and all these things will be given to you as well!"

What is truly necessary and useful must always be thought through and learned by the Christian community and all its members, especially by their leadership charged with assessing the various aspects, opportunities, and dangers. Daily bread and all that we need for body and soul in our life together should be prayed for; it is not unimportant for Jesus' disciples and the church, but we do not live by bread alone and all that it encompasses. At least in an affluent society that for decades has yielded to materialism in its most naked form, prophecy will have to speak out without regard to reaction. Church fellowships that imagine they are indispensable and whose thinking revolves about earthly and eternal survival will have to be told that God allows us all to die, that great churches have gone under, that only the bourgeoisie with its claim to ownership and permanence confuses the resurrection of the dead with its own survival. What is indispensable for our Lord is only that we follow him and shoulder the cross rather than shifting it to the back of our neighbor or stranger, only to make it heavier there. Put stiffly, but in genuinely evangelical fashion, the Crucified inspires all prophecy that has any right to genuine authority. It is not, as occurred in early Christianity according to 3 John, interchangeable with hierarchy, nor, contrary to 2 Peter 1:20, to be reduced to the message of the printed Scripture and needing official church interpretation. The Crucified is its legitimation at all times, and still is today. But the Crucified should not be made an edifying altar painting. He is present among the least. If that is so, then in our time the mistreated of the underdeveloped countries and continents are his representatives and the mirror in which the Christianity of the white race must be seen. What we are used to calling national church will not sustain this sight, to say nothing of surviving it. And here begins a new theme I believe I can no longer enter upon. But I cannot omit concluding with the statement that a prophetic authority that need not prove its identity by our rules but rather in face of the Crucified has its current criterion in defining our self-understanding from out of solidarity with the victims of white violence in the world of color.

Divine and Civic Righteousness

1. *Our ideal of righteousness.* Many of us are acquainted with the picture of that woman with the blindfold, holding a scale in her hands. This is how earthly righteousness is described. The woman is blindfolded so that her judgment is not affected by the pleasing or repulsive appearance of the parties contending for their rights. The opponents' rank or wealth can be of no significance, any more than the host of advocates brought in by both sides, and where possible bribed or extorted beforehand. Only the arguments of the disputants decide the trial. In addition, the judge may not look to his or her own advantage or, in difficult cases, to personal risk brought on by egotism or cowardice. The judge must remain impartial. The scales of judicial power may tip downward at proven guilt, upward at proven innocence. Justice would be unworthy of the name if the judge were not concerned with righteousness. Of course, blindfolded justice makes clear that everyday reality does not always correspond to ideal claims. Judges are not removed from human weaknesses. Mere appearance may often seduce them. The blindfold is to compel them to be, as it were, merely an ear for what the opponents and witnesses bring before them, and to weigh carefully what can endure.

This ideal of righteousness, designed to avert arbitrary diffraction of justice and award impartial judgment to all on the basis of merit, stems from classical Greece. For the devout Hellenes the goddess of righteousness is enthroned above all other gods and, more than ever, over all hu-

A lecture given on November 30, 1985, to the congregation at Sexau in Breisgau on the occasion of the conferring of the Sexauer Church Prize for Theology.

mans. All are subject to her power, her infallible verdict. Only in this way can there be order in heaven and on earth that holds all society together. Where there is no fixed norm, no unbreakable law, the whole world sinks into chaos, and neither what saves nor what hallows any longer exists. Naturally, we should note that, as early as for the Greeks, it was not merely the norm of requital that shaped the image of righteousness. She is not only the grim avenger. Her laws are not to be inhumanely applied, may not exceed reason, must serve life in community rather than destroying it. Thus it is necessary to weigh the cause of every transgression, just as to weigh the consequence of every judgment. The guilty shall not be permanently and pitilessly isolated. They must retain the chance for change and atonement in a new life. The punishment will thus be meted out more lightly or harshly depending on the circumstances. Justice must remain capable of clemency, be able helpfully to lift the fallen.

This ideal of righteousness has fascinated the Western world for over 2,000 years and at least been covertly dominant in it. Judges as well as those in authority have been tacitly measured by it, even when tyrannical arbitrariness subjected daily life to the justice of the more powerful. In modern times humanism and the Enlightenment established the democratic order of civic society on that basis. We must therefore have this ideal in mind when we ask what Christian righteousness means, and when we look for an answer to it in the Bible. Actually, the Bible connects the promise of salvation with the revelation of the righteousness of God on earth. How does this revelation of God's righteousness relate to the Greek ideal? In all the fluctuations of history, Christian theology has had to deal with this question. We may perhaps even say that it was determinative for the church whether theology harmoniously united or critically distanced the two types of perception. In my lecture obviously only a portion of this comprehensive and stimulating problematic can be treated. And in doing so, the New Testament scholar of the Reformation tradition has good reason for choosing Paul as chief witness.

2. *The offensive gospel.* It must be directly stated that the apostle Paul separated the righteousness of God from human justice in a highly offensive manner — that is, in sharpest contrast to what we in practice regard as proper, a human justice oriented to requital. For Paul, divine justice is not punitive but, paradoxically, a salvation-creating power. In this form Luther discovered it as the heart of the gospel and, if the gospel were inheritable, it should be the basis of every Reformation church and evangelical Christian

life. Unfortunately, it has not remained so. Just as before Luther's time, in Christianity everywhere the righteousness of God has been mingled with human justice, and the gospel thereby rendered equivocal. At this point we must all begin to learn again, and the principal task of every respectable theology is to point churches and their members to the righteousness of God as the genuine criterion of preaching and faith. The Bible, of course, does not make it easy for us to accept the message at its core. It would be useful if, on opening the Bible, we first shouted out the sentence from Luther's Small Catechism, "I believe that by my own understanding or strength I cannot believe in Jesus Christ my Lord or come to him."

Why is this so? Let us make it clear with a few parables of Jesus. We had best look first at the parable of the lost son in Luke 15:11ff., which actually deals with two lost sons. The elder son is also lost to the father when he sees the younger preferred to him. Is his indignation unjustified? He has already done his duty faithfully while the brother made merry with his inheritance and, in doing so, ruined body and soul. For this brother's homecoming a fatted calf was slaughtered, and his running off and dissolute living repaid with overwhelming goodness. But the older son never received so much as a little goat for a festival with his friends. Is this supposed to be righteousness? In Matthew 20:1-16, this is precisely the question of those workers who bore the burden of the day and the scorching heat in the vineyard. At the time of payment those who worked for only one hour come first and, into the bargain, are paid the same wages as the others. Is it not sheer mockery when the last word here reads, "So the last will be first, and the first will be last"? Further, is it not just as arbitrary and irritating when, in Luke 18:9-14, Jesus declares the tax collector righteous who can only pray, "God, be merciful to me, a sinner"? The Pharisee is not lying when he looks back in thanks over a devout life and distances himself from the despisers of God's commandments. What happens to us when the values and principles of a clean life are stood on their head? Is it blasphemous to ask whether God rewards immorality when he seems to prefer sinners to people who are steady and fear him? Finally, is not Jesus' praise of the unjust steward in Luke 16:1-9 totally incomprehensible? There a man criminally falsifies the notes due that belong to his master in order to make friends among the debtors for the coming evil days. How can one not only excuse but actually praise someone who in the last minute knows how to save his neck by evil means?

Enough examples are cited. The one whose eyes and ears they opened will find the most disconcerting, thoroughly shocking statements and stories all over the Bible. We read them only superficially if we are not irritated by the many examples we meet in them. Put very pointedly, whoever has not stumbled over God's word and does not do so again and again will never learn to proceed in true Christian fashion. Such a person will no longer stumble over needy sisters and brothers. Whoever draws from the Bible merely edifying froth does not penetrate to God's truth and will not hand it on to others. Such persons will continually draw from it only what they already know on their own and what suits their convictions or secret desires. But God's word, as the great Swabian pietist Albrecht Bengel[1] formulated it, intends the reverse. It intends to suit us to it. It comes to us as a strange word and draws us into a strange righteousness that does not measure us by our performance. Rather, it brings us to the point where we cease everlastingly to bother about ourselves, chasing after our worldly or pious goals as though we could manage life on our own and in daily existence dispense with the mercy of our Creator.

First of all, God's word quiets us, sets us to hearing and waiting, as Mary in Luke 10:38ff., who forgets all her usual cares and duties to allow the one thing needful to be said to her. This one thing means, "You do not live from your own powers or from what the earth offers you. By yourself you can only die. You live from the grace of the One who remains true to you as a parent to its child even when you run from him, substitute illusions for him, no longer allow him to be Lord alone, no longer allow his word alone to be the light on your dark paths, no longer allow his love alone to be the power that keeps you alive and wakens you each day to the praise of his glory." Evangelical faith does not mean that we hold miraculous events to be true but that we entrust ourselves and all the world to our Creator and ground ourselves and all the world in his mercy. He must retain his right over us and our earth. This takes place when he is allowed to act on us and shape us after the image of his Son. Then his righteousness is also our salvation, for it is salvation for all creatures to stand in the present, before the face of, and in the discipleship of the One to whom we belong. I realize that these sentences sound quite dogmatic. In reality, however, they describe the experiences we have when dealing with the gospel. The gospel is an offense because it removes us beyond our control and, for good or ill, sets our destiny along with the whole world in Another's hand. Neither pride nor despair will know anything of this. Both rather shout, "I myself will and must

---

1. Johann Albrecht Bengel (1687-1752), Lutheran scholar, celebrated for his edition of the Greek New Testament and for his *Gnomon,* an exegetical New Testament commentary.

be lord in my own house, must belong first of all to myself, personally answer for my doing or not doing. I claim my own right in good or evil but do not yield to an alien righteousness that robs me of independence."

3. *Who is actually our God?* What has been said till now must be given depth and width. The gospel becomes an offense because it reveals our God to us differently than we expect. This relates to the fact that we know and recognize human weakness and guilt, but only through God's word do we learn what sin is. Guilt fans out widely from infringing on sacred values to the breach of traffic rules. But sin concerns a humanity that no longer moves within the sphere of the first commandment, thus despises the one true Lord and Creator of life. Such occurs when we replace God with idols and honor or fear other powers besides him. Idols can be self-fabricated imaginings, traditions, ideologies, or persons accepted by the world around us, with whom we have fallen in love, to whom we cede the right to speak regarding our salvation. In any case, they are rivals of our God that, according to the first commandment, he does not allow because he makes undivided claim to his creatures and watches jealously over his right to us and our earth. With this statement we have used a term that needs our attention. Is there anything at all like jealousy on the part of the One we call God and Lord? Does not such a view drag the eternal Lord into the abyss of human emotions and errors? Here we have touched on a central question of Christian theology that each of us must answer. Do we really know who our God is, and do we live in such fashion that our neighbors are forced to recognize whom we have as God and Savior?

It is not true at all that this question is superfluous and easily answered by children. Rather, all who ask it find themselves on the path leading toward Pentecost. The main theme of our Pentecost hymns reads: "Lehr uns den Vater kennen schon, dazu auch seinen lieben Sohn!" (Teach us to know the Father and also his dear Son). Where this prayer is prayed, it is assumed that even Christians and Bible readers must always learn the true God anew. Only the Holy Spirit brings it about that we do not lose sight of God in daily life. Nothing is so easily lost as the one true God. For this reason we are all continually directed to the Spirit, who reveals God to us. Israel was scarcely in the wilderness when it danced around the golden calf. Throughout all its history prophets are called to indicate to the chosen people the presence of its Lord, since it continually tears loose from him in disobedience and worships idols. So, there is continuity in Christian life only when the idols in our hearts and round about in our daily existence are conquered every day anew. Christians and whole churches fall victim to demons if God's Spirit does not unmask their realities in time, a truth we should still remember from the years of Nazi rule. The Bible seldom has anything to do with atheists. Rather, the Old and New Testaments battle false piety within the community of God — as in Israel, so also among the disciples of Jesus. For our Lord is no settled possession, like an account in our savings bank. We keep him only so long as he keeps us in his grip. Nor can we make him a partner in a firm in which he takes his place alongside other shareholders, though we continually try to make him such. There is so much that lays claim to us among family and friends, in political, economic, and cultural existence, that keeps us on the move, fascinates or horrifies us, drives us to love or hate or to the dull habit of resignation. Everywhere there lurk about us hidden seducers or brutal power mongers, so that we tend to divide our heart according to their interests. What then is left for God is only Sunday or the prayer closet. For the most part, we are occupied territory before the Father of Jesus Christ can say to us, "You belong to me." He must conquer us ever anew if we are to be his alone, on the level of the first commandment.

Since this is so, the Bible describes God as a jealous God. He would surrender his lordship and right to his creature if he did not do battle for us. In time on earth God is nowhere else than in contest with the idols, and humans and earth are nowhere else than within God's struggle with the powers rebelling against him. God's righteousness is not the attitude of the impartial judge who, himself unimpeachable, decides over the right and wrong of the litigants in a trial subject to his judgment. God himself is most deeply involved in the process in which decision is made as to who is Lord over this world. His righteousness involves his right to his creatures. Therefore he must be jealous and, as such, partial. This may contradict our ideas of his omnipotence and actually appear scandalous. But let us not forget that at the center of this process stands the cross of Golgotha, and that because of this cross Paul in 1 Corinthians 1:18ff. called the gospel a scandal to Jews and Gentiles. Our God and all who confess him as Lord and serve him are involved in a worldwide scandal of historic proportions. Whoever wants to know and must proclaim what our God is really about may take no detour around the cross. All biblical truth is known from this point and from it alone. There, as nowhere else, it is clear that our God is partisan, and in a twofold way. He struggles and suffers for his right to his creature, a right he jealously cedes to no other. At the same time, he struggles and suffers for our salvation, for it can only be realized if God gains the right to his creature and wrests it from the demonic authorities that rule on earth. His right to his creation is our salvation, just as our ruin — as Hebrews 2:15 aptly puts it — consists in our being "all [our life] held in slavery by the fear of death."

In our generation, critical theology has lately discovered that the foundational saving event in the history of Israel was the deliverance from Egyptian slavery. From that point Old Testament faith interpreted the origin of humankind and the world. In liberating, the Creator brought his creation out of chaos into his rule, an event unceasingly repeated in the life of the elect. At all times the history of the people of God is an unbreakable chain of earthly deliverances. The New Testament also takes this view. For good reason Luke 4:18 allows Jesus in his so-called inaugural sermon at Nazareth to describe his task with a word from Isaiah 61:1-2, "to bring good news to the poor . . . to proclaim release to the captives and recovery of sight to the blind, to let the oppressed go free." According to the mighty words in Romans 8:21f. even inanimate creation, from out of its slavery to transitory existence, yearns for the glorious freedom of the children of God as the promise of the last day. At each Advent the Christian community sings: "O Heiland, reiß den Himmel auf . . . Reiß ab vom Himmel Tor und Tür, reiß ab, wo Schloß und Riegel für!" (O Savior, fling heaven wide . . . From heaven break down bar and door, break down what lock and bolt are for!). This would be the place to cite in its entirety Gottfried Arnold's magnificent chorale "O Durchbrecher aller Bande" (O Breaker of all Bonds). One verse may suffice: "Ach erheb die matten Kräfte, sich einmal zu reißen los und durch alle Weltgeschäfte durchzubrechen frei und bloß! Weg mit Menschenfurcht und Zagen! Weich' Vernunftbedenklichkeit! Fort mit Scheu vor Scham und Plagen, weg des Fleisches Zärtlichkeit!" (Oh, raise the feeble powers to tear loose all at once, free and pure to break through all the world's affairs! Away with fear of men and hesitation! Retreat, reason's consideration! Dread of shame and worrying, be off! Frailty of flesh, away!)

In this way the true God speaks as the merciful, which quite literally denotes the one who turns his heart to the poor. He is not the God "in and of himself," of whom philosophers speak, but a God related to his creation from eternity. We dare not speak of this God in the abstract or objectively. He is Immanuel, the God "for us," never to be isolated from us. Contrariwise, there is also no person "in and of himself or herself," but only the being created after the image of its Lord and as his earthly representative, called in the discipleship of Christ to reflect the truth, freedom, and love of this Lord. The world as it is assumed to be by politicians, economic leaders, and propagandists of all types has absolutely no legitimacy of its own. This world rests on God's mercy. When powers and forces sever it from that mercy and subdue it under their yoke, the world becomes a hell, as more than half of all humans experience it today in body and soul. Where we do not listen to the Bible, newspapers, radio, and television clearly witness to an earthly reality that seeks to avoid the grasp of its Lord. If divine mercy is despised as a basis for life, the demons gain power to ruin humanity worldwide, to make the cosmos the theater of war of all against all, and finally of universal suicide. We have been dragged far enough into this inferno. It is high time to be opened to the gospel. It points to the One who in mercy takes the part of all the exploited and enslaved, of the poor and those waiting for help, and wills to free us from the fear of tyrants and demonic seduction.

At the conclusion of this section we still need to ask what such a message has to do with God's righteousness. Why is it not enough to speak of his mercy? The answer follows from what was said earlier. That One is righteous who remains true to his covenant, even when his covenant partner is led astray to idols. What was applied to Israel in the Old Testament for the sake of the Sinai covenant is extended to all humanity in the New, clearly under the influence of the words and deeds of Jesus. Nor can humanity disavow this covenant with creation, since it did not make it. To it also is said, "I am the Lord your God." And just as Israel, it is commanded, "You shall have no other gods before me!" At issue, however, is not merely a command marking the limits of our thought and action. Because its Creator is committed to it, the creature need no longer admire or fearfully serve other gods, deliverers, lords, and ideals. It is loved and for this reason called again and again out of its earthly entanglements. God remains true to himself and thus does not surrender his fallen and erring creature to other powers. This is his righteousness, as the story of Jesus before and after Easter confirms by seeking out the lost and returning it to the Father's grace. The gospel proclaims God's liberating righteousness.

4. *Evangelical freedom and middle-class morality.* One would imagine everything is clear now. Our God loves what he has created and does not give up the right and claim to his creature. He does not act in this way only toward believers. If that were so, then his right to the whole earth would be abridged, he would hold only part of his creation in his hands. And before the One who sees into hearts and minds, it would be altogether doubtful as to what believer would survive impartial judgment. Lovers are never im-

partial. How should our God be impartial, thus requite us according to performance and merit as an avenger of evil? To word it with Paul in Romans 4:5, the gospel praises him on all its pages as the God who makes the godless righteous. For this reason it narrates all those strange stories that do not agree with our views of justice and righteousness, give such large space to shady figures in the Bible, and are annoying to us. For this reason the cross of Golgotha stands at the midpoint of the gospel, always a scandal to believers and heroes. There the Christ dies as lawbreaker and traitorous revolutionary among zealots, scorned, abandoned, and blasphemed by friend and foe. He dies on the cross because he had accepted those who did not satisfy the demands of the law and religious society and were thrust out. He dies because he preached and lived mercy toward every creature as the meaning and measure of the divine righteousness. Just as we must read and understand the entire Bible from the perspective of the first commandment, thus from that of the Golgotha event. Only then does it become clear. Only then do we see that the righteous God must be the God who is true to himself and thus frees and redeems his creation. The gospel gives us new eyes, a new heart, and a new mind. Under his reign we stop informing our God as to how he must act, what righteousness is, or where forgiving love is appropriate. We cease to shape him after our image and allow him to shape us after his image. From now on, piety means learning to believe, allowing oneself to be shaped and led by his word, no longer following current worldviews and ideologies but acknowledging Jesus of Nazareth as the only divine truth, viewing world history from the perspective of the cross, and from that point alone.

The great enigma is why offense at the gospel persists, not only outside Christianity, but even among its members and continually in our own life. Whoever wants to describe the history of the church as it really was must show without flinching that it too is dominated by misunderstandings, by a most unchristian tradition, by dogmatism, brutality, hardening, and superstition. For good reason, Luther's Small Catechism confesses that, by my own understanding or strength, I cannot believe in Jesus Christ my Lord or come to him and remain with him. Genuine discipleship of the Nazarene is a miracle of the Holy Spirit. We achieve evangelical freedom only by setting out on the never-ending wandering of the people of God. According to Paul's word in Philippians 3:13, we must forget what lies behind and strain toward what is daily held before us as the goal of our calling. But this is what middle-class morality resists.

Let the conflict between the righteousness of God and earthly righteousness be made clear once more, and applied to our situation in the most concrete and deliberate way. Of course, the bourgeois is not to be discredited or dismissed out of hand. Apart from the fact that we ourselves belong to it, our churches owe too much to it. Let the cathedral of the Middle Ages, Western theology, modern mission, and the diaconate serve as examples. On the other hand, it was a fateful development that the worshipping community (not only in Germany) should consist almost exclusively of citizens, among which women comprise the great majority. The Body of Christ is infinitely impoverished when considered against the declaration in Matthew 11:5, "The poor have good news brought to them." Where are the blind and lame, the lepers and deaf who gave evidence of this? Did we not become a sect when normally only respectable society finds a place at Jesus' table? In the Third World it may still be true that not many powerful or of noble birth represent the community, as 1 Corinthians 1:26ff. maintains of early Christianity. But we no longer recruit from the hedges and fences, to say nothing of tax collectors, zealots, and prostitutes. Even the needy, despairing, and helpless are hidden in the crowd of decent people respected by the world around them. Does this not contradict the promise and credibility of the gospel? Have we not become horrifyingly sterile and fallen into an edifying aloofness that reflects the past, but not the present and future? Would the Nazarene recognize in the Western congregation of today the host of the "poor" he once called blessed?

What is visible in Western Christianity, and more on Sunday and at festival times than in the everyday, is not a world set free by Christ, and in that variety as the Bible effectively describes it, but a substantially uniform religious society cut off from its environment. Here we have fairly distanced ourselves from earthly realities. And the church's internal side coheres totally with its outward appearance. I am tempted to recall the origin of European middle-class society. The hazards of agricultural life resulted in the first urban settlements, which lay under the protection of fortresses. In this way security for life, family, possessions, and goods was achieved, especially when firm walls were thrown up round about. Since these beginnings, citizens take care for their security and the preserving of their property. Even the constitution of our state confirms this. Such, of course, is not particularly evangelical. The Bible knows nothing at all of "human security." In possessions, which it may describe as God's gift, it continually perceives the thorn of selfish greed and demonic seduction. Even Christian citizens fiercely defend security and property because they feel continually threatened — and for good reason. It is hard to forget how slowly and difficult what we call our own was won. Pride in what was attained is completely understandable. So then, work is regarded as virtue, and unemployment seen not only as deprivation but usually as disgrace. Property is a basic value of our world, not accidentally coined by capitalism. Independence becomes our goal and the motive for universal competition, in which the weak lie by the side of the road. Caution toward unpredictable innovations appears as proof of our cunning and the basis for our success.

This sketch is superficial and drawn with broad strokes. For example, it lacks the many "no trespassing" signs of an almost omnipotent bureaucracy, lacks respect for those in authority whose duty it is to protect us in our living space, and it lacks trust in the judiciary and police, insofar as they are responsible for cleaning up the criminal element. In any case, this is not an atmosphere in which radicality thrives. Besides, in reaction to the French Revolution, people during the last century in Germany had grown conservative to the extent that business and upward mobility were not affected. The many small states generally spared the citizen any political involvement. The citizen could withdraw into so-called private life but, in doing so, lost connection with the emerging proletariat and the direction the world was taking. There was thus little room for revolution. The slogans read, "Order and Fatherland." Morality involved fulfilling one's obligations, civil decorum, and, where it could be seen, care for the neighbor and charity for strangers.

God has difficulty with a Christianity that emerges from such middle-class society. The first commandment is simply radical. It commands that we love God alone, above all earthly things and values; trust him alone in insecurity, anxiety, and temptation; fear him alone against all fear of the human and all so-called constraints; and resist the powers that violate. But the gospel is equally radical and most unsettling. Not even the Easter message gives first place to assuring us of our own persistence beyond the grave and death and last judgment, for the most part out of mind. According to 1 Corinthians 15:25, Christ must reign and conquer his enemies. Just as his disciples, so Christians belong to his victory. His kingdom alone is thus our hope. But it suffers from our theological dogmatism just as from our pious egotism when we do not make our way toward ecumenical fellowship from out of the confessional thicket, when we keep pitting our own inherited tradition at marriage ceremonies and the Lord's Supper against those with another history.

This kingdom neither knows nor endures the private edifying state to which liberals and pietists take flight from the evil world. None lives life alone. Each is a part of the world and, as such, obligated to a whole, an earthly representative of the Lord and, as Christian, a member of the worldwide Body of Christ. We must stop thinking and acting nationalistically. It is absurd that for centuries churches blessed their own wars of liberation in the name of God but hypocritically recoil at the fact that in South America, Africa, and Asia groups of the oppressed and persecuted, threatened by torture and murder, will not allow themselves to be murdered in godly fashion. Every decent theology was, is, and will be a theology of liberation. It does not end with color of skin but must be taught us again by the Third World. Our God does not allow himself to be fed with alms from our superfluity, when each day thousands of children in the developing countries die of hunger. Colonial exploitation ruined the raw material of these countries. Today, armament exports to military dictatorships plunge them into an abyss of debt. Not only our economic systems profit from this but our churches as well, and each one of us.

Wherever the gospel of God's righteousness as salvation for humankind and the earth is preached, Christians and churches of the Western world must repent. They must keep in mind how deeply they were trapped in the snare of middle-class tradition, ideology, and the morality of their environment, and how greatly evangelical freedom came to grief by it. Only that one has freedom who brings freedom to others, always only that one who, in discipleship of the Crucified, learns to serve brothers and sisters. Just as we all must die if God is to awaken us, so we must all be able to lose ourselves in order to win salvation for ourselves and others. God's grace is not to be had any cheaper than this. Otherwise, we do not really believe the gospel but continue in the heathen superstition that our God, just as the idols, endows his favorites with privileges and lets the rest of his creation go to waste. God's righteousness intends that every creature is to be aided, especially the poor and hungry, the erring and dying, and not least the godless, for whose sake he became man and descended into the inferno.

This is unintelligible to the old Adam. Against it he plays off his morality, "You've made your bed, now lie in it." He makes of piety a ladder on which to climb to heaven. He announces his claims, thumps away at his rights, compares them with the deficits of others, and reserves mercy for himself as though it did not belong to the poor and needy, who have nothing to show their Lord. Nevertheless, the traffic rules that apply on earth with the judiciary and police no longer apply where God's kingdom begins, and it will begin on earth, among, under, and through us. First Corinthians 14:33 reads that "God is a God not of disorder but of peace." It is the Holy Spirit alone who makes clear to us that in this sentence freedom does not, as in middle-class morality, denote a life in legally prescribed order. Biblically, freedom is the state of the free children of God under a heaven and earth opened for them by God's grace. God's righteousness works an evangelical freedom that does not aim at disorder but also cannot be caged by principles and powers of earthly order. The Nazarene was crucified because he breached the orders of the pious and moral when it was necessary to serve others and set them within the peace of God. The gospel does not proclaim middle-class or churchly order, but humanity as service and gift of the kingdom of God on earth. This is the inbreaking of a new world in which God's righteousness reigns. And we are called to break camp toward freedom and the peace of the children of God, so that our earth may experience something of this new world and the power of our Lord Jesus Christ.

Mark 1:16-20: On Discipleship of the Coming One

Beloved congregation! Once again we celebrate Advent. Once again we need to ask what Advent is and intends to be, what it can and should be for ourselves and our society. Generally, we are happy when there is something to celebrate but do not indulge in much thought as to why we are invited to do so. At Advent this is not enough. Here, only those can join in celebration who, with Christendom, can be told and, with Mary, ponder in their heart that "Christ, the Savior is here." "Advent" literally translated means "arrival." This is an event we daily experience when the newspaper or letters arrive. Sometimes we show that such an event is important to us and we say, "It has come for me." What we are saying is that something has struck us like an arrow, taken us aback, forced us to reflect. When the Latin term "Advent" is used, a solemn event is involved that arouses a public sensation such as in ancient times at the visit of a ruler to a city or the birth of a royal child whose divine ancestry and worldwide reign of peace court poets spoke of and prophesied. This explains why Christianity appropriated this term to proclaim the inbreaking of salvation for the earth: "The Savior is here!"

In this way Christianity proclaims the gospel, which envisages not merely an almost 2,000-year-old, once-for-all event. The gospel applies to every earthly age. Advent returns with each church year so that every generation may hear it afresh and accept it, every individual be reminded of it as of his or her own birthday. God's Savior is not only for the whole world.

A sermon preached on December 1, 1985 (the first Sunday of Advent), in the Evangelical Church in Sexau.

He has come also for me, not only to my forebears or his first disciples. He comes again and, as once in Bethlehem, will be born again in our time and among us. He remains the Coming One, always stands before our door and knocks. Now we have arrived at our Bible text. It is an Advent text. We will probably take note of it only when we consider that our story is set right at the beginning of the gospel of Jesus' earthly activity, and for good reason. What preceded is only the proclamation of the beginning of the rule of the One over whom the baptism narrative says the heaven opened that he might receive God's Spirit and be presented before all the world as God's Son. Now he announces his messianic Advent: "The time is fulfilled, and the kingdom of God has come near; repent, and believe in the good news."

At issue from now on till the end of days is that the kingdom of God is revealed on earth always and wherever the world has to do with this Jesus, and only where the gospel about him is preached and believed. This would not be possible if Jesus acquired no disciples whom he could send out as messengers and witnesses of his rule. To the messianic Advent of the kingdom of God essentially belongs that great mission in which people are called into service for this kingdom. The Lord is not without his community. The kingdom would be a utopia if it could not be visibly enfleshed on earth in members and instruments of his rule. Advent ties heaven and earth, ties the eternal God to his creatures, who continually seek to avoid him but whom he never leaves to themselves. When at Advent God's kingdom breaks into our world, it does so that, just as Israel at Sinai, we hear the first commandment with its promise and claim: "I am the Lord your God . . . you shall have no other gods before me!" The gospel is told so that it occurs where the poor, the sick, the despairing, and the possessed cry for help, where demons and tyrants play their evil game and afflict humankind, where in the midst of blindness, hate, scorn, blasphemy, and cowardice the cross of Golgotha makes visible God's rule as the self-humiliation of our Creator, that is, as love that seeks us out even in earth's inferno, sets itself alongside us, takes us in its supporting, comforting arms. As Israel once sensed the breeze or gale of freedom while in bondage to Egypt, so those who "all their lives were held in slavery by the fear of death" will sense it, and the redeemed will see the heavens above and the world around them opened to messengers of the gospel. This is what is taking place now if Advent is actually occurring among and for us.

Of course, we should not ignore the fact that, now as then, Advent begins in a most remarkable way. In the last 2,000 years, many kingdoms and dominions have been announced. Such news constantly swirls about humanity like leaves in the autumn forest, but we always hear, provided we have the ears to hear, "It is Advent." It was otherwise on the Sea of Galilee, which we usually call Gennesaret. Then, fishermen mended their nets by its banks for a new, hard day's work, hoping for a new catch to carry them and their families a step further on the hardscrabble of life. The redemptive history of the gospel begins in quite ordinary fashion, not at all with the hullabaloo we in the lands of the white race contrive at Christmas in our homes and even in our churches. The biblical Advent does not take place on festive stages like the miracles of fairy tales and legends. It takes place off to the side, in the desert, by the sea, in the province. Calendrists, newspapers, television, and radio take no notice of it. In the Gospel of Luke the heavenly light and angel choir over the Bethlehem stall, just as the wise men from the east, are already a preview of Easter morning and the Pentecost story. We should deeply engrave on our minds that it is characteristic of the revelations of our God to surprise us where we do not expect it. He does not dwell in churches and houses of prayer, though on Sunday he may appear and speak to us there. We cannot fix the places of encounter with him that we might prepare for him outwardly and inwardly, or that he might find us in festal garment and better disposed. His space is the whole world, but he necessarily prefers our everyday life, though we refuse to believe it, perhaps do not even fear it. Before the true God no one is ever secure, however many hiding places he or she may make. We are always within his field of vision. This is our definition, though no physician, psychologist, and certainly no police, and ourselves least of all are in agreement with it. We are creatures whom God sees; we stand, as the Bible says, in the light of his countenance. Advent, the seizure of the Coming One, the breaking in of his rule into our everyday life, is always possible. The watchers still call from their turrets at midnight: "Awake, city of Jerusalem!"

The hour in which God will encounter us is unpredictable. But when it occurs, our previous life is tossed into the heap as at the last Advent, that is, at the hour of our death. Ten minutes earlier the fishers by the sea faced their workday as they did a thousand others, and in their opinion would surely do a thousand others later. Then for Simon and Andrew, and for James and John the sons of Zebedee, occurred the great disturbance. Afterwards, nothing was as before. Nothing would ever be traceable to their past by the sea of Gennesaret, to their families, to their fishing and net mending. Just as Abraham, they had to be on their way toward an unknown future, Simon and James toward a martyr's death, and all of them before this toward a worldwide mission of their new Lord, for which they were not in the least prepared. It is something else to celebrate Advent in view of pious biblical stories, or to be suddenly exposed to the grasp of the Coming One.

What is most noteworthy about our story is that one single summons compels those now becoming disciples to a total break-up. Two words bring it about: "Follow me!" This erases whatever they had of plans, duties, or commitments. They no longer have, as it were, any will or power of their own. They are changed by an alien power, become the property of an alien will for time and eternity. They do not even roll up their nets. As though bewitched, they abandon father and servants by the boats. This will be and remain their life from now on. The Master calls, they follow. They were fishermen, now they will be those who are sent. Naturally, we may assume that the evangelist has deliberately stylized the scene in this way. He does not report that news of Jesus, the miracle man, had previously circulated about the sea, that his preaching of the breaking in of the kingdom of God had aroused attention. He is concerned to motivate discipleship solely by the messianic call. For him it is happening as at the creation. God said, "Let there be light!" and there was light. Here as there, a few words suffice. According to Mark 1:22, Jesus' speech was with authority and not like that of the theologians. In response, the only alternatives were obedience or obduracy. This should not be totally unintelligible to us. We too know words of love or anger that go directly to our heart and render us unarmed. Otherwise, we would not remember the happiest and worst experiences of our varied life. And otherwise, there would have been no Advent among us. Where Advent really dawns on us, we do not remain as we were but are set in motion by an irresistible force and have a mission overshadowing everything else, a destiny and salvation in one.

As with the first commandment, here too a promise is tied to the command. The promise sounds enigmatic, and the extent of it only gradually becomes clear. Entering upon discipleship, who knows what lies ahead? Each day keeps us in suspense, so that boredom does not emerge. Discipleship does not merely involve our own salvation. This too must be learned, since Christians, no less than others, incline to circle everlastingly about themselves, to incessantly feel their pulse and that of their friends, to regard their own navel as the center of the world, and to forget that our God is not only concerned with the salvation of pious people. He creates his kingdom on earth, and it does not grow where religious and brave citizens stay by themselves. Advent breaks into a demonized world in which humanity continually retreats before barbarism, in which so-called factual constraints drive us into the war of all against all — for example, in the capitalistic economy, where thousands of children die daily of hunger because the haves rake in power and money and harness all of us with our desires and duties to their wagons. God's salvation embraces the godless as well as the pious, counts the poor, abandoned, oppressed, despised, and dying dearer than the strong, satisfied, and self-secure. God's Advent stands as sign that humans must become more humane instead of competing with their Creator and outdoing one another.

In following Jesus, not only apostles fish for people but all the disciples whom the Christ forms after his image and calls to his mission, where over the wastes and the graves he wakens the community of those who become joyful companions of the needy, bearers of salvation. Only the one who is active in the service of freedom is free, a messenger and witness to the glorious freedom of the children of God. Freedom in and toward humanity is God's will for his people and the meaning of every Christian life. God became man in order to capture humans for his glorious freedom. His servants are not to become divine. Through his Spirit they must become more human to bring freedom to a world racked by tyrants. Their service is not needed for heaven, but for the earth, which for the majority of its inhabitants has become a hell from which there is no escape.

We have now come to the last thing to consider this hour with regard to our text. It has said to us that wherever Advent occurs, the summons to follow is heard. For many, perhaps even for us, this sounds so dogmatic or edifying that we have no idea how to begin with it or do not even wish to do so. Everyone propagating an ideology or party doctrine can speak dogmatically and edifyingly. It is not blasphemous if nowadays Christians give up the habit of pious jargon and turn human in their speech. According to good Jewish tradition, the Gospels describe discipleship in terms of the situation and action of the disciple. But the disciple, again typically Jewish, is before all else a pupil. To enter upon the discipleship of Jesus means to become his pupil, to have regard for his word as though it were a matter of life and death. It truly is such a matter when we allow this Master to speak to us. Then we become human. We learn to listen when the mother speaks to us. In this way the world began. God spoke and it was done. In this way community grows, and in this way also our inner self grows, so that we are moved to listen to each other and are encouraged toward our own development. In a time become inhumane, words become formulas and slogans boom out at us from loudspeakers, intent on recruiting us for an ideology or party. They make us objects to be conformed, to be used as fellow travelers. In face of this we need to hear the good voice that says to us, "I am the bread of life, the light of the world, the true way, the truth, the good shepherd, the beginning and the end." All this targets what we need, without which we cannot exist. And where it becomes ours to share, we do not go astray through darkness and waste, but we have support beneath our feet, a goal before our eyes, comfort in sorrow, and a firm heart because it is not we ourselves but Another who loves us and has us in his hands. We need no longer take care; we are taken care of. It is decidedly important to note that genuine discipleship does not begin with demands made of us, nor does it end with the results of our performance. Beatitude begins, and resurrection from the dead ends, our earthly journey. So we need not be keepers of the grail, as orthodox theology supposes, guarding a treasure entrusted to us; or as the more liberal prefer, we need not run after ethical ideals with our tongues hanging out. Our salvation is not a religious possession, it does not consist in pious models needing imitation. Our salvation lies in our encountering the Nazarene and allowing him to say to us, "Everything you truly need for life and death you find in me. Abide beneath my word, then even on earth you will be daily wakened from sleep, from impotence and demonic violence, and death will be for you only a crossing over to another, to my great day."

In discipleship we remain true to everyday existence and have nothing to do with tempting delights and seductions that carry us off into worlds beyond. After his exaltation our Lord will not abandon the world to itself so that it falls prey again to its enemies. As his disciples, we are the representatives of his presence and witnesses to his glory. Through us he continues to speak his gospel in all the corners of the earth: "I am the Lord your God," and all shall hear who in Egypt await their Liberator. Christians are needed in a time plagued by evil powers, because they can prepare the way for the Advent of the One who will be to all bread and light and protection and freedom and truth and resurrection. To follow this Lord means to find Lazarus at our door, to find our neighbors in the underdeveloped world, to shoulder their need on our hearts and backs and to resist their tormentors, just as our Lord did for us. So it is that in discipleship we are transformed into his image. We should not dreamily flee from the real world, make our salvation the measure of our piety, but open our eyes, ears, and hearts because our Lord leads us into his kingdom only by way of unknown sisters and brothers. As his pupils we learn that we are more deeply involved, cannot bypass Golgotha when he urges us on to become human by allowing us to be fishers for people. God's kingdom is nothing else but the kingdom and glory of a humanity regained. From the Christian perspective the Advent of heaven is a new earth in which righteousness, love, and peace seize a place. This is not said or meant in edifying fashion, for it does not occur except in struggle and resistance to the inhumanity at home round about and that grows and triumphs. The discipleship of Christ follows in the sign of the One who wrenched the possessed from earth's evil powers, who does not allow death its booty and, dying on the cross, was exalted. Advent sounds the breaking in of a new and better humanity, thus summons us as servants and witnesses of the Nazarene and the Crucified to war and to resistance against the despoilers of the good creation of our God. His kingdom will also come through us. Our life is to be an Advent of the coming Christ. Amen.

Prayer: Preserve us in the truth! Give everlasting freedom to praise your name through Jesus Christ! Amen. — Grace be with all who have an undying love for our Lord Jesus Christ! Amen.

Subject Index

327

Scripture Index